GRANDMAMA OF EUROPE

Also by Theo Aronson

ROYAL VENDETTA
The Crown of Spain 1829–1965
(*Oldbourne Press*)

THE GOLDEN BEES
The Story of the Bonapartes
(*Oldbourne Press*)

THE COBURGS OF BELGIUM
(*Cassell*)

THE FALL OF THE THIRD NAPOLEON
(*Cassell*)

THE KAISERS
(*Cassell*)

QUEEN VICTORIA AND THE BONAPARTES
(*Cassell*)

Grandmama of Europe

THE CROWNED DESCENDANTS OF QUEEN VICTORIA

THEO ARONSON

CASSELL · LONDON

CASSELL & COMPANY LTD

an imprint of
Cassell & Collier Macmillan Publishers Ltd
35 Red Lion Square, London WC1R 4SG
and at Sydney, Auckland, Toronto, Johannesburg

and an affiliate of The Macmillan Company Inc, New York

Copyright © THEO ARONSON 1973

First published November 1973
First edition second impression June 1974

ISBN 0 304 29063 7

Printed in Great Britain by
A. Wheaton & Co., Exeter

For
Nick, Sue, Liz and Jess

Contents

PART THREE 1918–1969

Illustrations

Between pages 148 and 149

Author's Note

The direct descendants of Queen Victoria occupy, or have occupied, ten European thrones. It is with this dynastic expansion that this book is concerned. However, in order to accommodate, and make intelligible, so immense a subject as the Queen's crowned descendants, I have found it necessary to set myself certain limits. The study is confined to those of the Queen's children, grandchildren or great-grandchildren who *first* occupied the various European thrones, and not with their descendants. I therefore deal with Queen Victoria's son Bertie, who became King Edward VII but not with his son, who became King George V; and with the Queen's daughter Vicky who – as the wife of the German Emperor Frederick III – became German Empress, but not with Vicky's son Kaiser Wilhelm II. I do, however, deal with Vicky's daughter Sophie, who married the future King of the Hellenes; for she, as Queen Victoria's granddaughter, was the first of Victoria's direct descendants to become a queen in Greece. Thus, with the exception of King Edward VII, this book is concerned with the various British or half-British princesses who became the queens and empresses of Europe.

Secondly, I have confined myself, very largely, to the personal lives of the characters concerned; this is a domestic history, not a political one. The focus throughout is on the royal courts; the political, economic and military events of the period are relegated to the background. Only when a subject – such as Vicky, the German Empress, or Alicky, the Tsaritsa – is closely involved in the political life of the country, are politics dealt with in any detail; otherwise they are simply mentioned *en passant*. This is a book about people. It is biography, rather than history.

I must thank Her Majesty Queen Elizabeth II by whose gracious permission certain extracts from the Journals of Queen Victoria are here published for the first time. For arranging this, I am indebted to Sir Michael Adeane, Her Majesty the Queen's Private Secretary and Keeper of the Archives, and Mr Robert Mackworth-Young, Librarian at Windsor Castle. I am grateful for the help I have received from Dr Anton Ritthaler of the Hausarchiv, Burg Hohenzollern, Munich, Dr Branig of the Geheimes Staatsarchiv, Berlin, and Don J. Almudevar of the Biblioteca

Nacional, Madrid. I must thank also the staffs of the British Museum, the Spanish Institute Library and the Hispanic Council Library, London; the Library of Congress, Washington; the Biblioteca Nacional, Madrid; and the Danish Ministry of Foreign Affairs, Copenhagen.

I owe a special word of thanks to Miss Myra Conradie, not only for drawing up the magnificent genealogical table from which I have worked (and of which only a simplified version appears in this book) but for helpful advice during the planning stages of this study. For information, material, advice and help, I am indebted to Don Ernesto La Orden, Don Manuel Garcia-Miranda, Dr Klaus Schmidt, Mr Anton Reinhardt, Mr P. Skovgaard Andersen, Mr Lars Jensen, Mr Christopher Lavrano, Mr Keith Killby, Mr André Bothner, Mrs Alma Holtzhausen, Mrs Dorothy Caine, Mrs Ilse Rooseboom, Miss Ann Seeliger and Miss Norah Henshilwood.

My chief thanks, however, are to Mr Brian Roberts whose assistance, encouragement and expert advice have been invaluable.

Four recently published books which have proved especially useful and to whose authors I am deeply indebted are *Nicholas and Alexandra* by Robert K. Massie (Gollancz), *Queen Mary* by James Pope-Hennessy (Allen & Unwin), *King Edward the Seventh* by Philip Magnus (John Murray) and *Louise Mountbatten, Queen of Sweden* by Margit Fjellman (Allen & Unwin). I should also like to thank the publishers of the following books for permission to quote copyright material: *Letters of the Empress Frederick*, edited by Sir Frederick Ponsonby and *Recollections of Three Reigns*, by Sir Frederick Ponsonby (Macmillan & Co Ltd, London and Basingstoke); *The Empress Frederick Writes to Sophie*, edited by Arthur Gould Lee (Faber & Faber); *The Letters of Queen Victoria*, 2nd series, edited by G. E. Buckle (John Murray).

1973

PROLOGUE

Golden Jubilee

Summer 1887

I

'The day has come,' wrote Queen Victoria on the morning of 20 June 1887, 'and I am alone . . . .'

By 'alone' the Queen meant that the Prince Consort, dead these twenty-five years, was not by her side to celebrate her Golden Jubilee. She could hardly have meant anything else. Buckingham Palace was crammed with royal guests, the majority of whom were closely related to the Queen. At every turn she could come up against a son, a daughter, a grandson, a granddaughter, a first or a second cousin. Although the Queen's husband might have been absent, their family, which she admitted was 'legion', was very much in evidence.

From all over Europe they had come to celebrate this fiftieth anniversary of the Queen's accession. Never before had such a galaxy of royalties been assembled in Buckingham Palace. There were kings, crown princes, archdukes, grand dukes and scores of princes – many of them with wives, children and grandchildren. The rooms were alive with Bourbons, Braganzas, Bernadottes, Battenbergs, Hapsburgs, Hohenzollerns, Romanovs, Coburgs, Glucksburgs, Savoys, Wittelsbachs and Hesses, as well as the royalties from various lesser states – limited in size but inexhaustible in the matter of providing consorts – such as Saxe-Meinigen, Saxe-Weimar, Mecklenburg-Strelitz, Mecklenburg-Schwerin, Schleswig-Holstein and Hohenlohe-Langenburg. And there were more exotic guests still: honey-skinned princes from such far-flung countries as India, Persia, Japan and Siam. There was even the irrepressible Queen of Hawaii, who had arrived with a piece of her own handiwork to present to the Queen: 'very rare feathers,' noted Victoria, 'but very strangely arranged as a wreath round my monogram, also in feathers on a black ground, framed'.

To Buckingham Palace, which had known so little gaiety since the Prince Consort's death, this cosmopolitan company brought a sudden

3

burst of brilliance. They might not all have been scintillating personalities but their presence created a decidedly kaleidoscopic air. The men were luxuriantly bewhiskered, superbly uniformed and dazzlingly bemedalled. The women were elaborately coiffured, tightly corseted and generously bustled. Little princes, kilted or sailor-suited, cavorted with princesses in frilled skirts and satin sashes. For a few days this royal throng was engaged in an almost ceaseless round of activity. Life was a succession of public appearances, presentations, receptions, luncheons and dinners. Crown Prince Rudolf of Austria complained that he did not even have the opportunity to speak to his father-in-law, King Leopold II of the Belgians. 'I am frightfully rushed . . .' he scribbled to his wife, at home in Vienna, 'no one has any free time.'

Busiest of all was the sixty-eight-year-old Queen Victoria. From the moment of her arrival at Buckingham Palace from Windsor on the morning of 20 June until her return three days later, she was on the move. With the King of Denmark on her right hand and the King of Greece on her left, she presided over a family dinner and noted how splendidly the gold plate gleamed under the blaze of lights. In the Small Ballroom she accepted a present from her assembled children and grandchildren: an immense and elaborate table decoration in gold, silver and enamel, fashioned in Berlin under the eye of her eldest daughter, the German Crown Princess. In the Large Ballroom ('half dead with fatigue') she received the *corps diplomatique*, foreign envoys and their suites. In the White Drawing-room, she granted audience to a deputation from the 'Women of England'. In the Green Drawing-room she held a great reception for the Indian princes and was almost overwhelmed by the splendour of their jewels and costumes. She had always had a *penchant* for dark, good-looking men; 'the handsome Rao of Kutch, most beautifully dressed,' she enthused, 'really he and his brother were like a dream . . .' At yet another dinner, wearing a dress embroidered with roses, thistles and shamrocks and her 'large diamonds', she listened to her eldest son, the Prince of Wales, propose the health of the sovereigns and royal guests crowded around the table.

The climax of these royal celebrations was the Thanksgiving Service in Westminster Abbey on 21 June. It was a day of brilliant sunshine; the longest of the year. The vast crowds lining the route had the satisfaction of seeing almost every member of the Sovereign's extensive family pass by. In the first procession drove the Queen's royal guests, not quite all of whom were her relations, but the second procession was made up entirely of her direct descendants. It needed ten carriages to accommodate her daughters, daughters-in-law, granddaughters, granddaughter-in-law and their ladies. They were followed by the men of the family. Splendidly mounted, glittering with gold, their accoutrements all a-jingle and their plumes all a-flutter, the Queen's three sons, five sons-in-law, nine grandsons and grandsons-in-law trotted by. It was a marvellous sight. Her eldest son, the forty-five-year-old Prince of Wales, was in the bright red tunic and plumed helmet of a British Field-Marshal; his eldest son, Prince Albert Victor, was in the blue and gold of the 10th Hussars; his second son, Prince George, was in the blue of a Lieutenant of the Royal Navy. Others were in scarlet and still others in green. Most spectacular of all was the German Crown Prince Frederick, husband of the Queen's eldest daughter Vicky. In his white uniform, silver cuirass and great eagle-crowned helmet, he looked, it was said, like 'one of the legendary heroes embodied in the creations of Wagner'. Dear Fritz, noted the Queen less poetically, 'looked so handsome and so well'.

The princes were followed by an escort of Indian cavalry, exotically turbaned, and then came the open landau drawn by six cream-coloured horses, in which sat the Queen, her eldest daughter Vicky, German Crown Princess, and her daughter-in-law Alexandra, Princess of Wales.

Whereas the Crown Princess looked attractive and the Princess of Wales superb (in cream and gold brocade with a toque of creamy-pink roses), the Queen looked hardly different from her everyday self. She had flatly refused to wear her robes of state for the great occasion. When the Princess of Wales, on behalf of the Queen's children, had tried to get the Queen to change her mind, she had been given short shrift. 'I was never so snubbed in all my life,' complained Alexandra. So the Queen drove to the Abbey in a dress of black satin, relieved by the blue Garter ribbon, several glittering orders and a few lace panels. One concession she did make, and this was in the matter of her bonnet. For the first time in twenty-five years she forsook a black bonnet for a white one. From a Marie Stuart-shaped brim, set with diamonds, a tuft of white feathers sprouted heavenwards, while a length of white Alençon lace was secured firmly under her chin. It was not notably regal but it was something.

Through the vociferously acclaiming, lavishly decorated streets the Queen drove to the Abbey. At the door she was met by a cluster of clergymen, all gorgeously robed. She started slowly up the nave to the strains of an overture by Handel. Preceded by the princes of her family and followed by the princesses, she made her way to the red-carpeted dais on which stood the Coronation chair. She was not too overwrought to spot various familiar faces in the congregation, but she was spared the sight of her *bête noire*, Mr Gladstone, 'though he was there'.

'I sat *alone* (oh! without my beloved husband, for whom this would have been such a proud day!)' wrote the Queen. But if Prince Albert was not there in person, reminders of him were in no way lacking. They played his *Te Deum* and they sang his chorale. At the end of the service ('to which all, even the natives of Asia, seemed reverently attentive,' ran one report) the Queen's – and the Prince Consort's – descendants passed before her to pay homage. Her sons, sons-in-law, grandsons and grandsons-in-law bowed and kissed her hand; her daughters, daughters-in-law, granddaughters and granddaughter-in-law curtsied and were embraced by her.

'It was a moving moment,' noted the Queen, 'and tears were in some of their eyes.'

For many, the sight of the old Queen embracing the members of her family was the most touching of the day's events. 'What Queen in the world has been so rich in offspring and has such good cause to rejoice in her many children?' asked one effusive observer. 'She was perfectly justified in kissing them all round. . . .'

The service over, the royal family drove once more in triumph through the streets. At the Palace the Queen thankfully exchanged her bonnet for her cap and distributed Jubilee brooches to the members of her family. Not until four in the afternoon did they sit down to luncheon. The rest of the day passed in a haze of presentations, greetings, speeches and gift-giving, and ended in the flash and shimmer of fireworks. Exhausted, the Queen slipped away to bed.

'Felt truly grateful that all had passed off so admirably, and this never-to-be-forgotten day will always leave the most gratifying and heart-stirring memories behind,' she wrote.

She had every reason to be gratified. Not only had her Golden Jubilee been a triumphant national event but it had emphasized her role as the head of a great royal clan. More than anything, Queen Victoria's Golden Jubilee was a family affair. Her Diamond Jubilee, ten years hence, was to have an altogether different atmosphere: it would be grander, more imperial, more stridently nationalistic. Then she would be hailed as the Queen–Empress of a mighty Empire; now she was being greeted as a European sovereign, head of a cosmopolitan family, the Grandmama of Europe.

She certainly had a right to this title. Not only was she Europe's leading monarch but, being part Coburg and having married a Coburg, she was related to almost every royal family on the Continent. Her Coburg cousins or second cousins reigned in Belgium, Portugal and Bulgaria and had married, or would one day marry, into the ruling families of France, Austria and Italy. Her son's wives were related to the Russian, Danish, Greek and Dutch monarchies. She was even to be connected to that most *outré* of dynasties, the Bonapartes. Had Crown Prince Rudolf not shot his mistress and himself at Mayerling, his wife – Queen Victoria's second cousin, Princess Stephanie of Belgium – would have been Empress of Austria. A mad and beautiful female cousin, now locked up in a Belgian castle, had once been the Empress of Mexico. Yet another second cousin, the jewelled and perfumed Ferdinand of Bulgaria, dreamed of having himself crowned Emperor of a new Byzantine Empire, in Saint Sofia in Constantinople.

But even without these various collatoral ramifications, through the marriages of her direct descendants alone Queen Victoria could claim to be Europe's royal grandmother. Through ten of her children, grand-children and great-grandchildren she came to be linked to the majority of the reigning sovereigns of the Continent. Her eldest son was to succeed to her own throne as King Edward VII. Her eldest daughter was to become German Empress, the mother of Kaiser Wilhelm II. One granddaughter would be the last, tragic Empress of Russia. Another would become Queen Sophie of the Hellenes, the mother of no fewer than three Greek kings and one Romanian queen. Other granddaughters would be Queen Marie of Romania, Queen Maud of Norway and Queen Ena of Spain. Her great-granddaughters would become Queen Marie of Yugoslavia, Queen Louise of Sweden and Queen Ingrid of Denmark. And most of these, in turn, were to be the mothers and grandmothers of kings.

It was thus with justification that a disgruntled Hapsburg archduke could complain that 'the Coburgs gain throne after throne and spread their growing power abroad over the whole earth'. And that Bismarck could refer to Coburg as 'the stud farm of Europe'. In the years between Queen Victoria's Golden Jubilee and the end of the First World War, the old Catholic monarchies were completely overshadowed; it was the Protestant royalties, and more particularly those with Coburg blood, who led the field. From snow-bound St Petersburg to stifling Lisbon, from rain-lashed London to sun-drenched Athens, the Coburgs wielded their influence. The *wagons-lits* were forever carrying yet another member of the family to a foreign capital: the *Orient Express* took them to Sofia, the *Star of the North* took them to St Petersburg. Stiffly they stood amongst the potted palms on station platforms waiting for trains to transport them to weddings in Madrid, house-parties in Copenhagen, christenings at Potsdam and funerals at Windsor. The Queen's Coburg relations exchanged gossip in the orchid houses at Laeken, they were piped aboard yachts on the Tagus, they opened balls in the Hofburg. In swaggering cavalcades they passed along the streets of Brussels or Berlin or Bucharest.

Indeed, this last great flowering of Europe's monarchy was very much a family affair: a royal aggrandizement presided over by the plump and imperious Grandmama of them all.

2

If, to the world, Queen Victoria was the remote and illustrious Grandmama of Europe, to her grandchildren she was every bit as awe inspiring. To them, whether they were youngsters, or men and women on the threshold of middle age, the prestige of Grandmama Queen was almost overwhelming. 'They spoke to her,' testifies one of these grandchildren, 'with bated breath, and even when not present she was never mentioned except with lowered voice.'

To be taken to see their grandmother was an event of extreme importance in the lives of the children. 'I have so much to do and have suffered so much from my head lately that I fear that I cannot undertake to see *you* this time,' wrote the Queen imperiously to the mother of one such brood of royal children, 'but if you will send Girdlestone [the nurse] with the children by herself at half past ten on Wednesday I could find a few minutes to see them – which I long to do.'

Along wide, silent and deeply carpeted corridors, like a flock of 'well-behaved little geese', the children would be driven by their anxious nurses towards the Queen's apartments. No one spoke above a whisper. Even reprimands were delivered in hushed tones. 'Mind you curtsy at the door and kiss Grandmama's hand and don't make a noise and mind you are good,' would run the scarcely audible instructions. Soundlessly, one after another, double doors would be opened by low-bowing, liveried footmen; 'it was like passing through the forecourts of a temple, before approaching the final mystery to which only the initiated had access.' The last door would open and there, sitting at her desk in an old-fashioned, elaborately flounced black silk dress with a snowy widow's cap on her head, would be Queen Victoria.

To the children, the Queen might be awesome but she was never frightening. She was certainly not the ogre of popular imagination. In fact, the more perceptive amongst her grandchildren realized that she was just as shy of them as they were of her. On seeing them, the Queen would smile her timid smile and give a little shrug of her shoulders. A quick, nervous laugh always preceded her opening remarks. Conversation was halting and made up, for the most part, of questions about the children's behaviour. Any report of naughtiness would be met with mock exclamations of horror on the part of the Queen. Yet she never raised her voice; her air was one of tranquillity.

Her rooms fascinated the children. They were always sweet with the scent of orange flowers and, as the Queen insisted on open windows, never stuffy or gloomy. They were crammed, not only with furniture, but with innumerable paintings, portraits and ornaments. In all of these, Grandpapa – the late Prince Consort – figured largely. He was portrayed in oil paintings, water colours, prints, photographs, busts and statuettes. In general's uniform, in Garter robes, in a kilt, in plaid trousers, on a mountainside, at his writing table, in the garden, with his dogs or his horses or his children, with his little wife gazing rapturously into his face, the shade of Prince Albert dominated the room. But there was a great deal more to be seen: Landseer's wonderful pictures of dogs and deer and horses, photographs of people long since dead, a glass ball shimmering with different colours, 'all sorts of delicious queer little objects made of

Scotch granite and cairngorm'. There was even a caged bullfinch who either screeched with rage or piped a gay little tune.

At Osborne or Balmoral, the Queen's grandchildren were more likely to see her out of doors. Sometimes they would be allowed to breakfast with her. Here, instead of carpets, the marvellously smooth, springy green lawns would muffle any footfalls. The Queen would be seated under a large ecru parasol tent, lined and fringed with green. All about, in nervous attendance, stood turbaned Indians, kilted Highlanders, liveried footmen and black-clad ladies-in-waiting. Dogs – collies, pomeranians, Scotch or Skye terriers – sprawled on the grass. The air would be pungent with the smell of coffee and of certain brown biscuits, imported from Germany, which the Queen might, or might not, offer to her grandchildren. As they often had difficulty in observing the obligatory silence or low-pitched conversation at the royal table, some of the children invented 'a kind of dumb talk'. This invariably led to fits of giggling followed by embarrassed explanations. The minute breakfast was over, the children would be packed off, the table cleared and the dispatch boxes brought out.

No less characteristic were the glimpses which the children would have of their grandmother out driving. Come wind, rain or sleet, the Queen would never miss her daily drive. 'I remember a morning when none of the family would accompany Grandmama Victoria in her little pony carriage,' recalled Princess Alice, afterwards Countess of Athlone, 'so, to my intense joy and pride, I was deputed and out we went, sleet pouring down on us, nothing daunted.'

Another of her grandchildren, the little girl who became the colourful Queen Marie of Romania, has left an even more vivid picture of the Queen taking her drive at Balmoral.

'There was a quite special thrill,' she writes, 'when from afar you saw Grandmama's outrider come trotting down the road ahead of her carriage. Grandmama never drove without an outrider.

'Solemn-faced, in a livery as impeccably black and neat as the clothes of a bishop, mounted on a stolid dappled grey, groomed to the superlative perfection only English stables can attain, this forerunner of the Royal Presence would appear round the bend of the road. Trot, trot, trot, trot, the very sound made your heart beat with expectation. That black-coated rider with a face that never smiled, never in fact expressed anything but almost magnificent reliability, was more uniquely royal and effective than any flare of trumpets or bright-coated military escort could have been. Trot, trot, trot, trot, and here was Her Majesty's carriage drawn by greys as superbly sleek and well-bred as the one who had heralded their coming; and seated within the open barouche, a wee little old lady with an exquisitely old-fashioned hat and antediluvian, sloping-shouldered mantle, black, with sometimes a touch of white. Nothing showy about her, no attempt at effect of any kind, the whole turn-out simple, unadorned, but what a thrill the passing of that simple carriage gave you.

'Trot, trot, trot, trot, deep curtseys, the waving of hands and hand-kerchiefs, smiles on every face, a responding smile from the little old lady in the carriage – only just a glimpse – but how the memory remained with you. Trot, trot . . . a diminishing sound. You stood staring after the carriage, the horses, the outrider, trot, trot . . . fainter, fainter . . . till it died quite away . . .

'Grandmama Queen!'

Although the Queen might only rarely be seen by her grandchildren, she was the dominant presence in their lives. No important step could be taken without the consent of the little old lady in black. She had to know about their education, their travels, their health and their person-alities. 'In a way she was the arbiter of our different fates,' wrote one of her granddaughters. 'For all members of her family her "yes" and her "no" counted tremendously. She was not averse from interfering in the most private questions. She was the central power directing things.'

Her cross-examinations were dreaded by the younger generation. 'I like Balmoral for about a fortnight,' complained one of the princesses, 'but I honestly think that longer than that is rather an ordeal as the everlasting questions and the carefulness of one's replies is extremely fatiguing . . . .'

Yet, for all her insistence on having her say, Queen Victoria was no virago. On the contrary, she was exceptionally kind, sympathetic and understanding. One could always go to her in trouble. So sentimental herself, she was quick to respond to a romantic situation. Her grand-children might stand in awe of her tremendous presence but on important issues they always found her tolerant, broadminded and far from prudish.

This compassion was well illustrated during the course of a scandal that set the small German courts a-quiver during the late 1890s. A young and unmarried royal duchess was discovered to be pregnant. The father of the child was a footman who, owing to some antiquated rule at the Grand Ducal court, had had the nightly task of bringing the lamps into the girl's bedroom. The parents, horrified at what they considered to be their daughter's plunge from grace, lost no time in turning her out. Queen Victoria was no less horrified at their lack of sympathy. 'It is too awful and shameful and almost sinful to send the poor Baby away,' wrote the Queen. 'I hear from a reliable source that the *family* have forbidden that poor unhappy girl's name ever being mentioned *in* the family . . . I think it too wicked.'

It was in the matter of her grandchildren's marriages, of course, that the Queen's influence was most clearly felt. On these she had very definite, and very sensible ideas. For one thing, she would never insist on marriage for the sake of marriage. 'Moretta has expressed a strong wish *not* to marry now,' she wrote to her grandchild Moretta's mother on one occasion, 'and I own – I think you should let it alone for the present. Let her *see* people – but *pray don't* force it on, for *if* she has no inclination, if she don't like anyone, it would *never* do . . . *don't force* or *press* her to marry for *marrying's sake*; that is dreadful.'

Such advice was rare in the courts of Europe.

Although she was always well enough pleased if a member of her family made a brilliant match, Queen Victoria was never one for talking anyone into a politically or dynastically advantageous marriage. In fact, the longer she lived, the less she cared about great foreign matrimonial alliances. In the case of her eldest children, they had led to endless friction. By the time her younger children, and her grandchildren, were ready for marriage, she always preferred a suitable match to a spectacular one. 'Great marriages do not make happiness,' she once warned her eldest daughter. In the face of considerable opposition the Queen allowed her daughter Louise to marry a commoner – the Marquess of Lorne. To her protesting eldest son, the Prince of Wales, she explained that marriage to some foreign prince would cause nothing but 'trouble and annoyances and unhappiness, and which I *never* would *consent* to'. What good, nowadays, were these 'great foreign alliances'?

Once, when a handsome young prince, having been refused permission to marry a suitable princess, married a beautiful singer instead, the Queen's daughter Vicky cried out that he had been 'driven to despair'. Victoria's comment was more sensible. 'Perhaps they love one another,' she answered.

Queen Victoria never shared the horror of the leading Continental royal families of marriage with a member of a morganatic branch. The German imperial family was appalled when the Queen sanctioned the marriage of not only one, but two, morganatic Battenberg princes into her own family. Both the German Empress and her son, the Crown Prince, wrote to the Queen to express their reservations. Victoria was furious. How *dare* they address her in that tone? How *could* they refer to the Battenbergs as not being *Geblüt* – pure-bred – as though they were animals?

'If the Queen of England thinks a person good enough for her daughter,' she quoted one of her Ministers as saying, 'what have other people got to say?'

For indeed, if the Queen was ready to allow her children and grand-children to ally themselves to Europe's less important and less pure-bred royalties, she was still extremely conscious of her own status as Europe's leading sovereign. Hers was still, she would claim blandly, 'the greatest position there is'. When her son Prince Alfred expressed a wish to marry the only daughter of Tsar Alexander II, Queen Victoria insisted that the Princess come to England for inspection. The Tsar did not see why she should. Why, suggested the Empress of Russia to the Queen's daughter Princess Alice, could the Queen not come to Germany and inspect the girl there? Princess Alice, in full agreement, passed the message on to her mother. The Queen exploded.

'I do *not* think, dear Child,' wrote the Queen to Princess Alice, 'that *you* should tell *me* who have been nearly *twenty years longer* on the throne than the Emperor of Russia and am the Doyenne of Sovereigns and who am a *Reigning* Sovereign which the Empress is *not* – *what I ought to do*. I think I know *that*. The proposal received on *Wednesday* for me to be at *Cologne* . . . tomorrow, was one of the *coolest* things *I* ever heard . . . I own *everyone* was shocked.'

Although Queen Victoria was not bigoted in this matter of her children's and grandchildren's marriages, it was very rarely that any of them married outside the charmed circle of European royalties. Some of their partners might be minor royalties but they were royalties all the same. To Queen Victoria, royalty was a race apart. It was inevitable, therefore, that with a family as large as hers, the Queen's descendants would be scattered throughout the palaces of Europe and that some of them, at least, would sit on thrones. She might have been able to ensure that her younger daughters married tame, uncommitted princelings who were content to live in England; she could hardly control the marriages of her grandchildren and great-grandchildren to the same extent.

Thus there was carried, into the courts of late nineteenth-century and early twentieth-century Europe, something of the atmosphere of Queen Victoria's England. A flock of English or half-English princesses introduced into the royal families of the Continent the taste, the ideas, the morals, the language and the way of life of Victoria's court. Into these foreign palaces they brought, sometimes quite literally, a breath of fresh air. They built homes that looked like Mayfair mansions or Tudor manor houses; they had them fitted with bathrooms and lavatories ('these really necessary affairs' as the Queen called them); they filled them with chintz-covered furniture from Maple and Liberty; they kept the vases full of flowers and the windows open. One could hardly believe, boasted Princess Alice to Queen Victoria on moving into her newly-built home at Darmstadt, that one was in Germany; 'the house and all its arrangements are so English'.

'The house would enchant you just now,' wrote Queen Victoria's daughter, Vicky, of her own daughter's improvements to her villa at Bonn, 'it is just like a pretty English country house . . . All in such good taste.'

In these cosy, chintzy, convenient houses, they tried to lead as English a life as possible. The day started with a hearty breakfast and, instead of having to change into full evening dress for dinner at four in the afternoon followed by a gargantuan tea at eight at night, the family sat down to luncheon in the middle of the day and to dinner in the evening. English manners were considered *de rigueur*. 'But my *dear*,' exclaimed the Queen's granddaughter, Princess Ena of Battenberg, to her husband, King Alfonso

XIII of Spain, on the morning after their wedding, 'you're dipping your toast in your tea!'

The children were brought up in the English fashion – simply, strictly and according to the maxim that they should be seen and not heard. They were fed on baked apples and rice puddings. Every nursery was presided over by that ubiquitous symbol of imperial Britain – the English nanny. There was a Mrs Orchard at Darmstadt, a Mrs Lorne at Athens, a Miss Green at Bucharest. (Sir 'Chips' Channon, in later years, claimed that all European royalties spoke English with a slight cockney accent from having been brought up by English nannies.) English was the language in which the German Empress Frederick wrote to her daughters – Princess Sophie of Greece, Princess Victoria of Schaumberg-Lippe and Princess Margaret of Hesse. English was heard in the Winter Palace in St Petersburg, in the Neues Palais at Potsdam, in the Palacio Real, Madrid. 'I am English by education and English is my language,' claimed the German princess who was the last Tsaritsa of Russia. And when Queen Olga of Greece asked one of her granddaughters why she prayed in English, rather than Greek, the little girl replied, 'I have arranged it with God. I told Him I liked to talk to Him in English best, and He said: "Please yourself, Marina!"'

And there were other, less tangible things that this bevy of princesses introduced into the courts of Europe. Although many of them were shy, inarticulate and a little too convinced of the superiority of all things English, they brought with them some of their grandmother's more admirable characteristics: her refreshing lack of bigotry, her fund of common sense, her high moral code, her transparent honesty and her unshakeable sense of duty. Different from each other in many ways, these princesses, grand duchesses, queens and empresses retained always something of the direct, practical, honest-to-goodness qualities of the plump old lady in the white widow's cap.

PART ONE

1887 — 1901

CHAPTER ONE

Vicky of Germany

I

Of all the marriages of Queen Victoria's nine children, that of her eldest daughter, Victoria, the Princess Royal, to Prince Frederick Wilhelm of Prussia, had been the most politically significant. It had been planned as a royal alliance on the grand scale: a traditional linking of two states by a match between their reigning houses. This joining together of the eldest daughter of the Queen of England to a prince who would one day be the King of Prussia had been designed as the first step towards an understanding between the two countries.

The idea had been Prince Albert's. Having grown up in a Germany that was fragmented into scores of states, some large, some tiny and most of them despotically ruled, the Prince had always dreamed of the day when these fragments would be united into a single, democratic country.

The lead for such a movement, reckoned Albert, would have to come from Prussia. For one thing she was the most dynamic of the states, for another she was Protestant. It would thus be her task to guide Germany towards a united, enlightened and influential future. This Greater Germany would then dominate the Continent, by holding the balance between fickle France and reactionary Russia.

Although Prussia, thus far, had shown unmistakable signs of vigour, she had shown precious few of liberalism. It was therefore up to Britain to give her all the encouragement she could. Injected with generous doses of British greatness and British enlightenment, Prussia could set about unifying and liberalizing Germany. Between them, Britain and Greater Germany would be able to set a shining example to the rest of Europe.

As a first step towards achieving this high-minded goal, Prince Albert – backed up to the hilt by his adoring wife – decided on a link between the royal houses of Great Britain and Prussia. Fortunately, there were two eminently suitable candidates to hand. The one was Prince Frederick Wilhelm of Prussia, the other was Vicky, the Princess Royal. Prince Frederick Wilhelm – known to his family as Fritz – was a tall, handsome, good-natured young man with suitably progressive views; Vicky was something of a prodigy.

From babyhood, almost, and in marked contrast to her brother Bertie, Vicky had shown signs of an exceptional intelligence. She was quick-witted, hard-working and eager to learn. As such, she had delighted Prince Albert. This earnest, liberal, conscientious Prince found in her the ideal pupil. To his tireless course of instruction she responded with an enthusiasm and a comprehension which was little short of amazing. No master could have wished for a more willing disciple. That this lively young princess (for in addition to being clever, she was attractive, viva-cious and energetic) would one day be capable of playing a significant role in European affairs, Prince Albert never doubted. To this end he instilled in her his Coburg brand of democracy; by the time he had finished with her, his concept of constitutional monarchy could hardly have had a more dedicated exponent.

In the autumn of 1855, when Fritz was twenty-four and Vicky a mere fourteen, Victoria and Albert invited the Prussian Prince to Balmoral. To the gratification of all concerned, the two young people fell in love. Not until after the Princess had turned seventeen, however, were they married. The four-day honeymoon at Windsor over, the two of them left for Berlin. The first step towards the realization of Prince Albert's dream had been taken. Through this idealistic young couple – and, more particularly, through Vicky – would his progressive ideas be introduced into Prussia.

Of this important vocation, Vicky was deeply conscious. She was determined not to fail her father. With her father-in-law, who ascended the Prussian throne as King Wilhelm I in 1861, already in his sixties, it was assumed that the young couple would not have long to wait before taking control of Prussian affairs. Together, they could then lead Prussia, and ultimately Germany, towards a radiantly liberal future.

Such had been the plan in theory; in practice, it had all worked out very differently.

In the first place, King Wilhelm I of Prussia would have no truck with any new-fangled liberal ideas. He was a firm believer in *Gottesgnadentum* – the Divine Right of Kings. A man of simple tastes and unaffected manners, King Wilhelm I was nonetheless an intransigent autocrat, determined that the crown should yield none of its rights. In his reactionary attitude, he was supported by the Prussian ruling caste – that conservative and insular class of landowning noblemen known as the Junkers. To them, no less than to the King, all talk of such things as parliamentary rule, constitutional monarchies and a united Germany was just so much nonsense.

Yet, at the start of Wilhelm I's reign, Vicky – now Crown Princess – could take comfort from the fact that, at sixty-four, the King could not be expected to live a great deal longer. Another reassuring factor was that King Wilhelm was not nearly as iron-willed as many imagined. His conservatism was that of a weak man who fears change; with patience and perseverance, he might yet be coaxed along a more enlightened path.

On both scores, the Crown Princess's hopes were destined to be dashed. King Wilhelm was to live for twenty-seven years after his accession; he was not to die until the age of ninety-one, in 1888. And, in the year after his accession, he appointed Otto von Bismarck as First Minister. With the assumption of power by this astute and ruthless Junker, all hope of the King being encouraged to follow a more democratic line could be forgotten. It did not take Bismarck long to get the King under his thumb; for the remainder of Wilhelm I's long reign, it was Bismarck who ruled.

And, paradoxically, it was Bismarck who turned Prince Albert's dream of a united Germany under Prussian leadership into a reality. He did it, not – as all liberals had hoped – by means of democratic example and parliamentary persuasion, but by the altogether more brutal method of 'blood and iron'. Three wars, one against Denmark, one against Austria, and one against France, established Prussia as the leading military power on the Continent. By January 1871 Bismarck had coerced the various German states into forming an Empire and the reluctant King Wilhelm of Prussia into becoming its Emperor. The Second German Reich, instead of being the enlightened *Kulturstaat* of the Crown Princess's fond imaginings, became an oppressive and powerful *Militarstaat*.

Thus, as year succeeded year, with the old King showing no signs of dying and Bismarck none of loosening his grip, so were the Crown Prince and Princess forced to sit by in helpless frustration while the state developed along lines utterly opposed to everything they planned one day to inaugurate. Against Bismarck's rock-like will, their liberal protestations dashed like so much froth. In the year of Queen Victoria's Jubilee, Vicky turned forty-six. Almost thirty years after first arriving in Berlin, she was still waiting to fulfil her mission.

2

But not quite all the blame for the unhappy position in which the Crown Prince and Princess found themselves could be laid at Bismarck's door. At least some of the fault lay in themselves. Their particular defects of character were the very ones which they could least afford in their delicate situation.

Prince Frederick, for all the soldierly magnificence of his appearance, was a weak man – fretful, irresolute, easily depressed. Nor was he quite as dedicated a liberal as had once been assumed. Humanitarian he certainly was, but – unlike his wife – he lacked the conviction that all his beliefs were necessarily the right ones. 'He is not born a free Englishman,' explained Vicky self-righteously to her mother on one occasion, 'and all Prussians have not the feeling of independence and love of justice and constitutional liberty they ought to have . . .' Indeed, Fritz was often plagued by soul-searing doubts. A dutiful son, he hated opposing his father. A patriotic Prussian, he could not help delighting in Bismarck's aggrandizing of his country. A proud Hohenzollern, he could not but approve of the fact that he would one day be Kaiser of the triumphant new Reich. Prince Frederick was an honest, well-meaning and high-minded man but he lacked single-mindedness of purpose.

Vicky, of course, was very different. There was never any doubt about the strength of either her character or her beliefs.

At forty-six, the Crown Princess Victoria was one of the most remarkable women in Europe. It was true that she was not much to look at. She was short, plump and high-coloured but her smile was radiant and her eyes a brilliant sea-green. Her hair, in contrast to the elaborately ridged, curled and fringed fashion of the day, was drawn neatly back into a braided coronet. Her clothes, in which she did not take an excessive interest, showed something of the same simplicity of style. In repose her air was tranquil, almost melancholy. At first glance, she could have been mistaken for a sensible, middle-class matron, hardly different from the Prussian *Hausfrauen* amongst whom she had spent almost thirty years of her life.

The reality was very different. A few minutes in the Crown Princess's company revealed her as a stimulating, assertive and highly individual personality: clever, diligent and dynamic. Her admiring father used to say that she had 'a man's head on her shoulders' and, compared with her fellow princesses, she was remarkably emancipated. In the Berlin of her day, when women were expected to confine themselves to *Küche, Kinderstube, Krankenstube und Kirche* – kitchen, nursery, sickroom and church – she never ceased to astonish her contemporaries by the range and unorthodoxy of her interests. She had a passion, not only for such things as painting, poetry and architecture, but for politics, economics and social reform. She took an active interest in prisons, hospitals, social welfare and sanitation. She read widely.

On the other hand, Vicky was no mere bluestocking. If she had a man's head, she had a woman's warmth and impetuosity. She might, in intellect, have been her father's daughter, but in ardour, she was very much her mother's. Like Queen Victoria, she was impulsive, partisan and emotional. Beneath that plain exterior beat a passionate heart. Her charm, when she chose to exercise it, could be prodigious; she was capable of extreme kindness.

But whereas Queen Victoria's emotionalism was tempered by a sound common sense, Vicky's was not. For all her brilliance, the Crown Princess completely lacked wisdom. The British statesman who once summed her up as 'always clever, never wise', knew exactly what he was saying. She was outspoken, dogmatic and assertive. A woman of strong opinions, she never hesitated to air them; nor did she ever doubt that they were the right ones. She was incapable of making allowances or of adapting her views. With her, it was always all or nothing. She could be extremely tactless. Of the art of handling people, she knew nothing. She would set out to win their heads, it was said, 'rather than their hearts'.

That this unconventional princess should have found life difficult at the hide-bound Prussian court is understandable. Amongst the narrow-minded bigots who made up the bulk of Prussian society she was extremely unpopular. They considered her cultural interests unseemly, her advanced religious views scandalous and her intellectualism positively dangerous. They distrusted her passion for open windows, modern plumbing and long walks. They never ceased to be affronted by the fact that such things as the number of quarterings, by which they set so much store, meant nothing to her: on making up her guest lists, she simply invited whoever she thought might be interesting. When she accepted the honorary chairmanship of a newly-founded orphanage for Jewish girls, they were appalled.

Most annoying of all, however, was her persistent Englishness. On Vicky's arrival in Berlin, Bismarck had announced that she would be a blessing to her new country only if she left the Englishwoman at home and became a Prussian. It was sound advice, but Vicky was incapable of following it. To her, England was always 'home', superior, in every possible way – were it politics or plumbing – to Prussia. It was, she claimed to her mother, 'my country which I shall love so passionately to my dying day and to have been too proud to have belonged to ever to let myself forget'.

In this regrettable attitude Vicky had been encouraged, during her early years in Prussia, by Queen Victoria. The Queen had insisted that her daughter remain as English as possible. If Vicky had suggested following some harmless Prussian custom, Victoria had replied that she could 'let the German ladies do what they like, but the *English* Princess *must not*'. She had instructed her daughter to sign her name *Victoria, Princess Royal and Princess Frederick Wilhelm of Prussia*; 'you are the eldest daughter of the Queen of England with a title and rights of your own,' she had written.

But whereas, in time, Queen Victoria came to show better sense, Vicky did not. With that grating lack of tact, she continued to sing the praises of all things English. Before long she came to be known (as the hated Marie Antoinette had been known as '*l'Autrichienne*') as '*die Engländerin*'.

The death of Prince Albert, in the very year of Wilhelm I's accession, robbed Vicky of the one person who would have been capable of keeping her vehement nature in check. Although Prince Albert's views had been no less strongly held than hers, he had been more tolerant, more able to compromise. He had always been able to see both sides of a question. This was something she never learned. She could never appreciate that by giving way on small issues one could yet hold to larger principles. Once Prince Albert died, there was no one to teach her these lessons.

The truth was that Vicky, no less than Fritz, was trapped in a dilemma. She had exulted in Prussia's march to greatness while being appalled at the way in which the march was being conducted. She had rejoiced in the unification of Germany but had disapproved of the manner in which it had been achieved. She was torn between pride in her native and her adopted countries. Her brother, the Prince of Wales, was not far off the mark when he claimed that she was always pure Prussian when she was in England and pure English when she was in Prussia. She even spoke English with a German accent and German with an English. At one moment she was claiming that the Prussians were a superior race; at another she was praising Britain to the skies.

That this inconsistency did nothing towards enhancing her reputation in Germany is understandable. Despite her bursts of patriotic fervour, Vicky remained as distrusted and unpopular as ever.

'To be friends with the present régime is impossible,' she complained to Queen Victoria, 'and yet to be in opposition is a thing as impossible. I always feel like a fly struggling in a very tangled web, and a feeling of weariness and depression, often of disgust and hopelessness, takes possession of me. . . .'

3

To Vicky's political difficulties were added domestic ones.

Her marriage was happy enough. She and Fritz had been in love when they married and they were to remain so throughout their life together. They suited each other very well. Both were enlightened, cultured, hard-working and conscientious; where there were differences, these were complementary. If she was quick, clever, impetuous and domineering, he was placid, serious-minded, reflective and tolerant. While she might dazzle guests by the force and mobility of her personality, it was he who won their hearts.

Their home life was extremely simple. The atmosphere in their town and country palaces – the Kronprinzenpalais in Berlin and the Neues Palais at Potsdam – was lively and natural. Of the formality, the friction and the philistinism of other Prussian royal households there was not a trace; guests were always struck by the unaffectedness, the tranquillity and the air of culture pervading the Crown Prince's *ménage*. In their role as host and hostess, Fritz and Vicky were charming: he, tall, bearded, superbly mannered; she small, graceful and vivacious. 'Nothing in the world is more natural and cordial than he is,' noted Disraeli on one occasion, while he pronounced Vicky to be 'most animated and entertaining'.

Between the years 1859 and 1872, Vicky bore her husband eight children – four boys and four girls. She raised them in as unaffected a fashion as possible and, in the early days, they made a delightful, harmonious family group. The harmony did not last long. One son died in infancy, another at the age of eleven. Vicky felt the death of these two sons keenly. Their passing left her, she sighed, with two stupid sons: 'good boys, but nothing in them'.

In fact, they were not even good. And, as they matured, so – as far as Vicky was concerned – did they become less and less good. The younger, Prince Henry, developed into a shallow, self-opinionated pup ('ignorant, green and misled,' complained his mother to Queen Victoria); the elder, Prince Wilhelm, was infinitely worse.

His was a difficult case. At his birth, in January 1859, a nerve in Prince Wilhelm's neck had been injured, leaving him with a poor sense of balance and a stunted left arm that was all but useless. To a large extent – for he was a determined boy – he overcame the physical aspects of his deformity: he learnt to ride, to shoot and to swim. If he kept his left arm bent, he looked hardly different from any other youngster.

How much his crippled arm had affected his character is another matter. Whether or not his arrogance, his bombast and his conceit were due to the fact that he, who longed to be thought of as a typically militant Prussian prince, was trying to compensate for the inadequacy of his body, is impossible to prove. Of perhaps more importance to the development of his character was his relationship with his mother.

An extremely sensitive person, Prince Wilhelm might, in childhood, have found his mother's obvious solicitude for his deformity somewhat embarrassing: the more she pitied him, the more conscious was he made to feel of his infirmity and the more he resented her concern. And then, as he grew older, so did he – a bright but by no means intellectual youth – begin to feel inadequate beside his brilliant, impatient and energetic mother. She wanted him to be a man in the mould of her father, Prince Albert; he wanted to be like his autocratic and soldierly grandfather, Kaiser Wilhelm I.

With each passing year Prince Wilhelm's manner became more lordly and his views more reactionary. At the Military Academy at Potsdam he became so stuffed with the currently fashionable, authoritarian, nationalistic and anti-British sentiments that he became insufferable. Each time he returned from these agreeably martial surroundings to the artistic and enlightened atmosphere of his parents' home, there would be a row. The Crown Prince might hold his tongue but the Crown Princess was not nearly so longsuffering. And Wilhelm, who found her liberal outlook no less intolerable, was quick to answer back. There were innumerable scenes. It was, in fact, the old story of a parent and a child having similar personalities and opposing views.

Queen Victoria, who was subjected to endless tirades against her grandson, did what she could in the way of giving her daughter good advice. When, during Wilhelm's schooldays, Vicky assured her mother that she watched over even 'the minutest detail of the boy's education', the Queen warned her that 'too great care, too much constant watching, leads to the very dangers hereafter which one wishes to avoid'. The Queen, no doubt, had her son Bertie in mind. She realized too, that her daughter's standards were probably too high and her approach too hectoring. But, as Wilhelm matured, so did Victoria come to appreciate that her daughter was grappling with an extraordinarily difficult situation. Wilhelm was clearly more than just a loutish young man.

Another reason for Prince Wilhelm's attitude was that he had grown up during the years of Prussia's surge to greatness. As a boy he had thrilled to the military triumphs of the Franco-Prussian War and the inauguration of the German Reich. One of his most exciting memories was of his grandfather, the newly proclaimed Kaiser, taking the salute at the march-past of his victorious troops after the war. His country's greatness had been achieved, not by a spread of liberal ideas, but by military conquest. As the young man's hero, Prince Bismarck, had once said, the questions of the day had been solved, not by majority votes, but by blood and iron. To identify himself with his parents' views, reckoned Prince Wilhelm, would be not only distasteful but extremely short-sighted. He thus gave the Iron Chancellor his full support. 'Bismarck,' he once wrote in his effusive fashion, 'was the idol in my temple, and I worshipped him.'

The Chancellor, of course, was delighted. Having always disapproved of the Crown Prince and Princess, he now made use of their son in his battle against them. He wanted to ensure that the young Prince, who would one day succeed his father as Kaiser, would rule according to the pattern laid down by Wilhelm I and himself. It did not need much to convince the old Kaiser of the need for this. Relieved to know that his son's liberalism had not been passed on to the next generation, Wilhelm I approved Bismarck's plans for involving young Wilhelm in affairs of state. For Fritz and Vicky, who had always been kept at arm's length, this was very galling.

In the year 1880, at the age of twenty-one, Prince Wilhelm had become engaged to Princess Auguste Viktoria of Schleswig-Holstein. The Princess was always known to the family as Dona. She was dispatched to Windsor for Queen Victoria's approval and the Queen pronounced her 'gentle and amiable and sweet'. That she was, and, as such, Dona suited the ebullient Prince Wilhelm very well. Unlike his mother, Dona would never involve herself in politics or try to influence her husband's policies. She was precisely the sort of submissive, church-going, child-bearing *Hausfrau* of which the Prussians approved, but with enough physical presence to play her public role. Bismarck, who entirely approved of his protégé's choice, always referred to Dona as 'the cow from Holstein'.

Thus, by the late 1880s, the German imperial family was split into two irreconcilable parts. On the one side stood the old Kaiser and his grandson Prince Wilhelm; on the other the Crown Prince and Princess, forming what Bismarck scathingly referred to as the Anglo-Coburg faction. Prince Albert's scheme, so optimistically initiated almost thirty years before, had been realized only in so far as that Germany had been unified. Of that model democratic state of the Prince Consort's imaginings, there was not a vestige in the militant, thrusting and powerful Second Reich.

Whether or not, when the old Kaiser finally died, Fritz and Vicky would be able to inaugurate their long-delayed plans remained to be seen. To many, it seemed extremely doubtful. For one thing Bismarck was as firmly entrenched as ever. Could Frederick afford to dismiss him? After more than a quarter of a century in power, he had blunted almost all sense of individual freedom and independence of mind in Germany. For the majority of Germans, brute force had become the most important thing in the state. It was quite probable that Bismarck's institutions were too strong and the German people's attitudes too ingrained for Crown Prince Fredrick to alter.

And in any case, with the heir, Prince Wilhelm, being so utterly opposed to everything his parents planned to do, would it be worth while making the effort? Would Fritz, already nearing sixty, be granted enough time to undo all Bismarck's work and set Germany along a different course? Would not Prince Wilhelm, on ascending the throne, simply nullify his father's efforts and revert to the autocratic rule of his grandfather's day?

It was a difficult situation. And by the summer of Queen Victoria's Jubilee, it had become more difficult still. Admittedly the old Kaiser, already in his ninety-first year, could not be expected to last much longer, but from this Vicky could not take a great deal of comfort. A further blow had fallen. Her husband was seriously ill.

CHAPTER TWO

Bertie of Great Britain

I

The Crown Princess's brother Bertie, the Prince of Wales, was also being kept waiting for a throne. He was waiting for it, however, in a far less anguished fashion. Indeed, not only in this, but in almost every possible way, did Bertie differ from his sister Vicky.

Prince Albert Edward was forty-five at the time of his mother's Golden Jubilee. By this stage he had developed fully the looks, the manner and the life style that were to characterize him until the day he died. He was stout; a condition which neither cures at Continental spas nor superbly cut jackets could successfully minimize. Behind his back, he was sometimes referred to as 'Tum Tum'. His baldness was offset by a full, greying, but neatly trimmed beard and moustache. His eyes were pale, bulbous, heavy-lidded and sensuous looking. They could be caressing if he were talking to some attractive young woman, dull if he were bored and steely if he became aware of some lapse of taste in dress or behaviour. An erect carriage and dignified bearing gave him an unmistakable aura of majesty; his manners were faultless. Yet his air, for the most part, was far from ponderous or unapproachable; it was relaxed, genial and charming. He looked, and was, a *bon viveur*.

By the 1880s, the Prince of Wales had established himself as the most fashionable figure in European society. He lived in great style. His clothes were elegant, his meals rich, his entertainments lavish. His wife, formerly Princess Alexandra of Denmark, had all the beauty, perfection and agelessness of a wax flower. His homes – Marlborough House in London and Sandringham in Norfolk – were comfortably and sumptuously furnished. He surrounded himself with the beautiful, the amusing, the wealthy and the worldly. Refreshingly free of racial, social or religious bigotry, he befriended anyone whom he considered interesting. He delighted in the company of financiers, men-about-town and actresses; he adored racing, shooting and gambling. Nothing pleased him so much as to be surrounded by smiling faces. Equally at home in London, Paris, the South of France or some Continental watering-place, he was renowned for his zest, his gregariousness and his licentiousness. As his disapproving mother only too frequently pointed out, the Prince of Wales lived purely for pleasure.

Sipping champagne, puffing cigars and trailing clouds of scandal, Bertie moved through the *beau-monde* of the late nineteenth century like some plump and stately Dionysus.

But there was another side to the coin. The Prince of Wales might have given the impression of an easygoing and warm-hearted rake, but his personality was not as resolved as it first appeared. Away from the café table or the roulette wheel, he was moody, irritable and impatient. His restlessness was a byword. Easily bored, he was the despair of his hostesses. Constant diversion was necessary to keep him from becoming depressed. Utterly without resources, he could not bear to be alone, even for a second. As he lacked application, nothing could hold his interest long; he seldom read a book and would merely skim through the newspapers. He was quick-tempered. For the most part, he would lose his temper over trivia: a decoration incorrectly worn, a hitch in an arrangement, a delay in some ceremony. Very conscious of his royal dignity, he was easily affronted. One never quite knew how far one could go with him. When a drunken friend once called him 'Tum Tum' to his face, he saw to it that the offender was ushered out of the company as soon as possible.

So seemingly a man of the world, Bertie was alarmingly immature in many ways. His indiscretions were always causing trouble. More than once his mother, or her Ministers, were obliged to cover up for him. He was too partisan, too impressionable and too susceptible to the influence of others. Often he simply reflected the opinions of the last person with whom he happened to have spent some time.

He had no intellectual curiosity and distrusted clever people. Of art and music he knew nothing and cared less. His taste, if not exactly vulgar, was philistine. His political creed was an unthinking conservatism, his religious beliefs those of a schoolboy, his sense of humour utterly un-sophisticated. 'Anything approaching a *practical joke*,' his pedantic father had once decreed, would be impermissible for the Prince of Wales; the fact was that Bertie came to adore practical jokes. Dummies in the bed, champagne down the neck, donkeys in nightshirts – all these were a source of side-splitting hilarity to the Prince of Wales. Something of this same boyishness was revealed in his passion for uniforms: he could never have enough of them – the brighter, the better. He was forever changing his clothes.

In a way, it was as though the Prince of Wales – and his beautiful wife, Princess Alexandra – were transfixed in eternal youth. To the end of her days, almost, the Princess of Wales looked and thought like a girl, while the Prince retained the tastes and habits of a young man. In middle age he was still living, as Queen Victoria once complained, 'in a whirl of amusements'; spending, for want of any more worthwhile occupation, the idle, frivolous and self-indulgent life of a young blood.

An example of his juvenile behaviour was provided during that Jubilee season of 1887. One night the Prince took a party of friends to supper in a public restaurant. Amongst them was Crown Prince Rudolf of Austria, a young man hardly notable for his prudishness. At about two in the morning Bertie asked the orchestra to play the famous can-can from *Orpheus in the Underworld*; with the beautiful Duchess of Manchester as his partner, he flung himself into the dance with embarrassing abandon.

'Tell the waiters to go,' whispered Crown Prince Rudolf to one of the company, 'they must not see their future King making such a clown of himself.'

2

That Bertie was leading so worthless an existence was not entirely his own fault. His upbringing had all but ensured this regrettable result.

Prince Albert, egged on by that high-minded *éminence grise* of the Coburgs, Baron Christian von Stockmar, had approached the problem of his eldest son's education with characteristic earnestness. To best control the rising tide of democracy, Albert and Stockmar had decided that it would be necessary to rear a set of enlightened princes: men who, by their breadth of vision, unimpeachable morals and high sense of duty, would win the respect and love of their people. They would be the examples of what could well be termed the Coburg ideal of constitutional monarchy: a race of wise, impartial and influential sovereigns, raised high above the hurly-burly of daily political life.

Of this proposed race of paragons, none would occupy a more important position than the prince who was destined to become the King of England. It was therefore essential that he be moulded, from babyhood almost, into a model constitutional sovereign.

With this ideal in mind, Prince Albert mapped out Bertie's future. The boy's character was to become an amalgam of all the virtues; he was to be fashioned, said Stockmar, into 'a man of calm, profound, comprehensive understanding'. Samuel Wilberforce, the Bishop of Oxford, was prepared to go even further. 'The great object in view,' declared his lordship solemnly, 'is to make him the most perfect man.'

To this end Bertie was subjected to a rigorous course of training. He was isolated from boys of his own age, surrounded by a team of upright, well-educated and serious-minded tutors, kept at his lessons from morning to night, bombarded with information and advice – usually in the form of ponderous memoranda – from his well-meaning father. Even his periods of relaxation were watched over by a keen, and usually disapproving eye. If the Prince were not turned into the *beau ideal* of a constitutional monarch, it would be through no lack of honest intention on the part of his elders.

It was all to no purpose. From the beginning Bertie revealed himself as an affectionate and amiable creature but one with whom very little could be done. He was lazy, he was slow, he was stupid. He was also completely unpredictable. At times his habitual geniality would give way to a mule-like obstinacy or screaming rage. The sad fact was that Bertie, unlike his sister Vicky, simply did not have the mental ability to cope with this intensive course of instruction. He was bored, bewildered and over-worked. Naturally gregarious and fun-loving, he was starved for company of his own age. Nor, once his weaknesses were exposed, was any attempt made to tailor his education to his personality. He was simply driven harder. A lighter touch might have encouraged him; the heavier hand crushed his initiative.

With each passing year his parents became more disappointed. Albert complained that the only thing in which the adolescent Bertie showed the slightest interest was clothes, while the Queen, who was never very relaxed in his company, could only beg the boy to try and be more like his father – if only in *some* ways. In no way, in fact, did Bertie resemble his father; he was very much his mother's son. 'Bertie . . .' the Queen once wrote to her daughter Vicky, 'is my caricature. That is the misfortune, and, in a man, this is so much worse. You are quite your dear, beloved Papa's child.' The Queen understood only too well that her son was developing into what she might have become had it not been for Albert's uplifting influence. In the tug-of-war between Coburg and Hanoverian for control of the boy's character, his Hanoverian ancestry was winning hands down. Every year these regrettable characteristics were becoming more and more pronounced.

Proof positive of what his parents considered his bad blood came in Bertie's twentieth year. By then, that nightmarish education almost completed (he was at Cambridge) the Prince was doing a spell of military training at the Curragh camp near Dublin. Here he was introduced to an easy-going actress named Nelly Clifden. Not unnaturally (and despite the fact that not until a mere two years earlier had he had the sex act fully explained to him) he slept with her.

When the news of this escapade reached the Prince Consort's ears, that high-principled man was appalled. The average Victorian father would have laughed, or at least shrugged the matter off, but Prince Albert saw it in the blackest possible light. His great dream of fashioning the perfect, unsullied heir had been finally shattered: Bertie was obviously about to go the way of Queen Victoria's unspeakable uncles. Could such a prince, having forfeited the respect of his future subjects, weather the democratic storms of the nineteenth century? Prince Albert did not think so. Assuring Bertie that he had inflicted on his father 'the greatest pain I have yet felt in this life', Prince Albert treated him to one of his most sanctimonious, if anguished, literary outpourings. He was too broken-hearted, he wrote, even to see his son.

After Bertie had expressed due contrition for his lapse, the Prince Consort forgave him. He even went so far as to pay his son a visit at Cambridge. The Prince Consort came back from this visit in a state of exhaustion. A week later he collapsed with typhoid fever. Less than a fortnight after this – on 14 December 1861 – he died.

The Prince Consort's death caused the Queen's long-simmering dissatisfaction with her eldest son to boil over. She was convinced that his 'fall' had killed her husband. The belief became an obsession. "I never can or shall look at him without a shudder . . .' she admitted in a letter to Vicky; indeed, she could not bear to look at him at all. Her antipathy towards him was such, she cried out, that 'I feel daily, hourly, something which is too dreadful to describe.'

Quite clearly, the Prince would have to be more or less permanently separated from his grief-demented mother. In her determination to adhere to every plan laid down by her late husband, the Queen was able to ensure this separation. The Prince Consort had decreed that his son should round off his education with a long journey to the Near East and, with that accomplished, to get married as soon as possible. Bertie duly made his journey and, on 10 March 1863, at the age of twenty-one, he married Princess Alexandra of Schleswig-Holstein-Sonderburg-Glucksburg, daughter of the heir to the Danish throne. She, too, had been approved by the late Prince Consort.

In the years that followed Bertie's marriage, the widely divergent ways of life of his mother and himself became an established part of the British scene. She withdrew from public life almost completely; he flung himself into an almost frenetic social round. From her seclusion at Windsor – or Osborne or Balmoral – she sent off a steady stream of letters in which she upbraided him for his extravagance, his frivolity, his idleness and his indiscretions. Tactfully – for until the day she died he was in awe of her – he would counter her strictures by pointing out that *someone* had to fulfil the social and ceremonial role of the monarchy.

This he certainly did. He not only lived and entertained in royal style but he performed many of those thankless royal duties which the Queen refused to carry out. He laid foundation stones, he opened schools, he presented prizes, he inaugurated exhibitions, he presided at dinners. He paid a highly successful state visit to India. All this was done with dignity, aplomb and apparent enjoyment. Particularly after his recovery from a serious illness in 1871, he was extremely popular with the majority of his mother's subjects. A great many people admired him for leading exactly the sort of life they would have led had they been as rich as he.

But it was, for all that, an unsatisfactory life. Bertie was just frittering away such talents as he had. Quite simply, he did not have enough to do;

nor, while his mother was alive, was there the slightest chance of his being given anything to do.

This exclusion of her heir from the more serious business of the monarchy had not always been the Queen's intention. During his infancy, Bertie's parents had resolved to initiate him into affairs of state as early as possible; they had been determined to show every confidence in him, to encourage him to work beside them. Had Bertie shown anything like his sister Vicky's abilities, Victoria and Albert would no doubt have implemented their resolution. When he did not, they kept postponing his political initiation. Once Prince Albert died, his broken-hearted widow was determined that no one, especially not Bertie, would play the political role that her husband had once done.

Thus the Prince of Wales was kept in almost complete ignorance of the business of government. His mother very rarely took him into her confidence and almost never consulted him. He must not see anything, she warned her Ministers, of 'a very *confidential* nature'. There must be no 'independent communication' between him and the government. For almost thirty years she refused to trust him with the Prince Consort's special golden key to the Foreign Office boxes. Even the most trifling decision concerning her heir's public activities had to be vetted by her. Any move on his part to involve himself in affairs of state was severely slapped down. 'He has *no* right to meddle,' the Queen would say.

And so Victoria, who would have been the first to claim that the Devil found work for idle hands, kept Bertie's hands resolutely idle.

Sometimes, in a desperate effort to involve the heir in the workings of the monarchy, a Prime Minister would induce the Queen to send the Prince a few unimportant state papers, or at least a précis of what was happening. In 1872, Gladstone came up with a more definite proposal. In a series of long-winded letters to the Queen, he pointed out the necessity of giving the Prince some active, useful employment. Could he not become the Queen's permanent representative in Ireland? That way he would learn something of the art of constitutional monarchy.

The Queen would have none of it. The Prince of Wales, she said, would never agree to it (in this she was correct); nor could any such artificially created position imbue him with the necessary sense of responsibility. Only when he was forced to assume full responsibility – when, in other words, he became King – would he tackle the job seriously.

In this, too, was Queen Victoria correct. The Prince of Wales was to make an admirable King, but he was to arrive at this goal by a very different route from the one mapped out by his exacting parents.

It was an impossible situation. Because the Queen considered her son to be so frivolous and incompetent, she refused to give him any employment; because he was given no employment, he became all the more frivolous and incompetent. A man of considerable diplomatic gifts, exceptional vitality and great panache, the Prince of Wales might have been of real service to his mother. On the other hand, the Queen was no fool; she had very good reason for her attitude. The defects of the Prince of Wales's character were not entirely due to his father's system of education or his mother's lack of confidence. He *was* feckless, he *was* self-indulgent, he *was* indiscreet. And every now and then yet another scandal, or another indiscretion, would serve to justify his mother's intransigent behaviour.

Yet she was fond of him. As she gradually overcame her conviction that he had been responsible for her husband's death, she began to appreciate his many good points. 'Really dear Bertie is so full of good and amiable qualities,' she wrote to Vicky on one occasion, 'that it makes one forget and overlook much that one would wish different.' And as the years passed, and the Prince Consort's shadow grew fainter, so did she come nearer to accepting her son for what he was. There were even times when – as frequently happened, he was in trouble – she gave him her active support. For this he was always very grateful.

Although he never mastered his feeling of inferiority in her presence, Bertie was no less fond of the Queen. As often as they found themselves at loggerheads over his way of life, they were in agreement on other matters. Both, for instance, were ardent imperialists, very conscious of the importance of upholding British prestige throughout the world. By the 1880s, with Britain the leading nation on earth, this shared imperialism was a very strong bond indeed. These were the years in which the Queen, having been coaxed out of her long seclusion by the romantic Disraeli, was becoming increasingly conscious of her role as ruler of a mighty Empire – *Victoria Regina et Imperatrix*. To the magnificence of her estate, the Prince of Wales was equally alive. Indeed, for much of the time and especially during Jubilee Year, a great deal of Queen Victoria's glory was reflected on him.

The Golden Jubilee brought mother and son as close as they had ever been. On New Year's Day, 1887, he presented her with the first of the specially designed Jubilee inkstands: an imperial crown which opened to reveal her portrait inside the lid. Victoria pronounced it 'very pretty and useful'. Throughout the celebrations the Prince of Wales bore the major part of the burden of entertaining what the Queen called 'the royal mob'. Later that year, in his mother's presence, he unveiled a Jubilee statue of her on the Balmoral estate.

The Queen's comments on her son's visit to Balmoral to perform this ceremony have a strangely touching quality.

'An early luncheon,' she wrote in her Journal, 'after which dear Bertie left, having had a most pleasant visit, which I think he enjoyed and said so repeatedly. He had not stayed alone with me, excepting for a couple of days in May '68, at Balmoral, since he married! He is so kind and affectionate that it is a pleasure to be a little quietly together.'

3

If the Prince of Wales, in Queen Victoria's estimation, was an unsatisfactory heir, *his* eldest son, Prince Albert Victor, was an infinitely worse one. Of all the Queen's grandsons, not one was less promising than the young man whom it was assumed would one day sit upon her throne.

The five Wales children – two boys and three girls – had been raised in the most informal and indulgent fashion. This was due, partly, to the Prince of Wales's determination that their childhood should in no way resemble his and, to an even greater extent, to the personality of the Princess of Wales. Not only would she have been temperamentally incapable of subjecting them to a rigorous course of training but she encouraged them to remain as childlike as possible as long as possible. So enduringly youthful, in both looks and personality, herself, the Princess was determined that they should not grow up too quickly. She might be socially accomplished and transcendentally smart, but to Princess Alexandra nothing was more important than her children. They were the centre of her world. Increasingly cut off from public affairs by her deafness, her domesticity and her immaturity, the Princess devoted herself to her children.

And they, in turn, adored her. To the Wales children, their mother – so gay, so spontaneous, so impractical and unpunctual – was always 'darling Motherdear': a delightful companion, hardly more grownup than themselves. It was as though mother and children lived in a make-believe world, in a state of eternal youth. Long after their childhood was over, the Wales children still spoke and behaved like adolescents. One of the princesses celebrated her nineteenth birthday with a children's party; in manhood, the second son would sign himself 'little Georgie'.

By no stretch of the imagination, however, could the blame for the backwardness of the eldest son, Prince Albert Victor, be laid at Princess Alexandra's door. Prince Eddy, as he was called in the family, had been subnormal from infancy. It was not that he was an imbecile; he was merely slow-witted. As a boy he had shown himself to be apathetic, listless, slow to react and quite unable to concentrate his attention on anything for long. His one positive characteristic being a devotion to his younger, and brighter, brother Prince George, it had been decided to keep the two princes together as much as possible. Some of George's liveliness was bound to rub off on Eddy. It did not. They spent years together at sea but neither that, nor a spell at Cambridge, could shake Eddy out of his lethargy. In one despairing report after another, his long-suffering tutors complained that there was simply nothing to be done with the Prince; 'he hardly knows the meaning of the words *to read*', wailed one of them.

After Cambridge, Prince Eddy joined the 10th Hussars and although the recreations – and dissipations – of army life held more appeal for him than study, he remained abnormally immature.

During Jubilee Year, Prince Eddy turned twenty-three. The Queen's complaint that the Wales children seemed to her 'a puny breed' was certainly justified in Prince Eddy's case. Not even his spectacularly flattering Hussar uniform nor his jauntily waxed moustache could make him look anything other than an indolent weakling. He was thin and pale, with an extraordinarily long neck and a vacant expression. His whole being was notable for an extreme lassitude; his air was that of a sleep-walker. With the best will in the world, his superior officers could find very little to say in his favour. They could only hope that he would prove to be a late maturer. With each passing year the hope became more remote.

Yet the Prince had his good points. He was a gentle, well-mannered young man, with an ability to charm and a complete lack of arrogance. He meant well. 'Kind' and 'dear' were the adjectives his family most frequently used when referring to him. Indeed, to some women his languid air was very attractive, almost seductive. His grandmother, Queen Victoria, treated him with great sympathy. He might be retarded but she appreciated him for his goodness, his simplicity and his sense of duty towards his parents and herself. Only later was she to learn something of his sexual escapades.

Prince Eddy's limitations would not have mattered nearly so much had he not been heir to the British throne. What sort of king was he likely to make? Anyone further removed from Prince Albert's ideal of an intelligent, enlightened, influential and unsullied monarch would have been difficult to imagine.

Very different from the lackadaisical Prince Eddy was his brother, the twenty-two-year-old Prince George. At the age of twelve, as a lively, intelligent and good-natured boy, he had joined the Navy. Since then he had spent almost all his life at sea. His character had formed early and by now he was already the steady, straightforward and conscientious person that he was to remain throughout his life. Unimaginative and unintellectual Prince George might have been, but the discipline of life in the Navy had incalculated him with one very valuable characteristic – a strong sense of duty. In this he was very much a Coburg.

Alone amongst Princess Alexandra's children, Prince George had inherited something of her good looks. Blue-eyed, suntanned, with a neatly trimmed nautical beard and moustache, he had none of the pallid, inbred appearance of his brother and sisters. Yet he, no less than the rest of them (and despite his more resolved personality) was still very much enmeshed in his mother's web. He adored her and she him. To read the letters between mother and son is scarcely to believe that she was the middle-aged future Queen of England and he a fully adult naval officer. How he wished, he wrote to her at this time, that he were going with her to Sandringham for the holidays. It almost made him cry to think of it. 'I wonder who will have that sweet little room of mine, you must go and see it sometimes and imagine that your little Georgie dear is living in it.'

It was no wonder that Queen Victoria could pronounce the young Prince to be 'so dear and amiable'.

The three Wales princesses – Louise, Victoria and Maud – had something of their brother Eddy's negative quality. Indeed, it was difficult to tell them apart. All three were pale and narrow-skulled with protruding eyes and tightly curled poodle fringes. Invariably, they were identically dressed. Diffident in public and boisterous in private, they had all suffered from the same happy-go-lucky system of education. Even their conversation had a similarity. They always talked, claimed one of their cousins, about people as 'the dear little thing' or 'the poor little man'. They always 'spoke in a minor key, *en sourdine.* It gave a special quality to all talks with them, and gave me a strange sensation, as though life would have been very wonderful and everything very beautiful if it had not been so sad.' Their rooms were like those of little children: jam-packed with an accumulation of tiny, pretty, dainty but far from aesthetic *objets* – miniatures, shells, little vases, diminutive paintings, tiny china ornaments. The three of them were sometimes referred to as 'the whispering Wales girls'.

All in all, the Wales family could not have afforded Queen Victoria much satisfaction. Amongst the lot of them, Prince George was the only one to show some promise. And he, unfortunately, was not in the direct line of succession. It was thus not surprising that the Queen, in thinking of her heirs – the dissolute Prince of Wales and the slow-witted Prince Eddy – sometimes despaired of the British monarchy outlasting her lifetime.

CHAPTER THREE

'My own dear *Empress Victoria*'

I

No one, seeing the fifty-five-year-old German Crown Prince Frederick riding in Queen Victoria's Jubilee cavalcade, would have imagined that he was seriously ill. So tall, so manfully bearded and spectacularly uniformed, Fritz looked the very picture of royal dignity and radiant health. Even the Queen, who knew that something was wrong, remarked on how well and handsome he looked. Indeed, Fritz himself had no real appreciation of the gravity of his condition.

His illness had first manifested itself during the previous winter. He had suffered from a persistent soreness in his throat. By March 1887 his personal physician, unable to alleviate the Prince's sufferings, had decided to call in a specialist, Professor Karl Gerhardt. Dr Gerhardt discovered a small growth on the left vocal cord. Having tried, without success, to remove the growth, Gerhardt advised the Crown Prince to take a holiday. He went to Bad Ems and from here the Crown Princess was able to assure Queen Victoria that Fritz was improving and that when, on his return to Berlin, the growth was removed, he would be quite well again.

She was soon disillusioned. On re-examining the Prince's throat, a panel of six leading German doctors decided that the growth was cancerous. They advised an immediate operation. This would involve the splitting of the larynx. Even if the patient survived the operation, he would probably be rendered permanently voiceless. Before going ahead, however, the doctors suggested that yet another specialist be consulted. They decided on one of Europe's leading authorities on diseases of the throat – an Englishman, Dr Morell Mackenzie. He was requested to come as soon as possible to Berlin.

Sick with worry, Vicky backed up the doctors' telegram to Mackenzie with one of her own to the Queen. Would her mother see that the doctor set off at once. 'Greatly distressed,' wrote the Queen in her Journal, 'and cannot bear to think of poor darling Vicky's anguish and sorrow.'

Dr Mackenzie arrived in Berlin on 20 May 1887. He examined the

Crown Prince's throat and sent several fragments of the growth to a German pathologist for examination. The report was negative. He therefore advised against the operation and suggested that the Crown Prince come to England for treatment. He should be able to cure him, reckoned Mackenzie, in a matter of months.

The Crown Princess was exultant. 'We are much more hopeful and reassured about Fritz's throat now,' she told her mother. The suspense, she admitted, had been agonizing, 'but I own the hope held out is a very great relief, and as I am sanguine by nature, I easily cling to it. . . .'"

The German doctors were distinctly less sanguine. Still suspecting that the growth was cancerous, they could not agree on what should be done. Some advised the operation; others suggested that Mackenzie's proposed treatment be carried out in Berlin; Dr Gerhardt thought it would be best if Mackenzie treated the patient himself. 'I now leave it to them to settle their minds amongst themselves and shall not interfere with them,' wrote Vicky. 'Fritz *ought* to be under [Mackenzie's] care and we must see *how* we can carefully effect this.'

She needed to be careful. A great many people at court, kept in ignorance of the seriousness of the Crown Prince's illness (he had no very clear idea himself) considered it quite wrong that he should think of absenting himself from Germany at a time when the health of his ninety-year-old father was far from good. Others were only too quick to say that the Crown Princess was anxious to whisk him away to her beloved England where he, who had always been putty in her hands, could be manipulated more easily.

But contrary to popular belief, she could not, and did not, simply insist that the Crown Prince go to England to be treated by Mackenzie. Only when Dr Gerhardt, albeit reluctantly, gave his permission, could she think of doing so. Queen Victoria's Jubilee celebrations provided them with the excuse. Fritz, who had a taste for ceremonial, was longing to represent the Kaiser at the Thanksgiving Service in Westminster Abbey. And the fact that his son, the officious Prince Wilhelm, was already suggesting that he take his father's place, acted as an added incentive.

An indication of the atmosphere of suspicion in which the couple lived in Berlin was provided when, prior to setting out for England, Vicky asked her mother whether she could bring over all their private papers for safe-keeping in Buckingham Palace.

A few days before the couple left Berlin, Dr Gerhardt warned the Crown Princess that he was becoming increasingly anxious about the Crown Prince's throat. He claimed that the hitherto healthy right vocal cord was now affected. If Dr Mackenzie's cure was not successful, then the operation would *have* to be performed – but in much less favourable conditions than before. Every day lost was dangerous. 'Of course you can understand this makes me utterly miserable!' wailed Vicky. She was being driven half distracted, she admitted, by the uncertainty; she simply could not bring herself to believe that the German doctors were right. For one thing, she could not bear the thought that her beloved husband might be fatally ill; for another, she could not face the fact that he might never ascend the throne. They had both lived for the day when his accession would mean the inauguration of their democratic ideas. Would all these years of waiting prove to have been in vain? Was the prize to be snatched away at the very moment of its coming within reach? Were her long-cherished ambitions about to turn to dust? Surely Fate would never be so cruel. Surely her husband would be cured.

It was in this tormented state of mind that the Crown Princess arrived in London to celebrate her mother's Golden Jubilee.

2

The Jubilee festivities over, the couple spent two months in England. During all this time the Crown Prince was being treated by Mackenzie. Twice the doctor removed further particles of the growth and sent them to the German pathologist for analysis. Again he could detect no sign of cancer. By the autumn, with Fritz at Balmoral, everyone – including the doctor – was convinced that his complete recovery was simply a matter of time. 'He is wonderfully better,' noted the gratified Queen, 'still hoarse, but not without any voice, as when he arrived in England. He seemed in excellent spirits.' In a rush of premature relief, Queen Victoria knighted Dr Mackenzie.

As Berlin was hardly the place for a convalescence, it was decided that, on leaving Britain in September, the couple would move on to Toblach in the Tyrol. When Toblach proved too wet, they made for Baveno, near Lake Maggiore. As the Crown Prince still showed no real sign of improvement, they moved on to an even warmer climate; this time to San Remo on the Mediterranean. Here, at the beginning of November 1887, the Crown Prince's little court established itself in a large villa set in an exotic garden.

During the course of these wanderings, public opinion in Berlin was becoming increasingly critical of the manner in which the whole business of the Crown Prince's illness was being conducted. Some said that he should return home at once. The Kaiser was not expected to last much longer and in certain liberal circles it was feared that Prince Wilhelm was gaining too much influence. Others suspected that the German doctors' diagnosis of cancer had been the correct one. No one had much faith in

Mackenzie. He was accused of being a fraud, anxious for the acclaim which having the Crown Prince under his care would bring him. Why indeed, was the German Crown Prince in the care of a British, and not a German, doctor? Because, ran the rumours, the Crown Princess – *die Engländerin* – had insisted on this.

Vicky, in fact, was being blamed for everything. Never had she been more abused than during this period of her husband's illness. Her main concern, it was said, was to keep her husband alive long enough for her to become Empress; she was determined that he should reign and not be passed over in favour of their son Wilhelm. This was why she had persistently minimized the seriousness of her husband's illness. This was why she had refused to concede that the growth was cancerous and had forbidden her husband to be operated on at a time when the operation might have saved his life. This was why she had insisted that an English, and not a German, doctor be called in. She had impressed on Mackenzie – a fellow-liberal – the importance of the growth not being diagnosed as cancerous. Together, she and Mackenzie had hurried the Crown Prince away to England and so kept him out of the hands of the German doctors whose proposed operation might have cost her husband his voice. By her persistent optimism she had buoyed up her husband with false hopes and misled the public about the seriousness of his illness. It was claimed that her passion for power and her hatred of her eldest son were costing her husband his life.

The accusations were entirely without foundation. Ambitious, wilful and highly emotional Vicky certainly was, but throughout her husband's illness her only concern was to save his life and alleviate his sufferings. Quite naturally, she looked forward to the day of his accession to the throne and was appalled at the thought that the splitting of his larynx might make him an Emperor without a voice. But she could never have believed that her husband would simply be declared unfit to reign; Bismarck himself admitted that there was no provision in Germany for altering the succession in the event of physical incapacity.

Nor was there any truth in the accusation that she had summoned Dr Mackenzie. She had merely backed up the German doctors' decision to do so. His doubts about the cancerous nature of the growth had delighted her. It is not surprising that she had put her faith in Mackenzie and his cure rather than in the German doctors and their operation: both Mackenzie and the German pathologist were pre-eminent in their fields, so why should she doubt their judgement? And then, far from insisting that her husband go to England to follow Mackenzie's treatment, she had confessed to her mother that the decision lay with the German doctors, not her. To the accusation that both she and Mackenzie were too optimistic by half, she insisted that it was her duty to remain cheerful. By a show of optimism, she would speed her husband's recovery. 'You know how sensitive and apprehensive, how suspicious and despondent Fritz is by nature,' she wrote to her mother; it was thus up to her to counteract his melancholy by remaining determinedly bright.

Indeed, far from behaving like some unfeeling, power-hungry virago, the Crown Princess was acting with exemplary nobility throughout this trying time. Her courage and devotion were of the highest order. At a time when she was tortured by the thought of her husband's fate, when she was forced to put on a smiling front lest he sink into an even deeper depression, when she was both physically and emotionally exhausted, she was being abused, privately and publicly, by her numerous enemies. She deserved all the sympathy and encouragement she could get.

But the worst was yet to come. Twenty-four hours after they had settled in at San Remo, there was an alarming deterioration in Fritz's condition. On examining the patient's throat, Dr Mackenzie discovered a new growth. This time he felt certain that it was malignant. The Crown Prince, begging to be told the truth, asked the doctor if it was cancer.

'I am sorry to say, Sir,' answered Mackenzie, 'it looks very much like it, but it is impossible to be certain.'

After a moment or two's silence, Fritz calmly thanked the doctor for his frankness. Only later, when he was alone with his wife, did the Crown Prince's control break down. Sobbing bitterly, he gasped out against the injustice of Fate. 'I had so hoped to be of use to my country. Why is heaven so cruel to me? What have I done to be thus stricken down and condemned?'

3

That Fritz had not much longer to live, there was now no question. A few days after Mackenzie's admission that the growth might be cancerous, his diagnosis was confirmed by a panel of German doctors. It was now simply a matter of whether the Crown Prince would outlast his ailing father or whether his son Wilhelm would be the next Kaiser. While the German public whispered a half-forgotten prophecy that Kaiser Wilhelm I would live to be ninety-six and be succeeded by a man with one arm, the official world began preparing openly for the next reign but one. With one sun sinking so fast, it would be as well to turn and face the coming dawn. Fritz was being treated, complained Vicky to Queen Victoria, as 'a mere passing shadow soon to be replaced by reality in the shape of Wilhelm'.

Yet she refused to accept the situation. She simply would not allow herself to believe that her husband was beyond recovery. She seems even to have convinced herself that he did not really have cancer. When the doctors, after their latest examination, had given the couple the choice of a complete removal of the larynx or a palliative measure whereby an incision would be made in the throat to avoid suffocation, they had plumped for the lesser operation. The doctors' opinion that the Crown Prince had less than six months to live, Vicky dismissed as nonsense, 'a mere guess and a conjecture'. The German doctors might convince the court and the public that Fritz was dying, but they certainly did not convince *her*, she declared.

In her stubborn belief, the Crown Princess was being backed up by the urbane Mackenzie. Despite the fact that he had concurred with the German doctors' recent verdict, within a few weeks he was assuring Queen Victoria that there was nothing malignant in Prince Frederick's throat. Did he really believe this? Or did he simply not know what to believe? He might well have been puzzled by the fact that the course of the disease was somewhat unusual, not really typical of cancer of the throat. Or was he perhaps concealing the true nature of the illness? Did the Crown Prince have syphilis of the larynx? One of the German doctors had suggested that he be given large doses of potassium iodide – the customary treatment for late syphilis – and with this the other doctors had agreed. He even went so far as to make a public announcement to the effect that the Crown Prince was suffering from a disease of a 'contagious origin'. Mackenzie himself is said to have confided to a close friend, Dr Pierce, that the Prince had 'syphilis of the larynx before the cancer appeared'. This opinion has recently been backed up by R. Scott Stevenson in his detailed study of the Crown Prince's illness. Given Fritz's character, it seems unlikely, but there was talk of his association with a Spanish dancer at the opening of the Suez Canal which he had attended some years before.

Bolstering Vicky's determination to remain sanguine about her husband's illness was her suspicion of a plot to force him to renounce his rights to the throne. She was convinced that the conservatives would go to any lengths to see that Prince Wilhelm gained power so that Bismarck's reactionary policies could be continued. To this end they were not only spreading alarming reports on the seriousness of the Crown Prince's illness, but were bent on getting his English doctor dismissed so that they could replace him with someone of their own choosing. This doctor would then convince the patient of the hopelessness of his case and of the necessity of renouncing his claim to the throne. It was the Junkers who wanted the Crown Prince's larynx removed; it was they who were trying to force an operation which would certainly cost the patient his voice, perhaps even his life. 'Against this,' declared Vicky to her mother, 'it is my duty to fight!'

The Crown Princess's suspicions could not be dismissed as mere hysteria; the imaginings of an ambitious and overwrought woman. Prince

Wilhelm's behaviour gave ample grounds for her fears. He was certainly making no secret of his impatience to ascend the throne. Already he had drawn up an Imperial Edict to be dispatched to the various German princes on the day of his accession. At this even Bismarck drew the line. Both the Kaiser and his heir apparent were still alive, explained the Chancellor to his headstrong protégé; it really would not do for the public to learn that the heir presumptive had drafted his Imperial Edict.

Disturbing, too, were Prince Wilhelm's visits to San Remo. Twice, during his parents' stay there, did he come to see them and on both occasions his manner was insufferable. Arrogant, conceited and unsympathetic, he behaved as though he were already Emperor. Making much of the fact that he was there as the 'Kaiser's representative', he insisted on giving orders to the doctors. He is even said to have claimed precedence over his mother as he entered the local Lutheran church.

However, Vicky was not one to put up with such high-handedness. Always ready to give as good as she got, she 'pitched into him,' she assured her mother, 'with considerable violence'.

'I will not have him dictate to me – the head on my shoulders is every bit as good as his,' she declared.

Still, Prince Wilhelm was able to return to Berlin with the German doctors' assurance that his father had not much longer to live. Wilhelm I might yet be succeeded by Wilhelm II.

He was not. On 9 March 1888, the old Emperor died, two weeks short of turning ninety-one. Fritz was walking in the grounds of the villa at San Remo when he received the news that he was now Kaiser Frederick III. Returning to the house, he entered the drawing-room in which his household stood assembled. His first task was to write out the announcement of his own accession. His second was to invest his wife with the highest decoration he could bestow – the Order of the Black Eagle. To underline further his appreciation of all she had done, he handed Dr Mackenzie a piece of paper on which he had written: 'I thank you for having made me live long enough to recompense the valiant courage of my wife.'

Queen Victoria's reaction to the news was more effusive. 'My own dear *Empress Victoria*,' she wrote to Vicky, 'it does seem an impossible dream, may God bless her! You know *how* little I care for rank or Titles – but I cannot *deny* that *after all* that has been done and said, I am *thankful* and *proud* that dear Fritz and you should have come to the Throne.'

Two days later, on a bitterly cold night, the stricken Emperor arrived in Berlin to begin his long-deferred reign. 'I pray,' wrote the new Empress to her mother, 'that he may be spared to be a blessing to his people and to Europe.' By now, even she must have realized that there was little hope of that.

At last, and in this sad and untriumphant fashion, did the first of Queen Victoria's descendants come to sit upon a throne.

CHAPTER FOUR

Ninety-eight Days

I

On the day after Crown Prince Frederick's accession to the throne –
10 March 1888 – the Prince and Princess of Wales celebrated their silver
wedding. Queen Victoria, having made a somewhat disgruntled entry
in her Journal to the effect that she and Albert had not been 'permitted' to
celebrate this happy anniversary, presented the couple with a huge silver
loving-cup. That night she attended a family dinner at Marlborough
House. Princess Alexandra, in white and silver, looked radiant: 'more like
a bride just married than the Silver one of twenty-five years,' noted the
Queen.

By now the forty-three-year-old Alexandra, no less than her husband,
had perfected the appearance that was to characterize her throughout her
life: the crown of elaborately coiffured brown hair, the creamy complexion, the jewelled 'dog-collars' (to hide a girlhood scar), the tiny waist,
the superbly elegant clothes. She already walked with the famous 'Alexandra limp', an affliction caused by a stiff knee and converted by her into
a movement of such grace that it was copied by a number of society
ladies. 'To the very end,' wrote one of her nieces, 'there was about Aunt
Alix something invincible, something exquisite and flower-like. She
gave the same joy as a beautiful rose or a rare orchid or an absolutely
flawless carnation. She was a garden flower that had been grown by a
superlative gardener who knew every trick of his art.'

How had Alexandra managed to retain this aura of youthful perfection? Her life, after all, had not been a particularly easy one. To be the
wife of so restless, mercurial and licentious a man as the Prince of Wales
would have tested the resilience of the most angelic of women.

Angelic the Princess certainly was, but she had, in addition, certain
qualities that created a sort of immunity from her domestic problems.
Even before Alix's marriage to Bertie, the Queen – with characteristic
perspicacity – had noted that 'there is something frank and cheerful in
Alix's character, which will greatly assist her to take things without being

too much overpowered or alarmed by them.' Immature, impractical and happy-go-lucky, Princess Alexandra was never one to fret about things which could not be helped. Even her one political passion – an undying hatred of Prussia – came from a child-like pig-headedness rather than from any real appreciation of the nature of the Prussian state. Prussia had once waged war against her native Denmark; therefore she was prepared to hate Prussia to her dying day.

Creating a further barrier between Princess Alexandra and the realities of life was her increasing deafness. This hereditary affliction, known as otosclerosis, was worsening with the years. It forced her to cling to the company of those whom she knew well and to avoid meeting new people. Not being a reader, she never learnt much from books; by now she was no longer able to learn by listening to intelligent conversation. More and more did she submerge herself in the things she anyway liked best – her children, her horses, her dogs and her homes.

This, in turn, kept her away from that gregarious society so loved by her husband; the two of them spent less and less time in each other's company. Yet, she rarely complained. She took Bertie's absences, as she did his infidelities, in her stride. Unlike Queen Victoria, Alix simply accepted that there was one code of behaviour for men and another for women. She had been born into a family in which masculine unfaithfulness had been the rule rather than the exception and she never made a fuss. On the contrary, she always behaved extremely graciously towards such of her husband's mistresses as she met. So goodnatured, she rated jealousy a worse sin than licentiousness.

Bertie was always grateful to his wife for her understanding attitude. In this way he was very fond of her and treated her with unfailing chivalry and protectiveness. 'After all,' she is reported to have said after his death, 'he always loved me the best.'

Thus, if the marriage was not an especially happy one, then neither was it especially unhappy. There might have been no close bond between Bertie and Alix such as there was between Fritz and Vicky, but the two of them suited each other well enough. Not entirely without justification could Queen Victoria, on the occasion of their silver wedding, wish that God might give them 'many more happy years together!'

The silver wedding celebrations, which were to have embraced more than that family dinner at Marlborough House, had been cut short by the death of Kaiser Wilhelm I. For one thing, the court had to go into mourning; for another, the Prince of Wales had to attend the old Kaiser's funeral. Four days after his silver wedding, Bertie, accompanied by his eldest son, the apathetic Prince Eddy, was in Berlin. They put up at the British Embassy.

At Charlottenburg Palace, in which the new Emperor and Empress had taken up residence, the Prince of Wales – together with other dignitaries in Berlin for the funeral – was received by the Kaiser. Fritz looked deceptively well. 'In full uniform with quick steps, dignified and upright as usual, he went to meet everyone,' claimed Vicky. All were 'astonished to see him like that after all they had heard'. But Bertie was not taken in. Although Fritz did not look ill, he was much thinner and was quite unable to speak. He had, moreover, 'a hunted, anxious expression, which was very distressing to see'.

Vicky was delighted to welcome her brother. In the past, the two of them had not always been in accord, but maturity, and Vicky's present plight, had improved their relationship. 'To have dear Bertie here,' wrote the Empress to her mother, 'was a great comfort.'

The Prince of Wales attended the funeral service and took part in the procession from the cathedral to the mausoleum at Charlottenburg. Chief mourner was Prince Wilhelm, as the new Kaiser was not strong enough to brave the bitter weather. Forced to stand by his window to see the magnificent cortège wind its way through the Tiergarten, Fritz scribbled a note to Dr Mackenzie. 'That is where I ought to be,' he wrote as he watched the proudly strutting figure of his son behind the hearse.

While in Berlin, the Prince of Wales received Prince Bismarck at the British Embassy. The extraordinarily enthusiastic reception given to the Chancellor by the crowd outside brought home to Bertie something of the great man's popularity. It was obviously to Bismarck, and not to the new Kaiser, that the people were looking for guidance.

Four days after the funeral, the Prince of Wales was reporting to the Queen at Windsor. His news was hardly reassuring. 'I am determined . . .' wrote the Queen in her Journal after he had left, 'to visit dear Vicky and Fritz, if only for a day.'

2

Some six weeks later Queen Victoria arrived in Berlin to pay her promised visit to the new German Emperor and Empress. She was on her way home from a holiday in Florence. The visit was being made in the face of violent opposition on the part of Prince Bismarck and his circle. The Chancellor, assuming that the Queen was coming to force through a marriage of one of Vicky's daughters to a Battenberg prince of whom Bismarck disapproved, had been determined to keep her away. Whether the Chancellor really objected so strongly to the proposed match or whether he feared that the Queen's presence would encourage the Emperor and Empress to dismiss him from office, was uncertain. He certainly did everything in his power to stop her coming.

The projected marriage, he announced heatedly, would unite France and Russia against Germany (the Battenberg Prince was anti-Russian); it would estrange England; the German government resented this 'foreign interference' in her affairs; the Queen would be faced with hostile demonstrations in Berlin. Who could say to what friction, both national and international, the Queen's visit to Berlin might not lead?

This artificially created furore Queen Victoria dismissed as 'absurd'. Russia, she declared firmly, did not care a *straw* about the marriage; the whole *fracas* was simply a nefarious plot on the part of Bismarck, Prince Wilhelm and their '*cercle vicieux*' to undermine the position of the Emperor and Empress and to keep her from visiting them. In any case, she herself did not favour the Battenberg marriage and had already told Vicky this. 'How Bismarck, and still more Wilhelm, *can* play such a double game is impossible for us honest, straightforward English to understand,' she declared. 'Thank God! we are English!' She was determined to go to Berlin.

To Berlin, therefore, she went. The visit was a tremendous success. Despite the campaign of vilification in the German press, the Queen was vociferously welcomed when she arrived on 24 April 1888. At the sight of that plump but imperious figure, all traces of hostility melted and she was met, reported her somewhat astonished ambassador, by 'dense crowds and hearty cheers'. The Queen herself was impressed by the 'great crowds, who were most enthusiastic, cheering and throwing flowers into the carriage'. The people, she claimed, were 'very friendly'.

The situation at Charlottenburg Palace was distinctly less encouraging. Although Fritz looked well, he spent almost all his time in bed. Dr Mackenzie told the Queen that he could not last for more than a few weeks. When Sir Henry Ponsonby, the Queen's private secretary, assured the Empress that her husband was looking better, her eyes filled with tears. 'No, he is not really better,' answered Vicky, 'but it has done him a temporary good to see Mama.' The Empress herself was in a pathetic state. She looked, thought her mother, 'careworn and thinner' and was liable to burst into tears whenever she was alone with the Queen. 'Her despair at what she seems to look on as the certain end is terrible,' noted Victoria.

Her husband's illness, however, was merely one of the many difficulties with which Vicky had to contend. Chief amongst these was the behaviour of Prince Wilhelm. Relations between mother and son were as bad as ever. 'William,' complained the Empress to her mother, 'fancies himself completely the Emperor – and an absolute and autocratic one.' He was, she said, 'in a "ring", a *côterie*, whose main endeavour is, as it were, to paralyse Fritz in every way'.

The Queen claimed that she had no words to express her 'indignation and astonishment' at the conduct of Prince Wilhelm. He and his 'odious ungrateful wife', Dona, should be packed off on a long journey.

Vicky's political difficulties were as bad as her domestic ones. Her husband's régime was simply a travesty of what they had once planned.

Because of his helpless state, the Emperor had been obliged to confirm Bismarck in office. There had been nothing else that he could do. Since then the Chancellor had lost no opportunity of asserting his authority. Even Frederick III's most moderate attempts at reform were nullified or ignored by Bismarck. No one dared give Fritz any help or encouragement. Even the members of his entourage worked against him by repeating to Bismarck exactly what the Chancellor wanted to hear: that the Emperor was weak, apathetic, little better than a corpse. All the Emperor's schemes for the gradual identification of the throne with liberalism rather than conservatism came to nothing. However strongly he might feel, he could insist on nothing for fear of Bismarck handing in his resignation and leaving him with a situation with which he would not have the strength to cope.

Worse than the Chancellor's high-handed treatment of the Emperor was his persecution of the Empress. Realizing that in her he had a more formidable opponent, he did everything he could to whip up public feeling against her. Readers of the Bismarck-controlled press were reminded that *die Engländerin* was always ready to sacrifice German to British interests. To her, he claimed, the Kaiser was 'as dependent and submissive as a dog, you'd hardly believe to what extent'.

And if it was not Bismarck himself who was reviling the Empress, it was one of his, or Prince Wilhelm's, adherents. The reactionary Count Waldersee claimed that the Empress now ruled the land and when a liberal politician tried to refute this allegation in the Prussian parliament, he was simply howled down. The fact that the Empress always had to be present to speak on behalf of her dumb husband seemed to confirm the view that she was now the power in the land. She was very quick, it was said, to point out to his visitors how well he was looking; she hoped thereby to give the impression that his reign – under her influence – would be a long one. She was accused of forcing him to make public appearances, of plying him with wine and other stimulants to get him through these occasions, of not caring one jot that the effort left him utterly exhausted. It was even whispered that she was demanding that the Emperor should appoint her Regent. To this suggestion her son lost no time in replying that not the Hohenzollerns, nor Prussia, nor the German Reich would allow a woman to rule over them.

The deplorable situation in Germany was summed up by Colonel Swaine, the British Military Attaché in Berlin. 'We are living in sad times here in Berlin . . .' he wrote in April 1888. 'It seems as if a curse had come over this country, leaving but one bright spot and that is where stands a solitary woman doing her duty faithfully and tenderly by her sick husband against all odds. It is one of *the* most tragic episodes in a country and a life ever recorded in history.'

The visiting Queen Victoria did what she could to alleviate her daughter's suffering. By her prestige, her assurance and her sound common sense, the Queen brought a breath of fresh air into the embittered atmosphere at Charlottenburg. She sat talking to the Kaiser; she listened to her daughter's tearful outpourings; she gave Wilhelm some grandmotherly advice. Appreciating the prickliness of his nature, she did not scold; she merely asked him to be more considerate towards his mother. This Prince Wilhelm, who always stood in awe of his grandmother, promised to do.

The Queen's greatest achievement, however, was the audience which she granted Bismarck. The momentous interview between them took place on 25 April, the day after Victoria's arrival. At the prospect of coming face to face with the formidable old lady, all Bismarck's self-confidence evaporated. He felt sure that he was in for a difficult time. The Queen's aide-de-camp reported him as being 'unmistakably nervous and ill at ease'; he wanted to know exactly where she would be in the Audience Chamber and whether she would be seated or standing. The British aide felt 'proud that this great man evidently realized that he was about to be received by an equally great, or even greater, woman'.

The meeting passed off admirably. Queen and Chancellor were charmed with each other. The Queen, expecting to meet a monster, was 'agreeably surprised to find him so amiable and gentle'. The Chancellor, expecting her to insist on the Battenberg marriage, was gratified to find that she did not mention the subject. They discussed their one previous meeting, over thirty years before; they spoke about the state of Europe. The Queen appealed to Bismarck to stand by 'poor Vicky' and, for the sake of 'dear Fritz', not to appoint Prince Wilhelm as Regent. They agreed that Wilhelm was painfully inexperienced, although Bismarck believed that 'should he be thrown into the water, he would be able to swim', as he was certainly clever. Queen and Chancellor parted on cordial terms and Bismarck emerged from the interview mopping his brow and exclaiming, 'That was a woman! One could do business with her!'

If only England would follow the Queen's sensible views, he afterwards declared, Europe would be in a much happier state. Indeed, so impressed was Bismarck by Queen Victoria that he was even prepared to behave towards the Empress with unaccustomed – if temporary – gallantry. At the state dinner that evening he set himself out to be as agreeable as possible. Drawing Vicky's attention to a sweet wrapper which carried her likeness, he unbuttoned his coat and, with a graceful remark, placed the bonbon beside his heart.

The Queen left for home the following evening. After an early dinner she went to take leave of the Emperor. It was a poignant parting, for both of them must have known that they would never see each other again. For his sake, however, the Queen remained cheerful, 'I kissed him as I did every day, and said I hoped he would come to us when he was stronger.'

The Empress, too, was determined not to give way to her feelings. She drove with her mother to the station and kept control of herself as the Queen took leave of the various people assembled on the beflagged platform. Only on following her mother into the carriage, where the heartbroken Queen kissed her 'again and again', did she break down. By the time she had returned to the platform to take up her position as the train started up, she was in floods of tears.

'It was terrible,' wrote the equally anguished Queen, 'to see her standing there in tears, while the train moved slowly off, and to think of all she was suffering, and might have to go through. My poor, poor child. . . .'

3

The reign of Kaiser Frederick III lasted for less than seven weeks after Queen Victoria's departure from Berlin. During that time Fritz was able to undertake only one political act of any significance: he insisted on the dismissal of a particularly reactionary Minister. For the rest, it was as much as he could do to sit up for a few hours during the day. Occasionally, if he were feeling stronger, he might be taken for a drive and once, on the occasion of the marriage of his second son, Prince Henry, to Princess Irene of Hesse, he was able to attend an official function. Dressed in full uniform ('so handsome and dignified but so thin and pale', reported Vicky) Fritz got through the ceremony without coughing. But the effort had obviously been too much for him. That night he ran a high temperature and had to spend the following day in bed.

Yet the Empress persisted in maintaining that he was not really as ill as everyone imagined. That she should always show him a cheerful face was understandable; that she should keep up this insouciance with others seemed inexplicable. To Prince Hohenlohe, who found her 'frank and cheerful' manner astounding, she once said that 'it is perhaps possible that the illness will be of long duration. The expectation of a speedy end has not yet been confirmed'.

Even Queen Victoria was treated to encouraging reports from her daughter. During the month of May 1888, she was receiving 'very good accounts of beloved Fritz' from the Empress. He was 'gaining strength', he was 'continuing to improve' and, on the last day of the month, a mere fortnight before Fritz's death, Vicky told her mother that Mackenzie had said that the Kaiser might live for six months, a year, or might even recover. The doctor had had the good sense to add that although this was possible, it was not probable.

On the day after the Queen had received this reassuring report, the Emperor and Empress left Berlin for the Neues Palais, their home at Potsdam. They travelled by steamer up the Havel, and all along the river banks cheering crowds collected to see the Emperor pass by. On arrival at the Neues Palais – the home which Fritz had spent some of the happiest days of his life – he scribbled a note to the effect that he would like the palace to be known, henceforth, as Friedrichskron.

Even now Fritz insisted on doing as much as his weakened state would allow. He made entries in his diary, he wrote letters, he studied the newspapers, he signed documents, he issued instructions. When the King of Sweden visited Friedrichskron, the Kaiser put on his uniform and received him in correct fashion. It was such instances of her husband's devotion to duty that caused Vicky to be so incensed by the slanders of his enemies. They, who knew nothing of his courage, spoke of him as a listless, bemused, half-imbecile creature, propped up and goaded on by his ambitious wife. There were even wild rumours to the effect that he had already died and that she and her liberal coterie were concealing the fact from the nation.

An additional anxiety for the Kaiser was the thought of what would happen to his wife after his death. He realized that she could expect very little sympathy from their son Wilhelm. Thus one day, when Bismarck was visiting him, the Emperor had the Empress called into the room. Taking hold of his wife's hand, Fritz laid it in Bismarck's. The dumb and dying man looked from one to the other; both realized that he was committing his wife to the Chancellor's care. Bismarck murmured an assurance to the effect that he would never forget his obligations towards the Empress.

But Vicky refused to be taken in. She appreciated that Bismarck might harbour a certain feudal loyalty to his master, the Emperor, but she knew that this feeling did not extend to her. How little she trusted him – or her son Wilhelm – was clear from her actions during the last days of her husband's life. She had already seen to it that her own and her daughters' share of her husband's property would be made over before Wilhelm assumed control of the family revenues; now she put into operation a plan which she had been contemplating for some time.

Determined that the full story of the campaign against her husband and herself should one day be revealed and that justice should be done to their memory, she had to make sure that their private papers did not fall into unsympathetic hands. The only way to ensure this was to smuggle the papers out of Germany. Already, during their visit to England for the Queen's Jubilee the year before, she had deposited three boxes of papers in a safe at Buckingham Palace. Now, on 14 June, she arranged for yet more personal papers to be secreted to England. A Mr Inman Bernard, special correspondent for the *New York Herald*, was invited to call at Friedrichskron. There he was handed a parcel by Dr Mackenzie. He was asked to deliver it to the British Embassy in Berlin with instructions for the Ambassador to send it on to Queen Victoria. Presumably this was done, for a few days later the Queen noted that the Military Attaché had arrived from Berlin with some of Kaiser Frederick III's papers for her safe-keeping.

The move had been made just in time. On 13 June the Queen had received a telegram from the British Ambassador in Berlin to say that Fritz was sinking fast. 'The worst is feared within the next twenty-four hours,' he wired. On receipt of this the Queen sent a telegram to her grandson, Prince Wilhelm. 'Am in great distress at the terrible news, and so troubled about poor, dear Mama. Do all you can, as I asked you, to help her at this terrible time of dreadful trial and grief. God help us!'

Kaiser Frederick III died on the morning of 15 June 1888. 'I cannot, cannot realize the dreadful truth,' wrote the anguished Queen on receipt of the news. 'The misfortune is awful. My poor child's whole future gone, ruined, which they had prepared themselves for for nearly thirty years.'

To her grandson, now Kaiser Wilhelm II, the Queen wired, 'I am broken-hearted. Help and do all you can for your poor dear Mother and try to follow in your best, noblest, and kindest of father's footsteps.'

Her advice fell on deaf ears. Wilhelm was planning to follow a very different course. The minute his father died, he put a long-premeditated plan into action. The palace was sealed off from the outside world by a regiment of hussars and orders given that no one, not even members of the imperial family, were allowed to leave without a signed permit. Once the palace had been successfully cordoned off, it was thoroughly searched. The new Kaiser was anxious to lay his hands on his late father's private papers; he probably hoped, imagined the Empress, that he would uncover traces of 'liberal plots'. While one of his generals ransacked the late Emperor's desk, the Kaiser himself, in his red hussar's uniform, searched his mother's rooms. They found nothing. The late Emperor's personal papers, for what they were worth, were stored at Buckingham Palace.

Foiled in this attempt to obliterate as much as possible of the late Emperor's aspirations and achievements, Wilhelm struck out in other directions. In defiance of his father's instructions, he permitted a post-mortem to be conducted on his body; this was simply to underline the fact, as publicly as possible, that the German doctors had all along been right in their diagnosis of cancer and the Empress and Mackenzie wrong. Next, ignoring his father's written wish that his daughter Moretta be allowed to marry Sandro of Battenberg, Wilhelm sent a letter to Sandro forbidding the match. His father's wish that his name be perpetuated in the name of his palace Wilhelm also disregarded: he gave orders that henceforth the newly named Friedrichskron would again be known as the Neues Palais.

And, as a final insult to his father's memory, Kaiser Wilhelm II made a public announcement to the effect that he intended to follow in the footsteps of his late grandfather, Kaiser Wilhelm I.

Kaiser Frederick III's reign, which the late Prince Albert had designed to be one of the most glorious in history, had lasted for less than a hundred days. It had been, in the words of his Empress, 'a mere passing shadow'.

'We had a mission,' wrote the embittered Vicky to her mother, 'we felt and we knew it – we were Papa's and your children! We were faithful to what we believed and knew to be right. We loved Germany – we wished to see her strong and great, not only with the sword, but in all that was righteous, in culture, in progress and in liberty. We wished to see all the people happy and free, growing and developing in all that is good. We tried hard to learn and study and prepare for the time in which we should be called to work for the nation. We had treasured up much experience! Bitterly, hardly bought!!! – that is all now wasted. . . ."

CHAPTER FIVE

Eddy, Georgie and May

I

By the year 1891 Queen Victoria had decided that something would have to be done about the future of her heir presumptive, the apathetic Prince Eddy. Now twenty-six years of age, the Prince was leading an utterly worthless existence. His military career having proved, in the words of his father the Prince of Wales, to be 'simply a waste of time', the young man had been sent off on a tour of India. From this he had returned in a state of near collapse, having indulged, it was said, in all forms of dissipation. Nor were these dissipations confined to India. The feckless Prince lived entirely for pleasure and he took it wherever he could, not least of all in London. There was even some talk of a *male* brothel. If the Prince of Wales had not proved quite as dissolute as the Queen's wicked uncles, Prince Eddy was showing every sign of making good the deficiency.

Bertie's solution to the problem of his eldest son (created, in 1890, Duke of Clarence and Avondale) was that he be sent off on a series of colonial tours. He had done India, so why not South Africa, Australia and New Zealand? The further he travelled and the longer he stayed away from the temptations of London life, the better.

With this the Queen could not agree. In an attempt to salvage some scrap from the ruins of the late Prince Consort's plans for a set of cultured, cosmopolitan and informed heirs, she suggested that Eddy be sent to Europe instead. For one of Europe's future kings, he knew far too little about the Continent and almost nothing of its courts. He was too exclusively British. In the colonies he would learn nothing of art or history, nor would he acquire that polish so necessary in his position. Travel in Europe would rub off 'that angular insular view of things which is not good for a Prince', she declared.

To this outpouring of matriarchal advice, the Prince of Wales had to reply very carefully. He could not tell the Queen his real reasons for wanting to pack Eddy off to the farthest-flung corners of the Empire. The

tour was to be in the nature of a punishment for the young man's transgressions, as well as a means of keeping him, as Bertie's private secretary
put it, 'out of harm's way'. The capitals of Europe, on the other hand,
would be the worst possible places for someone of Prince Eddy's lax
and licentious habits. Think of Vienna; think of *Paris*. The Prince of
Wales had therefore to defend both his idea of a colonial tour and his
son's Englishness. It would be an excellent thing for Eddy to take an
interest in 'the great Empire over which you rule'; as for his Englishness, it
was a good fault and would make the young man more popular at home.

As it was, Bertie was in no position to throw stones in this matter of
his son's behaviour. Throughout this period he himself was involved in
not only one but two major scandals. The first was the Tranby Croft
affair – an episode which started when one of Bertie's fellow guests at a
house party was accused of cheating at baccarat and ended in a lawsuit in
which the Prince was called as a witness. The second concerned Bertie's
current mistress, Lady Frances Brooke, who had talked the Prince into
demanding the return of a compromising letter which she had written to
a previous lover. The previous lover, resenting this royal interference,
insulted the Prince and the whole sordid affair was made public.

In these circumstances, Bertie could hardly afford to be censorious about
his son's failings. It was, he admitted in a letter to the Queen, 'difficult to
explain' the reasons why Eddy should be kept away from the capitals of
Europe.

Bertie had underestimated his mother. The Queen knew the reasons
well enough. Rumours of her grandson's way of life had reached even
her seemingly inaccessible ears ('who is it tells the Queen these things?'
wrote an anguished secretary) and she assured the Prince of Wales that
there were just as many 'designing pretty women' in the colonies as
anywhere else.

Perhaps the most sensible suggestion to emerge from this exchange of
letters between mother and son on the question of Eddy's future came
from Bertie. 'A good sensible wife – with some considerable character is
what he needs most – but where is she to be found?'

Where indeed? Prince Eddy, it seems, was himself on the lookout for a
bride. His excursions into the *demi-monde* had not blinded him to the
attractions to be found in his own class. With his adolescent-like ability to
fall in and out of love in the same week, he had already embarked on a
series of love affairs. In 1889 he had fallen for his cousin, Princess Alix of
Hesse, daughter of the late Princess Alice, Queen Victoria's third child.
The Queen was delighted. Alicky was exactly the sort of serious-minded,
sensible girl that was needed. In addition, she was a German princess (her
father was the Grand Duke of Hesse) and, as the Queen so often said, the
'German connection' was the one which she wished her family to maintain. On this occasion, however, Alicky proved a shade too sensible. She
turned Eddy down. She would marry him if she were *forced* to do so, she

declared, but they would not be happy together. For this show of resolution on Alicky's part, the Queen was all admiration. It needed great strength of character, she said, to refuse 'the greatest position there is'.

Alicky's Aunt Vicky, the newly widowed German Empress Frederick, was somewhat less resigned to the refusal. 'I regret it very much,' she wrote, 'and hope that *she* may not regret it later.' Alicky, in later years, was to have good reason for regret. She married, instead, Tsar Nicholas II, and ended her life in that blood-stained cellar at Ekaterinburg.

With Alicky no longer in the running, the Queen came up with a suggestion of her own. What about Mossy? Mossy was yet another of Prince Eddy's cousins – Princess Margaret, the youngest child of the Empress Frederick. She might not be 'regularly pretty', but she had a good figure, an amiable disposition and, besides being German, was very fond of England. Would *she* do? She would not. This time it was the normally complaisant Eddy who refused to consider it. Although he had only just been turned down by Alicky, he was already in love with someone else.

His latest choice was Princess Hélène of Orleans, the twenty-one-year-old daughter of the Comte de Paris, at present living in exile in England. Dark and distinguished-looking, Princess Hélène was, in almost every other way, a highly unsuitable candidate for the future Queen of England. On both religious and political grounds, the thing was impossible. The Princess was a Roman Catholic and her father was a pretender to the French throne. On first hearing of Prince Eddy's infatuation, the Queen had written to explain the dangers of the attachment; he should avoid meeting Princess Hélène as much as possible, she cautioned.

Ignoring this sound advice, Eddy continued seeing Hélène in secret. In his unwise courtship, he was being backed up by his adoring mother and three sisters. The Princess of Wales was especially touched by the idea of this clandestine affair. It was all so romantic, and how nice that Hélène was a French, as opposed to a German, princess. When Princess Hélène, who seems to have been besotted by this languid, seductively-mannered Prince, agreed to change her religion in order to marry him, the couple became engaged.

How was the news to be broken to Grandmama Queen? Princess Alexandra, in her astute and feminine fashion, provided the answer. The young couple were to go at once to the Queen and let her into their secret. They were to ask for her blessing and advice. This they did, and the Queen, an incurable romantic, promised to do what she could to help.

There was, in fact, very little that she could do. While Victoria's advisers delved into constitutional problems, Princess Hélène informed her father of her decision to renounce her religion. The Comte de Paris would not hear of it. Nor, when Princess Hélène made a personal appeal to the Pope, would he. And so, as Prince Eddy could not marry a Roman Catholic without renouncing his rights to the throne, the engagement had to be broken off. The bitter-sweet romance was over. 'I loved him so much,' Princess Hélène afterwards admitted to Queen Victoria, 'and perhaps I was rash but I couldn't help myself, I loved him so much. . . .' He was, she added with a singular choice of word, 'so good'.

It would take years, imagined the sentimental Queen, for her grandson to recover from this disappointment. It took, in fact, no time at all. While everyone imagined that the Prince was still pining for his lost love, he was under the spell of yet another beauty – Lady Sybil St Clair Erskine. To her he was penning, in his laborious fashion, a series of naïve, if barely comprehensible, letters. He would not at one time have thought it possible, he assured her in one of his notes, to be in love with two people at the same time, but he had to admit that he now found himself in this exceptional position. He hoped that she, who so charmed and fascinated him, loved him a little in return? Would she, by the way, always be sure to destroy the crest and signature on his letters?

Needless to say, the lady did nothing of the sort.

It was no wonder that the Prince of Wales was so anxious to find his frivolous son a 'good, sensible wife, with some considerable character'.

2

While Prince Eddy was still writing his muddled letters to Lady Sybil, his elders and betters had made up their minds as to what was to be done with him. He would tour neither the Empire nor the Continent; instead, he would be married off to yet another of his relations, Princess May of Teck.

Princess May was the only daughter of the Duke and Duchess of Teck. The Duke of Teck was the son, by a morganatic marriage, of Duke Alexander of Wurtemburg, while the Duchess was Queen Victoria's first cousin; like the Queen, the Duchess of Teck (who had been Princess Mary Adelaide of Cambridge) was a granddaughter of King George III. The Tecks were thus members, albeit fringe members, of the British royal family. And whereas the Duke and Duchess might not have been above criticism – he was moody, irascible and obsessed by the morganatic 'taint' in his blood, while she was extravagant, irresponsible and enormously fat – Princess May was considered eminently suitable.

She was a good age, having turned twenty-four in the spring of 1891 and, for her age, she was remarkably mature. Life with her cantankerous father and capricious mother had brought out all the stability of her own nature: she was calm, even-tempered and unemotional. Her manner was reserved, even shy, but when one penetrated this façade, she revealed considerable depth of character, surprising self-confidence and a fund of common sense. As Queen Victoria put it, May was '*very* sensible and well-informed, a *solid girl* which we want. . . .' She was also – and this would be important as far as Prince Eddy was concerned – very good-looking. Her bearing, as befitted a future queen, was dignified.

The choice having been made, Princess May, without her ebullient mother, was summoned to Balmoral for inspection by the Queen. Victoria was enchanted. 'I think and hope that Eddy will try and marry her,' she wrote to her daughter the Empress Frederick, 'for I think she is a superior girl – quiet and reserved *till* you knew her well . . . she is the reverse of *oberflächlich* [superficial]. She has no frivolous tastes, has been very carefully brought up and is well informed and always occupied.'

That Princess May was something of a paragon there was no doubt, but what would Prince Eddy think of her? Would he be prepared to marry her? On this score, the household at Marlborough House had no fears. They understood the young man only too well. If Prince Eddy were 'properly managed and is told he *must* do it', then do it he would, was the candid opinion of the Prince of Wales's private secretary.

And so it turned out. The fickle Eddy, having been instructed to marry May, obliged everyone by falling in love with her and proposing a month before he was due to do so. They became engaged, at a house party in Bedfordshire, on 3 December 1891. Everyone, including Princess May, was delighted. Not only was she fond of Prince Eddy but for a young woman with her strong sense of royal obligation, she was only too anxious to do something for the monarchy. And with her relatively humble background, the prospect of becoming the Queen of England was a heady one. It is hardly surprising that, on the evening of the engagement, she so forgot her habitual reserve that, in full view of her fellow female guests, she lifted her skirts a fraction and danced around the room.

'We are much excited and delighted at the happy event of May Teck's engagement to dear Eddy,' wrote the Empress Frederick to one of her daughters. 'May he be very happy, he so fully deserves it. Aunt Mary [the Duchess of] Teck will be in the 7th heaven, for years and years it has been her ardent wish, and she has thought of nothing else. What a marriage, and what a position for her daughter!'

This euphoric mood did not last long. Just over a month later, when Princess May and her parents were at Sandringham to celebrate Prince Eddy's twenty-eighth birthday, he fell ill. It was influenza. This quickly developed into pneumonia and for six days, in his tiny bedroom, the Prince lay dangerously ill. By the dawn of 14 January 1892, it was realized that he was dying. Soon after half past nine that morning, surrounded by the shocked and exhausted members of his family, he died.

Prince Eddy was buried at Windsor on 20 January 1892. On his coffin lay Princess May's bridal wreath of orange-blossom.

3

If Queen Victoria had been worried about the succession when her heir presumptive, Prince Eddy, had been alive, she was even more worried about it now that he was dead. The crown would go to Eddy's only brother, Prince George. At the time of Prince Eddy's death, Prince George was twenty-six years of age, unmarried and in poor health. In November 1891 he had been dangerously ill with typhoid; at one stage it was thought that he must die. Were he again to fall ill while in his present state of weakness and depression (his brother's death had left him desolate) Prince George might never survive. The succession would then pass to his sister – the eldest of those 'whispering Wales girls' – Louise, who had recently married the Duke of Fife. They had only one child, a daughter. As immature, ill-educated and diffident as her sisters, and married, moreover, to a commoner, Princess Louise was not really of the stuff of which successful queens regnant are made.

Queen Victoria's hopes, therefore, were pinned on the pale, unhappy figure of her grandson, Prince George. His present despondency apart, Georgie was certainly a more suitable candidate for the throne than his brother Eddy. Not only was he more intelligent but he was stable, diligent and conscientious. 'I think dear Georgie so nice, sensible and truly right-minded, and so anxious to improve himself,' said the Queen. A few months after Eddy's death, she created him Duke of York ('Fancy my Georgie boy . . . now being a grand old Duke of York,' wrote Princess Alexandra) and tried, unsuccessfully, to get him to change his name to Albert. Some belated efforts were made to equip him for his new role.

It was with the matter of Prince George's marriage, however, that his grandmother's mind was most actively engaged. Georgie must marry and produce a family as soon as possible.

This was not, of course, the first time that thoughts of a marriage for Prince George had crossed his grandmother's mind. A year before Prince Eddy's death, the Queen had written to Prince George, suggesting that he do something about finding himself a bride. He had not shown much enthusiasm for the idea. Unlike his brother Eddy, George was sexually unprecocious ('I must say it is good of you to have resisted all temptation so far,' wrote his possessive mother to him on one occasion) and he had answered his grandmother with a little homily on the dangers of marrying too early.

If, however, the Prince had little experience of sex, he did have some of love. Indeed, it might have been his youthful infatuation for a girl by the name of Julie Stoner that helped the Prince resist temptation during his years in the Navy. The girl's mother had been a lady-in-waiting to the Princess of Wales and on Mrs Stoner's death in 1883, the generous-hearted Princess had taken the attractive young orphan under her wing. Julie Stoner had spent a great deal of time with the Wales children and in due course Prince George had fallen in love with her.

It had been a difficult situation. Prince George, unlike his brother Eddy, was capable of feeling things deeply and the Princess of Wales did not want to hurt these feelings by simply forbidding her son to have anything to do with Julie. But that there could be no thought of his marrying her had to be made quite clear. For one thing the girl was a Roman Catholic, for another she was a commoner. Princess Alexandra handled the delicate affair with great tact. She allowed the romance to run its course, taking care to express both her affection for Julie and her regret at the impossibility of the match. 'I only wish you could marry and be happy,' she sighed, 'but alas, I fear that cannot be.'

And that had been that. Prince George, supported by his strong sense of duty and his deep love for his mother, had renounced the pretty Miss Stoner and kept himself available for a more acceptable bride.

Queen Victoria was not long in suggesting one. Indeed, on the question of Prince George's marriage, his grandmother had 'gone mad' complained the Princess of Wales. Having failed to marry Prince Eddy to either of his cousins, Alicky or Mossy, the Queen tried to interest Prince George in yet another of her grandchildren, Missy. Missy was Princess Marie, the eldest daughter of Queen Victoria's son Alfred, Duke of Edinburgh. In the year 1891, the fair-haired Princess Marie was only sixteen or, as the disapproving Princess of Wales put it, 'not in long petticoats yet!!!' For Princess Alexandra's taste, the Edinburgh girls were all far too German (they had been educated in Germany) and remembering that her son had once mentioned a preference for an English, as opposed to a German, consort, she made a point of stressing Missy's strong German accent.

By this time, however, Prince George was not quite so ready to be guided by his mother. German accent or no, the lively, golden-haired Princess Marie was not unattractive to the shy Prince George; he was quite ready to marry her if she would have him. In 1892, some months after Prince Eddy's death, Princess Marie was asked if she would consider marrying Prince George. She would not. She looked upon her cousin as a 'beloved chum' and nothing more. This fact, and the promptings of her violently anglophobe German governess, caused her to reject the proposal. Prince George, who had not really been in love with Missy, was not unduly cast down. 'Poor Georgie . . .' as Queen Victoria put it, 'is not bitter.'

Prince George might not have been bitter but by now his grandmother was almost frantic. 'She is in a terrible fuss about your marrying,' wrote the Prince of Wales to his son, while the Queen herself confided to her private secretary the fear that something quite dreadful would happen if Prince George did not hurry up and marry. But who was to be his bride? With Missy out of the running, the Queen fell back on the plan which she had formulated soon after poor Prince Eddy's death: Prince George must marry Princess May.

4

The idea that Prince George should marry Princess May was welcomed by everyone; by everyone, that is, other than the two principals themselves. It was not that they were indifferent to each other; it was simply that they were both acutely distressed and embarrassed by the situation in which they found themselves. Prince George had been devoted to his brother and even if Princess May had not been in love with Prince Eddy, there was something unseemly about the haste with which she was expected to transfer her affections to Prince George.

'Aunt Mary Teck was here with May whom I thought very nice indeed,' wrote the Empress Frederick to one of her daughters. 'Her position is most difficult and embarrassing. She is still in mourning for our poor darling Eddy, and the newspapers are constantly writing about her becoming engaged to Georgie, and the whole of the public seem to wish it ardently. Of course not a word has been mentioned in the family, but there is a universal feeling among them all that it is almost sure to take place sooner or later. There is so much for it . . . in many ways she is very much suited for the position, and everyone praises her.'

During the year that followed Prince Eddy's death, these two modest, somewhat inarticulate young people found themselves being drawn together. At first they shared a common sorrow; later they developed a respect and warmth for each other. When they were apart they exchanged affectionate letters; when they were together, they indulged in friendly, if rather halting, conversation. Not until sixteen months after Prince Eddy's death, in May 1893, did Prince George propose to Princess May.

Queen Victoria was delighted. 'Let me now say,' she wrote to her grandson, 'how thankful I am that this great and so long and ardently wished for event is settled and I gladly give my consent to what I pray may be for your happiness and for the Country's good. Say everything affectionate to dear May, for whom this must be a *trying moment* full of such mixed feelings. But she cannot find a *better* husband than you and I am sure she will be a good, devoted and useful wife to you.'

The couple were married in the Chapel Royal, St James's Palace, on 6 July 1893, amidst scenes of great splendour. The bride wore a dress of white and silver brocade with a sweeping train and a short lace veil. The bridegroom was in naval uniform. An awkward moment occurred when, by some miscalculation, the Queen was the first, instead of the last, of the royalties to reach the chapel. The bride's mother, the elephantine Duchess of Teck, who had driven in the Queen's carriage, suggested that she wait in a small room to the left of the chapel until such time as everyone else had arrived. The suggestion made, the Duchess of Teck and her lady-in-waiting started up the aisle. But the Queen was having none of it. Coming up behind the Duchess's lady-in-waiting and giving her dress a sharp tug, the Queen announced firmly, 'I am going first.' With that she rapidly overtook the two figures ahead and advanced imperiously to her place by the altar.

She afterwards admitted that it had been most amusing to be able to watch, for once, all the other royal guests making their entrances.

The honeymoon was spent in the couple's future home, York Cottage, a cramped and hideous little villa on the Sandringham estate. The Queen regretted the choice of Sandringham ('rather *unlucky* and sad') and, indeed, the place was heavy with memories of the recent death of Prince Eddy. The Prince's room was kept exactly as he had left it. On his dressing-table were his watch, his brushes and his combs; in a glass-fronted cupboard were his clothes and his photographs. Only the bed looked different. It was now covered with a vast silk Union Jack. 'No one,' said the approving Empress Frederick of this death chamber, 'is to live in it again.'

But neither this, nor the ugliness and inconvenience of York Cottage itself, could diminish the Duke of York's enthusiasm for Sandringham. He loved it, and for the following thirty-three years, York Cottage was his country home.

It was not in one of its poky rooms, however, but in a more spacious one at White Lodge in Richmond Park – the home of Princess May's parents – that her first child was born on 23 June 1894. It was a boy. On the subject of the baby's name, the Queen had very strong ideas. She lost no time in letting Prince George know that she would like the boy to be called Albert. The country, she said, 'would expect that dear Grandpapa's name should follow mine in future to mark the Victorian era'.

But the Duke of York was not having it. 'Long before our dear child was born, both May and I settled that if it was a boy we should call him Edward, after darling *Eddy*. *This is the dearest wish of our hearts*, dearest Grandmama, for Edward is indeed a *sacred* name to us and one which I know would have pleased *him* beyond anything; it is in loving remembrance of him and therefore *not* painful to us.' Of course, he added, one of the boy's names would certainly be Albert, but the *first* name must be Edward.

For this particular line of reasoning, the Queen had a ready answer. Dear Eddy's name, she pointed out, had *not* been Edward: it had been Albert Victor. She was especially anxious, she went on to say, that the name *Albert* should *mark* the dynasty; that the kings of the Coburg line – beginning with her own son, Prince Albert Edward and continuing with George himself, one of whose names was Albert – should all bear the name.

But the young couple held firm and the Queen, who was never quite as intransigent as many imagined, had to give way on the understanding that the name Albert would feature somewhere amongst the others. In fact, it featured second, after the parents' own choice of Edward. By neither of these names, however, was the boy ever known. To his family and friends he was always David. When he finally succeeded to the throne, it was as King Edward VIII.

But no disagreement over the choice of name could lessen Queen Victoria's delight in this birth of her great-grandson. To her daughter, the Empress Frederick, she pointed out that 'it has never happened in this country that there should be three direct Heirs as well as the Sovereign alive!'

Some eighteen months later she had further cause for gratification. On 14 December 1895, the Duchess of York gave birth to a second son. The actual date – 14 December – was unfortunate, as this was the anniversary of the death of the Prince Consort in 1861. 'The terrible anniversary returned for the thirty-fourth time,' noted the Queen in her Journal that evening, although she was not as put out by the timing as Prince George had feared. 'I have a feeling it may be a blessing for the dear little boy and may be looked upon as a gift from God,' she wrote. After all, had the child not entered this life on the very day that his great-grandfather had entered an 'even greater life'?

This time there was no haggling about a name. The baby was christened Albert Frederick Arthur George. In time he, like his grandfather the Prince of Wales, became known as Bertie. Yet, when he succeeded to the throne, on the abdication of his brother Edward VIII, in 1936, it was not as King Albert I, but as King George VI.

CHAPTER SIX

Sophie of Greece

I

With the accession of her eldest son as Kaiser Wilhelm II in 1888, the Empress Frederick withdrew from public life almost completely. This was not, by any means, from choice. As energetic, as idealistic, as politically aware as ever, Vicky would have enjoyed nothing more than to have been involved in affairs of state. But the new Kaiser was having none of it. He simply brushed her aside as being of no consequence. No one consulted her, no one deferred to her, no one confided in her. Her husband's death was not mourned; her own eclipse not regretted.

'I am completely cast off from the official world;' she complained to her mother Queen Victoria, 'not a single official person ever comes near me and what used to be *mein tägliches Brot* [my daily bread] has quite ceased. How I used to work for Fritz and how he used to tell me everything! Now I might be buried alive . . . Influence on the course of events I have not the smallest or faintest . . . Now that my experience is perhaps worth something there is a dead silence and one's existence is forgotten.'

Denied any political outlet, the Empress busied herself with the affairs of her home and family. With almost indecent haste, the Kaiser had turned her out of the Neues Palais, in which she had lived for most of her married life, and had offered her, instead, the use of two inconvenient castles. Not wanting to spend the rest of her days in some state-owned building and so be at the mercy of her son's whims, Vicky decided to build a home of her own. About a year after her husband's death, she bought an estate at Kronberg, near Homburg. Here, in the chestnut-covered Taunus hills, she built a vast country mansion. Ever *die Engländerin*, she packed her German architect off to England to look at Elizabethan architecture and Victorian plumbing. As a result, there was erected, 'not a Schloss according to German ideas', as she assured her mother, but an outsize country house in the mock-Elizabethan style so dear to English Victorian hearts. In this steep-roofed, many-windowed, multiple-chimneyed home were collected her paintings, her furniture, her *obiets d'art* and her books. She even kept the little scraps of paper on which her voiceless husband had scribbled his last messages. In his memory, she named her home Friedrichshof.

'His spirit shall rule there,' she declared, 'and in that way alone can his poor, forsaken, broken wife have any peace in her loneliness and sorrow.'

It was a touching prospect but, with the best will in the world, the Empress could not give herself up entirely to revering the memory of her dead husband. For one thing, she was far too active; for another, she still had three unmarried daughters on her hands. The eldest was Victoria (Moretta) whose projected marriage to Prince Sandro of Battenberg had been opposed with such vehemence by Wilhelm and Bismarck; the second was Sophie, known to the family as Sossie or, in moments of even greater intimacy, as Fozzie; the youngest was Margaret (Mossy) whom Queen Victoria had once suggested as a possible bride for Prince Eddy.

These three girls, in contrast to the Empress's three eldest children (Kaiser Wilhelm II, Prince Henry and Princess Charlotte) were devoted to their mother. Throughout the months of their father's tragic illness and brief reign, these three princesses had remained by their parents' side, dispelling some of the gloom by their youth, their loyalty and their liveliness. Since Kaiser Frederick III's death, they had been a source of great comfort of the Empress. 'My trio', '*my Kleeblatt*', 'my three sweet girls', she called them.

The girls' grandmother, Queen Victoria, was hardly less fond of them. She loved having them to stay with her and took the closest interest in their welfare. To help Moretta recover from her disappointment at not being allowed to marry the dashing Sandro of Battenberg, Queen Victoria invited her to spend a few weeks at Windsor and Balmoral. The calm and well-ordered atmosphere of the English court, together with the sage and sympathetic presence of Grandmama Queen, soon restored Moretta's spirits. To the girl's mother, Queen Victoria had some sound advice to give on the matter of not forcing Moretta into another marriage against her will.

Of these three granddaughters of Queen Victoria, Sophie was possibly the most engaging. Small-waisted, plump-cheeked, fair-haired and with a fashionably frizzed fringe that was the despair of her mother, she was also the first of the three girls to get married. In the autumn of 1888, when Sophie was eighteen, Crown Prince Constantine, the son of King George I of the Hellenes, asked for her hand. The young couple had known each other for some time. Constantine, the Greek *Diadoch* or Crown Prince, had studied in Germany – at Leipzig and at Heidelberg – and was now a sub-lieutenant in the 2nd Prussian Guards. He and Sophie seem to have been very much in love.

Constantine's father, King George I of the Hellenes, was the son of King Christian IX of Denmark. Like so many descendants of the Danish

King, Constantine (or Tino, as he was called in the family) was attractive, good-natured and high-spirited. The Empress Frederick assured her mother that he was 'very nice and charming and well brought up'; her only reservations about the match were Tino's youth (he was twenty-one) and the precariousness of the Greek throne.

Some months after the young couple had become engaged, the Empress took Sophie to Copenhagen on holiday. Staying at Fredensborg Castle with their grandfather, the Danish King, were Tino and some of his brothers. The Empress was thus able to get to know him better. The young Greek princes, she informed the interested Queen Victoria, were 'the finest of young men, and also the most intelligent'. They were also the liveliest. Their simplicity, their cheerfulness, their complete lack of inhibition must have served as a refreshing change from the formality of the German imperial court or the correctness of the English. 'The noise they all made, and the wild romps they had were simply indescribable . . .' reported the Empress. They carried each other, they flung each other about, they 'seemed happier and to enjoy themselves more thoroughly than children of five or six'.

It was no wonder that pretty Princess Sophie, who had spent the last few years in an atmosphere of such *Sturm und Drang*, was taken with the blond and square-jawed Tino, whom the Empress described as 'a young Hercules'.

The match between Tino and Sophie even satisfied Kaiser Wilhelm. After all, it meant that his sister would one day be Queen of the Hellenes. With his capacity for self-deception, Wilhelm managed to convince himself that it was he who had arranged it – for reasons of state. With one masterly stroke he had united five ruling houses: those of Germany, Britain, Greece, Denmark and Russia. Was the bride not the sister of the German Kaiser and granddaughter of the Queen of England? Was the bridegroom not the grandson of the King of Denmark, the son of the King of the Hellenes and the nephew of the Tsaritsa of Russia? Wilhelm had every reason to be satisfied.

The wedding, in Athens on 27 October 1889, was one of those splendid late nineteenth-century royal jamborees; a coming together of that inter-related crowd that Queen Victoria always referred to as the 'Royal Mob' ('than which,' she would add, 'I dislike *nothing more*.') The sunlit waters of Piraeus were crammed with royal yachts; the summit of the Acropolis was a-swarm with sightseeing royalties. Besides the Greek and German royal familes, there were the King and Queen of Denmark, the Tsarevich of Russia and, representing the bride's grandmother, the Prince and Princess of Wales. The weather was perfect, sunny but not too hot, and there was no wind to coat the city with dust from the Plain of Attica.

The Prince of Wales's yacht, *Osborne*, was escorted by the entire British Mediterranean fleet. This afforded the Kaiser, whom Queen Victoria had recently made an honorary admiral, the ideal opportunity to air his views on his grandmother's Navy. At an official luncheon aboard the *Dread-nought*, he warned his hosts that their Mediterranean fleet was far too weak. This uncalled-for advice he followed up with a lengthy mem-orandum on the state of Britain's Navy; the fleet, he instructed his grandmother, 'must be reinforced'. Bertie, not allowing himself to be annoyed at his nephew's officious behaviour, merely assured Queen Victoria that 'Willy' had been in 'high good humour' and that, for once, there had been no *contretemps*.

The wedding itself was a spectacular affair. The royalties, ablaze with jewels and orders, drove in open carriages (hastily borrowed from the wealthier *bourgeoisie* of the town) through the sunbright streets to the new Greek cathedral. The theatricality of the Orthodox ceremony – the candles, the crowns, the bearded and mitred bishops – was offset by the simplicity of the service, in a specially arranged Protestant chapel, which followed it. Princess Sophie wore an elaborate dress of white and silver with a long, lavishly embroidered train. Because her bridal veil was nowhere to be found, she was obliged to wear a simpler one, of tulle. 'My darling Sophie looked so sweet and grave and calm . . .' reported the Empress to Queen Victoria. 'How much I thought of you and dear Papa and my wedding when I saw the dear young people standing at the altar. . . .'

The ceremonies over, Princess Sophie changed into a dress of white and gold, and, with her husband standing beside her, drove to the little rented villa which was to be their home. They were vociferously acclaimed. The Greek crowd – so excitable, so patriotic, so proud and so superstitious – saw, in the marriage of this attractive young couple, the beginnings of the fulfilment of an old prophecy: when a Constantine shared his throne with a Sophie, Greece would once again rise to great-ness. 'The Great Idea', that of a new Byzantium in which all the Greek people would once more be united, would become a reality. Greece would once again know glory.

2

For Crown Princess Sophie, life in Athens was a far cry from life in Berlin. Although, since the accession of her brother Kaiser Wilhelm II, the German imperial court had become more showy, it was still extremely formal, hidebound and pompous. The German imperial family had always taken themselves very seriously. In contrast, the Greek royal family was charmingly informal. The dynasty was very new. Sophie's father-in-law, King George I, was the first of his line. Before him, and since the establishment of a monarchy in Greece after the War of Independence in 1830, the country had been ruled by King Otho I, who had been a Bavarian. After a turbulent, twenty-nine-year-long reign, King Otho had been overthrown. The finding of a monarch to replace Otho had been no easy task; not every prince had been prepared to face the caprices of Greek politics.

Amongst those whom the Greeks had fondly imagined would be prepared to do so had been Queen Victoria's second son, Prince Alfred, Duke of Edinburgh. By a massive majority in a nation-wide plebiscite, Prince Alfred had been elected the new King of the Hellenes. The Greeks could have saved themselves the trouble. Britain announced that, according to an earlier agreement, no member of her reigning house was eligible for the Greek throne. So Prince Alfred withdrew from the scene. Not until over fifty years later, when Queen Victoria's granddaughter Sophie became Queen of the Hellenes, did one of her descendants come to sit on a Greek throne.

The crown was eventually accepted by Prince Wilhelm, the eighteen-year-old son of King Christian IX of Denmark. He was proclaimed King George I of the Hellenes on 30 March 1863. Thus his father, King Christian IX of Denmark, had the satisfaction of adding the Greek to the thrones which his children would one day occupy, for one of King George I's sisters was Alexandra, Princess of Wales and future Queen of England, and the other Dagmar, future Empress of Russia. If Queen Victoria was the Grandmother of Europe, then King Christian IX of Denmark was certainly the Grandfather.

At the age of twenty-two, King George I of the Hellenes married the sixteen-year-old Russian Grand Duchess Olga (she brought with her to Athens a trunkful of dolls) and during the following twenty years they raised eight children. The eldest of these was Crown Prince Constantine, who became the husband of Princess Sophie.

The royal family into which Sophie married was one of the most natural in Europe. King George I, still in his early forties, was a slender, blue-eyed, exotically moustached extrovert; sensible, unpretentious and full of fun. Queen Olga was a beauty, fair-skinned, plump and sweet-tempered. Their eight children had been brought up (and, indeed, were still being brought up) in the simplest possible fashion. The uncomfortable rooms of the palace in Athens and the grounds of their country place at Tatoi resounded to the noise of the royal children at play. They roller-skated through the ballrooms, they cycled along the corridors, they charged across the flower beds. They played elaborate practical jokes. The atmosphere, in other words, could hardly have been more different from that of Windsor or Potsdam.

Something of this same informality marked the family's public life. Athens – small, dusty, poor and provincial – was the most democratic of towns; there were few social distinctions and almost no formal entertaining. The relatively exclusive state banquets were usually followed by the far from exclusive court balls. To these, all and sundry crowded in. One of Crown Prince Constantine's brothers tells the story of a visitor to Athens who hired a carriage to take him to a ball at the palace: 'Do you mind going rather early,' asked the coachman, 'because I'm going to the court ball myself and shall have to go home and change?' And Prince Constantine, on having a young woman presented to him, recognized the vaguely familiar face as belonging to the daughter of his valet. She had married a naval officer and had every right to be presented.

To be granted an interview with the King, one had merely to write one's name in the audience book. The monarch would stroll about the streets of the capital attended only by an aide or one of his sons. 'Here comes Constantine' or 'Here comes Nicholas' the townspeople would call to each other as the princes walked by.

For Princess Sophie, life was even less formal than it was for the King and Queen. The sovereigns, at least, lived in a palace; it was inconvenient, smelly, stifling in summer, freezing in winter and with not more than two bathrooms for its three hundred and sixty-five rooms, but it was undeniably a palace. Sophie and Tino, on the other hand, lived in a rented house in the town – a small, unpretentious villa hardly better than those of the *bourgeoisie*. But Sophie loved it. Shy, and somewhat ill at ease amongst the rough and tumble of King George's household, she was delighted to have a home of her own. The house, like those of most of Queen Victoria's descendants, was cheerfully and comfortably furnished. 'I cannot tell you how intensely happy I am here with my Tino,' she told her mother, 'and how I enjoy this dear little house, the lovely English furniture . . . .'

The Empress, always ready with advice, was soon giving her hints on how to improve it and run it. Indeed, there were few subjects on which the Empress Frederick was not anxious to advise her daughter and it was fortunate for Princess Sophie that this advice was always practical, sensible and gracefully tendered. In a steady stream, the Empress's ideas on such diverse subjects as drains, cookery, gardens, books, paintings, choirs, ladies' colleges, travel and the necessity of making oneself popular poured forth. As Princess Sophie had been blessed with neither her mother's boundless energy nor her wide-ranging intellect, one cannot altogether blame her for not acting on quite every one of the Empress's suggestions.

For the moment, Princess Sophie, who had inherited Queen Victoria's taste for domesticity, was happy enough to be running her little home and devoting herself to her husband. The better she knew him, the more she appreciated him. Crown Prince Constantine was an honest man – open, straightforward, incapable of insincerity or dissimulation. At times, this frankness could lead to difficulties: he was often outspoken, intolerant and undiplomatic. Yet he was never autocratic; like his father, the King, he was friendly, unaffected and thoroughly at ease with the least of his countrymen. With the army, he was especially popular; his vocabulary of Greek oaths, they say, had to be heard to be appreciated.

In addition, the Crown Prince had two qualifications which his father, no matter how capable or popular, could ever equal. To a people such as the Greeks, these were all-important. The one was Constantine's Orthodox faith, the other his Greek birth.

To escape the heat and dust of the town, Tino and Sophie would join the rest of the family at their country place at Tatoi. Here, on a forty-thousand-acre estate, some fifteen miles from Athens, King George had built a family home in what was claimed to be the 'English cottage style'. In fact, it was more like an English suburban villa. The house boasted a flower garden, a kitchen garden, a home farm, an orchard and an evergreen plantation. From the balconies of the house one could look out over the trees to a distant view of the shimmering Aegean. Life at Tatoi was even more informal than it was in Athens. Meals were served at the most unfashionable hours: luncheon at eleven and dinner at three. To the Greek royal family, Tatoi meant home. 'We children just loved it,' wrote one of Tino's brothers. 'It was the one place where we could live a real home life and forget, for a short time, that we were not supposed to be ordinary human beings!'

On 19 July 1890, almost exactly nine months after her marriage, Princess Sophie gave birth to a son. He was named George, after his grandfather. The event brought forth a positive avalanche of suggestions from the Empress Frederick. Prominent amongst them was the advisability of the mother surrounding herself with English faces – an English doctor, an English midwife, an English nanny and an English governess. On this score, the Empress need have had no fears. Very much Queen Victoria's granddaughter, Sophie was determined that her household should be run on English lines. Tino's family was confusingly cosmopolitan: his father was Danish, his mother was Russian; the parents spoke to each other in German and to their children in English. In addition to these four languages, the family spoke French, Italian and, of course, Greek. But it was as an English family that the Crown Prince and Princess raised their children.

Between 1890 and 1913, Princess Sophie bore six children; three boys and three girls. The language used in the home was English. The simple, almost spartan way of life was considered to be English. English furniture, from Maple and Liberty, filled the rooms. Princess Sophie, reported one German official, 'is the most English of all the Empress Frederick's children; she talks English to her husband and her own children, to whom that language comes more natural than any other. I had the opportunity of hearing the Greek children speak English many times at Friedrichshof and they seemed to me to have no foreign accent at all.' They had English governesses and English tutors and spent frequent holidays at that most

English of resorts, Eastbourne. In time, some of them attended English schools.

And, of course, presiding over the entire household like some distant but all-powerful deity was that personification of all things English – the children's great-grandmother, Queen Victoria.

3

A few months after the birth of their first son, Tino and Sophie travelled to Berlin for the wedding of Sophie's sister, Moretta. With Moretta's old love, Prince Sandro of Battenberg, having married a far less illustrious bride – a singer by the name of Joanna Loisinger – Moretta had accepted the proposal of a much less glamorous suitor, Prince Adolf of Schaumburg-Lippe. It was while in Berlin that Princess Sophie told her family that she had decided to enter the Orthodox Church. The announcement precipitated a violent crisis.

Sophie's brother, the Kaiser, was furious. His wife, the pious and narrow-minded Dona, was even more outraged. Sending for Sophie, Dona (about to give birth to a sixth strapping son) primly announced that Wilhelm would never stand for the change of religion. If Sophie persisted in this headstrong course, she would end up in Hell. Flaring up, Sophie told Dona to mind her own business and slammed out of the room. At this the pregnant Dona became so excited that the doctors were sent for and her baby was born three weeks prematurely. 'If my poor baby dies it is solely Sophie's fault and she has murdered it,' wrote the agitated Kaiser to his grandmother, Queen Victoria, who was, of course, following this *fracas* between her grandchildren with deep concern.

But the baby flourished and Sophie, ignoring her brother's disapproval, returned to Greece determined to embrace the Orthodox faith. Wilhelm, suddenly alive to his sacred duties as Head of the Church, threatened to expel her from both Germany and the Hohenzollern family.

His high-handed behaviour led to a positive snowstorm of family letters. From Grandmama at Windsor, from the Empress Frederick at Homburg, from Crown Princess Sophie in Athens, even from Princess Moretta, honeymooning in Cairo, the indignantly worded reactions criss-crossed Europe.

'Good gracious, have they gone clean mad?' asked Moretta of Wilhelm and Dona. 'To think of sweet Sophie and Tino having these disreputable scenes makes me boil with indignation. The audacity of Dona to speak like that.'

The threat of expulsion caused a violent scene between Wilhelm and his mother. 'William is convinced that I tried to persuade you to become Greek,' reported the Empress to Sophie. 'He is so firmly convinced that I am always in some "intrigue" against him . . .' Her arguments had no effect. The Kaiser sent King George of the Hellenes a telegram announcing his decision to cut Sophie off if she defied him.

The Empress described her son's telegram as 'preposterous'. 'It makes me quite furious,' she went on to say to Sophie, 'and yet I am obliged to laugh. He seems to be copying Peter the Great, Frederick William I, Napoleon or some such conspicuous tyrant. To a free-born Briton, as I thank God I am, such ideas, so little in harmony with the XIX Century and personal liberty and independence, are simply abhorrent; and this my own son!'

Queen Victoria was less vehement but no less disturbed. 'I cannot say how grieved and upset I am at what has happened, and which was so entirely unnecessary and uncalled for,' she wrote, with customary sagacity, to Vicky. 'I think it was all Dona's love of interference . . . I myself do not understand such narrow-mindedness. I could not, even though I may be against a person changing their religion, if they do it willingly and out of conviction and without compulsion, I could not blame them or be angry with them for it.'

Sophie, in a final effort to smooth things over, wrote her brother a long conciliatory letter, explaining her reasons for entering the Orthodox Church and asking him to retract the ban. He refused. 'Received answer,' Sophie informed her mother in an open telegram, sent through the post offices at Athens and Homburg. 'Keeps to what he said in Berlin. Fixes it to three years. Mad. Never mind. Sophie.'

Princess Sophie was received into the Greek Orthodox Church in the spring of 1891. A few months later, defying Wilhelm's ban, she visited her mother at Freidrichshof. The Kaiser made no move to stop her. He was about to pay his first state visit to Queen Victoria; for all his arrogance, Kaiser Wilhelm II did not dare incur the wrath of his formidable grandmother.

CHAPTER SEVEN

Marie of Romania

I

Few of Queen Victoria's grandchildren were to prove more exotic than Princess Marie, eldest daughter of the Queen's second son, Prince Alfred, Duke of Edinburgh. Having, at the age of sixteen, rejected a proposal of marriage from her cousin Prince George of Wales, and so missed the opportunity of one day becoming Queen of England, Princess Marie, or Missy, accepted a second proposal and ended up as the Queen of Romania instead.

Of the characters of the two royal houses represented by Marie's parentage – matter-of-fact British and mystical Russian – the Princess took her colour, almost entirely, from her mother's side of the family. In the Coburg aviary, she was to be a very rare bird indeed.

Her father, the Duke of Edinburgh, was a bluff, handsome, uncomplicated and unquestioningly patriotic Englishman. Having made a career of the Navy, he spent long periods away from home. Her mother was the Grand Duchess Marie Alexandrovna, the only daughter of Tsar Alexander II of Russia. The Duchess of Edinburgh's plump figure and softly pretty face belied the strength of her character: she was an energetic, proud, autocratic and masterful woman, spartan in her way of life, fanatically religious and devoted to her native Russia. Even in surroundings as uncompromisingly British as Clarence House and Eastwell Park, she carried with her the flavour of imperial Russia. Her private rooms glittered with jewelled icons; she was never without a Russian priest and two chanters. England, she never liked. To her, English was an ugly language and, after the gorgeous, almost barbaric splendours of the Russian court, life in various British naval stations seemed strange indeed. Nor was she, the daughter of the Tsar of all the Russias, satisfied with her British rank. She was obliged to give precedence, not only to all Queen Victoria's daughters, but to the Danish Princess of Wales.

As a result, the Duchess of Edinburgh kept very much to herself, living amongst her icons and bringing up her family of five children (one boy and four girls) strictly, simply and – for all the apparent haughtiness of her manner – not unkindly.

But not even the stand-offish Duchess of Edinburgh could hope to live a life quite independent of her mother-in-law, Queen Victoria. Grandmama Queen was the sun around which her life, and the lives of her children, revolved. The girls were taken to visit their grandmother in her fascinating rooms at Windsor; they breakfasted with her on the lawns at Osborne; they drove out with her at Balmoral. In the summer the Queen would lend the family Osborne Cottage; in the autumn, they moved into Abergeldie, on the Balmoral estate. The old Queen followed her grandchildren's careers, says Missy, 'with grandmotherly affection, but also with the anxious severity of one who wished that those of her House should do it every honour, no matter where they were placed.' For all the smallness of her stature, the dowdiness of her clothes and the softness of her voice, Queen Victoria was 'a tremendous, sometimes almost a fearful force' in their lives. 'Even Mamma, who, according to us, was omnipotent,' says Princess Marie, 'had to count with Queen Victoria, had to listen to her, and if she had not exactly to *obey*, had anyhow to argue out all differences of opinion. But as she was strong-willed and autocratic, I can imagine that these arguments were tough.'

By the end of the 1880s, a complicated dynastic issue, known as the Coburg Succession, finally ensured that the Duchess of Edinburgh need live under the shadow of Queen Victoria no longer. At that time, the dukedom of Saxe-Coburg-Gotha was held by the Prince Consort's only brother, Ernest. Duke Ernest was everything that Prince Albert had not been: he was an ugly, uncouth and licentious old roué, whose life had by now been given over, almost entirely, to the seducing of young women. He had a wife – a sad, faded creature – but no children. An heir to what Queen Victoria looked upon as this most precious of duchies had therefore to be provided and it had long ago been decided that the dukedom would go to the Queen's second son, the Duke of Edinburgh. Already, the Edinburghs' only son was being educated in Coburg; now the Duke moved his entire family there. They took up residence in the mock-Gothic, ochre-coloured Schloss Rosenau (once so beloved of the Prince Consort) and there sat waiting for terrible old Duke Ernest to die.

Happy at last amidst the simple formalities of this little German court, the Duchess of Edinburgh was able, as her daughter Marie puts it, 'to live entirely according to her desires, uncontrolled by Grandmama Queen and uncriticized by those who were inclined to find her ways foreign and out of keeping with British traditions'. She could also put her children in the care of German tutors and governesses so that, according to her sister-in-law, the Princess of Wales, 'they won't *even know* that they have ever been English'.

Thus it was that when Prince George of Wales made his tentative proposal of marriage, the Duchess of Edinburgh did nothing towards encouraging her daughter Marie to accept it. Although the Duke of Edinburgh was all in favour of the match (it was the dream of his life, maintained Queen Victoria) the sixteen-year-old Missy – influenced by her anglophobe Russian mother and encouraged by her anglophobe German governess – turned down her cousin's offer. Prince George married Princess May instead and gained himself a wife who was just about as different from Princess Marie as it was possible to be.

Even at sixteen Missy was a romantic. She was an emotional, impressionable, impulsive girl, given to what she, in her always selfconscious way, referred to as 'ecstasies'. There seem to have been few things that did not bring forth some rapturous reaction; she appears to have been in an almost permanent state of enchantment. She delighted no less in the scent of violets beneath her window than in some spectacular scene in her mother's Russia – 'the fantastic, gorgeous Russia, almost Asiatic in splendour, a pageant of might and power' as she so characteristically described it.

She was, she claims blandly, a great 'lover of beauty'; not only of her own, which was considerable, but of everything around her. She had 'an irresistible instinct, or shall I call it urge, towards beauty. I *must* have something about me that satisfies my eye . . .' Yet the more beautiful the object, the more likely was that very eye to spill over with tears. 'If I look hard enough at anything in this world,' runs one of her singular observations, 'it brings tears into my eyes.'

That the Duchess of Edinburgh was anxious to marry off this impetuous and passionate creature is understandable. The Duchess had, moreover, very definite views on the advisability of princesses marrying young. 'When they are over twenty,' she used to say, 'they begin to think too much and to have too many ideas of their own which complicate matters.' It did not take much insight to appreciate that a girl such as Marie would very soon be developing a great many strong ideas of her own; it would be as well to arrange a marriage before her character was too well formed.

With this in mind, the Duchess of Edinburgh took the sixteen-year-old Missy and her younger sister Victoria Melita (who was known by another of those arch family nicknames – Ducky) to a royal house-party at Wilhelmshöhe, near Cassel, in the autumn of 1891.

Presiding over the royal gathering at Wilhelmshöhe was yet another of Queen Victoria's grandchildren: Marie's first cousin, Kaiser Wilhelm II. (His mother, the Empress Frederick, and Marie's father, the Duke of Edinburgh, were sister and brother.) Missy, for all her theatricality and self-satisfaction, was no fool, and her powers of observation were always acute. On her cousin the Kaiser, she had some very telling remarks to make. 'William was, of course, much older than we were,' she wrote, 'and though an interesting personality, he was not a favourite cousin. He was no doubt full of good feelings but his attitude towards his family in general was brusque and at times boisterous.' He did not, she went on to say, 'exactly intimidate you, but he "put your back up" the moment he addressed you in his overloud and deliberately [aggressive] manner; you felt all prickly with opposition, there was something about him that roused antagonism'.

It was not, however, in order to be patronized by Kaiser Wilhelm II that Princess Marie had been brought to Wilhelmshöhe. Among the guests was Crown Prince Ferdinand of Romania. He was a good-looking young man but with a shy, diffident manner and a nervous laugh. He was known, inevitably, as Nando. Whether or not the twenty-five-year old Prince knew that he had been brought to Wilhelmshöhe to meet Princess Marie is uncertain; what is certain is that Missy herself knew nothing of her mother's plans. 'In those days,' she says, 'girls were kept in ignorance of the marriage plots of their parents.' Prince Ferdinand went out of his way to be amiable although, surprisingly, the one topic the two of them never discussed was Romania. The young Princess was not even too sure where it was.

They met again, the vivacious Missy and the unpretentious Nando, in Berlin later that year and, once more, the following spring, in Munich. 'The young prince was excruciatingly shy and laughed more than ever to mask his timidity,' says Marie. 'Curiously enough, it was his extra-ordinary timidity which attracted me most; there was something so young, so suppressedly eager and just a little helpless about him. It gave you a longing to put him at his ease, to make him comfortable; it aroused your motherly feelings, in fact you wanted to help him.'

This was all very well, but it was not love. Not, that is, on Missy's side, although she assures us that Nando was passionately in love with her. None the less, encouraged by her mother's 'happy, expectant face', Princess Marie accepted Prince Ferdinand's halting proposal; or, as she so flamboyantly puts it, 'I just said "Yes" . . . and with that "Yes" I sealed my fate, opened the door upon life . . .'

The engagement was announced early in June 1892 at the Neues Palais at Potsdam, and celebrated with a huge banquet given by the Kaiser. 'I was excited, believed that I was very happy,' noted the slightly bemused Missy, 'but beneath all the noise, glamour and glory there was a feeling of *angoisse* . . .'

She was not alone in her distress. Her father, for one, was not at all happy about the engagement. It had been contrived while he was stationed at Devonport in England and his permission not sought until it was too late. 'Papa', admitted Marie, 'said very little, though his face was rather glum.'

Grandmama had rather more to say. 'I have been expecting to get a telegram from you about Missy's engagement, which has us all by surprise,' wrote Queen Victoria to the Empress Frederick, 'it seems to have come very rapidly to a climax. The Country [Romania] is very insecure and the Society – dreadful – and she is a mere Child, and quite inexperienced . . .'

Victoria admitted, however, to hearing that Crown Prince Ferdinand was 'very nice'.

Soon, the Queen would be able to judge for herself for, as the apprehensive Marie says, 'she would have to approve of my future husband; none of her granddaughters married without her approval.'

2

The Romanian royal family was German. Indeed, like Kaiser Wilhelm II himself, the Romanian royalties were Hohenzollerns. They sprang from the Catholic branch of the German imperial family – the Hohenzollern-Sigmaringens, who lived in a picturesque old castle in southern Germany, near the source of the Danube. In the year 1866, one of the Hohenzollern-Sigmaringen princes had been elected King of the recently created country of Romania. At the time of Princess Marie's engagement this Hohenzollern still reigned there as King Carol I.

King Carol of Romania was a short, dignified, self-assured man, luxuriantly bearded, hook-nosed and eagle-eyed. His manner was polite but cold, cordial but masterful. He had an unshakable sense of duty. Very different was his wife, Queen Elisabeth of Romania, for she was that most bizarre of nineteenth-century royalties, the romantic poet-queen, who wrote under the name of Carmen Sylva. As this ill-assorted pair had no children, they had adopted, as the heir to the Romanian throne, the son of one of the King's brothers: this was the present Crown Prince of Romania, the modest and unassuming Ferdinand, who was to marry Princess Marie of Edinburgh.

Unbeknown to the starry-eyed Missy at the time of her engagement was the fact that her fiancé was in disgrace. Not long before, Nando had scandalized royal circles – not because of any licentious behaviour – but by falling in love with a commoner; and not only by falling in love with her but by proposing to marry her.

That this should have happened is understandable. Life, in the Romanian capital of Bucharest, had been no bed of roses for the young Prince Ferdinand. He had arrived there direct from the military academy at Potsdam when hardly more than a boy and had at once been plunged into a rigorous course of training by his uncle, the King. Faced, on the one hand, by the unsmiling, exacting, hard-working King Carol (*Der*

Onkel as he called him) and the dreamy, warm-hearted and theatrical Carmen Sylva on the other, the young man had been drawn to the latter. In her spell-binding company, his hesitancies, deficiencies and inferiorities were much less apparent.

Nor was this the only reason for Nando's addiction to her company. The Queen delighted in surrounding herself with pretty girls; to their adoring and uncritical eyes, this silver-haired queen in her trailing draperies was, as Missy once wrote, 'the soul of poetry, the Muse, the inspirer'.

Her favourite amongst these girls was a dark and hot-blooded beauty by the name of Hélène Vacarescu. The Queen never moved without Hélène. In 1890, the two of them had even paid a visit to Queen Victoria at Balmoral. Victoria had been enchanted by Carmen Sylva ('a wonderful and charming personality, unlike other people') and hardly less impressed by Hélène ('a bright little person of twenty-four, a poetess, very oriental-looking'). The Romanian Queen had treated the English Queen's court to one of her famous readings of her own work – a Greek play in German: 'Many of course could not understand . . .' noted Queen Victoria, 'but all were interested.' Mlle Vacarescu, said Victoria, 'helps the Queen in her writings' and her own work had been 'crowned by *l'Académie française* – a very rare distinction for so young a person'.

It was with this talented favourite that Prince Ferdinand fell in love. The Romanian Queen, far from resenting the romance, actively encouraged it. The idea of it fired her fevered imagination. The lovely Hélène, her protégée, would lead this awkward young man to greatness: she would mould him, transform him. She would one day be for him a glorious Queen. Caught up in what was described as 'an atmosphere of palpitating romance', Carmen Sylva 'idealized the lovers, she threw them together, encouraged, stimulated, helped, gloried them; caring little for the morrow, she lived entirely for the excitement of the moment . . . .'

The moment did not last very long. When the Crown Prince, plucking up courage, announced to his uncle, the King, his intention of marrying Mlle Vacarescu, he was given short shrift. Once King Carol regained control of his temper, he gave Ferdinand a choice: the throne with its attendant advantages or Mlle Vacarescu without them. Ferdinand chose the throne. The Queen, her dream – and nerves – shattered, fled to her mother's home at Neu Wied, while the unhappy Nando was packed off in search of a more suitable bride.

He found her, of course, at Wilhelmshöhe, as King Carol and the girl's mother, the Duchess of Edinburgh, had planned he would. 'But *I* did not know,' protested Missy afterwards, 'that he was supposed to be travelling about with a broken heart.'

Once the Crown Prince had become engaged to Princess Marie, he was obliged to introduce her to the architect of his earlier romance, the poet-queen, Carmen Sylva. As the Queen was still in quasi-banishment, it was to Neu Wied that Marie, with her mother and sister Ducky, had to go and meet her.

Carmen Sylva was ready for them. Indeed she had set the scene for this momentous meeting with customary care. 'To her poetical temperament acting came quite naturally . . .' wrote Marie, 'to her the world was a vast stage, she saw all things as a series of scenes out of a drama in which she had the leading role; and today, this receiving of me who was usurping the place of the girl she had chosen, was drama indeed. Innocent though I was, I was the rival; the winning rival, and that wide gesture of welcome was on her part a gesture of heroic abnegation: she felt it as such and she meant to act it magnificently, which she did.'

While making allowance for Marie's own tendency towards the dramatizing of every situation, there is no doubt that Carmen Sylva was fully alive to the potential of this particular scene.

The Queen was lying in a large, low bed which took up the greater part of a small room (she had a passion for tiny, oddly-shaped rooms) which was lit by a skylight. The whole impression was of whiteness. White light, reflecting the snow outside, poured through the skylight onto the white bed with its mounds of soft, white pillows. Carmen Sylva was dressed all in white, her hair was white, her skin was white, her teeth – as she smiled with ineffable sweetness at the timid Marie – were magnificently white. The only colour came from her deep blue eyes, and they, says Marie, were full of pain. Calling the girl '*lieb Kindchen*', she clasped her in her arms and gazed at her in a way that Marie could only describe as 'hungry'. In no time the impressionable girl had fallen completely under the older woman's spell. 'She was a romantic personage,' admitted Missy, 'and I loved romance.

'She was so fascinating, so charming, the things she said were so sweet, so touching; her voice was music, everything was in keeping with the poetical atmosphere emanating from her . . . .'

They spoke of the Queen's painting (she was busy on a vivid flower study at the time), of faraway Romania, of Marie's future life there, of Nando and of how the Queen had tried to bring some happiness into his life. On this last topic, the Queen was careful not to be too specific; Missy knew nothing of the Hélène Vacarescu affair.

Only once was there a pause in Carmen Sylva's effusive flow. This was when Marie's strong-minded mother, embarrassed by the other woman's performance, tried to bring the conversation down to a more matter-of-fact level. But the Queen was having none of it. She had no intention, says Missy, 'of being decoyed from the part she meant to play'. Just for a second the perceptive Princess became aware of an outspoken antagonism between the two older women; 'like flint on steel [this antagonism] seemed to draw sparks'. This slipping of the Queen's mask, or what Marie calls the 'silent passage of arms' lasted hardly any time at all and Carmen

Sylva, resuming her charming, if sad-eyed pose, carried on as if nothing had happened.

'Her voice,' wrote the enraptured Marie, 'was music, but her language often too high-flown for my immature mind; I did not always understand what she was talking about, there was nothing positive I could grasp, it was just music, poetry; her words sank into my brain. A curtain was being lifted, giving me a glimpse into a world unknown to me, where all things had other names, other meanings, an unreal world which only existed while she was talking, and which dissolved like mist when I left her bedside.

'But she was wonderful, herself a poem, a white apparition, born to be adored.'

The visit to Queen Victoria was very different.

Missy, accompanied by her fiancé, went to Windsor with considerably more trepidation that she had to Neu Wied. She knew that her English relations did not really approve of the engagement. Why, when she could have had her cousin Georgie and so have remained in the family, did she choose a foreigner? A foreigner, moreover, who would one day sit on so rickety a throne.

She need not have been so apprehensive. Grandmama Queen proved extremely sympathetic. Marie tells of the occasion when she, Nando and other members of the family stood waiting for the Queen in the Great Corridor at Windsor. A distant tap, tap of a stick and the rustle of stiff silk preceded the Queen's arrival. She rounded the corner, looking astonishingly small. The Queen's shyness, to those who did not know her well, always came as a surprise. On meeting anyone new, she gave a quick nervous laugh and a little shrug of her shoulders; her smile, 'with teeth small like those of a mouse', was sweet and diffident. She now paused in front of Crown Prince Ferdinand (who was, of course, even more shy than she) and, in her beautifully modulated voice, asked, in German, after his parents. Ferdinand's mother was a Portuguese Infanta – a daughter of Queen Maria da Gloria of Portugal, whose husband had been a Coburg prince. Nando was thus blessed, as Queen Victoria would have regarded it, with some Coburg blood. The Queen told the blushing young man that she always kept a picture of his mother in her private rooms.

'*Sie war so wunderschön*,' said the Queen.

Victoria's comments on Marie were equally generous. 'Missy looked very pretty, and seemed very happy about her engagement,' she wrote.

That the unsophisticated, German-bred Nando should make a *faux pas* at Queen Victoria's strange English court was inevitable. As he broke his rolls into his coffee at breakfast on his first morning there, he noticed that he was the only one doing so. The Queen had noticed it as well. Later that day, in the most tactful way possible, she drew his attention to the unacceptability of the custom. 'You must come and breakfast with me in my *private* apartment,' she said sweetly, 'and *then* we will break our rolls into our coffee together *in the good old German fashion.*'

At a later stage during this visit to Windsor, the Queen invited Missy and Ferdinand to her rooms. The Munshi, explained Victoria, was anxious to make the Prince's acquaintance.

The Munshi was the Queen's current favourite. An Indian, whose real name was Abdul Karim, the Munshi had taken the place of the late John Brown in the Queen's affections. Part personal servant, part secretary, part confidant, the twenty-nine-year-old Munshi held a special and much resented position in the royal household. Having heard that one of the Empress of India's granddaughters had given her hand to a foreign prince, the Munshi had expressed a desire to meet the man; no sooner expressed than fulfilled. That same day Missy and Nando were ushered into the Queen's private drawing-room. Victoria was sitting at her writing desk; all about her the air was sweet with the scent of orange flowers. On an easel beside her was Winterhalter's portrait of Ferdinand's mother. With her shy, captivating smile, the Queen drew the young man's attention to the painting.

'*Wunderschön,*' she said.

'*Wunderschön,*' repeated the tongue-tied Nando.

The silence that followed this far from animated exchange was broken by the click of the door handle. A second later the Munshi stood framed in the doorway. He was dressed in gold, with a white turban. Without moving from the doorway, he greeted the young couple by putting one honey-coloured hand to his heart, his lips and his forehead. He neither moved into the room nor spoke.

Nor did anyone else. No one knew what to do. The Queen sat smiling and hunching her shoulders. Nando simply stared at the golden figure in the doorway. Missy stood in an agony of indecision. The Munshi, as an Oriental, 'manifested no sort of emotion at all, simply waiting in Eastern dignity for those things that were to come to pass'. The impasse was finally broken by the sixteen-year-old Marie. Fractionally less shy than her grandmother and Prince Ferdinand, she moved towards the Munshi and shook him by the hand. Nando followed her example and Victoria, relieved that all was over, dismissed the equally relieved young couple.

The Queen had been anxious for the wedding to take place in St George's Chapel, Windsor, as all her English grandchildren had been married there. But as Ferdinand was a Catholic and Marie a Protestant, there would have to be two ceremonies, and neither Church would agree to its ceremony being the second, less important one. The idea of Windsor, therefore, had to be abandoned. Nor could the marriage be celebrated at Coburg. Old Duke Ernest's court, composed, for the most part, of pimps, adventurers and *demi-mondaines*, was far too dissolute. The final choice, therefore, was the castle of Sigmaringen, seat of the bridegroom's family.

So it was in this romantic old castle on the Danube, early in the year 1893, that Marie and Nando were married. To represent the bride's grandmother, Queen Victoria, came the Queen's son, Prince Arthur, Duke of Connaught; from Romania came King Carol I (his Queen, Carmen Sylva, was still in exile from the court); from Russia came the Duchess of Edinburgh's brother, Grand Duke Alexis; from Belgium came King Leopold II's sister-in-law, herself a Hohenzollern-Sigmaringen. And from Berlin, of course, came the bullying, overbearing and neurotic Kaiser Wilhelm II, determined to dazzle the other royal guests by the number and brilliance of his uniforms. On the day of the wedding itself, the little bride, in her white dress and tulle veil, was completely outshone by her cousin the Kaiser in his white uniform, huge gauntlet gloves, gleaming boots and towering, eagle-crowned helmet.

The honeymoon, spent in a snow-bound *Jagdschloss* not far from Sigmaringen, was a dismal failure. The young couple had nothing to say to each other; the husband simply did not know how to amuse or handle his childlike wife. 'He was terribly, almost cruelly in love,' says Marie. 'In my immature way I tried to respond to his passion, but I hungered and thirsted for something more . . . .'

A few days later, bewildered, anxious and desperately homesick, Princess Marie arrived by train in the Romanian capital. Her mother, with her uncertain taste, had chosen her clothes for this important occasion. Over a willow green velvet dress, Missy wore a long mantle of violet velvet shot with gold, its white fox collar so vast that the girl's head all but disappeared into it. On her blonde hair, enthusiastically frizzed in imitation of that model for all late nineteenth-century princesses, Marie's Aunt Alexandra, Princess of Wales, was perched a small golden toque studded with amethysts. Dressed in this inelegant fashion, Queen Victoria's little granddaughter stepped down from the train to a roar of welcome from the Bucharest crowd.

'Looking back upon myself as I was then, is as looking back upon a rather shadowy, very timid and exceedingly silly younger sister in whom I find none of myself today,' wrote Marie in later years. 'I must have looked exactly what I was, an innocent little fool with a head stuffed full of illusions and dreams.'

CHAPTER EIGHT

Alix of Russia

I

Queen Victoria, denied the opportunity of attending the wedding of one of her Edinburgh granddaughters, was able to be present at another. In the spring of 1894, Marie of Romania's sister, Victoria Melita, or Ducky, married Grand Duke Ernest of Hesse and by the Rhine. On this occasion, the Queen was able to preside over the marriage of not only one, but two of her grandchildren, for the bridegroom, Ernest of Hesse, was the son of Queen Victoria's daughter, the late Princess Alice, Grand Duchess of Hesse.

The fact that the bride and the groom were so closely related bothered the Queen not at all. When the Empress Frederick wrote of her reservations about this union between first cousins, Queen Victoria's blithe rejoinder was that 'the same blood only adds to the strength and if you try to avoid it you will marry some unhealthy little Princess who would just cause what you wish to avoid'.

It was to Coburg, the cradle of the dynasty, that the seventy-five-year-old Queen travelled for the wedding. That Coburg should have been chosen was due to the fact that lecherous old Uncle Ernest, Duke of Saxe-Coburg-Gotha, had finally died the year before. Queen Victoria's son, Prince Alfred, Duke of Edinburgh, was now the Duke of Saxe-Coburg-Gotha. 'Aunt Marie,' wrote the Empress Frederick of her haughty Russian sister-in-law, the Duchess of Edinburgh, 'will love being No. 1 and reigning Duchess, I am sure.' Her daughter Ducky's wedding certainly gave the Duchess the opportunity of playing hostess at one of the most brilliant royal occasions of recent years.

The normally sleepy little town of Coburg had been transformed. Its narrow, cobbled streets were gay with flags and bunting; a triumphal arch graced the *platz* in front of the ducal palace; a squadron of Queen Victoria's Prussian regiment of dragoons cantered to and from the station. The town was crammed with royal guests. 'I never saw so many,' commented Queen Victoria's private secretary, Sir Henry Ponsonby, and

82

he had experienced a great many royal gatherings. Amongst them were Queen Victoria, the Prince of Wales, Kaiser Wilhelm II, the Empress Frederick, Prince and Princess Henry of Prussia, the Tsarevich Nicholas, the Grand Duke Vladimir, Prince Ferdinand and Princess Marie of Romania and an assortment of Coburgs, Connaughts, Hesses and Battenbergs.

Yet, throughout the festivities, the limelight was to be stolen by a shy, serious and relatively unimportant princess: the bridegroom's sister, Princess Alix of Hesse.

Queen Victoria had always taken a special interest in the Hesse family. After the death, in 1878, of her second daughter Alice, Grand Duchess of Hesse, the Queen had taken the five motherless Hesse children under her wing. As their father, Grand Duke Louis IV, was an easygoing sort of man, it was Queen Victoria who had the most say in their lives. She paid frequent visits to Darmstadt; the children made prolonged annual stays in Britain. She had seen to it that their nanny, Mrs Orchard, and their governesses, Miss Jackson and Miss Pryde, posted her regular reports on their behaviour and education. Even the patterns for their dresses had to be sent to Grandmama for approval. 'The Grand Ducal family looked upon themselves almost as a branch of the English royal house,' wrote one observer. 'They felt one with it, and took part in all the family festivals.'

To forge a still closer link with the Hesse family, it had at one stage been suggested that the children's father, the widowed Grand Duke, marry his sister-in-law, the Queen's youngest daughter, Princess Beatrice. But the bill which would have made possible a marriage with a deceased wife's sister was thrown out by the House of Lords. ('Incredible!' had been Queen Victoria's comment.) When the Grand Duke died in 1891, at the early age of fifty-four, the Queen hurried across to Darmstadt to teach his twenty-three-year-old son, now Grand Duke Ernest Louis, something of the art of governing.

The youngest of the five Hesse children was Alix, or Alicky. Six at the time of her mother's death, Alix had developed into a shy, introspective young woman, deeply religious, obstinate, sensitive and self-critical. She was an intelligent, almost intellectual girl. She was also something of a beauty, with a pale skin, sea-green eyes and a head of red-gold hair. Queen Victoria had taken a particular interest in her reserved young granddaughter. 'Have you not been as a mother to me since beloved Mama died?' the Princess once asked of her grandmother, and indeed, the Queen had treated the girl as her own. She had succeeded in moulding her into the prototype of a young English lady: modest, conscientious and well-behaved. 'What a charming girl she was!' remembered one princess. 'A simple English girl in appearance, in a skirt and blouse, utterly unaffected, warm-hearted, and fresh as a rosebud touched with dew.'

This was why, when the feather-weight Prince Eddy fell in love with his cousin Alix in 1889, their grandmother had been so delighted. What an excellent foil she would make for the rudderless young man. But it was not to be. Not only was Alix not attracted to Eddy but she was in love with someone else.

The young man in question was the Tsarevich Nicholas, son of the Tsar Alexander III of Russia. One of Alicky's sisters, Ella, had married one of the Tsar's brothers, Grand Duke Serge, and it had been while Alix was in St Petersburg for the wedding that she had first met the Tsarevich Nicholas. They had met again, some years later, when she had spent six weeks with her sister in St Petersburg. She had been seventeen then and he twenty-one, and the two of them had fallen in love. Nicholas, with his 'gentle charm and that kind, caressing look in his eyes' was an extremely handsome young man; Alix found him all but irresistible. And the quiet, diffident Nicholas had been no less attracted to her. 'My dream is some day to marry Alix H.' he wrote in his diary in the year 1892. 'I have loved her a long while and still deeper and stronger since 1889 when she spent six weeks in St Petersburg. For a long time, I resisted my feeling that my dearest dream will come true.'

There were several reasons why the Tsarevich had felt obliged to resist his feelings for Princess Alix. In the first place, his parents did not really approve of her. The great, bear-like Tsar Alexander III and his tiny, elegant wife, the Empress Marie (she was sister to Alexandra, Princess of Wales) were both anti-German. Not only this, but they considered Alix to be too withdrawn, too unsmiling, too unsophisticated for a future Tsaritsa. Nor was she really important enough.

The Tsar, moreover, had a couple of candidates of his own. Both were favourites in the marriage stakes that season; their names had already been bandied about in several European courts. One was the tall, dark, distinguished Princess Hélène, daughter of the Comte de Paris, whose romance with Prince Eddy of Wales had come to nothing. The other was Princess Margaret of Prussia, the Empress Frederick's daughter Mossy, whom Queen Victoria had once suggested for Prince George of Wales. The first would not forsake her Catholicism, nor the second her Protestantism. And even if either of them had been prepared to embrace the Orthodox faith (and this, for a future Tsaritsa, would be essential) the Tsarevich Nicholas was not interested in them. He might be gentle but he could be stubborn. If he could not marry Alix, Nicholas told his parents, he would not marry at all.

Another stumbling block was Alicky herself. Inclined to think deeply about most things, she thought most deeply about her religion. In 1888, at the age of sixteen, she had been confirmed in the Lutheran faith. Like her mother, Princess Alice, Alix took her religion very seriously; it was not something which one could lightly discard for the sake of marriage. If others were ready to barter faith for a crown (and the Coburgs were readier about this than most) she was not. But, on the other hand, a nature which could be so passionate about religion could be just as passionate about love. Alix was in love with Nicky and anxious to marry him. This was her dilemma. In the spring of 1894, when Alix was twenty-one, things reached a climax. For Nicholas had finally talked his formidable father into allowing him to propose to Alix.

The marriage, at Coburg, of Alix's brother, the Grand Duke Ernest of Hesse, provided the ardent Nicky with his opportunity. Half the royalties of Europe were converging on this old German town for the ceremony; to represent Russia came the Tsarevich Nicholas.

He lost no time. On the morning after his arrival, Nicky proposed. For two hours he tried to persuade Alicky to marry him. She refused. Nothing would make her change her religion. Sobbing bitterly throughout the session, she could only keep repeating, 'No, I cannot.'

By now all the royal wedding guests had been caught up in the drama. The marriage of Ernie and Ducky had been completely overshadowed by the question of Nicky and Alicky. One by one Alix's relations tried to talk her into accepting the Tsarevich's proposal. Most pressing was Alix's cousin, Kaiser Wilhelm II; to this megalomaniac, the idea of a German princess as future Tsaritsa of Russia was very attractive indeed. Wilhelm's mother, the Empress Frederick, remembering the furore created by him when his sister, Crown Princess Sophie of Greece, had changed from Protestantism to Orthodoxy, admitted that she 'could not help chuckling to myself that William did not think Alicky so very sinful to accept Nicky, and with him, the necessity of conforming to the Orthodox Church'.

But it was probably the reassurances of Alix's sister Ella, who had married Grand Duke Serge of Russia, that carried most weight. Ella had changed her religion to Orthodoxy; this change, she assured her tortured sister, was not really so drastic a step.

On the day after the wedding, Alix gave in. Her capitulation enraptured Nicky. 'A marvellous, unforgettable day,' he wrote in his diary. 'Today is the day of my engagement to my darling, adorable Alix.' Alicky, too, now that she had finally given her consent, was filled with joy. 'She is quite changed,' reported Nicholas to his mother, the Empress Marie. 'She is gay and amusing, talkative and tender.'

As Queen Victoria was finishing her breakfast that morning, Alix's sister Ella burst into the room. 'Alicky and Nicky are engaged!' she announced. The Queen professed herself 'thunderstruck' by the news. But she could not really have been so surprised: everyone at Coburg had been following Nicky's pursuit of Alicky. Hand-in-hand the young couple came in to make their announcement to the Queen. She gave them her blessing. Although, as she had so often declared, she did not 'care for rank or Titles', she could not help being impressed at the magnificent way in which her matriarchy was being enlarged. It seemed impossible, she said, that 'gentle simple Alicky should be the great Empress of Russia'.

From that moment Queen Victoria set about grooming her grand-daughter for her future role. The girl was brought over to England so that the Queen could supervise her health, her Russian lessons and her religious instruction. As Alix suffered from sciatica she was sent to Harrogate for a cure. While she was taking it, she began to learn Russian. Religious instruction came, first, from the Bishop of Ripon, who was at pains to point out the similarities between Protestantism and Orthodoxy, and then from the Tsar's own confessor, Father Yanishev, whom – one imagines – took no such pains. In May 1894, Nicholas himself arrived with the engagement gifts: a dazzling selection of jewellery, including a magnificent *sautoir* of pearls, created by Fabergé and representing the most expensive item ever ordered by the imperial family from the renowned jeweller.

'Now Alix,' warned her grandmother, 'do not get too proud.'

While the Tsarevich was in England, he saw a great deal of his English relations. 'He has lived this month with us like one of ourselves,' wrote the Queen to her daughter Vicky, 'and I never met a more amiable, simple young man, affectionate, sensible and liberal minded . . . .' To hear Nicky described as liberal-minded is somewhat unexpected: when, at the invitation of his mother's sister, Alexandra, Princess of Wales, Nicky spent a few days at Sandringham, he proved himself to be anything but liberal. In his Uncle Bertie's home, the Tsarevich found himself in a completely strange *milieu*. Having been raised in a thoroughly bigoted atmosphere, Nicky was shocked by the Prince of Wales's house guests. He had never had anything to do with people like this – financiers, Jews and what he called 'horse dealers'. His more enlightened English cousins were greatly amused by his stand-offishness; 'but I tried to keep away as much as possible,' he assured his approving parents, 'and not to talk'.

Already, the worldly and relatively democratic Prince of Wales was becoming conscious of the flaws in his nephew's character: his autocratic outlook, his narrow-mindedness, his hesitation. He was later to describe the Tsarevich as amiable but 'weak as water'.

At this stage of his life Nicky bore a strong physical resemblance to his cousin Georgie, the Duke of York. In fact, on the occasion of Prince George's wedding to Princess May of Teck, the Tsarevich had frequently been mistaken for the bridegroom. Both were short, both wore full, neatly trimmed beards and upswept moustaches and both had clear blue eyes. However, where George's eyes were slightly protruding, Nicky's were narrow and sensuous-looking. Of the two young men, Nicky was the more handsome.

During this visit, Princess May, the Duchess of York, gave birth to her first son, afterwards King Edward VIII. As Nicholas and Alix had been invited to be godparents, they travelled with Queen Victoria to White Lodge in Richmond Park for the christening. The Tsarevich was interested to note that the baby was not, as in the Orthodox ceremony, completely immersed in water, but merely sprinkled with it.

After a six weeks' stay, the Tsarevich was obliged to return to Russia. If anything, their time together in England had deepened the love between Nicholas and Alix; by now they felt passionately for each other. 'I am yours, you are mine, of that be sure,' wrote the reserved but ardent Princess to her fiancé. 'You are locked in my heart, the little key is lost and now you must stay there forever.'

It was arranged that they would marry in the spring of the following year, 1895.

But by the autumn of that same year the position had radically altered. Tsar Alexander III, usually so virile, so powerful, and only forty-nine, became seriously ill. The doctors diagnosed nephritis. They advised the patient to make for the warmer climate of the Crimea; by October 1894 the imperial family was established in the summer palace at Livadia. But it would have needed more than a change of air to save the life of the Tsar. By the middle of the month it was obvious that he was dying. Realizing what was happening, Nicholas sent for Alix. She crossed Europe by train, travelling as an ordinary passenger.

The dying Tsar, conscious of the fact that the future Empress of Russia had arrived in the country, insisted on getting out of bed and putting on full dress uniform for her reception. He seems to have been alone in his appreciation of her future position. During the following ten days – the last of the Tsar's life – his court all but ignored the shy young girl from Darmstadt. All attention was focused on the Tsar and his wife, the beautiful Empress Marie. Even the Tsarevich, because of his unobtrusive nature, tended to be perfunctorily treated by the doctors, the ministers and the officials.

If he, with his lack of self-confidence, did not resent this, his fiancée did. Alicky might have been reserved but she had a certain steeliness of character. Before many days had passed, she gave the first indication of her strength of will.

'Be firm and make the doctors come to you every day and tell you how they find him . . .' she instructed her fiancé, 'so that you are always the first to know. Don't let others be put first and you left out. You are your Father's dear son and must be told all and asked about everything. Show your own mind and don't let others forget who you are. Forgive me, lovy.'

In this manner did the withdrawn and nervous Princess set the pattern for the future relationship between Nicholas and herself.

Tsar Alexander III died on 1 November 1894. His twenty-six-year-old son now became Tsar Nicholas II. For him, it was an appalling prospect. 'Sandro, what am I going to do?' he asked of a brother-in-law, with tears spilling from his blue eyes. 'What is going to happen to me . . . to all of Russia? I am not prepared to be a Tsar. I never wanted to become one. I know nothing of the business of ruling. I have no idea of even how to talk to the Ministers.'

Queen Victoria was hardly less appalled. She was desperately worried about her granddaughter. 'May God help them all!' she wrote. 'What a terrible load of responsibility and anxiety has been laid upon the poor children! I had hoped and trusted they would have many years of comparative quiet and happiness before ascending to this thorny throne.'

The first thing to do was to secure the succession. The Dowager Empress was all for Nicholas and Alix marrying immediately. The young couple were quite willing, but the late Tsar's brothers were not. They felt that the wedding ceremony should take place publicly, after the funeral. No time was lost, however, in the receiving of Alix into the Orthodox faith. On the morning after Tsar Alexander III's death, the ceremony of conversion took place. The new Tsar's first imperial decree was to proclaim the new faith, title and name of the former Princess Alix of Hesse. She became the Grand Duchess Alexandra Fedorovna.

Now began the long, sad journey of the Tsar's remains from the Crimea to St Petersburg. For thirteen hundred miles, from the balmy air of Livadia to the snow-bound capital, the funeral train, draped in black and carrying the mourning family, rolled north across the vast Russian Empire. To the tens of thousands of Russians who watched the Tsar's remains pass by, it seemed ill-omened that their future Empress, all in black and heavily veiled, should come to them behind a coffin.

In St Petersburg were gathered a host of royalties. To represent Queen Victoria came the Prince and Princess of Wales and their son Prince George, the Duke of York. For seven days the body of the Tsar lay exposed in its coffin in the Cathedral of the Fortress of St Peter and St Paul. There were innumerable, elaborate and prolonged services (the Prince of Wales's equerry complained to Queen Victoria of the '*thirty-ninth* repetition of the same mass') which the long-suffering royal mourners were obliged to attend. The most severe ordeal of all was having to kiss the Holy Picture which the dead man held in his hand. 'It gave me a shock when I saw his dear face so close to mine when I stooped down,' wrote Prince George to Princess May, 'he looks so beautiful and peaceful, but of course the face has changed very much, it is a fortnight today.'

At the final ceremony, which lasted for four hours, an even worse ordeal faced the mourners. The Tsar, dead by now for almost three weeks, had to be kissed on the lips. His face, reported a member of the Duke of York's suite, 'looked a dreadful colour and the smell was awful'.

A week after the funeral, Nicholas and Alexandra were married in the chapel of the Winter Palace. To Alicky her marriage seemed no more than a continuation of the masses for the dead but with one difference: 'now I wore a white dress instead of a black'. Her wedding-dress, in fact, was more elaborate than she made it sound. It was one of those opulent Russian court garments, made of rich silver brocade and covered by a trailing mantle of cloth of gold, lined with ermine. On her copper-coloured hair she wore a nuptial crown, all flashing with diamonds. This combined weight was such that, without help, she simply could not move. Yet she is said to have looked radiant. The Princess of Wales was in raptures about her appearance and Prince George assured his grandmother that 'Nicky is a very lucky man to have got such a lovely and charming wife and I must say I never saw two people more in love with each other and happier than they are.'

To celebrate her granddaughter's wedding, the Queen gave a large dinner party at Windsor Castle. She proposed the health of the imperial couple and stood to attention during the playing of the Russian national anthem. 'Oh! How I do wish I had been there!' she exclaimed.

The wedding ceremony over, Nicholas and Alexandra drove through cheering crowds to the Anitchkov Palace which was to be their home. Because the court was in mourning, there was no reception and no honeymoon. The couple went to bed early that evening and came down to breakfast the following morning looking, according to Alicky's Uncle Bertie, the Prince of Wales, 'as if nothing had happened'.

But something had indeed happened. There had been consummated, that night, a deep and passionate love which was to last for the rest of their lives. 'Never did I believe that there could be such utter happiness in this world,' wrote Alix in her husband's diary that morning, 'such a feeling of unity between two mortal beings.'

CHAPTER NINE

Missy and Alicky

I

For Alicky's cousin, Princess Marie of Romania, there was no marital bliss to alleviate the misery of her first few months in her new country. Her husband, Crown Prince Ferdinand, remained a withdrawn and negative figure, utterly incapable of providing her with the companionship she craved. Nor could she find anyone else from whom to draw comfort. Her husband's uncle, the intimidating King Carol, was totally absorbed in his work. His Queen, Carmen Sylva, was still absent from court. Missy was allowed no intimate friends; royalties, commanded *der Onkel*, must remain aloof. In so new, so Eastern and so politically unstable a country as Romania, friends could be positively dangerous; intimacy would encourage intrigue. The Princess thus came into contact with others on official occasions only: at dull tea parties, at enormous banquets, at receptions in which rows of opulently dressed people stood waiting to be spoken to. With her heart sinking and with Nando trailing behind, Missy would move along beside the King, all the while racking her brains for something to say, in her inadequate French, to these hundreds of strange people.

Nor could Marie take any delight in her surroundings. The Bucharest palace was a squat, undistinguished building of no particular style. Her rooms were hideously furnished; 'German *mauvais goût* at its worst,' she called it. Everything was dark, pompous, over-ornate, completely lacking in elegance or comfort. For one of Queen Victoria's grandchildren, accustomed to open windows, flower-filled rooms, crackling fires and cosily screened-off corners, the atmosphere in these ostentatious rooms was stifling. She was not even allowed to go out for a walk. The little she saw of Bucharest she found dull. It seemed to her a city of no special character or mood, simply a poor imitation of other European capitals.

Worst of all, perhaps, was the denial of any independence for the young bride. Neither she, nor her husband, was allowed any say in the running of their lives and certainly none in the running of the country. King Carol controlled everything. They could make no move without his permission. Not even the humblest chambermaid could be employed unless he had approved her first. He was obsessed by the fear of political conspiracies within the palace. Any suggestion the young couple might make for a brightening of their circumscribed lives was invariably vetoed.

To this state of affairs, Prince Ferdinand had long since accustomed himself. Such little spirit as he had ever had had been entirely crushed. He was, says Charles Hardinge, the British chargé d'affaires in Bucharest, 'a very stupid young man with large protruding ears'. Amongst the diplomatic community Ferdinand was nicknamed Prince Doch – Prince Just-so – because of his habit of saying '*Doch! Doch!*' in answer to almost any remark. 'He listened to his uncle in all things,' complains Marie, 'blindly following his lead, submitting to his every demand, never revolting . . . he remained pliant, acquiescent and patient.'

With Marie it was different. She might, in these early days, have been unsure of herself but she was never as compliant as her husband. Not for nothing was she the granddaughter of the Queen of England. Through her veins there ran a great deal of Coburg tenacity, of Coburg obstinacy, of Coburg resilience. Moreover, she was young, high-spirited and blessed with a great lust for life. Like her aunt, the Empress Frederick, she was something of a rebel; she enjoyed nothing so much as a good fight.

Before long, she was beginning to kick against King Carol's restrictive régime. 'His one object,' she says, 'was to fit me into his scheme of things . . . while mine was to remain a free agent, to be my own master, to develop along my own lines a being with thoughts of her own, a life of her own.' There were endless disagreements. Once, after a particularly bitter argument, Marie wrote the King a letter in which she attacked him for his dictatorial and repressive behaviour; she was determined, she told him, not to have the best years of her life ruined by his joylessness. His answer had been concise. 'Only the frivolous consider youth the best years of life,' he wrote.

Side by side with Marie's surge of revolt against the King's behaviour came something else: a gradual awareness of the attractions of her new country. She had always been a lover of the outdoors; the first time that the King permitted her to venture beyond the capital she felt the beginnings of what would one day be her great love for the Romanian countryside. This first outing was simply a drive to a nearby monastery and convent but it fired her always vivid imagination. She had never seen a country as open or as melancholy as this; she had never seen a people as proud and picturesque as the gypsies that thronged the dusty roads. 'All this I saw and my eyes opened wide, the artist within me rejoiced,' she wrote. 'Yes, this was Roumania, the land of the Rising Sun. These endless roads, this dust, these peasants, these villages, these files of carts, these long-poled wells painted against the enormous sky, all those fields, that wide, wide view over the plain . . . Roumania . . .'

In the summer they went to Sinaia, the King's country estate, and again those irrepressible spirits soared heavenwards. The castle itself might have been too grandiose and its furnishings too sombre for her taste but with the setting she had no fault to find. She loved the mountain backdrop, the great trees, the fresh air and, above all, the lush green meadows starred with thousands upon thousands of flowers. 'After the hot dusty ugliness of Bucharest,' she effuses, 'it was release, rapture, enchantment.'

She had further cause for satisfaction that summer: she was pregnant. Earlier in the year, when she had started feeling sick, she could not – in her innocence – imagine why this should be. Her mother had told her nothing. A lady-in-waiting had had to explain it all to her and since then she had been acutely embarrassed by the open fashion in which the ladies of the royal household questioned her about her condition. As a British princess, she had been brought up to believe that it was improper to refer to pregnancy in company. Here, such things were obviously discussed quite naturally.

If the Duchess of Edinburgh had neglected to enlighten her daughter on the early stages of her pregnancy, she was determined to give her all the help and advice she could in the final stages. In October 1893 she arrived in Romania. The advent of this practical, autocratic and strong-willed woman led to immediate trouble. In her, King Carol met his match. So accustomed to having his own way, the King was determined to have his say on every aspect of the coming birth. The Duchess was having none of it. She could not see what such matters as the choice of doctors, wet-nurses, names and suitable rooms had to do with him. Her stand led to innumerable battles, with poor Nando caught in the cross-fire.

In her fight, the Duchess of Edinburgh had one formidable ally: her mother-in-law, Queen Victoria. The Queen put an end to some of the controversies by sending an English accoucheur, Dr Playfair, to Romania. 'We want to be on the safe side,' was her imperious comment; Romania was 'so near the East . . . so uncertain . . .' Faced with her intervention, even the resolute King Carol had to submit.

Princess Marie's baby was born on 15 October 1893. It was a boy. 'Listen to the cannon,' whispered the Duchess of Edinburgh to her daughter as she laid the newborn baby in her arms, 'think of how delighted the people will be when they hear the hundred and one salutes.'

The news was wired to Grandmama Queen immediately. 'When I got up and went to my dressingroom I found telegrams from Marie [of Edinburgh], from Sinaia, announcing that dear Missy had been safely delivered of a son. . . .' she wrote in her Journal.

The royal heir safely delivered, Dr Playfair returned home to report to Queen Victoria. A family council was called at Buckingham Palace to discuss the matter of a reward for the doctor. After all, he had delivered, not only the Queen's great-grandson but a future King of Romania. As the doctor's elder brother was already Lord Playfair, the assembled royalties could not decide on a suitable title for him. Finally Princess Alexandra, who shared the family weakness for punning, came up with a suggestion. 'I know,' she said, 'why not call him Lord Deliver-us?'

A year or two later, when Missy was visiting the Queen at Osborne, Victoria suddenly asked her if she had been given chloroform during childbirth. The young woman was disconcerted by the question. Would her grandmother think less of her for having had chloroform? Was she one of those spartan creatures who disapproved of the easing of pain during childbirth? Did she, like Carmen Sylva, consider that 'bringing a child into the world was a moment of such poetical rapture that nothing must be allowed to allay the ecstasy of the pain'?

Timidly, Marie confessed to having been given just a whiff of chloroform. She had not been put to sleep, she added defensively; it was simply that the edge of her suffering had been blunted.

Her shamefaced admission was greeted with peals of laughter from the Queen. 'Quite right, my dear,' said her grandmother. 'I was only given chloroform with my ninth and last baby; it had, alas, not been discovered before, and I assure you, my child, I deeply deplore the fact that I had to bring eight children into the world without its precious aid!'

Marie's child was baptised, in the Orthodox faith, on 29 October 1893. It was the mother's eighteenth birthday. In honour of his great-uncle, the King, the boy was given the name of Carol. As King Carol II of Romania, he was to lead an extraordinarily eventful life.

2

The Empress Alexandra's happiness, so joyously proclaimed in her husband's diary on the morning after her wedding, was confined to the hours she spent alone with him. For the rest of the time, she was desperately unhappy. Even her home life was disheartening. Because the young couple had married in such haste, no palace had been prepared for them; therefore, for the first few months of their marriage, they shared the Anitchkov Palace with the Empress Marie. That the Dowager Empress was still mistress of the house, there was no question. Nicky and Alicky did not even have a dining-room of their own and were obliged to dine at the Empress Marie's table.

In addition to this, the young Tsar, feeling sorry for his widowed mother, spent a great deal of time with her. It was to her, rather than to his inexperienced wife, that he looked for encouragement, example and advice. These, the Empress Marie was only too ready to give. Although she, like her sister, Alexandra, Princess of Wales, was not an assertive or domineering woman, the Dowager Empress was quite prepared to remain in control of family affairs. To her, Nicky was little more than a schoolboy while Alicky appeared pathetically timid and unsophisticated.

Nor was the Empress Marie's dominant position confined to the private life of the imperial family, As, according to Russian court protocol, a dowager empress took precedence over an empress, Marie quite naturally continued to act as first lady. It was she, and not the Empress Alexandra, who took the place beside the new young Tsar; his wife was obliged to follow after. And, of the two women, Marie was much better equipped for the role of Empress. She had served a fourteen-year-long apprenticeship before becoming Empress (and she had been an Empress for thirteen years) whereas Alexandra had been pitched into the position almost overnight. Where Marie was soignée, vivacious and assured, Alexandra was awkward, immature and painfully shy. Public appearances were a nightmare for Alexandra. She loathed what her British relations referred to as *cercle-ing* – that slow round of guests when one was expected to speak a few words to each of them. She blushed, she stammered, she could never think of anything to say. Every face was a strange one. Her poor French became poorer. Numb with nerves, she could not even smile. As a result, she made no effort to speak; she simply stood there, stiff, silent, and solemn-faced. Before long, she was being described as hard, haughty and uninterested.

Some years later Alicky's cousin, Princess Marie of Romania, who was as extrovert as Alicky was withdrawn, gave her impressions of the new Tsaritsa at this time of her life. 'The young Empress never relaxed this severely aloof attitude which was in part, no doubt, timidity. Nothing ever seemed to give her pleasure, she seldom smiled, and when she did it was grudgingly as though making a concession. This of course damped every impulse towards her. In spite of her beauty, no warmth emanated from her; in her presence enthusiasm wilted. Serious, earnest-minded, with a high sense of duty and a desire towards all that is good and right; she was nevertheless not of "those who win"; she was too distrustful, too much on the defensive, she was no warming flame. Life, like all else, needs to be loved; those who cannot love life are vanquished from the very start.'

Even allowing for hindsight, for antipathy towards a totally different character and for the customary underlay of self-satisfaction, Princess Marie's picture of her cousin Alexandra is perceptive.

If Alicky was overshadowed by her accomplished mother-in-law, Nicky suffered in the same way in the presence of his formidable uncles, his father's brothers. Beside these giant and assertive grand dukes, small, gentle, vacillating Nicky seemed insignificant indeed. 'Nicholas II spent the first ten years of his reign sitting behind a massive desk in the palace and listening with near-awe to the well-rehearsed bellowing of his towering uncles,' wrote one of Nicky's cousins. 'He dreaded to be left alone with them.'

No wonder then, that the young couple found happiness only in each other's company. More and more did they cut themselves off from other people, withdrawing into their own private world. The lavish entertainments and decadent morals of the Russian aristocracy were not to their taste; they preferred a simple, domestic, almost *bourgeois* life. For this, of course, Alicky always had the example of her grandmother, Queen Victoria. Victoria, too, had been deeply in love with her husband and had resented any time spent away from him. Regarding home life as all-important, the Queen would have no truck with what she looked upon as a wicked and worthless aristocracy. During all the years that Alicky had known her grandmother, Queen Victoria had lived a quiet, secluded life, shunning, not only society, but all public duties which she did not consider absolutely essential.

A move, in 1895, to the Alexander Palace at Tsarskoe Selo, some fifteen miles south of St Petersburg, gave the young couple their first real home. They needed it, for the Empress was pregnant. The parents hoped for a male heir but the child that was born in November 1895 was a girl. Their disappointment was short-lived. With both Nicky and Alicky still in their twenties, there was plenty of time for more children. The girl became the Grand Duchess Olga Nicolaievna.

Just over five months later, in May 1896, the Emperor and Empress travelled to Moscow for their coronation. It was an occasion of overwhelming splendour, of almost barbaric magnificence. The scene in the Ouspensky Cathedral was breathtaking. 'Wherever the eye rested,' enthused one observer, 'gold, nothing but gold, with here and there the flash of a precious stone, red, blue or green . . . Alone the figures of the Emperor and Empress stood out in symbolic significance, two shining apparitions imbued for an hour with transient glory. And the thousand tapers reflected in the glittering *iconostas* were like stars in God's Heaven.'

Of these two almost god-like figures standing in all this blaze of light, that of the Tsaritsa was the more impressive. She seemed transported. For the intense, emotional, mystical Alexandra, the coronation was a ceremony of deep personal significance: a symbolic union between herself and Holy Russia. When the Tsar lifted the nine-pound, jewel-encrusted Imperial Crown of Russia from his own head and placed it for a moment on hers, Alexandra felt that she had been transformed. She had become *Matushka* – the Mother of the Russian people.

'How well I can still see Alexandra standing in all her glory, side by side with the Emperor in the golden cathedral in which they were crowned,' wrote her cousin, Marie of Romania. 'The very atmosphere seemed golden, a golden light enveloped the glittering assembly come to render homage to these youngest amongst the sovereigns of Europe, golden also were Alexandra's robes. All eyes were fixed upon her; a beautiful woman is always a source of interest and how much more so when she stands, crowned before all eyes, a figure apart, raised above her sisters, anointed, imbued with a glamour few ever achieve. And Alexandra was beautiful, she was also tall and dignified, actually dwarfing the Emperor standing beside her. The heavy vestments he wore seemed to overwhelm him, the prodigious crown of his ancestors to be too heavy for his head; instinctively one remembered the giant stature of those gone before him; his face was pale, but there was the light of the mystic in his eyes. But his young wife stood steadily upright, her crown did not appear to crush her, and the golden flow of her mantle, cascading from her shoulders, made her appear even taller than she was. Her face was flushed, her lips compressed; even at this supreme hour no joy seemed to uplift her, not even pride; aloof, enigmatic, she was all dignity but she shed no warmth. It was almost a relief to tear one's gaze from her to let it rest upon the Emperor, whose caressing eyes and gentle expression made every man feel his friend.'

The glories of the coronation gave way, almost immediately, to stark tragedy. On the day after the ceremony, the Tsar was due to attend a vast open-air gathering, held in a field outside Moscow. Hundreds of thousands of people were encamped on the field, anxiously waiting for the free coronation mugs, cake and beer that were to be distributed amongst them. The distribution began at about six in the morning. At first slowly and then more and more insistently, the people pressed forward to receive their gifts. A rumour to the effect that there would not be enough for all started a panic. The crowd surged forward. As the field, which was normally used for military manoeuvres, was criss-crossed with shallow trenches, people stumbled into them, fell and were trampled on by those coming behind. A squadron of Cossacks proved helpless against the frantic mob; within minutes hundreds of people had been trampled to death and thousands more injured. Only the arrival of more soldiers prevented further disaster.

The Tsar was appalled. His first thought was to cancel the ball which was being given by the French Ambassador that evening. He could not possibly attend a ball while the ditches were packed with dead and the hospitals crowded with wounded. But his uncles decreed otherwise. They insisted that he attend. France was Russia's ally and the French government had spent vast sums of money on that evening's entertainment. To offend France would be to make matters worse. The irresolute Nicholas gave way and within hours of the disaster, he and Alexandra were dancing in the opening quadrille. They did so with anguish in their hearts. 'The Empress appeared in great distress, her eyes reddened by tears,' reported the British Ambassador to Queen Victoria. But to those who did not witness the grief of the imperial couple – and even to some of those who did – the presence of Nicholas and Alexandra at the ball that evening was taken as a sign of their callousness. Not only were they ill-fated, they were obviously heartless.

A complete change from the dramas of the coronation came later that year, when Nicholas, Alexandra and the ten-month-old Olga visited Queen Victoria at Balmoral. Although there was some attempt at ceremonial (the Prince of Wales, not the Queen, had insisted on this) it was very much of the matter-of-fact, Highland variety. As the carriages splashed through the rain-lashed dark from Ballater station to the castle, bonfires blazed on the surrounding hillsides, church bells pealed and the Crathie and Ballater Volunteers, together with the Balmoral Highlanders, held flaming torches. To the music of the pipes, the imperial couple entered the castle.

Although the Tsar was able to assure his mother that Queen Victoria was 'kinder and more amiable than ever', the visit was not an unqualified success. The Prince of Wales insisted on dragging his nephew out to shoot in all weathers; Nicky was almost permanently drenched and had 'on top of it, no luck at all'. Political talks between the Queen, the Tsar and the British Prime Minister, Lord Salisbury (Victoria would not allow her fifty-four-year-old heir to attend them) proved unsatisfactory. The British found Nicholas far too indecisive. One of Alicky's sisters (Princess Victoria of Battenberg), who was at Balmoral for the visit, once heard Nicky saying that he envied a constitutional monarch, 'on whom the blame for all the mistakes made by his Ministers was not heaped'. The Tsar, she went on to say, 'would have made a remarkably good constitutional sovereign.' And indeed, if Nicky could have changed places with his cousin Georgie, there is little doubt that he, too, would have died peacefully in his bed after a successful reign, instead of in that cellar at Ekaterinburg after a turbulent one.

Alicky enjoyed the visit to her grandmother rather more. Looking handsome in white serge, she was able to display both her plump-cheeked little daughter and her spectacular jewellery ('all her own property', noted the approving Queen). To mark the visit, they were all photographed: Grandmama looking benign, the Prince of Wales jovial, the Tsar handsome and the Tsaritsa – with her baby on her knee – lovely but as cold as ice.

At the end of September, the imperial couple quitted the relative simplicities of royal Balmoral to face a magnificent reception by republican France. 'It has been such a very short stay and I leave dear kind Grandmama with a heavy heart,' wrote Alicky to her old governess. The Queen was no less depressed. The fact that her granddaughter would no longer be able to pay her regular visits upset the old Queen considerably. 'I have a right to her,' she would complain.

Indeed, with each marriage, it seemed as though her Continental granddaughters were moving farther and farther away. Germany, in which many of them had spent their childhood, had been so reassuringly close. Only the Channel had separated the Queen from those familiar, *gemütliche* German courts. But with them going to such far-off, and improbable, countries – Sophie to Greece, Marie to Romania, Alicky to Russia – those frequent visits between the Queen and her granddaughters had become a thing of the past. That her matriarchy was spreading to the farthest rim of Europe was not a source of unmixed satisfaction to the matriarch herself.

CHAPTER TEN

Maud of Norway

I

In 1896 Bertie, the Prince of Wales, turned fifty-five. In the same year his mother, Queen Victoria, turned seventy-seven. She had been Queen for almost sixty years; indeed, the following summer would see her celebration of her Diamond Jubilee. Yet even now she was not prepared to involve her heir in the workings of the monarchy. He was kept at arm's length as much as ever. His position was made still more humiliating by the fact that while his opinion counted for almost nothing, the world listened attentively to whatever his nephews – the bombastic Kaiser Wilhelm II and the irresolute Tsar Nicholas II – might care to say. In vain he protested to the Prime Minister, Lord Salisbury, and to the Colonial Secretary, Joseph Chamberlain, that he was not kept well enough informed; they, with the example of the Queen to guide them, rarely thought of telling him anything and certainly never of consulting him. Once, when in his frustration the Prince exploded at not being informed that his candidate for a diplomatic post had been rejected in favour of another, his secretary assured Lord Salisbury that the Prince of Wales 'really only requires to have things properly explained to him, and he is then always most reasonable'.

But Bertie could still give his mother grounds for doubting his political wisdom. During the last decade of the nineteenth century, Britain was becoming increasingly isolated in Europe. She was engaged in fierce colonial rivalry with France and, largely through Kaiser Wilhelm II's blundering behaviour, was at odds with Germany. Deciding that Britain should make a gesture of friendship towards Germany, the Prince begged his mother to send a telegram of congratulation to Prince Bismarck on his eightieth birthday. She refused to do any such thing. Somewhat tartly, she pointed out that she had never sent Bismarck congratulations before, that he was no friend of hers or, for that matter, England's, and that any such telegram would infuriate the French, who loathed Bismarck. The Prince's impulsive idea was dropped.

More and more, as the years went by, did the Queen come to rely on her youngest daughter, Princess Beatrice (whose husband, Prince Henry of Battenberg, died early in 1896) rather than on the Prince of Wales. The Queen's eyesight was failing but, in her determination to keep control of things, she insisted that Princess Beatrice read out all telegrams, dispatches and memoranda. She would not even allow her private secretary to do this for her. 'Apart from the most hideous mistakes that occur . . .' complained one of the Queen's assistant private secretaries, 'there is the danger of the Queen's letting go almost entirely the control of things which should be kept under the immediate supervision of the Sovereign.'

And the one person who should have been helping her – the Prince of Wales – she refused to take into her confidence. Only once, during his long period of waiting, did the Prince stand in for his mother on a constitutional occasion. This was when, at the age of fifty-seven, he presided over an urgent ten-minute Privy Council meeting to sign a British declaration of neutrality in the Spanish-American War of 1898.

If Bertie was no more actively engaged in affairs of state, socially he was as occupied as ever. Yachting and horse-racing were his chief sporting activities during the 1890s. His enthusiasm for yachting ensured that the season at Cowes was always brilliant, and in 1896, amidst thunderous cheering, his horse *Persimmon* won the Derby. As money always opened the doors to Marlborough House, new fortunes brought him new friends: besides the Rothschilds and the Sassoons, he now befriended men like Ernest Cassel, Louis Bischoffsheim, Horace Farquhar and Thomas Lipton. Nor was his love life in any way less active. When his long-standing mistress, Lady Warwick, forsook his arms to embrace socialism instead, the Prince turned to another beauty, the twenty-nine-year-old Mrs George Keppel. Alice Keppel was to remain with him to the end.

Unaltered, too, were the looks and the way of life of Alexandra, Princess of Wales. Now in her early fifties, she looked, says Lord Carrington, 'too pretty – about thirty-five apparently'. Her figure was still extraordinarily youthful, her face unlined and her clothes superb. Her manner was as abstracted as ever; she was just as charming, as impulsive, as unpunctual and as scatter-brained. She would donate huge sums to charity yet insist that her maids darn her stockings. She would treat her daughters, whom she loved dearly, with a shameful lack of consideration, yet lavish attention on a servant. That sense of the ridiculous, so characteristic of the Danish royal family, she never lost. Once, at a court ball, the tubby Prince of Wales and the enormously fat ex-Queen Isabel of Spain were followed in by the stork-like King Leopold II of the Belgians and the slender Princess of Wales – both of whom walked with a stiff leg; 'a *pretty sight* indeed!' reported Alexander to her son Prince George, 'we all waddled and limped together – you would have laughed . . . .' And when the Princess once caught sight of her husband and his mistress

Alice Keppel – both distinctly plump – sitting solemnly side by side in an open carriage like two pouter pigeons, she was suddenly overcome by a fit of helpless laughter.

Alexandra's relationship with her son, Prince George, now married to Princess May of Teck, was not quite as close as it had once been. Princess May, in her quiet, tactful, determined fashion, had succeeded in weaning her husband away from his adoring mother. The days when the entire Wales family had come bounding uninvited into York Cottage, Sandringham or York House, St James's Palace, were over. The tone of the Princess of Wales's letters to her son were now, if no less affectionate, somewhat less possessive.

Yet Alexandra was fond of her daughter-in-law. Sometimes thoughtless in her treatment of others, the Princess of Wales could appreciate thoughtfulness towards herself. And Princess May was invariably attentive. Princess Alexandra was always grateful for the subtle way in which her daughter-in-law would help when her deafness was proving especially distressing. 'You my sweet May are always so dear and nice to me,' she wrote on one occasion, 'and whenever I am not quite "*au fait*" on account of my *beastly ears* you always by a *word* or even by a move towards me make me understand – for which I am *most grateful* as nobody can know what I often have to go through . . . .'

This frustrating deafness ensured that the Princess spent her time almost entirely amongst people whom she knew well. When she was not at Sandringham, she would be paying extended visits to her relations – to her parents, King Christian IX and Queen Louise, in Denmark; to her sister, the Dowager Empress Marie, in Russia; to her brother, King George I, in Greece. She had a very strong sense of family, and nowhere, of course, was this sense stronger than in her own home. Although this home no longer held her son George or her eldest daughter Louise, now Duchess of Fife, in it were still her two unmarried daughters: Princess Victoria and Princess Maud.

By 1895, Princess Victoria was twenty-seven and Princess Maud twenty-six. 'Like Juno's swans, still coupled and inseparable,' ran one lyrical description, while their aunt, the Empress Frederick referred to them, with rather more accuracy, as 'two such Ducks!' Indeed, the two princesses were seldom seen apart. Pale carbon copies of their mother, but without her marvellous beauty, they looked alike, they dressed alike, they spoke alike. In company they were diffident although, according to Mary Gladstone, not at all 'stuck up') and in private they were playful. The two princesses, says one effusive observer, 'appeared so invariably together that they became a suggestive symbol of that close family life which is typical of our nation at its best, and nowhere finds greater expression than in the home life of the Royal Family'.

This was all very well, but several members of the royal family were not at all satisfied with the unmarried state of the two Wales girls.

'Coupled and inseparable' they should not be allowed to remain forever. In 1894, the Empress Frederick had written to the Queen on the subject. Giving, first, the names of a couple of princelings whom 'darling Bertie's sweet girls' could not possibly marry, she gave the names of two whom they could; 'it *would* be desirable that they should marry some one of a reigning family,' she thought. In any case, she continued, 'it really is *not* wise to leave the fate of these dear girls *dans le vague*'.

To this the dear girls' grandmother replied that the Prince of Wales had assured her that he was 'powerless' to do anything about it. His wife, finding them 'such good companions', did nothing towards encouraging them to get married; nor, he added, had the girls themselves shown any inclination to do so. 'I think he is mistaken as regards Maud,' commented the perceptive Queen.

It was indeed the Princess of Wales who was standing in the way of her daughters getting married. With her fierce hatred of Germany, Alix was determined that no daughter of hers should marry a German. As most Protestant princes were German, this firmly held prejudice considerably narrowed the field. In addition, she had become far too dependent on her daughters to bear the thought of them leaving her. She loved them but this simply made her all the more possessive, demanding and inconsiderate. Princess Victoria, wrote one of her cousins, 'was just a glorified maid to her mother. Many a time a talk or a game would be broken off by a message from my Aunt Alix, and Toria would run like lightning, often to discover that her mother could not remember why she had sent for her, and it puzzled me because Aunt Alix was so good.'

'That dear Victoria is an angel of a girl,' claimed the Empress Frederick, 'so good and unselfish, so helpful and useful and true. Of all the nieces I have, I love her the best. And Maudie is a perfect duck and so bewitching. I long to squeeze her when I see her.' The Empress preferred them to their cousins – the Hesse girls, Ella and Alicky. She considered them more graceful and more natural, and so much more agreeable. 'How I wish they would marry,' she sighed. 'It does seem a shame for such nice charming girls not to have homes of their own. They would make such perfect wives and mothers.'

In truth, Princess Victoria was not entirely without experience in affairs of the heart. She is said to have wanted to marry a member of the Baring family, and to have fallen in love, in later life, with one of her father's equerries. There was also a story that Lord Rosebery, at one time Prime Minister, had thought of asking for her hand. Not by any stretch of the imagination, however, could any of these men have been thought suitable for the daughter of the future King of England. So Victoria remained unmarried. She stayed with her mother and gradually developed into a hypochondriacal, embittered and sharp-tongued old maid.

It was the younger daughter, the slightly prettier, livelier and sweeter-natured Princess Maud, who married.

Princess Maud of Wales was known, in the chaffing way of her family, as Harry. The nickname derived from the fact that of the three Wales girls – all of whom were happiest when out of doors or playing some knock-about family game – she was the most boyish. 'As an all-round sportswoman few of her own sex can touch her,' writes a member of her parents' household. 'With horses, dogs and birds she is wonderful, and she is the one amongst her sisters who is really fond of yachting.' She could also lay claim to the distinction of being the only royal lady to have thus far 'ridden a bicycle through the public streets'.

None of this is to imply that Princess Maud was in any way mannish. Indeed, for all her love of outdoor sports, she was a rather gentle creature. She might not have been especially cultured or intellectual, but she had a kind and cheerful disposition. Of the three Wales girls, she was the most attractive. 'She did look so pretty and fresh,' wrote the Empress Frederick of Princess Maud in 1895, 'like a little rose, with her bright eyes and dear intelligent expression.'

At that time, this bright and natural creature was suffering from the most bitter-sweet of ailments – unrequited love.

The object of Princess Maud's affections was one of her sister-in-law Princess May's brothers – Prince Frank of Teck. Twenty-five years of age in 1895, Prince Frank was as unlike his sister, Princess May, as it was possible to be. Where she was modest, discreet and conscientious, he was flamboyant, feckless and brimful of life. Tall and handsome, with dark hair and bright blue eyes, Frank had inherited much of the vitality, charm and extravagance of his mother, the Duchess of Teck. He gambled, he lived on credit, he was alarmingly outspoken. Time and again, he had to be rescued from some scrape.

That the tomboyish Princess Maud should fall in love with so exotic a *beau* was indeed unfortunate. Prince Frank might be good-natured, affectionate and well-intentioned but he could certainly not return poor Maud's love. In fact, he hardly gave her a thought. He certainly never bothered to answer her letters. His affections, it seems, were otherwise engaged. Prince Frank had embarked on a liaison with a married woman much older than himself and, despite his fond mother's wishes, was prepared to waste no time on the likes of the immature Princess Maud.

To teach the errant Frank a lesson, his parents applied the customary Victorian remedy: in 1895 he was packed off, in disgrace, to India. And there, until after Princess Maud was married, he remained.

If the Princess of Wales was likely to favour one suitor above another for the hand of her daughter, then he would have to be a member of her own – the Danish – royal family. At one stage there had been some talk of Maud, or even Victoria, marrying their cousin, Prince Christian (afterwards King Christian X) of Denmark. 'Alix,' wrote Queen Victoria, 'to whom I said I had hoped for something for the girls, said she would be very glad and would like it, but she feared the girls thought him too young for them.'

The idea petered out but in the following year, 1895, Prince Christian's younger brother, Prince Charles of Denmark, began paying court to Princess Maud.

Charles and Maud had known each other all their lives. On the Princess of Wales's frequent visits to her father's court, her children and the children of her brother, the Danish Crown Prince, had always played their boisterous games together. They had bicycled, they had ridden, they had indulged in those practical jokes which were such a feature in the life of the Danish royal family. Three years younger than Maud, Charles had entered the Danish Navy at the age of fourteen. Since then, the Navy had been his career. In 1893 he had passed out as a second lieutenant and not until three years later, after his engagement to Princess Maud, did he become a first lieutenant. On being asked why he had remained a second lieutenant for so long, his unblinking reply was, 'lack of strings and influence'. Indeed his father, in true Danish democratic fashion, had refused to allow him to be favoured in any way.

In 1895, Prince Charles was twenty-two years of age: a tall, fair, slender, good-natured and level-headed young man. The Duchess of Teck considered him very goodlooking. '[He] seems *charming*!' she wrote, 'but looks *fully three years* younger than Maud, has *no money* . . . .'

Nevertheless, during one of those Danish family gatherings at Fredens-borg, Prince Charles proposed and Princess Maud accepted. He might not have set her pulses pounding to the extent that Prince Frank of Teck had once done, but he would certainly make her a better husband. The couple were officially engaged in October 1895. 'The announcement . . . caused much excitement here yesterday,' wrote one of Queen Victoria's ladies from Balmoral, 'and has been the cause of endless telegraphing. The Queen is delighted and healths were drunk at dinner.'

As Prince Charles was due to set off on a five-month-long cruise to the West Indies, the marriage date was set for July the following year.

The wedding, on 22 July 1896, was a relatively small one. It was held in the chapel at Buckingham Palace and public display was confined to the drives between Marlborough House, Buckingham Palace and St Pancras station. It was essentially a family gathering. From Denmark came the bridegroom's parents, the Crown Prince and Princess of Denmark, and their other children (the old King, Christian IX, could not attend); from Athens came the Crown Prince Constantine and the Crown Princess

Sophie of Greece (he was cousin to the bridegroom and she cousin to the bride); and from Windsor, of course, came Queen Victoria.

'Never,' wrote the London *Times* effusively on the day of the wedding, 'has a more charming and graceful bride issued from an English home, and never has a Royal Princess looked happier upon her wedding day than Princess Maud of Wales.' This might have been carrying deference a little too far but it was true that Princess Maud, thanks to her mother's unerring taste, was considerably better dressed than most royal brides. Her dress of ivory satin was unusually simple and she wore no jewels. On her hair was a crown of orange blossom and as she passed, 'the perfume of orange blossom escaped from her dress and filled the air round her'. Followed by her bridesmaids, in white trimmed with red geraniums (the national colours of Denmark), the bride moved up the aisle on the arm of her father, the Prince of Wales. At the altar, in the uniform of the Danish navy, stood the tall, straight and slender Prince Charles.

The ceremony concluded, the newly married couple made their obeisances to the seated figure of Grandmama Queen.

The marriage service was followed by a wedding breakfast. At the end of it, with the Queen about to take her leave, an Indian servant wheeled in her chair. But Her Majesty waved it away. 'Behind the door,' she said imperiously and, leaning on her stick, went stumping out of the room. Bride and bridegroom left from St Pancras station at a quarter to six that evening. They were bound for Appleton House, near Sandringham, which the Prince of Wales had given his daughter for use as an English home. They were to spend a short honeymoon there before leaving for Denmark.

The honeymoon lasted, in fact, for five months.

Before Princess Maud's marriage, the Duchess of Teck, with some perspicacity, had written, 'My feeling is, Maud does not care for him enough to leave England for his sake and live in Denmark, and I dread her finding this out when too late.' The Duchess of Teck was proved right. Fond as Maud might have been of her husband, she was more fond, by far, of her country. For years she had been kept tucked under the wing of her possessive mother; now she could not face the thought of leaving home and family. Already almost twenty-seven at the time of her marriage, Maud had become too accustomed, not only to the company of her mother, but to the life of an English princess. How could she live without her dogs, her horses and all the other outdoor delights of Sandringham; without Cowes week; without her visits – under the improbable alias of 'Miss Mills' – to her old governess in the West of England? How could she, who had no taste or talent for public life, who was so shy in strange company, face the demands of life in a different country?

During the first few months of her marriage, Maud decided that she could not.

Once established in Appleton House, nothing could induce her to leave it. By mid-August – three weeks after the wedding – the Danish royal family were all assembled at Bernsdorff Castle to welcome the newly married couple. There was no sign of them. By the end of August, the Princess of Wales and her daughter Victoria joined the family in Denmark. Still Maud refused to move from Appleton. By early September, King George of Greece was at Bernsdorff; by mid-September the Tsar and Tsaritsa of Russia were there. And still Maud would not budge. There could be little doubt that the Prince of Wales, instead of losing a daughter, had indeed gained a son.

In October the Princess of Wales came home. King George I returned to Greece. The Tsar arrived at Balmoral. The Danish royal family trooped back to Copenhagen. But Maud stayed put. She could not think of leaving England. The couple rode, they drove, they cycled, they sat for portraits, they received congratulatory addresses, they inspected the Technical and Cottage Schools on the Sandringham estate, they went up to London to the theatre, they listened to the band in Green Park, they visited Queen Victoria at Windsor, at Osborne and at Balmoral. They were still in England when that melancholy anniversary of the deaths of the Prince Consort and Princess Alice – 14 December – came round, and were able to join the rest of the family at the service in the Mausoleum at Frogmore. Not until Prince Charles's six months' leave from the navy was almost up could Princess Maud be coaxed into making a move. She would, no doubt, have dearly loved to have spent Christmas with her parents at Sandringham, but on 21 December she steeled herself to set off.

In Copenhagen they were received with relieved enthusiasm. As their train steamed into the gaily decorated station, a military band struck up the Danish National Anthem. On the platform were gathered the royal family, the ministers, the *corps diplomatique* and a galaxy of dignitaries. They drove through cheering crowds to their new home beside the Amalienborg Palace. That night they attended a state banquet. Princess Maud, sporting the Danish colours in her white dress trimmed with red roses, sat beside her husband's grandfather, old King Christian IX. In proposing her health, the King expressed the hope that 'as my dear daughter Alexandra has won all British hearts, so may my granddaughter win the hearts of the whole Danish nation'.

But Maud's own heart was in England.

CHAPTER ELEVEN

Vicky, Willie and Sophie

By the mid-1890s, relations between the widowed Empress Frederick and her son, Kaiser Wilhelm II, were hardly better than they had ever been. Although she played no part in public life and lived, for most of the year, in her new home, Friedrichshof, near Homberg, Vicky could not reconcile herself to her son's conduct. She resented both her own eclipse and his increasing megalomania. She could not forget his outrageous behaviour at the time of her husband's death; nor the way he had subsequently humiliated her by publicly associating himself with the various accusations levelled against her.

'I *cannot* forgive or forget all his *deeds* . . .' she admitted to her daughter Sophie, Crown Princess of Greece. '*I* am the sufferer, not he . . . and *he* is the offender, let him ask and wish for forgiveness and he shall have it, but *not* in the way he goes on now!'

She was expecting the impossible. Wilhelm was too much his mother's son to admit that he was ever wrong. 'My mother and I,' he wrote with some sagacity, 'have the same characters. I have inherited hers. That good stubborn English blood which will not give way is in both our veins. The consequence is that, if we do not happen to agree, the situation becomes difficult.'

In her wisdom, Queen Victoria realized that the fault did not lie entirely with her grandson. The Queen always did what she could to sweeten relations between mother and son. When Vicky's sister, Princess Helena, once visited Germany, she decided that the Kaiser's rudeness to his mother was more a matter of thoughtlessness than intention. He meant well, it was simply that his manner was unfortunate. Nor did the Empress make the slightest effort to meet him half-way. Princess Helena, who came to a quick understanding of the young man's character, advised her sister to flatter him by consulting him about little things; this way she would win his confidence and gain considerable influence over him.

But things had gone too far for such remedies. Besides, with her transparently honest nature, Queen Victoria's eldest daughter was incapable of such guile. As the years passed she did, however, learn to keep a check on herself in his company; to live, as she put it, 'with a padlock on my mouth'.

Her self-control was helped by the fact that she did not very often see her son. His occasional visits to Friedrichshof, always marked by great state and bustle, were merely formal calls. Outwardly, their behaviour towards each other became more decorous. But if experience had taught the Empress to hold her tongue in his presence, in private she aired her views on his arrogance with all her old spirit. She was still capable of flinging a newspaper to the floor and of stamping about in exasperation. His provocative public statements, his sudden whims, his appalling lack of finesse, distressed her considerably. If only, she declared, he would make no more of those terrible speeches and would not write those braggartly messages in books and on photographs of himself. It was enough to 'make one's hair stand on end'.

If Queen Victoria was prepared to make allowances for her grandson in some cases, she was certainly not prepared to do so in all. Indeed, there were times when she found his behaviour no less insufferable than did his mother. Particularly irritating was that sense of his own importance. With his notoriously thin skin, Wilhelm could never quite shake himself free of the suspicion that some of his relations, and the British royal family in particular, did not take his status quite seriously enough. Not long after his accession, the Kaiser complained, through official channels, to Queen Victoria, that the Prince of Wales tended to treat him as a nephew rather than as an Emperor.

This impertinence earned him one of his grandmother's most withering replies.

'This is really too *vulgar* and too absurd,' wrote the Queen to Lord Salisbury, 'as well as untrue, almost *to be believed.*

'We have always been very intimate with our grandson and nephew, and to pretend that he is to be treated *in private* as well as in public as "his Imperial Majesty" is *perfect madness*! He has been treated just as we should have treated his beloved father and even grandfather, and as the Queen *herself* was always treated by her dear uncle King Leopold. *If* he has *such* notions, he [had] better *never* come *here*.

'The Queen will not swallow this affront.'

More and more, during the last decade of the nineteenth century, did the Empress Frederick devote herself to her home and her three youngest daughters. Friedrichshof, by now, was a house of considerable charm and character. The rooms, furnished with Vicky's superb taste, were always filled with flowers from her garden; its atmosphere was cultured, relaxed, quite free of the fustiness of so many royal German homes. To the people of nearby Kronberg, the Empress was a kindly châtelaine and, to her guests, an informed, enlightened and intelligent hostess.

When Vicky was not in residence, she would be travelling. For so active a personality, movement was essential. She would visit her daughters Moretta and Mossy, both of whom were now married and living in Germany; she would travel to Athens to stay with her daughter, Crown Princess Sophie. 'In sheer beauty *nothing* comes up to the Greek landscape for colour, purity of outline, transparent atmosphere, and everywhere the lovely sea . . .' she enthused. She was devoted to Italy. Each summer found her scrambling about its ruins, wandering through its *palazzi*, studying its sculpture or sitting in its hot, white sunlight, painting in the bright colours she loved so well.

But perhaps, most of all, she enjoyed her visits to England. London's shops and museums were a source of endless delight. In the rooms at Windsor, Osborne and Balmoral, with their brightly blazing fires and their bowls of freshly picked flowers, she felt eminently at home. 'Really dear old England is a *most* fascinating place and it is indeed hard to leave it,' she admitted to one of her daughters. 'There is so much to be seen, and so many kind friends to see, that the time seems to pass like a dream and one cannot do half what one intended . . . Dear England! How I love it! I cannot help it!'

With her mother, Queen Victoria, she always remained on affectionate terms. Throughout Vicky's turbulent life, the Queen had provided understanding, sympathy and support. 'I have had my very last drive with beloved Grandmama before she leaves for Florence,' she once wrote to Princess Sophie from Windsor. 'It was a glorious evening without a cloud or a breath of wind, and the dear old Park looked so fine. But I felt sad. At her age partings seem doubly melancholy, as you can imagine, and the thought of living far away from her in her old age is very painful. However, I must be thankful to have seen her.'

It was because of this deep love for her mother and her country that the Empress Frederick watched, with increasing anxiety, the maladroit behaviour of her son, Kaiser Wilhelm II, towards England.

The Kaiser's attitude towards his grandmother's country had always been ambivalent: rather in the nature of a love-hate relationship. He admired England, he envied her, he was attracted to her, he feared her. He criticized her with characteristic vigour yet his criticisms had never quite rung true. They had been shafts aimed at his Anglophile parents rather than at England herself. Now that his father, Kaiser Frederick III, was dead and his mother of no account, the Kaiser could allow his latent respect for Britain to emerge. In fact, of all the countries of Europe there was none with which he would rather be associated. What was more natural than that these two great Teutonic nations should stand together?

Two years after his accession to the throne, Wilhelm had forced his mentor, Prince Bismarck, to hand in his resignation. With the Chancellor out of the way, the Kaiser felt free to shape his own foreign policy. He thus began thinking in terms of a closer friendship with Britain.

The fact that the Queen of England was his grandmother gave Wilhelm opportunities for friendly overtures denied to other sovereigns. Indeed, once he had paid his first state visit to Britain there seemed to be no keeping him away. Every year saw him yachting at Cowes and every visit was followed by a gushing letter of thanks to his grandmother in which he would hint at a possible alliance between their two countries. Should 'the Will of Providence lay the heavy burden on us of fighting for our homes and our destinies,' ran one typically flamboyant out-pouring, 'then may the British fleet be seen forging ahead, side by side with the German, and the "Redcoat" marching to victory with the Pomeranian Grenadier!'

Enamoured of uniforms, Wilhelm was always angling for yet another one. The Queen, who had already made him an Admiral of the Fleet, considered this 'tireless fishing for uniforms' regrettable. When, on giving way to his importunings, she made him an Honorary Colonel of the 1st Royal Dragoons, his delight was almost overwhelming. 'I am moved, deeply moved,' he enthused, 'at the idea that I now too can wear beside the Naval uniform the traditional British "Redcoat".'

Not quite everyone, though, shared Kaiser Wilhelm II's enthusiasm for closer relations between the two countries. Britain was determined to remain aloof from any Continental entanglements and a great many Germans, conscious of their country's growing might, saw no reason for allying themselves to anyone. Then, on a more personal level, the Kaiser's English relations were not nearly so enamoured of him as he seemed to be of them. Queen Victoria, finding his ebullience somewhat exhausting, once suggested that the British Ambassador in Berlin drop a hint to the effect that her grandson need not come to England *every* year.

And there was little love lost between the Kaiser and his Uncle Bertie – Britain's future King. It was largely his nephew's braggartly behaviour at Cowes that forced the Prince of Wales to abandon yachting in 1897. In fact, the Kaiser's arrogance tended to make the urbane Prince of Wales increasingly Francophile.

There was as yet no suggestion, however, that King Edward VII's England might one day look to France rather than Germany for friend-ship; during the 1890s such a possibility seemed remote indeed.

Yet Wilhelm, having decided to win Britain's friendship, was in-capable of carrying through his scheme. He was too tactless, too boastful and too bellicose to win British confidence. With almost every step he took he seemed to bring the German Reich into conflict with British interests. The two countries clashed over colonial policy in Africa and the Far East; German promotion of a Berlin-to-Baghdad railway line roused British antagonism; the Kaiser's plans to build a powerful navy alarmed the Mistress of the Seas. In 1896, when Dr Jameson led his un-successful raid into the Transvaal Republic, the Kaiser saw fit to send a telegram to President Kruger, congratulating him on having repelled the band of British invaders. Willie's rashness earned him a stinging rebuke from his grandmother (it would have been more stinging still had she known that he had suggested sending German troops to the Transvaal) and raised a storm of indignation throughout England.

Although the Kaiser's fears that the incident had put an end to his little visits to Cowes were not justified, it did put an end to any hope of an alliance. Some politicians, in Britain and Germany, might still favour co-operation, but from now on public opinion in both countries was against it.

One of those most ardently in favour of an alliance was Wilhelm's mother, the Empress Frederick. Such an alliance was to have been the cornerstone of her husband's foreign policy; it had always been the Prince Consort's dearest wish. In mounting alarm Vicky watched the friendship which was developing between Russia and France. On the face of it, the association between reactionary Russia and republican France seemed an unlikely one, but the two countries had one powerful factor in common: a fear of Wilhelm II's Germany. The French and Russian fleets exchanged visits (Europe was diverted by the spectacle of the Tsar of All the Russias standing bare-headed while a French naval band blared out the revo-lutionary strains of the *Marseillaise*) and a secret military convention was agreed upon between the two nations.

When the French fleet, having just paid its visit to Russia, was invited to Portsmouth and its officers presented to Queen Victoria, the Empress immediately grasped the significance of the occasion. The fact that her mother had had to stand up while the 'horrid *Marseillaise*' had been played, appalled Vicky; not, one suspects, because of its violently revolutionary sentiments, but because of the fact that the incident pointed to the coming *entente* between Britain and France.

In the year 1898, forsaking for once her negative role, the Empress made one more effort to bring about the cherished alliance. In secret, she approached both her son and the British Ambassador, claiming that she had information to the effect that the time for a formal alliance was never more opportune than at present.

In this, as far as Britain was concerned, she was correct. Certain British statesmen were indeed ready for an approach to Germany. But by now Germany had lost interest. The Reich was becoming more self-sufficient by the day and its politicians resented what they considered to be Britain's patronizing attitude.

When the Empress Frederick spoke to the new Secretary of State, Bernhard von Bülow, of her fears that the building of a great German navy would put paid to all hopes of an *entente* with Britain, he treated the warning as another instance of her Anglomania. She was speaking, as usual, as Queen Victoria's daughter. 'She believed' he wrote in his memoirs, 'the best Germany could do was to make herself useful to England and England's high aims and at the same time ennoble herself by keeping in the course of English policy, like a tiny boat in the wake of a great frigate . . . .'

By the summer of 1899 the Empress had to admit the final fading of her dream. The gulf between the two nations was widening too fast. 'Such a thing as an alliance is too good to be true,' she sighed. Her beloved father's plans, mulled over at such length and with such optimism half a century before, had come to nothing.

2

Of absorbing interest to the Empress Frederick during the last decade of the century were the affairs of her daughter Sophie, Crown Princess of Greece. There was no aspect of Sophie's life in which her mother did not feel deeply involved. On her visits to Greece, Vicky had been enchanted by the country. Its landscape, its politics, its finances, its possibilities, all interested the Empress profoundly; her flow of advice to Sophie and her husband Crown Prince Constantine reveals the extraordinary extent of her knowledge. On no subject did the Empress Frederick not have a strong, original and practical opinion. She was forever sending the young couple suggestions for the improvement, not only of their own surroundings, but of the country's always precarious financial state. She could advise on babies, drains, furniture, shrubs, pottery, hospitals, water supplies, orange trees, marble quarries, roads, railways and military instructors. That Greece did not blossom into instant prosperity was through no lack of directives on the part of the Empress Frederick.

How many of her mother's suggestions Crown Princess Sophie acted upon one cannot say. Her subsequent work for hospitals and afforestation were certainly inspired by the Empress but Sophie would have had to have been an exceptionally energetic person to have carried through all her mother's various schemes.

This she was not. Her health was delicate, she was easily depressed and her interests centred on her home and family rather than on national issues. For someone of Sophie's temperament, there were so many things to be despondent about. During the first years of her marriage, she had no real home of her own. A palace was being built for the Crown Prince but the country's perennially bankrupt state meant endless delays. When the couple finally moved in, in the autumn of 1898, work on the palace was still not finished and the household was obliged to put up with numberless inconveniences.

The furniture, too, was a disappointment. Princess Sophie had ordered it, *en bloc*, from an agent of that indispensable supplier of furniture to Queen Victoria's Continental grandchildren, Maple of London. At the time of ordering, the Empress Frederick had warned her daughter of the dangers of such bulk buying. 'If the furniture is too much alike everywhere, the house easily has the appearance of a hotel or steamer. The charm of a house is, I think, to see that objects of furniture have been carefully and well selected, and not bought wholesale to save thought and trouble.'

But wholesale the furniture was bought and, once installed in the rooms of the new palace, it looked – as the Empress had said it would – undistinguished.

At the royal family's country estate at Tatoi, things were hardly better. The Crown Prince and Princess and their children were housed in a little cottage near the main building. As the cottage boasted neither bathrooms nor lavatories, Sophie was anxious to build another, more convenient one. She asked for plans of what she called her grandmother's 'adorable' cottage on the Osborne estate and of her cousin Georgie's cramped little house at Sandringham. She wanted to 'compare which is best'. Here, too, the building was subject to frustrating delays.

In addition to what the Empress called *les petites misères de la vie* ('which poison one's existence and sap one's strength for overcoming the serious trials one has to bear') Sophie battled against other problems. She was often homesick, bored and dispirited; her work for such things as hospitals and almshouses was frequently disheartening; she complained that she had no friends, that no one wanted to make the inconvenient journey to Athens to visit her. At times, she felt utterly overwhelmed by her difficulties.

Princess Sophie's occasional bouts of depression were as nothing, however, when set against the alarms of the year 1897: the year in which Greece went to war against Turkey.

The island of Crete, lying south of the Greek mainland and having a large Greek population, was ruled by Turkey. Greece was anxious to free the islanders from Turkish domination; on this subject public opinion in Athens was becoming increasingly voluble. Princess Sophie, caught up in the clamour, decided to appeal to Queen Victoria. Here, surely, was the opportunity for putting to good use the fact that she was the Queen of England's granddaughter. Sophie begged her mother, who was visiting Osborne at the time, to put the Greek case to Queen Victoria. The Empress, always quick to take up what she considered a just cause, suggested that Sophie approach her grandmother directly as well; 'do tell her how distressing the condition of the Greeks and Christians on the island is . . .' she instructed.

The Queen did not need much convincing, but there was very little that she could do. That Sophie was her granddaughter affected the Greek position not at all. Grandmama 'hopes and trusts affairs in Crete will be satisfactorily settled,' the Empress assured Sophie, 'but she does not say how.'

Victoria's hopes and trusts were ill-founded. In February 1897 the Cretans, encouraged by the Greeks, rose up against their Turkish masters. At once Greece sent troops, commanded by Tino's brother George, to help the insurgents. The Great Powers of Europe, anxious to preserve peace, dispatched naval patrols to Cretan waters and landed an international force on the island. Prince George of Greece was ordered to withdraw. When he failed to comply, he was issued with an ultimatum.

Throughout this turbulence, reactions amongst the members of Queen Victoria's family were hardly less stormy. Crown Princess Sophie was furious that British ships should be amongst those involved in restraining the insurgents. As for Vicky, her feelings were at fever pitch. 'Though there is no better Englishwoman than I am, and I am a devoted German too,' she exclaimed, 'yet on this occasion I feel more Greek than either! Yet, if there is *one* nation in the world that understands national liberty, that feels for others, it is just England . . . That it should be *England* that should have to "warn off" dear Georgie is too distressing'.

Queen Victoria's son and daughter-in-law, the Prince and Princess of Wales (whose brother was King George of Greece) were equally distraught. Still further complications arose from the fact that Sophie's brother, Kaiser Wilhelm II, favoured Turkey above Greece. Sophie's appeal for his help in 'this mass-murder of Christians and Mohammedans' fell on deaf ears. The Kaiser was courting the Sultan of Turkey at that stage; indeed, the Turkish army was in the process of being reorganized by German instructors. In his bombastic and self-righteous fashion, the Kaiser was making violent denunciations of Greek behaviour. His pronouncements enraged his sister Sophie still more.

Queen Victoria alone kept her head. To her, this battling between her children and grandchildren was a reminder of those terrible days when Bismarck's wars of unification had split her family into two just such warring sections: Vicky and Fritz on the one side and Bertie and Alix on the other. Again, she did what she could to keep the peace. 'Grandmama writes me to tell you how awfully sorry she is for you and Tino and Papa and Mama,' wrote the Empress to Sophie. 'She is so anxious and troubled, and as far as she *may*, and as she *dare*, she tries at ways to make peace and to soften asperities and cool down angry spirits.'

While protesting, through her ambassador, at Kaiser Wilhelm's public castigation of Greece, the Queen was anxious for Greece to comply with the ultimatum of the Great Powers. If Greece did not, she would find herself involved in a full-scale war with Turkey. This she could not afford.

But this is what happened. Greece, stubbornly refusing to evacuate Crete, encouraged her countrymen in Turkish-ruled Macedonia – on the Greco-Turkish border – to revolt. They did, and on 17 April 1897, Turkey declared war on Greece.

It was a short, inglorious campaign. The Greek army simply melted away in the face of the German-trained and officered Turks. Within three weeks all Greece lay open to the Turkish army. Both Queen Victoria and Kaiser Wilhelm II sent battleships to Pireaus in case the royal family needed to be evacuated.

Soundly beaten, Greece could do nothing other than accept the armistice terms arranged by the Great Powers. In these, the Kaiser had the chief say. In a telegram which Queen Victoria described as 'very grandilo-quent', Wilhelm informed his grandmother that he was taking steps to initiate the armistice. Greece was obliged to withdraw her troops from Crete immediately and, by the terms of the peace which was signed later, had to pay Turkey four million pounds.

While still suffering from the humiliation of the Greek defeat, Crown Princess Sophie was faced with an even more dismaying experience: the sudden, and to her inexplicable, loss of popularity of the Greek royal family. The very people who had urged the King to go to war (the 'café politicians' as the Empress Frederick scathingly called them) now turned against him. The feeling was so violent that Tino was obliged to relinquish his command of the army. Worse still, public antagonism fixed itself on Sophie. The victorious Turkish army had been trained by Germans; therefore, as the Kaiser's sister, Sophie was partly to blame for the Greek defeat. To those who knew nothing of her appeals to Wilhelm, of the always unsympathetic relationship between brother and sister, of her fury at his public statements on the war, Sophie was little less than a traitor.

The accusations upset her considerably. Here again, she was given sound advice by her mother. The Empress knew all about unpopularity. It was, she told her daughter, a most fickle thing; it was easy 'to get a cry up against anyone'. Sophie was to take no notice of 'this rubbish'. One must remember, she told her daughter, 'that as gold tried in the fire comes out brighter and purer still, so those who are noble show their grandest qualities in misfortune'.

Crown Princess Sophie managed to survive this particular bout of public hostility; she was not to be so fortunate a second time.

With the war over, Crown Prince Constantine set about trying to reorganize the Greek army and to regain his lost reputation. It was no easy task. One of the chief stumbling blocks was his father, King George I. As so often happened between a sovereign and his heir, King George could not appreciate that his son was a grown man, capable of thinking for himself. In 1898 Tino turned thirty; three of his brothers were in the second half of their twenties. Yet the King insisted on treating his sons as children. Like his sister Alexandra, Princess of Wales, King George could not realize that his children had matured. He never took them into his confidence; he never asked their advice. About the government of the country, they knew almost nothing.

Even the Princess of Wales was alarmed by her brother's short-sighted and tyrannical behaviour. 'Aunt [Alix] thinks that *Tino* has been *most* unjustly used . . .' confided the Empress Frederick to her daughter Mossy. 'Aunt says the King has often *very good reasons* for what he thinks and does but never explains them to Tino!!'

As a result, the sons felt increasingly antagonistic towards their father. In his turn, the King resented the way in which his sons seemed to be in league against him. Princess Alexandra reported that 'the King complains that when the sons are together or with their Mama, and talking in an animated way, the moment he comes in the conversation ceases and every one is silent, or that they get up and go away and he feels that very much indeed.'

Yet when Tino wished to discuss his ideas for army reform with his father, the King refused to give him a hearing. 'I would go on and on in some way or another until attention is paid to Tino and he is listened to,' the Empress advised Sophie. 'Has your Papa-in-law no confidential friend to whom you could both speak?'

Vicky herself tried to soften the King's attitude towards his eldest son and to get him to involve his heir in the workings of the monarchy. 'I ventured to say [to the King] at the end,' she told Sophie, 'that I hoped Tino would find work worthy of him at Athens, and the means of actively serving his country, and gaining the popularity he so justly deserves.'

She advised Tino, in the meantime, to gather around him the best men in the army and the best heads in the country. He should remain in constant touch with public life and to develop his own particular sphere of interest. 'I do so want him to become in himself a "pillar of the State" he will some day be called upon to rule over,' she said to her daughter. 'I want him to have success and satisfaction after he has suffered so much injustice and ingratitude. Help him, like a good and admiring and helpful faithful little wife, wherever you can.'

This Princess Sophie always tried to do. Indeed, the one reassuring spot in Sophie's often difficult life was her love for her husband and her family. Husband and wife were devoted to each other and they delighted in their children. Their home life was harmonious and unpretentious; the children were raised strictly but lovingly. By 1901 – the year of the deaths of both Sophie's grandmother, Queen Victoria, and her mother, the Empress Frederick – the couple had four children: three boys and a girl. The girl would one day become a queen and each of the three boys, through the caprices of their country's politics, would in turn be King of the Hellenes.

CHAPTER TWELVE

'Sweet Grandmama'

By marrying into the senior branch of the family into which her cousin Sophie had married – the Danish royal family – Princess Maud of Wales had joined one of the most unaffected royal houses in Europe. At the time of Maud's arrival in Copenhagen, her husband's grandfather, King Christian IX, was seventy-eight and had reigned for thirty-three years. His wife, Queen Louise, was a year older. Of the two, the Queen was the more forceful ('false, intriguing and not wise' was Queen Victoria's blunt opinion) but the marriage was a happy one. Husband and wife were both simple in their tastes, unquestioningly religious and devoted to their family. During his reign, King Christian IX, largely through the marriages of his attractive children, had risen to a position of considerable importance and influence in Europe. If he was not yet the Grandfather of Europe, he was certainly Europe's Father-in-law. His eldest son, Crown Prince Frederick (Princess Maud's father-in-law) would one day reign as King of Denmark; his daughter, Princess Alexandra, would be Queen of England; another son was King George I of the Hellenes; a second daughter was now the Dowager Empress Marie of Russia; a third daughter had married the son of the ex-King of Hanover; his youngest son was married to an Orleans princess and had once been offered, and had declined, the crown of Bulgaria.

These brilliant connections had in no way gone to the head of this modest and gentlemanly King. Manners at the Danish court might have been somewhat stiff but life remained as simple and as unsophisticated as it had ever been.

In the Amalienborg Palace in Copenhagen there might occasionally be some state entertaining but in the country castles of Bernsdorff and Fredensborg everything was on the homeliest scale. The most illustrious royal guests were obliged to live *en famille*. Visiting queens had to share sitting-rooms; breakfast and luncheon were taken without servants, the food being set out on sideboards and guests helping themselves. Some unimportant princess was quite likely to find herself being attended to by the Tsar of Russia or the Prince of Wales.

Dinner was served at the unfashionable hour of six in the evening. Before the meal, the old King would move solemnly from guest to guest, saying a few words to each. Dinner, at which the food was reported to be 'heavy, not to say indifferent', lasted for an hour and a half, after which the guests would file into the drawing-room where again the King would make his agonizingly slow circle. This would be followed by cards or artless parlour games. At nine o'clock there would be a further spread of country fare: tea, sandwiches, sour milk and *øllebrød*. It was all very provincial. The worldly Prince of Wales is reported to have once said that there was only one more boring place on earth than Fredensborg, and that was Bernsdorff.

But the family loved it. Close-knit, clannish, unsophisticated, the children and grandchildren of King Christian IX adored these family gatherings. Princess Alexandra is said to have enjoyed being in her Danish home 'much more than anything else'. Under the eye of the patriarchal old King, the family seemed to live in an atmosphere of per-manent adolescence: they pedalled their bicycles, they rode their horses, they played their jokes. They went picnicking and boating and walking. Of cultural or intellectual pursuits there was no trace. Anyone attempting to write a letter or read a book would be mercilessly teased. Even the Princess of Wales, by then almost stone deaf, complained of not being able to concentrate on her letters because of the obligatory racket raised by the others the minute she sat down.

As the park of Fredensborg Castle was often open to the public, visitors were quite likely to find themselves face to face with members of the royal family. On one occasion a man who had lost his way in the woods came across the King of Greece, the Tsar of Russia and the Prince of Wales. Not realizing who they were, he asked them to show him the way out of the park. The illustrious trio accompanied him to the gates, talking all the while of the weather, crops and politics.

'I've very much enjoyed my walk with you gentlemen and I hope we shall meet again,' said the stranger as he parted from them. 'May I ask your names?'

'Certainly,' answered King George. 'I'm the King of Greece, this is the Prince of Wales, and this is the Emperor of Russia.'

'And I,' said, the stranger with a sceptical smile, 'am Jesus Christ.'

One of the chief characteristics of the members of the Danish royal family was their devotion towards one another. Queen Victoria, on referring to the disharmony so prevalent in most royal families, once claimed that 'one remarkable exception is the Danish Royal Family; they are wonderfully united – and never breathe one word against each other, and the daughters remain as unspoilt and as completely Children of the Home as when they were unmarried.'

All in all, one would have imagined it to be a highly suitable *milieu* for the newly-married Princess Maud. So unworldly, so unaffected, so fond of outdoor amusements, she could hardly have wished for more congenial company. But she was not happy. She disliked Denmark and she longed for England. Although her Copenhagen home – a suite of twelve rooms in what was known as King George's Palace, beside the Amalienborg Palace – was furnished 'to reflect English taste', she was dissatisfied. She was forever bemoaning the fact that her husband's naval duties kept him at sea for long periods. Such complaints brought an uncharacteristically sharp rejoinder from her mother: Princess Maud must 'on no account forget that she married a *Danish* Prince and a *naval* man and *he owes* his first duty to *his country* and his profession', wrote Princess Alexandra.

But before many months had passed, Princess Maud and her husband were back in England. In buttercup yellow satin she attended a state concert; in white serge and a boater, she boarded the *Osborne* at Cowes; at the Chamberlains' great party she was all but torn to pieces by an unruly mob on the pavement. When Prince Charles was obliged to return to Copenhagen at the end of the summer, his wife remained at Appleton. She seemed, indeed, to be spending almost as much time with her mother and sisters as she was with her husband.

'The Princess of Wales and her daughters look very seedy,' wrote one of Queen Victoria's ladies on seeing them in the South of France the following Easter, 'and Princess Maud has dyed her hair canary colour which makes her look quite improper and more like a little milliner than ever.'

Well might an observer write that 'it is indeed remarkable how little the marriages of the Royal Family have interfered with their old family life, for when the [Prince and Princess of Wales] are in residence, their children are near to them, proving unmistakably the deep affection which unites them. Such a close family life with their parents, after marriage has claimed princes and princesses, is unique in history.'

And while Princess Maud remained the wife of a relatively unimportant Danish Prince, she could afford to indulge her passion for England and her family. She was not to know that before many years had passed, she would suddenly become a Queen.

In the summer of 1897, the Empress Frederick travelled to England for Queen Victoria's Diamond Jubilee celebrations. The Diamond Jubilee differed from the Golden Jubilee, ten years before, in that it was a manifestation of British imperial power rather than a gathering of Europe's royalties. No crowned heads were invited. The thought of all those kings and emperors crowding into Buckingham Palace was more than the seventy-eight-year-old Queen could bear. It also meant that her grandson, the exhausting Kaiser Wilhelm II, need not be invited. Never the less, there was no shortage of lesser royalties. Princes and princesses from every court in Europe came swarming into London: 'Buckingham Palace is like a beehive,' reported the Empress, 'the place is so crammed we do not see very much of each other.'

Celebrations on Jubilee Day – 22 June 1897 – were restricted to the Queen's magnificent procession through the streets of the capital. At the steps of St Paul's Cathedral the procession halted and, with the lame old Queen remaining firmly in her carriage, a short thanksgiving service was conducted in the open air. 'No!' exclaimed the Queen's cousin, the English-born Grand Duchess of Mecklenburg-Strelitz, on first hearing of this plan, 'that out of doors Service before St Paul's! Has one ever heard of such a thing! after 60 years Reign, to thank God in the Street!!!'

But thank God in the street Queen Victoria did, and the unusual proceedings in no way detracted from the brilliance of the occasion. 'The celebrations were no less magnificent than ten years ago . . .' wrote the Empress to her daughter Sophie. 'The streets were *most* beautifully decorated, the crowds immense, the enthusiasm great, and the perfect order was marvellous, all so well arranged and organized. The scene in front of St Paul's was most impressive, and when the bells pealed out from the dark old Cathedral, and the cheers rang out again, and the sun shone on all the glitter of the escort and carriages and the countless spectators, it was as fine a sight as you could wish to see.'

After an exhausting round of luncheons, dinners, soirées, garden parties and receptions, the Empress returned to Friedrichshof. As always, she hated leaving England; more particularly now, as her mother was growing so old and frail. But within a year, Vicky's own health, which had always been so good, began to trouble her.

In the autumn of 1898, at the age of fifty-seven, the Empress was thrown by her horse and was obliged to spend a few days in bed. It appears that the doctor who was called in to examine her after the accident discovered that she had cancer. Whether or not he advised an operation is not certain; a specialist, examining her six months later, claimed that an operation at the time of the discovery might have been successful.

But she would do nothing about it. She imagined that her body was strong enough to withstand the ravages of the disease for as much as ten years, by which time she would have lived her allotted span. She therefore swore the doctor to secrecy and gave out that she was suffering from lumbago.

'To have all the world know it would be to make my life utterly *wretched* and deprive me of all peace and independence,' she wrote to Sophie. 'You know how indiscreet people at Berlin are. I am not much loved, so I should not like to have people most likely *rejoicing* over my misfortune and speculating on my coming decease before it is necessary.'

Not until the following year did the Empress tell the Kaiser, her other children, the marshal of her household and one or two close friends. Her mother, Queen Victoria, was never informed.

But the Empress Frederick's estimate of ten more years of life had been too optimistic. The disease spread rapidly and by the end of the year 1900 she was in almost continuous pain. 'The terrible nights of agony are worse than ever, no rest, no peace,' she confided to her daughter Sophie. 'The tears rush down my cheeks when I am not shouting with pain. The injections of morphia dull the pains a little for about quarter of an hour, sometimes not at all, then they rage again with renewed intensity, and make me wish I was safe in my grave, where these sufferings are not. So my nights are spent.'

In addition to her own health, the Empress was worried about that of her mother. For the Queen, too, was sinking. 'How I wish I could see her soon,' wrote the Empress. 'I long to be with her, but am a stupid useless thing, like a log of wood.'

Life, for Queen Victoria, had been particularly sad during the last few years. The Boer War, which broke out in October 1899 and in which the British initially suffered terrible reverses, filled her with anxiety. She was distressed by the almost general European sympathy for the Boer cause; so vociferous was French condemnation of Britain's action in South Africa that the Queen was obliged to cancel her customary journey to the South of France in the spring of 1900. The German Press was no less insulting. 'The Anglophobian fever, which seemed to have deprived the German press of its reason, gives me great pain,' admitted Vicky to her mother. Further away than ever seemed any realization of Vicky's dream of an Anglo-German alliance.

Family deaths further saddened the old Queen. In February 1899, her grandson, 'young Alfred', only son of Prince Alfred, Duke of Edinburgh (and brother to Princess Marie of Romania) died at the age of twenty-five.

The following year the Duke of Edinburgh himself died. 'Oh God! my poor darling Affie gone too . . .' cried the Queen. 'It is hard at eighty-one!' In October 1900 yet another of her grandsons, Prince Christian Victor of Schleswig-Holstein, son of her daughter Helena, died of enteric fever in South Africa. It had been, as the Queen put it, a 'horrible year'.

Making it yet more horrible for the Queen was the thought of her daughter Vicky's illness. The Queen still believed that her daughter was suffering from lumbago. 'Darling Vicky's sixtieth birthday,' ran the entry in the Queen's Journal for 21 November 1900. 'To think of her, who was so wonderfully active and strong, now so ill and suffering, is heart-breaking . . . We pray daily that she may suffer less.'

But the Empress's sufferings were worse. By the beginning of the year 1901 it was realized that she did not have many more months to live. With the old Queen growing more feeble by the day, it was wondered which of the two would go first. By the middle of January it was clear that it would be the Queen. Her children were summoned to Osborne on 18 January; with them came her grandson, Kaiser Wilhelm II. At four o'clock on the afternoon of 22 January 1901 a bulletin was issued to say that 'The Queen is slowly sinking'.

Queen Victoria lay in her great white bed, her pillows supported by a touchingly solicitous and uncharacteristically mute Kaiser Wilhelm. Around her stood her children and grandchildren. In an effort to rouse the dying Queen, they called out their names. There was no response to their appealing voices.

Queen Victoria died just after half past six that evening.

The news was broken to the Empress Frederick the following day by her daughter Mossy. Vicky was desolate. She wished, she said, that she too were dead.

'Words cannot describe my agony of mind at this overwhelming sorrow,' she wrote to Sophie. 'Oh, my beloved Mama! Is she *really* gone? Gone from us all to whom she was such a comfort and support . . . It *breaks* my heart. My Sophie darling, you have lost a most dear and kind and sweet Grandmama, who was ever so full of love for you all, taking an interest in all that concerned you.

'What a Queen she was, and what a woman!'

PART TWO

1901 — 1918

CHAPTER THIRTEEN

Europe's Uncle

King Edward VII was in his sixtieth year when he ascended the British throne in January 1901. That Queen Victoria's son looked every inch a king, there was no denying. Impressively corpulent, impeccably dressed, supremely self-assured, King Edward VII cut an unmistakably regal figure. On state occasions he wore his robes with immense authority; in private, with his hat stylishly tilted, a carnation in his buttonhole and a cigar between his fingers, his air was no less majestic. Not even in the most brilliant company did he ever look anything other than the most important person present.

And not only did Edward VII look like a king, he behaved like one. Into those public duties which his mother had so long neglected, he threw himself with gusto. The ceremonial aspect of the monarchy was not only restored but expanded. Parliament was once more opened with great pageantry, spectacular state visits were exchanged, glittering courts, balls and banquets were held at Buckingham Palace, carriages bowled in colourful procession along the course at Ascot. No capital in Europe – not the barbaric splendour of St Petersburg or the showy militarism of Berlin – could match the assured magnificence of King Edward VII's court. With the decorative and perennially youthful Queen Alexandra by his side, King Edward restored to the British monarchy a lustre that it had not known since the days of the Stuarts.

'Nothing,' wrote one of his Continental nieces, 'is more irreproachably perfect in every detail then the King of England's Court and household, a sort of staid luxury without ostentation, a placid, aristocratic ease and opulence which has nothing showy about it. Everything is run on silent wheels that have been perfectly greased; everything fits in, there are no spaces between, no false note. From the polite, handsome and superlatively groomed gentleman-in-waiting who receives you in the hall, to the magnificently solemn and yet welcoming footman who walks before you down the corridor, everything pleases the eye, satisfies one's fastidiousness. When I call up before my eye the royal English abodes I always have a vision of softly carpeted picture-hung corridors, with a silent-footed servant walking ahead of you, discreetly impersonal and yet belonging to the whole; I have the feeling of mounting shallow-stepped stairs leading towards rooms as perfectly "groomed" as were the horses of the royal carriage which brought you up to the front door, as perfectly groomed also as the tall sentry presenting arms before the gates . . . .'

That this blend of magnificence and perfection should be the hallmark of the Edwardian court was due, very largely, to the new King's highly developed sense of style. His taste might not have been faultless – or even, for that matter, good – but he had an eye for the right setting. He knew how a king should present himself. 'I don't know much about art,' he once said in his gutteral fashion, 'but I think I know something about arrangement.' He did indeed, and his arrangements ensured that he was always seen against a suitably regal background.

He lost very little time in sweeping away the graces of his mother's dowdy court. Her black-clad ladies-in-waiting were pensioned off. Her favourite Indian servant-companion, the Munshi, was sent packing. The innumerable busts, statuettes and memorials to an earlier favourite, John Brown, were likewise got rid of.

There was a drastic reorganization of all household departments. The sedate afternoon 'Drawing-rooms' were replaced by evening 'Courts'. Osborne House was given to the Navy, on the understanding that the central part would be preserved as a family shrine. Balmoral Castle was centrally heated and the famous tartan stripped from the drawing-room walls (Lord Rosebery once remarked that he had always considered the drawing-room at Osborne to be the ugliest in the world until he saw the drawing-room at Balmoral.) Firm measures were taken to stop the excessive drinking of whisky at Balmoral. Windsor Castle was modernized and redecorated: the elephants' tusks, the marble busts, the cumbersome mahogany furniture were replaced by porcelain, jade and long-forgotten pieces from the Brighton Pavilion. Buckingham Palace became once again a home worthy of a monarch who held, as Queen Victoria used to say, 'the greatest position there is'. The King ordered its façade and its setting to be redesigned. Its galleries and staircases were recarpeted. Its chandeliers were electrified. Its reception rooms were regilded, refurnished and fitted with enormous looking glasses; on state occasions, they were filled with pyramids of roses, carnations and hydrangeas.

The stage having been set, King Edward VII played his part with customary verve. Far from confining himself, as his mother had done, to the more inaccessible royal homes for the greater part of the year, Edward kept himself in the public eye. He was forever on the move. His annual routine was strenuous, if unvarying, and would have exhausted any man less energetic than he. Yet despite his restlessness, he kept to a strict timetable; he never broke an engagement. 'The punctuality and regularity of his yearly programme,' says his assistant private secretary, Ponsonby, 'is perhaps the most striking tribute to that love of order and sense of decorum which was one of his most marked characteristics.'

The New Year found the King playing host to a stream of guests at Sandringham. At the end of January he moved to Buckingham Palace for the Opening of Parliament. Every night in February was given over to dinner parties or after theatre supper parties. March and April he spent abroad – in Paris, at Biarritz and cruising the Mediterranean. In May he returned to London for the Season. This entailed an unending succession of dinners, balls, receptions and presentation parties. In June he moved to Windsor for the racing at Epsom and Ascot. In July he visited some provincial centre. The end of that month found him at the Goodwood races; the beginning of August at Cowes. Then followed a month at Marienbad for a much-needed cure. By September he was back in England for the Doncaster races; in October he was at Balmoral. During November and December he moved between Buckingham Palace, Windsor and Sandringham, always spending Christmas and New Year – again amongst a host of guests – at Sandringham.

If, since his accession, the King's life had become somewhat more formal, it was still far from staid. 'We shall not pretend,' lectured the London *Times* on his accession, 'that there is nothing in his long career which those who respect and admire him would wish otherwise.' If *The Times* imagined that the King was about to turn over a new leaf, it was being too optimistic by half: Bertie's behaviour might be a shade more circumspect but it was no less self-indulgent. He still ate enormous meals. He attacked them all – breakfast, luncheon, tea, dinner and supper – with equal zest. His dinner never consisted of anything less than twelve courses, with each course richer and more elaborate than the last. His favourite drink was champagne; he smoked almost continuously. On the very day of Queen Victoria's funeral, an assistant private secretary was horrified to find the King, the Kaiser, the King of the Belgians and the King of Portugal smoking cigars in the Great Corridor at Windsor Castle; 'no one had ever smoked there before', runs his shocked comment.

The King dined out – in restaurants or in private homes – as frequently as he had ever done. His suppers in the private room behind his box at the Royal Opera House, Covent Garden, were as lavish and as indiscreet as they had ever been. His liaison with the voluptuous Mrs Keppel continued; when in London, he visited her almost every day. The Pompadour of this Edwardian court, Alice Keppel was a figure of considerable importance; she could always be relied upon to keep the notoriously tetchy King in a sweet temper. 'Thank God,' exclaimed Sir Arthur Nicolson on joining the King's yacht for a cruise, 'Alice will be on board.'

Nor was Mrs Keppel the only woman capable of diverting the King. Edward loved the company of beautiful, well-dressed women. 'What tiresome evenings we shall have!' he sighed when Queen Alexandra's mourning for the death of her father obliged him to hold a series of men-only dinner parties. He 'was never happier', claims Ponsonby, 'than in the company of pretty women.' During his continental holidays, his equerries were quite likely to come across him grappling with some picture-hatted, full-breasted beauty in a secluded arbour. And it is said that on one occasion a ship's officer, passing the porthole of the royal cabin, heard his sovereign's deep voice saying, 'Stop calling me Sir and put another cushion under your back.'

To his credit, and unlike so many of his contemporaries, Edward was never hypocritical about his private life. Once, at Marienbad, he walked out of a revue called 'The Underworld' simply because he was bored by it and not because he was shocked by its somewhat improper tone. Within a day or two he was inundated with letters of congratulation for having made 'a firm stand in the cause of morality'. One of the most fulsome came from the Bishop of Ripon. When Ponsonby asked the King how he should reply to the Bishop's letter, Edward's answer was concise. 'Tell the Bishop the exact truth,' he said. 'I have no wish to pose as a protector of morals, especially abroad.'

With his other duties – the private as opposed to the public aspects of monarchy – King Edward was less at ease. He had no taste for, and no experience of, desk work. Easily bored, lacking in concentration, hating to be alone, he was not nearly as conscientious or as well informed as his mother had been. Formal meetings with Ministers irked him; he much preferred to discuss things with them over a balloon of after-dinner brandy. Thus, when his Ministers proved uncongenial, matters tended to go undiscussed. As a result, the King complained, with justification, that they did not keep him well enough informed and that they did not trust his judgement.

Edward was none the less capable, if the subject interested him, of applying himself to it with considerable zeal. Every detail of such things as the State Opening of Parliament or a foreign visit would be attended to by him personally. In these he was meticulous, demanding, almost tyrannical. He had very little interest in domestic or colonial politics; on the other hand, for foreign affairs and the armed forces he showed great enthusiasm. Here his influence – and influence was all that he was allowed to exert – was considerable. That the British Navy was reformed during the first years of the century was in no small measure due to the King's interest in the matter. And although his much vaunted diplomatic activity was never quite as effective as a great many people then, and since, imagined, it was certainly useful. His *bonhomie* oiled many a political wheel; his charm created a sympathetic climate. The ease and authority with which he moved amongst the diplomats, statesmen and sovereigns of Europe enhanced his own, and thus his country's, status.

Having failed to match up to the exacting standards of his father, the Prince Consort, in almost every sphere, King Edward VII, by exercising the two attributes never considered important by his father – personal magnetism and a sense of showmanship – developed into an influential and impressive monarch.

Edward's diplomatic endeavours were made easier by the fact that he was so closely related to the various kings and queens of Europe. In an age when sovereigns still wielded considerable influence (and almost all the monarchs of Europe were in a position to exercise more personal power than he) King Edward's status proved very useful. Through his mother's wide-ranging connections he could claim relationship to almost every monarch on the Continent. To several of them he was very closely connected indeed. His sister Vicky was the Dowager German Empress. Her son – his nephew – was Kaiser Wilhelm II; her daughter – his niece – would one day be Queen Sophie of the Hellenes. Another of his nieces was the Empress Alexandra of Russia. Yet another would be Queen Marie of Romania. During Edward's reign his daughter Maud was to become the Queen of Norway and his sister Beatrice's daughter, Ena, the Queen of Spain.

Although, when the great test came in 1914, these family relationships proved to be of very little value, this unhappy fact was largely unsuspected during this high summer of European monarchy. The sovereigns of Europe, patriarchal, colourful and moving always in a blaze of glory, were still looked upon as representatives of their people. They were considered to be the most important figures on the European scene. Their state visits were regarded as acts of considerable political significance. What better guarantee of international goodwill than this close relationship between the royalties of Europe? Were they not all members of a royal clan, the descendants, or at least the relations, of the great Queen Victoria? How could Uncle Bertie ever allow his country to go to war against his nephew Willie's Germany? Surely cousin Willie would never think of taking up arms against cousin Nicky's Russia?

And of all these inter-related monarchs, none moved across the European stage more reassuringly and with greater majesty and aplomb than Queen Victoria's eldest son. It was no wonder that people not only called King Edward VII, but believed him to be, 'The Peacemaker'.

3

Edward VII's first journey abroad as King was to visit his dying sister, the Empress Frederick, at Kronberg. On 23 February 1901 he crossed the

Channel in the *Victoria and Albert*. At Flushing, and at several stations *en route* to Homburg, he was greeted by crowds singing what his entourage assumed to be the same hymn over and over; 'a very proper way of spending a Sunday evening', noted Frederick Ponsonby. Only on inquiry did Ponsonby discover that they were singing the Boer National Anthem. This particular show of hostility was preferable, none the less, to the singing of the British National Anthem, which was done by a party of schoolgirls, on Düsseldorf station, at two in the morning. The girls were said to have been bitterly disappointed at the non-appearance of the King in response to their earnest serenading.

The King was met at Homburg by his nephew, Kaiser Wilhelm II, and from there they made for Friedrichshof. Vicky was delighted to see her brother. With the passing years these two very dissimilar personalities had grown closer. 'There is not a kinder brother in the world,' said the Empress to her daughter Sophie, 'and I cling to him in my loneliness very much.'

Deeply distressed by his sister's sufferings, King Edward urged his own doctor, Sir Francis Laking, to induce the German doctors to prescribe larger doses of morphia. This the Empress's doctors refused to do. The King, appreciating how often his sister had been criticized for her supposed preferences for all things English, including English doctors, did not press the point.

If, in the mind of Frederick Ponsonby, there was any doubt about the Empress's distrust of German doctors, there was soon none about her distrust of her eldest son, the German Emperor. Sending for Ponsonby one evening, the Empress, looking 'as if she had just been taken off the rack after undergoing torture', asked him to do her a favour. She wanted him to take some of her letters back with him to England. These were bound copies of her letters to Queen Victoria which the Empress had once borrowed, possibly with a view to publishing them. As they formed such an indictment of the Kaiser and such a vindication of her own behaviour, the Empress possibly suspected that her son would never allow them to be made public. They were her one means of clearing her name; of correcting Bismarck's presentation of her as an anti-Prussian and politically ambitious virago. Remembering how the Kaiser had ransacked the rooms of the Neues Palais on the death of the Emperor Frederick, the Empress was obviously determined that these letters should not fall into his hands. 'I don't want a soul to know they have been taken away,' she said to Ponsonby, 'and certainly Willie must not have them, nor must he know that you have got them.'

Late that night two enormous boxes were delivered to Ponsonby's room. He claims that only by the exercise of considerable ingenuity was he able to get them past the Kaiser and out of Friedrichshof the following day. Almost thirty years were to go by, however, before – in 1928 – a selection of the correspondence was published. This Ponsonby did on his own initiative. With the publication of the *Letters of the Empress Frederick* the world was able to learn, for the first time, something of the sufferings of this impetuous but high-minded woman at the hands of Bismarck and her eldest son.

The Kaiser, by then in exile in Holland, did his utmost to prevent publication of the letters but, being unsuccessful, insisted on writing a preface to the German edition of the book. His mother, he wrote, was 'very sensitive and everything wounded her; she saw everything in shadows, everything hostile, saw want of sympathy and coolness where there was only helpless silence, and her temperament made her use bitter words about everybody. Therefore the reader should not believe implicitly everything she wrote.'

For five months after King Edward's return to England, the Empress lived on. In July, Princess Sophie of Greece joined her sisters, Moretta and Mossy, at Friedrichshof and on 4 August, Wilhelm and his wife Dona arrived. The following day, 5 August 1901, was one of brilliant sunshine. As the Empress lay dying, a butterfly flew in by the open window and fluttered about her head. As it returned to the window and floated out into the sunlit garden, Vicky died. She was sixty years of age.

Calumnies pursued her beyond her death. Despite the fact that her orders for a simple funeral were faithfully carried out (she was buried beside her husband at Potsdam) the most scurrilous stories about her dying wishes circulated Berlin. She had insisted, they whispered, that she be buried, not as a German sovereign, but as an English princess. An Anglican bishop was to conduct the funeral service according to the rites of the Anglican Church. She was to be laid naked, wrapped in a Union Jack, in a coffin specially brought over from England and the body then sent back to England for burial at Windsor. Only an admirable firmness on the part of the beloved Kaiser had prevented such scandalous proceedings. One could imagine, clucked one of her enemies, how hurt the people of Berlin had been by the behaviour of the Princess 'who in dying showed her contempt of everything that was German'. She was *die Engländerin*, it seemed, to the very end.

The legend of Vicky's unremitting Anglophobia, carefully fostered by Bismarck, continued for many years. Her enemies refused to see in her undeniable love for her native country anything other than a hatred of Germany. Yet all Vicky had wished to do was to introduce into the national life of her adopted country all that was best in her own. Where other British princesses were content to bring the language and the customs of their homeland into their husband's households, Vicky had been determined to inculcate more important values into her husband's country.

Her championship of Britain was not mere jingoism; she believed that it was the only country 'that understands liberty, the only one that understands true progress, the only happy, the only really free and above all the only really humane country.' It was these virtues that she tried, so tirelessly, to reproduce in Germany. Her overwhelming urge, says one of her biographers, was 'to help others, to better them, to guide them towards those material, moral and social standards that she had first imbibed in England'. In this, she had come up against, first, the blood and iron autocracy of Bismarck, and then the militarily dominated autocracy of her eldest son.

'Why were we, so to speak, in opposition?' she once explained after the death of her husband. 'Because our patriotism wanted to see the greatness of our fatherland connected with the noble sense of right, morality, for freedom and culture, for individual independence, for the improvement of the single person as man, as German, as European and as cosmopolitan. Improvement, progress, ennoblement – that was our motto. Peace, tolerance, charity – these most precious possessions of mankind, we had to see them trampled upon, laughed at . . . *Blood and iron* alone made Germany great and unified – all national vices were called patriotism.'

That these passionately expressed ideals were never put into practice in Germany is one of the great tragedies of the nineteenth century. Had Kaiser Frederick III come earlier to the throne or reigned longer than ninety-eight days, the Second Reich would have taken a very different road. The régime would have been liberalized and Germany would almost certainly have formed an alliance with Great Britain. These had always been Vicky's fondest hopes. But it was not to be. Almost every one of those schemes with which, as a young, idealistic bride Vicky had arrived in Berlin, had turned to ashes. Her crown, more so, perhaps, than that of any other of Queen Victoria's descendants, had turned out to be what the Queen used to describe as 'a crown of thorns'.

4

Of the many ways in which King Edward VII differed from Queen Victoria, one of the most valuable was in his treatment of his heir. From the very start of his reign, the King ensured that his only son, the thirty-five-year-old Duke of York, was closely involved in the workings of the monarchy. And not only did the King initiate him politically, he encouraged him, he sympathized with him, he drew him out. Unlike his worldly father, Prince George was a shy and self-doubting young man; it is greatly to the father's credit that the son's personality was not permanently undermined by the contrast between them. The Duke of York could so easily have become even less confident than he was; instead, the King's warm and tactful handling brought out the best in him.

'My room opens out of Papa's and is on the ground floor,' wrote the Duke proudly from Windsor to his wife, Princess May, in 1901, 'then I have got a writing table next to his in his sitting room, he wished it so. Sidney is now doing boxes while I am writing this. Fancy that being possible in dear Grandmama's time; anyhow it shows that Papa and I are on good terms with each other.'

They were indeed. The King not only understood his son, he loved him dearly, while the Duke of York was no less devoted to his father. In later life, when speaking of his relationship with his father, King George V's voice was quite likely to break and his blue eyes to spill with tears.

Evidence of these strong emotional family ties was provided when, in March 1901, the Duke and Duchess of York set off from England to open the Australian Federal Parliament. At a farewell luncheon aboard the *Ophir* at Portsmouth, Queen Alexandra and her unmarried daughter, Princess Victoria, cried throughout the meal, while the King could scarcely propose the toast for sobbing. The Duke of York, no less upset, only just managed to reply before he and Princess May hurried down to their cabins for 'a good cry'.

Despite this melancholy start, the Australian tour was a great success. Prince George gained more confidence and Princess May, away from the brittle gaiety of King Edward's circle, blossomed into a charming, assured and attractive personality. The cruise on the *Ophir* did not, however, permanently cure her shyness; back in England, in November 1901, Princess May proved as reserved as before.

Just a week after his return from Australia, Prince George was proclaimed Prince of Wales. The King had delayed conferring this title on the grounds that it was still too closely associated, in the public mind, with himself. Queen Alexandra, too, was loath to relinquish the title by which she had been known for almost forty years. She proved even less amenable when it came to giving up her home, Marlborough House. At first, in her wayward fashion, she would not hear of moving to Buckingham Palace at all. That, she assured Prince George, would finish her. 'All my happiness and sorrow were here, very nearly all you children were born here, all the reminiscences of my whole life are here, and I feel as if by taking me away a cord will be torn in my heart which can never be mended again.'

None the less, the King finally prevailed upon her to make the move and Prince George, Princess May and their four children moved into a redecorated Marlborough House.

The first great state occasion which the couple attended as Prince and Princess of Wales was the State Opening of Parliament in January 1902.

The second was to be the Coronation. A date had been set for 26 June 1902. By the middle of that month the streets of London were hung with red and gold and almost every boat train was delivering yet another foreign prince or colonial deputation. In superb weather carriage processions clattered to and from the stations and all day visitors from the provinces surged through the decorated streets.

One thing only rendered the prospect less than perfect: a rumour that the King was not very well. He seemed tired, depressed and irritable; he looked more bloated than ever. On 16 June he was too ill to attend the ceremonial review at Aldershot; the next day he could not take part in the drive from Windsor to Ascot. On 23 June he drove, in agonizing pain, through cheering crowds from Paddington Station to Buckingham Palace, but was unable to attend the banquet and reception that evening. By now his doctors had diagnosed appendicitis but the King was proving an extraordinarily difficult patient. He would not hear of a postponement of the Coronation. He swore that he would go through with the ceremony even if it killed him.

This show of determination was all very well but by now the chances were that, unless he were operated on immediately, he would be dead before he reached the Abbey. And as the operation for appendicitis, in 1902, was still an extremely dangerous one, there was a strong possibility that he would die anyway. However, an operation was at length agreed upon and the Coronation postponed.

The operation, performed on 24 June, was a complete success. The King, who on the second day was sitting up in bed smoking a cigar, made a rapid recovery and spent three weeks convalescing aboard his yacht off Cowes. A new date for the Coronation was set for 9 August by which time, unfortunately, the majority of foreign royalties had already left London. The ceremony was none the less spectacular for that. The crowds were enthusiastic; the decorations were superb; the processions were magnificent. Within the Abbey itself there were one or two inevitable, but minor, mishaps. Princess Beatrice dropped her prayer book and sent a wealth of gold plate clattering across the flagstones; the Duchess of Devonshire tripped over her train and fell headlong down some steps, thereby losing her coronet but not, fortunately, her red wig. The Marchioness of Londonderry, having decided to repair to the lavatory before facing the lengthy ceremony, remained there for such a long time that a queue of fidgeting peeresses outside the door became increasingly alarmed. They became distinctly more so when they heard the Marchioness calling out for a pair of forceps. What *could* she be doing? Emerging, triumphant if dishevelled, the Marchioness explained that while bending to adjust her train, her tiara had gone clattering into the pan. She had needed the forceps to retrieve it.

The King, looking slimmer for his illness and his corsets, played his part with great dignity and obvious enjoyment. He had felt, he assured someone afterwards, not the slightest fatigue. 'Marvellous, isn't it?' he exclaimed. The Queen, in a dress of golden Indian gauze, shimmering with diamonds and pearls, and trailing a richly embroidered, ermine-lined violet velvet train, looked radiant. As the crown was placed on her towering false coiffure, the peeresses, in a graceful, simultaneous movement, placed their coronets on their own heads. Of all the impressive scenes in the Abbey that day, this was the one which most impressed the King. 'Their white arms arching over their heads,' he afterwards said, had resembled 'a scene from a beautiful ballet.'

Amidst scenes of gratifying acclamation, the newly crowned King and Queen drove back to Buckingham Palace. Here Queen Alexandra took off her dazzling crown and, much to the delight of her Greek nephews, allowed them to try it on.

CHAPTER FOURTEEN

'An Invincible Joie de Vivre'

I

Of all King Edward VII's nieces, the one who would come to resemble him most in his lust for life and his sense of royal showmanship was Princess Marie of Romania. It is not surprising that she was amongst those royalties who had managed to remain in London for the postponed Coronation. Not for the world would she have missed this particular piece of pageantry. With her husband, the pliant Crown Prince Ferdinand, in tow, Missy of Romania flung herself into the round of Coronation festivities. She was determined to make the most of her temporary escape from the petty tyrannies of *der Onkel* – King Carol of Romania. To her, this Coronation summer was all enchantment.

It was during these opening years of the century that Marie of Romania began developing into a personality in her own right; to gain her reputation for frivolity, flirtatiousness, wilfulness and theatricality. She was in her late twenties by now, with her looks in full flower. 'I thought Missy a dream of beauty,' the Empress Frederick had written a year or two before her death, 'I have seldom seen so lovely a creature, so graceful and with such complexion and hair. She is a perfect picture.' Of those ravishing blond looks, no one was more conscious than Missy herself. 'I felt all eyes following me, male as well as female,' runs one typical observation, 'and it was not a disagreeable sensation.'

It certainly was not. Marie found the contemplation of her beauty a highly agreeable sensation. Once, when one of her nephews asked for her portrait, the gratified Marie summoned a lady-in-waiting to bring over a silver salver piled high with photographs of herself. Slowly, one by one, she scrutinized them. For each, she had an appreciative comment: 'This one is *divine*'; 'The beauty of that profile'; 'The nobility of that pose'; 'Oh! those *eyes*!'

To make certain that her beauty did not pass unnoticed, Marie let slip no opportunity of drawing attention to herself. She dressed in the showiest fashion – in black tricorn hats, in red shoes strapped *à la grecque*, up to the ankle, in diaphanous, lavishly embroidered gowns. At a ball at Devonshire House during Coronation summer, the train of her gauzy white dress was so long that it wrapped itself round the waltzing figure of her cousin, Crown Princess Sophie of Greece, and brought her crashing to the ground. The incident could hardly have improved the always edgy relationship between the two of them. To the unpretentious Sophie, the flamboyant Marie was anathema. 'If that woman doesn't leave tomorrow,' she once threatened a few hours after Missy's arrival in Athens, 'I will kick her out of the palace myself.'

From having always dressed fashionably, if somewhat daringly, Marie gradually developed a style of her own that had very little to do with fashion. She affected a bizarre, picturesque, self-consciously romantic way of dressing: she moved in a cloud of veils, cloaks and trailing draperies. 'I had an imaginative and daring mind . . .' she assures us, 'and adopted my own ways and style, regardless of criticism, rather dangerously indifferent to anything but my passion for beauty.'

She adored being photographed in her *outré* costumes. Sometimes it would be in a flowing chiffon dress amidst the part-Byzantine, part-Art Nouveau splendours of her palace at Cotroceni, outside Bucharest. At others it would be in Romanian national costume in the woods around the country palaces at Sinaia. Yet again it would be on horseback, in the red tunic, black braid and gold buttons of her hussar uniform, against the vast plains of her adopted country.

'The Crown Princess of Romania outshone all the other Princesses in beauty and grace,' wrote one of the guests at a garden party at Buckingham Palace that season, 'clad in a Byzantine-looking gown with an immense cross of jewels as only ornament.'

Hand in hand with this exotic appearance went what Missy called 'a profound and invincible *joie de vivre*' but which others tended to give less complimentary names. Having come to appreciate the particular qualities of Romania, Marie began to enjoy herself. She discovered that Bucharest was not nearly as dull as she had once imagined, and there was a magic about the Balkan countryside that set her always vivid imagination aflame. She visited gypsy encampments, she organized lavish picnics, she gave spectacular balls, she joined the late afternoon parade on the 'Chaussée' in the capital. She was never happier than when out riding. In her specially designed riding habit she was forever galloping across the landscape. The reluctant King Carol had been induced to create her honorary chief of a cavalry regiment and she carried out her military duties with characteristic zest. Her regiment, she says, adored her.

Nor, it seems, were her soldiers the only ones in whom she inspired such devotion. 'I was too vital, too magnetic also, not to attract friendship . . .' she protests, 'wherever I went, I carried with me this air of enjoying life, everything was interest and stimulation for me, so I quite naturally also stimulated those with whom I came in contact.' That she saw herself as a *femme fatale* there is no question. One of her most difficult tasks, she sighs, was to keep her clouds of admirers at bay. She discovered that the best way of dealing with some ardent, lovesick young officer was to pretend that she did not in the least understand what he was trying to tell her. That, she says, soon took the wind out of his sails.

It was hardly surprising that this indiscreet, high-spirited and un-conventional granddaughter of Queen Victoria was soon the talk of Europe. Her aunt, the Empress Frederick, once claimed that the 'beautiful and gifted' Missy was like a butterfly who, 'instead of hovering over the flowers, burns her pretty wings by going rather near the fire!' Missy herself always (and not without a touch of pride) claimed that her reputa-tion for fast living was greatly exaggerated. 'The wildly, worldly life that I have been supposed to live is a legend invented by those who vaguely heard rumours about my fine clothes and so-called eccentricities. For I was 'la Princesse Lointaine', living in a country near the Rising Sun; this fired the imagination, as the moment a woman is spoken of as "pretty" people want to know all about her, she excites interest more than anything else and gossip would have it that I was tremendously gay . . . .'

There was certainly some justification for this gossip: Marie was living in one of the gayest capitals in Europe. Romanians were fond of referring to Bucharest as the Paris of the East, and if the city was no match for Paris in some things, it was more than a match in others. Its atmosphere was notoriously licentious. A French education, says one tight-lipped Englishman, gave Romanians 'an external French veneer which con-cealed their natural Oriental characteristics'. Morals were loose, divorce was easy, extra-marital affairs commonplace. Princess Marie would have had to have been exceptionally strong-minded not to have fallen for the attractions of this free-and-easy existence. Her cousin, Kaiser Wilhelm II, went so far as to debar 'that English harlot' from his court.

About her domestic life there was nothing very exciting. Her husband Nando remained, as the Empress Frederick once put it, 'as unprepossessing as ever': a dull, diffident creature, completely under the thumb of his uncle, King Carol. The King even insisted on choosing the governess for their children; a woman who lost no time in reporting to King Carol that Princess Marie was having an affair with a 'dark-eyed lieutenant'. Whether or not she was, one does not know, but the King warned Marie to have nothing more to do with the man. The indignant Missy insisted that the tale-bearing governess be dismissed. This King Carol refused to do and Marie promptly quitted the country. She made for Coburg. Not until she received news of a near-fatal illness of her eldest son did she return to Romania.

By the year 1902, Missy and Nando had three children (they were to have six in all): Carol, Elizabeth and Marie. Missy was a devoted and, of course, highly emotional mother. Because she had suffered under the restrictive régimes of her own mother – the autocratic Princess Marie of Edinburgh – and of King Carol, Marie tended to be too indulgent with her own children. Her eldest son, Carol, would one day become the controversial King Carol II of Romania. Her second child, Elizabeth, would marry the eldest son of Princess Sophie and so become Queen of the Hellenes. The third child Marie, known as Mignon, would one day become the Queen of Yugoslavia.

Between Marie and her husband's aunt, the Queen of Romania, there was very little *rapport*. Indeed, one suspects that the poet-queen, Carmen Sylva, now returned from exile, resented the presence of this younger and hardly less exotic creature. '*Ach lieb Kindchen*,' the Queen would exclaim, pressing the younger woman to her bosom in an extravagant gesture. 'Sit down here at my feet and listen, darling.' Yet the Queen's fulsomely expressed affection never prevented her from a ruthless interference in the upbringing and education of Marie's children. Missy claims that she often went to bed in tears because of the Queen's meddling in the affairs of her household.

Returned from exile, Carmen Sylva had once more resumed her pose as 'the soul of poetry, the Muse, the inspirer'. In her flowing, shapeless, vaguely medieval clothes, she presided over a court of young people – aspiring painters, poets and writers – to whom she would hold forth in her high-flown way, regardless of whether or not they understood what she was saying. 'Nothing,' says Marie, 'was ever taken calmly, everything had to be rapturous, tragic, excessive or extravagantly comic.'

The Queen was always full of hare-brained schemes and new enthusiasms. She was forever championing imagined geniuses or encouraging ill-matched lovers. She dreamed of building a great white city where all the blind of the world would congregate, listening to music and learning crafts. On the end of the pier at the entrance to the Romanian port of Constanza on the Black Sea, she built herself a quaint little wooden house. At dead of night, with her white robes and long silver hair streaming in the wind, the poet-queen would stand on her balcony, waving a long white scarf at the passing ships. Through a megaphone, and above the screeching of the gulls, this ghostly figure would call out poetically phrased greetings and blessings to the doubtless startled crews.

It was against the iron will of King Carol, however, that the independently minded Princess Marie most frequently beat her wings. Able to handle both her complaisant husband and the romantically minded Queen, she could never get round *der Onkel*. He remained always unsmiling, unsympathetic, unemotional. She could take no step without his permission; she was allowed no say in even the most trivial matters. He was forever criticizing her behaviour. 'I was considered too English,' she complains, 'too free-and-easy, too frivolous, I was too fond of dress, of riding, of outdoor life, I was too outspoken, I had not enough respect for conventions or etiquette.' He, who was so Germanically self-disciplined and correct, looked upon her as *die Fremde* – the Stranger – a dangerously liberated creature, 'distressingly English in tastes and habits'.

That, indeed, was at the heart of the trouble. Marie might not, in many ways, have been a typical English princess, but in others – in her frankness, her emancipation and her lack of bigotry – she was. 'Don't you understand,' she once shouted at the King during the course of one of their many rows, 'that I am a transplanted tree, that my roots were torn out of my own ground?'

For no matter how much Marie had identified herself with her new country (and, in years to come, she was to be completely identified with it) she could never forget that she was Queen Victoria's granddaughter. She had only to return to her native land to feel overwhelmed by her love for it. 'The sensation of coming home, to what is no more "home", is both wonderful and unbearable,' she once wrote, 'it seems to tear apart your heartstrings, to fill you to the very brim with all the tears you never dared weep, with all the world-wide *Sehnsucht* – yearning – you never dared express.'

She loved it all: the ordered opulence of King Edward VII's court, the quiet elegance of the great country houses, the sound of the birds in a wood carpeted with bluebells, the jam, the cream, the scones and the cake of an English tea. Once, when she was strolling with Queen Alexandra across the green lawns at Sandringham, she suddenly felt weak with nostalgia for everything she had given up by going to live in faraway Romania. 'An immense desire came over me to fall down on the ground and kiss this green, green grass, to roll on it, to feel it, to possess it, make it mine once more,' runs her impassioned admission.

The Queen looked at her and took her hand.

'You love it?' she asked quietly.

'Yes, I love it,' answered Marie, 'and it hurts to love quite so hard . . . .

2

Despite the fact that King Edward VII paid visits to almost every monarch in Europe during the course of his reign, it was his state visit to republican France in 1903 that was to prove the most significant.

During the closing years of the nineteenth century there had been a gradual shift in continental alliances; a shift quite independent of ruling family, or even monarchical, ties. The old Three Emperors' Alliance – an agreement between the autocratic rulers of Russia, Germany and Austria – had fallen away and Tsarist Russia was now allied to republican France.

With Britain anxious to emerge from its long period of splendid isolation and with a proposed German alliance having come to nothing, British statesmen were obliged to look towards France for friendship.

The realization of such a friendship was going to be no easy task. The two countries had been at loggerheads for years. Various factors – colonial rivalries, French pro-Boer sympathies, the Anglophobe rantings of the French press – had poisoned Franco-British relations. Considerable diplomatic skill would be needed to overcome the hostility of French public opinion towards Britain. The politicians might be ready enough to come to an agreement, but would the public be as amenable? How was the right atmosphere for a *rapprochement* to be created?

To this problem King Edward VII applied himself with gusto. The proposed *entente* between Britain and France had his enthusiastic approval. He had always loved France; of all continental capitals, Paris was the one in which he felt most at ease. This did not mean that his admiration for France was unqualified. He would undoubtedly have preferred an Orleans or a Bonaparte to a president as Head of State and he could hardly approve of recent French behaviour towards his country. His well-known love of Paris did not blind him to what he considered certain shortcomings of the French nation, any more than his equally well-known dislike of his nephew, Kaiser Wilhelm II, blinded him to certain German virtues. Edward VII's approval of an *entente* with France was the result neither of his antipathy for Wilhelm II nor his taste for Parisian life; it was due to his lifelong sympathy with what he regarded as the most civilized nation on the Continent.

The delicate negotiations between the representatives of the two countries having got under way, the King decided to do something to help. What was needed was *le grand geste*, some spectacular proof of Britain's good intentions. He would visit Paris in state. His Ministers, apprehensive of the sort of reception he might be given by the Parisians, were not very enthusiastic; perhaps an incognito visit would be wiser? But Edward was having none of it. He would go to Paris as the King of England, in state, or not at all. He had already decided to embark on a grand tour of Europe in the spring of 1903; he would visit Paris for a few days on his way home. With this plan President Emile Loubet was in full accord and the King was formally invited to visit the French capital from 1 to 3 May 1903.

Travelling without a Cabinet Minister in attendance (there was not one with whose company the King could bear to put up for several weeks) Edward set off in the *Victoria and Albert* on 2 April 1903, for Lisbon. Here the stout English King, in an embarrassingly short jacket of a colonel of a Portuguese cavalry regiment, was met by the even stouter Portuguese King, Carlos I, and lavishly entertained. For several days the British party moved in an almost eighteenth-century atmosphere: a world of rococo carriages, gilded barges, 'magnificently ugly' salons, theatrical bullfights (they were gratified to discover that the bulls were never killed and the horses never hurt) and stiff ceremonial. After the customary exchange of decorations, with which the King, as always, had some fault to find, he remarked that Portuguese noblemen looked like nothing so much as 'waiters at second-rate restaurants'.

From Lisbon he sailed, via Gibraltar and Malta, to Naples. On 27 April he was welcomed to Rome by the diminutive King Victor Emmanuel III and two days later paid a visit to the Pope. This visit was made in the face of considerable opposition on the part of the British Government, but, as always, the King carried it off with great aplomb.

The scene in the Hall of Tapestries at the Vatican was brilliant: cardinals in scarlet robes, chamberlains in sixteenth-century costume, the Swiss Guard in gleaming armour and the Noble Guard in red and gold. The King, having decided that it would 'never do' for the members of his suite to kiss the Pope's ring, had told them that they must simply bow to the Pontiff. Thus, when, on the approach of the aged Leo XIII, the rest of the company fell to their knees, the British party remained firmly on its feet. The adroit Pope, appreciating their predicament, eased the situation by saying, 'I am so pleased to see you here today that I must shake you by the hand.'

On 30 April, amidst scenes of great enthusiasm, the King boarded a special train for Paris. He was joined, at Dijon, by his apprehensive Ambassador, Sir Edmund Monson, and was met, at the Gare du Bois de Boulogne, by the no less apprehensive President Loubet.

For King Edward VII, this visit to Paris was a great personal triumph. During the course of it he was able, by virtue of his tact, his charm and his geniality, to convert the scarcely veiled hostility of the crowds into vociferous enthusiasm. On his first drive along the Champs Elysées to the British Embassy, he was assailed with shouts of '*Vivent les Boers!*', '*Vive Fashoda!*' and even, strangely enough, '*Vive Jeanne d'Arc!*'; when he left, three days later, it was with thunderous cries of '*Vive Edouard!*' ringing in his gratified ears.

He never put a foot wrong. He melted the iciness of the audience at the Théâtre Français by saying, during the first interval, to the beautiful Jeanne Granier, 'Mademoiselle, I remember applauding you in London where you represented all the grace and spirit of France.' He charmed his hosts at the Hôtel de Ville by assuring them, in the sort of extempore speech he did so well, that it was always with the greatest pleasure that he returned to their charming city, in which he always felt so much at home. At a race-meeting at Longchamps, he delighted the *beau monde* by arranging to excuse himself, with impeccable politeness, from the worthy but dull presidential party ('Get me out of this at once!' he hissed to Frederick Ponsonby) in order to spend some time in the Jockey Club stand. And at a glittering banquet at the Elysée he so 'captivated' the guests by the ease, audibility and warmth of his address (so different from the mumblings of the nervous President) that he was given a long and enthusiastic ovation.

When he left Paris on 3 May, his cortège could hardly make its way through the press of wildly cheering people. The visit, wrote the astonished British Ambassador to the British Foreign Secretary, had been 'a success more complete than the most sanguine optimist could have foreseen'.

The subsequent *entente cordiale* between Britain and France, made more tangible by the signing of an Anglo-French agreement in April 1904, was not, of course, solely due to the success of King Edward VII's visit to Paris. Indeed, certain British Ministers considered that it was very little due to him; with or without his active encouragement, the two countries would probably have come to some arrangement. But there is no doubt that the King's state visit created the right climate for such an agreement. 'It was all very well,' argued Frederick Ponsonby, 'for Lord Lansdowne [the Foreign Secretary] to claim afterwards the credit for the *entente cordiale*, but neither he nor the Government could ever have got the French people round from hostility to enthusiastic friendship the way King Edward did.'

In this affair, the King acted as a catalyst. By his dignity, his assurance, his friendliness and his very apparent love of the French people, King Edward VII stilled their suspicions and won their hearts. With that achieved, the politicians could more easily carry public opinion with them. As Paul Cambon, the French Ambassador in London, afterwards remarked, 'any clerk at the Foreign Office could draw up a treaty, but there was no one else who could have succeeded in producing the right atmosphere for a *rapprochement* with France.'

CHAPTER FIFTEEN

The Tsarevich

I

The death of Queen Victoria came as a severe blow to her grand-daughter Alicky, the Empress of Russia. Alicky's first thought on hearing the news had been to travel to England for the funeral but, as she was pregnant, she was dissuaded from doing so. 'How I envy you being able to see beloved Grandmama being taken to her rest,' she wrote to one of her sisters. 'I cannot really believe she has gone, that we shall never see her any more . . . Since one can remember, she was in our life, and a dearer, kinder being never was . . . England without the Queen seems impossible.'

Although apparently such different types, the Queen and her grand-daughter had had certain similarities of temperament. 'The Empress Alexandra,' wrote one of her intimates, 'had the Queen's warm heart, her capacity for great enthusiasms, both for ideas and for people, the same intense sense of duty, the same fidelity in friendship.' Alicky had inherited, too, her grandmother's shyness and her preference for a quiet, well-ordered domestic life.

And Queen Victoria's death had robbed her granddaughter, not only of the woman who had been, as she once said, 'as a mother to me', but of an extremely beneficial influence. Since Alicky's marriage, the two of them had been in regular correspondence. The flow of advice from the practical, sensible and experienced Queen had been of inestimable value to the withdrawn, intense and highly emotional Empress. Queen Victoria's down-to-earth qualities had been the very ones which her grand-daughter lacked; with her gone, there was no one of superior, or even equal rank, to whom Alicky felt that she could look for encouragement.

She was certainly in need of it. Although, by the time of Queen Victoria's death, Alicky had been Tsaritsa for over half a dozen years, she did not yet know how to act the Empress. She remained painfully ill at ease in company; she loathed public appearances. Yet in no court in Europe were sovereigns on such merciless display. The Winter Palace in

St Petersburg, with its magnificent *enfilade* of state rooms, gleaming with marble, porphyry and malachite and glittering with gold, glass and crystal, made an unrivalled setting for the most formal and exacting ceremonial in the world. Everyone moved in strict order of precedence; everything was acted out according to long-established custom. Nicholas and Alexandra were the central figures in a set piece of almost barbaric splendour. From the moment that the great double doors opened and the entire, brilliantly dressed company bowed or curtsied in their honour, the imperial couple were on show. Every move, every gesture, every word was noted and criticized.

For Alicky, it was all a form of torture. In her lavishly embroidered dresses of gold or silver brocade, her waist-long ropes of pearls and a diamond tiara flashing on her red-gold hair, she was breathtaking in her beauty, but her manner lacked all grace and charm. With set mouth, hooded eyes and erect carriage, she moved through all the kaleidoscopic brilliance of the St Petersburg winter season like an automaton. She never relaxed; she never enjoyed herself. She was incapable of saying a gracious word or of making a spontaneous gesture. It was all too obvious that she could hardly wait for the moment when she could take her leave.

And it was not only her shyness that made her appear so unsympathetic in public. Added to it was her hearty disapproval of the majority of the people with whom she was obliged to mix. To this serious-minded young woman, raised under the eye of Grandmama Queen, the decadence of St Petersburg society was abhorrent.

The aristocracy was just as quick to disapprove of her. They found her cold, prudish and provincial. To them, with their French gloss over their Russian barbarism, she was too 'English': with relish they repeated the witticism that whereas Queen Victoria's subjects were gloomy on only one day a week, she kept gloomy on seven. Her piety they found equally disconcerting. The Orthodox religion was something which court and society took for granted. In fashionable St Petersburg, religious observance had become little more than another social diversion; the Easter midnight service was more remarkable for the chic than the fervour of the congregation. Yet here was the Empress taking it all so desperately seriously: studying theology, collecting icons, making pilgrimages and hunting for relics. Already there were stories about the visits of bizarre miracle-workers to the palace – bands of blind nuns, deaf and dumb holy men, dabblers in the occult.

To the Tsaritsa, this aristocratic disapproval meant very little. She felt that she could ignore their opinion. They were not, by her reckoning, real Russians at all. In the Empress's mind, says one of her biographers, Holy Russia meant 'Church, dynasty, nation – in that order.' And by nation Alicky did not mean these amoral aristocrats, any more than she meant any of those other 'undesirables': the striking workers, the fiery students, the pen-pushing clerks or the frock-coated Ministers. To the

Empress, the Russian nation meant the peasants – the humble, simple, devout, unspoilt, unquestioning millions who worked the land. It was to this Russia that she must dedicate herself.

And dedicate herself she did. For if Alexandra had no taste for the public part of her duties, she was beginning to develop an interest in what she, quite rightly, considered to be the more important aspects of the monarchy. In this, she was very much a Coburg; very much Queen Victoria's granddaughter.

Utterly at odds with normal Coburg thinking, however, was her outright rejection of all idea of political reform. Of the enlightenment of her grandfather, Prince Albert, or the passionate liberalism of her aunt, the Empress Frederick, she had inherited nothing. From the beginning Alicky had accepted the principle of autocracy root and branch. One of Nicholas II's first public pronouncements, to the effect that he would 'maintain the principle of autocracy just as firmly and unflinchingly' as had his father, would have had her full approval. Her political creed was simple. The Russian people, who were 'deeply and truly devoted to their sovereign' were none the less 'utterly unbalanced and childlike' and had to be ruled firmly and autocratically. Therefore anyone wanting to destroy this autocracy was automatically an enemy of Russia. And not only an enemy of Russia but an enemy of God. The autocratic Tsar was God's anointed; thus the revolutionaries, or even the reformers, were God's enemies.

None of this is to say that the Empress Alexandra was the hard-hearted, power-hungry virago of her critics' imaginings. She sincerely wanted what was best for Russia. That she was too inexperienced, too straightforward, too simple-minded to appreciate what this best should be would be her undoing. There was nothing wrong with her intentions; it was the way in which she thought they should be made manifest that was to prove so disastrous. She saw the vast Russian Empire, says E. M. Almedingen, 'in terms of a magnified private household'; a household in which her husband was the master and she his right hand.

Nothing could have better epitomized Alexandra's naïve view of Holy Russia than Tsarskoe Selo – the Tsar's village – in which the imperial family lived. Lying some fifteen miles south of St Petersburg, Tsarskoe Selo was an elaborate, self-contained little world, effectively and quite literally sealed off from the harsh realities of life in the capital. Behind the tall, ceaselessly patrolled iron railings of its enormous park, the imperial family could live their make-believe life, unhampered by the presence of either the worthless nobility, the disgruntled proletariat or the sinister revolutionaries. At Tsarskoe Selo one really could believe that God was safely in his heaven, the Tsar safely on his throne and a nation of loyal peasants safely hoeing their fields.

Amidst the ornate splendours of Tsarskoe Selo the imperial family lived a relatively simple life. As was gradually becoming customary all over Europe, life within the private apartments of the Alexander Palace was run on English lines. With their loose covers of brightly coloured cretonne, their white-painted panelling, their lemon wood furniture and their great bowls of freshly picked flowers, the imperial apartments were not unlike those of an English Edwardian country house.

Slightly more exotic was Alexandra's famous mauve boudoir, in which everything – curtains, carpets, furniture, cushions, flowers and the wealth of *objets* – was in shades ranging from the palest lilac to deep violet. The room had, though, (in addition to a reassuringly English cosiness) two undeniably English features: a large photograph of Queen Victoria and a disagreeable Scotch terrier named Eira.

But the room's most striking, if less tangible, reminder of Grandmama Queen was its temperature. It was always cold. 'Like her grandmother, Queen Victoria,' says one of the Empress's ladies, 'she could not stand a temperature that was even moderately warm.'

In this boudoir, in which she could feel safe from the sneers of sophisticated St Petersburg society, Alicky spent a great deal of her time. Wearing unfashionable, but becomingly fluid, dresses in pastel colours, she would lie stretched out on her mauve chaise-longue, writing, reading, doing handwork or drinking tea with her husband. Thus relaxed, Alexandra revealed herself as a charming, compassionate, utterly unaffected woman, deeply interested in everyday things: books, flowers, her children's lessons, her husband's recreations, her household's problems.

The pity of it all was that only those in the immediate imperial circle could appreciate the Empress's good qualities. Even members of the Tsar's family were kept at arm's length. As for the millions upon millions who made up the Russian nation, they knew nothing of their Tsaritsa, except what they were told: that she was arrogant, unfeeling and unpopular.

And there were more sinister tales about her than this. 'Some people say that Alexandra Feodorovna is mad,' wrote Princess Catherine Radziwill, safe behind her pseudonym of Count Paul Vassili, 'and that her madness takes an erotic direction, which accounts for the seclusion in which she is kept.' Of course, continues the Princess self-righteously, 'I do not believe this rumour.'

Unsuccessful in so many ways, Alicky had made an unqualified success of her marriage. She and Nicky were devoted to each other. 'Nicholas II was much more than a loving and devoted husband,' says Mussolov, a member of the imperial household. 'He was literally the lover of his life's partner.' Throughout their married lives, they shared the same bed. Their letters to each other, even in middle age, were love letters. 'When a man likes nothing better than to remain at home with his wife, it is a sure sign that he is very much in love with her,' wrote the visiting Infanta Eulalia, who had known Alicky as a girl. 'Judged by that test, there is no happier couple in Europe than the Emperor and Empress of Russia.'

Nicholas and Alexandra spoke to each other, and to their children, in

English. When the Empress spoke Russian, it was with a strong English accent.

'I will say no more here,' wrote one British Ambassador to St Petersburg, 'than that the Emperor, had he been an Englishman, would have been the most perfect type of English gentleman, and that the Empress, though shy and reserved, was devoted to England and thoroughly English in all her tastes.'

Higher praise, one feels, His Excellency could not possibly have bestowed.

Nowhere was this 'Englishness' of the imperial household more apparent than in the bringing up of the children. They were being raised in what was generally regarded as the British fashion: that is, simply and strictly. They slept on camp beds, they bathed in cold water, they ate plainly cooked food. They were watched over by English nannies. Meals were served on the dot and the day rigidly organized. By the year 1903 Nicky and Alicky had four daughters – Olga, Tatiana, Marie and Anastasia – with only six years separating the eldest from the youngest. Differing in personality, they were none the less all affectionate, obedient and good-natured girls. As their unsociable mother discouraged them from mixing with other children, the four young grand duchesses remained closely attached to each other and to their parents. Together, the six of them made a delightful family group. Amidst all the turbulence of the reign, Tsarskoe Selo remained a haven of peace.

One thing only was lacking to complete this picture of domestic bliss: the Emperor and Empress had no son.

This was not for any want of trying. To present her husband with a son, and the Empire with an heir, was Alicky's dearest wish. The birth of each of their four daughters had meant sharp disappointment for the parents; indeed, after the birth of her last daughter, Anastasia, the Empress had begun to despair. She prayed with increased fervour, she made pilgrimages to little-known sanctuaries, she gave audience to half-crazed prophets, she consulted dubious 'soul doctors'. By the winter of 1903 she was once more pregnant. Finally, on a sultry day in August the following year, and with surprisingly little suffering, she gave birth to a son.

'A great never-to-be-forgotten day when the mercy of God has visited us so clearly,' wrote the jubilant Tsar in his diary on 12 August 1904. 'Alix gave birth to a son at one o'clock. The child has been called Alexis.'

The thirty-two-year-old mother was radiant. Her prayers had been answered: God had given Holy Russia an heir. He was an heir, moreover, who looked the very picture of good health. 'I saw the Tsarevich in the Empress's arms,' wrote one observer. 'How beautiful he was, how healthy, how normal, with his golden hair, his blue eyes, and his expression of intelligence so rare for so young a child.'

The Tsar was no less ecstatic about his son's appearance. 'I don't think you have seen my dear little Tsarevich,' he said to a member of the court

Queen Victoria, the 'Grandmama of Europe', at the age of seventy-five

Queen Victoria's eldest daughter, the brilliant and emotional Vicky, aged forty-seven, in the year that she became German Empress

Queen Victoria, photographed for
her Golden Jubilee. Behind her
stand her eldest son, the
forty-five-year-old Bertie, Prince
of Wales, and her daughter-in-law,
the forty-two-year-old but
perennially youthful-looking
Alexandra, Princess of Wales

Queen Victoria's son-in-law Fritz,
German Crown Prince and later
Kaiser Frederick III, preparing to
take part in the Golden Jubilee
procession

A painting, by Tuxen, of the Grandmama of Europe, surrounded by her enormous family, at the time of her Golden Jubilee

The Wales family in 1889. (Standing, left to right): Eddy (The Duke of Clarence), Maud (later Queen of Norway), the Princess of Wales, Louise (later Duchess of Fife), the Prince of Wales. (Seated): George and Victoria

Queen Victoria, on the arm of her grandson, Willie, German Crown Prince, arriving in Berlin to visit her dying son-in-law, Kaiser Frederick III. Behind her walk her daughter Vicky, the German Empress, Crown Princess Dona, and three of Vicky's daughters

Four generations: Queen Victoria
holds Prince Edward of York (later
King Edward VIII and Duke of
Windsor). Behind stand Bertie, the
Prince of Wales and Georgie, the Duke
of York

The wedding of Tino and Sophie in
the cathedral in Athens. Eddy, the
Duke of Clarence, holds the crown
above his cousin Sophie's head

Sophie, daughter of the Empress
Frederick, and Crown Prince
Constantine of Greece, at the time of
their marriage in 1889

Queen Victoria's granddaughter, Alicky, the intense and introspective Empress of Russia, during the early years of her marriage

Queen Victoria with the Prince of Wales, Tsar Nicholas II, the Tsaritsa Alexandra and their baby, the Grand Duchess Olga, during the visit of the Russian imperial family to Balmoral in 1896

Nando, Crown Prince Ferdinand of Romania, holding his eldest son, Carol (afterwards King Carol II of Romania)

The beautiful and theatrical Marie of Romania, in one of her exotic rooms at Cotroceni Palace in 1907

King Alfonso XIII and Queen Ena
of Spain, in the early days of their
marriage

King Alfonso XIII and Queen Ena,
photographed on the way back from
their wedding, seconds before the
bomb was thrown at their carriage

The Empress Alexandra of Russia, at the height of her beauty and power

The bizarre Queen Marie of Romania, in her specially designed crown and robes, at her coronation in 1922

The funeral procession of Edward VII, attended by nine monarchs and a gathering of other royalties from all over Europe

Princess Maud of Wales and
Prince Charles of Denmark
(later King and Queen of
Norway), at the time of their
marriage

The first coronation ever
photographed; the enthronement of
King Haakon and Queen Maud in
Trondheim Cathedral in June 1906

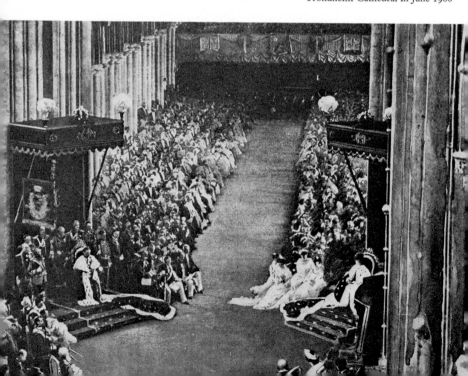

The spartan and soldierly King Alexander of Yugoslavia

The honest-to-goodness Queen Marie of Yugoslavia, with her sons Peter, Andrej and Tomislav

The scene after the assassination of King Alexander of Yugoslavia in Marseilles in 1934

Princess Sophie of Greece at
the time of her conversion to
the Greek Orthodox faith and
subsequent banishment from
Germany by her brother,
Kaiser Wilhelm II

Mignon, daughter of Queen Marie of
Romania and wife of King Alexander,
holding her eldest son Peter, afterwards
King Peter II of Yugoslavia

Princess Louise of Battenberg, afterwards
Queen of Sweden, painted by Philip
Laszlo

Queen Ena of Spain, painted by
Philip Laszlo

Crown Prince Frederik of
Denmark and Princess Ingrid of
Sweden after their marriage in
Stockholm in 1935

King Frederik IX and Queen
Ingrid of Denmark later in life

The scholarly King **Gustav** VI Adolf of Sweden

The vivacious Queen Louise of Sweden

a few months after the boy's birth. 'Come along, I will show him to you.'

The baby was being bathed. Standing him up in the palm of one of his hands, Nicholas showed him off. 'There he was,' says the admiring visitor, 'naked, chubby, rosy – a wonderful boy!'

'Don't you think he's a beauty?' asked the Tsar proudly.

2

For Nicholas and Alexandra, the birth of the Tsarevich Alexis was the one shaft of light in a frighteningly stormy sky. Abroad and at home, the Russian Empire was in serious trouble. February 1904 saw the beginning of a disastrous war with Japan; January the following year saw the beginning of a revolution.

Lying just off the farthest-flung rim of the Russian Empire, almost half a world away from St Petersburg, was the burgeoning island empire of Japan. For some years the two empires had been squabbling over the Pacific seaboard of yet a third empire – the decaying Chinese Empire. By the year 1903 Russia, much to the chagrin of the Japanese, had already bullied China into handing over its most valuable Pacific coast possessions. When the Russians began advancing into the Korean peninsula as well, Japan decided that she could stand for no more. In February 1904, without a formal declaration of war, Japanese ships attacked a Russian squadron lying off Russian-controlled Port Arthur.

The war that followed was a disaster for Russia. The Japanese, fighting so near home, were in a much better position than the Russians whose lines of communication (restricted to the still incomplete Trans-Siberian railway line) stretched for some four thousand miles. Again and again the Russians were obliged to fall back before the Japanese forces. By the summer of 1904, Port Arthur was in a state of siege.

At sea, the situation was even worse. With the Russian Far Eastern Fleet immobilized at Port Arthur, the Russian Baltic Fleet was sent to its aid. Leaving St Petersburg, it was obliged to sail through the North Sea, all the way round Africa and across the Indian Ocean to Japan. As it finally steamed through the Strait of Tsushima, eight months after setting out, it was attacked by the Japanese. In an engagement that lasted for less than an hour, the Russian Fleet was all but annihilated.

In the meantime Russian-held Port Arthur, having withstood the Japanese bombardment for months, finally surrendered in January 1905.

Both on land and at sea, Russia had been humiliatingly defeated. The loss of Russian lives had been tremendous.

News of the surrender of Port Arthur intensified the feeling of discontent throughout the country. Not only were there demands that the war, with its frightening death toll, should end, but that the shocking conditions in factories and on the lands should be improved. In addition, the people wanted some say in their government. It was considered iniquitous that in the year 1905 they should be at the mercy of the Tsar's will, or rather, of that will implemented by a harsh and repressive government. They wanted a fully representative assembly – a Duma.

By January thousands of workers in St Petersburg were on strike. As yet, their demands could hardly be called revolutionary. Their anger was directed, not at Tsar Nicholas II, but at his government. Appreciating this fact, a sympathetic priest named Father George Gapon decided to take control of the situation. He would rally the workers and lead them in peaceful procession to the Winter Palace. Here he would hand a petition, listing their grievances, to the Tsar. The Tsar, he assured the workers, would listen to their plea. Was he not the father of all Russians?

On the morning of Sunday, 22 January 1905, Father Gapon led his march through the snowy streets towards the Winter Palace. The crowd was good-natured and expectant. They carried flags, icons, crosses, religious banners and pictures of the Tsar and, as they tramped along, they sang the imperial anthem, 'God Save the Tsar'.

Within seconds, however, the cheerful scene changed to one of tragedy. The troops guarding the approaches to the Palace lost their heads and opened fire. In their hundreds, the bullet-riddled corpses of men, women and children crumpled to the ground; before the Tsar's Palace, the white snow was red with blood. From thenceforth the day, which had started so optimistically, was to be known as 'Bloody Sunday', and Nicholas II as a blood-stained tyrant.

But he was not directly to blame. Unsuspected by Father Gapon and his marchers, the Tsar was not even in the Winter Palace that day. He was at Tsarkoe Selo. Nor had he known anything about Father Gapon's petition. Whether or not he would have accepted the petition is uncertain but he certainly did not, as was generally believed, order the troops to open fire on the crowd. The news of the massacre upset him terribly: 'Lord, how painful and sad this is!' he wrote that evening.

The Empress was no less upset but her reaction tended to be more defiant. In a letter to her sister, Princess Victoria of Battenberg, she tried to justify their position: the Tsar lacked good advisers, foreign newspapers were exaggerating the casualties, the crowd had refused to retreat when told to do so. St Petersburg was 'a rotten town, not one atom Russian', the petition had made 'atrocious' demands, Russia could not possibly be given a parliament, the people were not ready for a constitution.

The troubles did not end with 'Bloody Sunday'. On the contrary, it marked their beginning. For a year all Russia was in turmoil. The Tsar's uncle, the reactionary Grand Duke Serge, who was married to Alicky's sister Ella, was blown to bits in Moscow. The Black Sea Fleet mutinied. There were murders, strikes, riots and uprisings throughout the Empire. Russia, soundly thrashed by the Japanese, was forced to make peace. By October the country was crippled by strikes. No trains ran, schools and universities were closed, shops were empty. The streets of the capital resounded to the cries of 'Long live the Workers' Soviet!' and 'Down with the Tsar!' as banner-waving students and workers clashed with sabre-slashing Cossacks.

To avert a full-scale revolution, something had to be done. Daily the anguished Tsar conferred with his most able Minister, Count Sergius Witte. Witte gave his master a choice: the rebellion must be crushed by force or the country given a constitution. Nicholas, who hated having to make choices, was urged by Witte to grant a constitution. Reluctantly, the Tsar agreed.

By the Imperial Manifesto of 30 October 1905, Russia ceased to be an absolute autocracy and became a type of constitutional monarchy. Although this granting of a constitution by no means ended all unrest, it did avert a revolution.

The first Duma was opened in the throne room of the Winter Palace in the spring of 1906. Into this magnificent setting, and looking distinctly out of place amongst the gorgeously uniformed councillors of state, senators, diplomats and courtiers, came the newly-elected members of the Duma, some of them in workers' blouses and breeches. In front of his great gilt throne stood the Tsar and beside him the Tsaritsa, looking superb in white with a single strand of pearls about her neck.

But neither husband nor wife had much faith in the régime which the Tsar was about to inaugurate. 'I hear everybody talking about a new era,' said Alexandra afterwards, 'but I see no signs of it. They all talk about the Duma as though its opening were to be some kind of re-birth. They'll merely talk and talk.'

She was right. But she was quite wrong in imagining that the imperial throne would be made safer for her son in any way other than by the relinquishing of what she looked upon as a God-given autocracy.

CHAPTER SIXTEEN

Revolutionary Queen

Very different from the introspective Empress Alexandra was her cousin Maud, the daughter of King Edward VII and the wife of Prince Charles of Denmark. By the summer of 1905 Princess Maud was thirty-five years old and had been married for nine years. She and her husband, the gangling, good-natured Prince Charles, had only one child, Prince Alexander, who had been born in 1903. The responsibilities of marriage and motherhood had made very little difference to Maud's looks, personality or way of life. With her piled coiffure, her high collars and her small, slim-waisted figure, she was still like an echo of her mother, Queen Alexandra. She remained as unaffected, as tomboyish and as fond of the outdoors as she had ever been. She still divided her time between her little palace in Copenhagen, and Appleton, her adored English country home near Sandringham.

Of all Queen Victoria's granddaughters living on the Continent, none remained more persistently English than Princess Maud. Her talk, interests and pursuits were those of English county society; she was never happier than when gardening, riding, bicycling or driving a wagonette. Although ill at ease in public, in her intimate circle she was said to be 'full of chaff'. Her tone was bantering and her conversation peppered with words like 'rotter' and 'bounder'. 'That's rot. It's because you funk,' she once shouted to a companion who had protested that his horse was incapable of jumping a hedge.

On King Edward VII's spring cruises in the Mediterranean, she was full of what her companions considered to be the greatest fun. Knowing that the commodore of the royal yacht was terrified of monkeys, she once played a leading part in an elaborate practical joke whereby the poor commodore was convinced that a monkey was being brought on board. Such escapades were guaranteed to reduce the members of the party, including King Edward and Queen Alexandra, to fits of uncontrollable laughter.

With her family, and particularly with her mother and her unmarried sister, Princess Victoria, Maud kept on the closest terms. 'The habit of relying on her mother's taste and judgement has remained with Princess Maud even since she has a home of her own,' wrote one member of the royal circle, 'and every opportunity of spending time with her parents is eagerly seized.'

However, the days of such complete freedom from responsibility were about to come to an end. A somewhat gentlemanly revolution in Denmark's near neighbour, Norway, was to bring about a change in the life of the hoydenish Princess Maud.

Ever since the end of the Napoleonic wars, in 1815, Norway had been tied to Sweden by an Act of Union. It was an unsatisfactory arrangement. Although Norway enjoyed a certain degree of autonomy (it had its own parliament, the Storting) Sweden was the dominant partner. The King of Sweden reigned over both countries. Throughout the nineteenth century, relations between the two countries had become increasingly bitter. The independent-minded Norwegians were anxious for more say in the running of their own affairs and the Swedes were just as anxious to keep control of both countries in their own hands. Early in 1905, things came to a head.

The particular point at issue was whether or not Norway should have its own consular representation. Having agitated, for years, for such representation, the Norwegians finally lost patience. In March 1905 the Storting defiantly passed a bill by which Norway would in future have its own consuls. The bill was sent to King Oscar II of Sweden for his sanction. This the King refused to give. Thereupon the Norwegian government resigned. The King, finding himself unable to form a new government, refused to accept their resignation. This meant, argued the Norwegians, that as their country had no government and as the King was incapable of forming one, the King of Sweden had ceased to function as King of Norway. In other words, the Act of Union between the two countries had been dissolved. The Storting then instructed the Norwegian Council of State to take over the government of the country. In June 1905, the President of the Storting formally announced the dissolution of the Union and the independence of Norway.

As revolutions went, it had not been much of one, but a revolution, nevertheless, it had been. However, to soften the blow, Norway offered its now vacant throne to a member of the Swedish King's family. To this conciliatory offer, the unresigned King Oscar gave no immediate reply. As far as he was concerned, the Union had not yet been dissolved and the throne – whatever Norway might claim – was not yet vacant.

The fact that Norway intended to remain a monarchy came as a great relief to Europe's family of kings. There was a strongly republican element in the country that saw no reason why, having rid itself of one king, Norway should saddle itself with another. On the other hand, even among republicans, it was appreciated that the monarchies of Europe would look more kindly on the newly independent country if it were headed by a monarch. A king would give the revolution an air of respectability. This was how revolutionary Italy had managed things a generation before; 'like Garibaldi,' wrote one prominent Norwegian republican in an open letter to another, 'we two old republicans have no choice but to serve a king'.

But who was this king to be? Although, unofficially, King Oscar of Sweden had indicated that no member of his house would accept the throne, the Norwegian offer had not been formally rejected. Nor would it be, until Norway had fulfilled one Swedish condition: Sweden would recognize Norwegian independence only after the parliaments of the two countries had formally negotiated the dissolution of the Act of Union. Until such time, Sweden maintained that Norway had no right to offer the throne to anyone.

Norway, on the other hand, was determined that the throne be filled before negotiations began. A king, setting the seal on Norwegian independence, would gain the country international recognition and thus strengthen its hand in the negotiations with Sweden.

While this vexed question of priorities remained unsolved, Norway started looking round for a monarch. A prince from the ruling house of one of the Great Powers was out of the question: it would make things far too complicated. There was some talk of a Greek or even a Spanish prince but, in the end, it was agreed that the candidate would have to come from either Sweden or Denmark. With the King of Sweden unlikely to accept the offer for a member of his family, the field was narrowed to the Danish House of Glucksburg.

Here there were two likely candidates: Prince Waldemar, the youngest son of old King Christian IX of Denmark, and Prince Charles, second son of the Danish Crown Prince and the husband of Princess Maud.

As Prince Waldemar was already forty-seven years old, with a Roman Catholic wife and grown-up children; he was not considered very suitable. Prince Charles, on the other hand, was still in his early thirties, with a son not yet three years old and a wife who was the daughter of King Edward VII of England. An added advantage was that Prince Charles's mother, the Danish Crown Princess, was a member of the Swedish royal family. In every way, Prince Charles seemed eminently suitable.

The candidate himself was not quite so sure. When approached, in confidence, by the Norwegian emissary, Baron Wedel, the unassuming Prince Charles was hesitant. He protested that he did not want to be a king, that he was quite happy with his position as an officer in the Danish Navy and that he hated the idea of leaving Denmark. His reluctance was shared by his wife, Princess Maud. If Charles had no desire to become a king, she had even less to become a queen. She had no taste for ceremonial and no talent for public life. Amongst strangers, she was painfully shy. And would it not spell the end of her comfortable life: those months at Appleton, that bicycling through the streets of Copenhagen, those cruises in the Mediterranean, in short, the whole informal, unpretentious, countrified atmosphere of her days? If Maud did not actually discourage her husband from thinking of accepting the throne, she would certainly have done nothing to encourage him.

However, they were both royalties and, as such, conscious of what they considered to be their duty. However distasteful the idea might seem, it would not have occurred to them to reject a formal offer of a crown. Princes had obligations which could not be shirked; royal blood entailed royal duties. Both Prince Charles and Princess Maud came from houses with an unshakable sense of royal dedication.

Thus, stifling his own inclinations, Prince Charles assured Baron Wedel that he would accept an offer of the crown but only, he protested, if he could be of real service to Norway. And then it must be with the approval of Sweden, Denmark and Great Britain and, of course, with the whole-hearted consent of the Norwegian people. He had no wish to behave like an ambitious adventurer or what his wife would no doubt have called a 'bounder'. In any case, until the crown had been definitely refused by the Swedish royal house, Prince Charles was prepared to make no move whatsoever.

Not everyone shared the couple's somewhat lukewarm approach. By now the various sovereigns of Europe were becoming distinctly agitated. As summer turned to autumn and the King of Sweden still refused to give an answer until the formal dissolution of the Union had been negotiated, the situation became increasingly tense. There was talk of war between the two countries; there was evidence of a growing republicanism in Norway.

Maud's cousin, Kaiser Wilhelm II, who must needs have a finger in every pie, was becoming more and more alarmed. At first, on the Norwegian declaration of independence, he had been all in favour of the King of Sweden taking firm measures. A fellow sovereign, he maintained, had been grossly insulted; he could not condone what he somewhat wittily described as 'kings being dismissed by registered letter'. Broken rights, thundered the Kaiser, must be restored by force. The Crown was 'sacred above all else'. But now, with Norwegian republicanism becoming more voluble by the day, he climbed down somewhat. He urged King Oscar to recognize Norwegian independence and to accept the throne for a member of his house. In his yacht, *Hohenzollern*, Wilhelm sailed to Finland to confer with Tsar Nicholas II. Both agreed that King Oscar should accept the Norwegian offer. It would be one sure way of preventing what they disliked almost as much as the idea of a Norwegian republic: that is, a Norwegian king whose father-in-law would be King Edward VII of England.

Yet when the Kaiser, who was as false and fickle as the wind, visited

Copenhagen on his way back, he pretended that he was all in favour of Prince Charles accepting the throne. Nothing, he assured his cousin Maud, would delight him more. He even lifted the little Prince Alexander onto his knee and addressed him as 'Der Kronprinz Norwegens'.

For this particular piece of duplicity, Prince Charles was prepared. His father-in-law, King Edward, had warned him what to expect. 'Am quite aware of double game going on to prevent your going to Norway,' he had wired the day before the Kaiser's arrival. 'Pray warn your Grandfather and Father when the German Emperor comes to be firm. I strongly urge that you should go to Norway as soon as possible to prevent someone else taking your place.'

Indeed, of all the royalties involved, none was more determined that Prince Charles should become King of Norway than King Edward VII. He was in a state of high excitement about the affair. Prince Charles, he urged, was not to wait for a decision by the King of Sweden: he was to set off immediately for Norway to claim the throne. Hardly a day went by without yet another frantic telegram from King Edward, begging his son-in-law to go to Norway before it was too late.

To this barrage of telegrams, the circumspect Prince Charles replied that he could not go until his grandfather, old King Christian IX of Denmark, had given him formal permission to do so. This the old monarch refused to do until the King of Sweden had officially renounced the throne. And this, in turn, the King of Sweden stubbornly refused to do until negotiations on the dissolution of the Union had been concluded.

But King Edward would not be put off. He tried another approach. He wrote to the Swedish Crown Prince, asking for Prince Charles to be given some sort of provisional recognition so that he could go to Norway and take part in the negotiations. To this suggestion, the Swedes refused to listen. Until agreement had been reached on the dissolution of the Union, answered the Swedish Crown Prince, the question of the throne could not be discussed.

It was as well, perhaps, that the notoriously short-tempered King Edward was at Marienbad, taking his cure, when this answer arrived.

Eventually, Norway was obliged to give in. She agreed to negotiate. The talks opened in September. With these successfully concluded, Sweden recognized Norwegian independence and refused the offer of the throne for a Swedish prince. The crown could at last be offered to Prince Charles of Denmark.

Yet once again Prince Charles proved hesitant. Worried by the apparent strength of republican sentiment in Norway (he was being inundated with republican literature) he insisted on a plebiscite. Only if the great majority of the Norwegian people wanted him would be become their king. He did not want to force himself on Norway; he had no wish to become a party king. In the face of considerable opposition, including that of his exasperated father-in-law ('King Edward furious at idea of referendum,' wired Baron Wedel from London) Prince Charles held firm.

The plebiscite was held on 12 and 13 November 1905. Some 260,000 voted in favour of a monarchy and some 70,000 against: a majority of more than five to one. Five days later the Storting met to elect Prince Charles of Denmark as King of Norway. Henceforth Prince Charles was to be known as King Haakon VII (the last King Haakon had died in 1380) and his little son Alexander as Crown Prince Olav.

Baron Wedel, rushing to Prince Charles's palace in Copenhagen to congratulate him on his election, was ushered into a charmingly domestic scene. Princess Maud was at her desk, sorting through a pile of papers; how on earth, she exclaimed, was she going to be ready to leave in a week's time? Across the room, at another desk, sat her husband, diligently practising his new signature – Haakon.

On 20 November 1905, in the Throne Room of the Amelienborg Palace in Copenhagen, Prince Charles of Denmark formally accepted the Norwegian throne. By his side, small, stiff and dressed all in white, stood Princess Maud. The ceremony concluded, the new King and Queen drove through cheering crowds to their own palace where they held a reception for the members of the Norwegian delegation. Four days later, aboard the *Dannebrog*, they sailed into the Norwegian capital of Christiania – later Oslo. In swirling snow, they stepped ashore.

King Edward was highly gratified. Both Charles and Maud, he assured his son George, the Prince of Wales, 'have won golden opinions and Charles's speeches are *very* good'.

Not everyone shared the King's gratification. 'So Maud is sitting upon her unsafe throne . . .' wrote the outraged old Duchess of Mecklenburg-Strelitz to her niece, Princess May, 'he making speeches, poor fellow, thanking the revolutionary Norwegians for having *elected* him! No really, it is all too odd!' Besides, added the old lady sourly, 'they have but that one *peaky* Boy.'

It was all 'too horrible,' she thought, 'for an English Princess to sit upon a Revolutionary Throne!'

2

That her throne was a 'revolutionary' one, would not have bothered Queen Maud unduly; much more unnerving for her was the fact that she was sitting on a throne at all. She was not cut out to be a queen. Like so many of Queen Victoria's descendants – and, indeed, like Queen Victoria herself – Maud was inordinately shy. Whereas her husband, King Haakon, soon developed an easy public manner, she did not. Amongst strangers, she appeared stiff, reserved, even cold. She seemed incapable of making a relaxed or spontaneous gesture. Dressed with all the rich elegance, but none of the flair, of her mother, Queen Alexandra, she had the look, in these early days, of a marionette. The Swedish Minister (not, admittedly, an impartial observer) was delighted to report that on the occasion of his first audience with her, she simply stood before him, as mute and immobile as a statue.

Her domestic life, too, had its problems. Transported, almost overnight, from a twelve-roomed apartment in Copenhagen to the immense Kongens Slot – Royal Palace – in Christiania, she was obliged to make considerable adjustments. Not only did her days become busier, more complicated and more formal, but she had to organize her new home. The vast, pillared, butter-coloured palace had never been designed as a permanent residence. The Swedish royal family, whose home was in Stockholm, had had it built for ceremonial purposes only. Comfort and convenience had been sacrificed to prestige. The rooms were magnificent but utterly uninhabitable. The entire building boasted only one bath and that had been installed a mere half a dozen years before. Not even in the royal apartments was there a lavatory. The household was expected to manage with wash-hand stands, basins and buckets. All the meals and all the water had to be lugged up from the kitchens in the basement and all the slops carried down. Most of the furniture, which had been the personal property of the King of Sweden, had been taken back to Stockholm. Queen Maud's furniture, brought over from those twelve rooms in Copenhagen, made very little impression on these gigantic apartments.

Luckily, in the attics and servants' quarters, the Queen discovered a wealth of long-discarded, Empire-style pieces which were, at that time, coming back into favour. As she shared the contemporary interest in Napoleon, this furniture suited her collection of Napoleonic portraits and *objets* very well. But as even those pieces did not fully equip the vast palace, the government solved the problem by buying up all the furniture when the contents of the mansion of a wealthy banker were sold.

If Queen Maud had little taste for her public duties, she had a real talent for creating a cheerful domestic atmosphere. The Norwegian royal ménage was one of the happiest and most harmonious in Europe. Life within the palace was run, inevitably, on English lines. Husband and wife spoke to each other in English and little Olav was in the care of two English nannies, Miss Butler and Miss Jones. The private apartments, a-clutter with family photographs, family gifts and conventionally pretty paintings, were extremely comfortable. The Queen busied herself with her rose garden, her English horses and her dogs. She took Norwegian lessons and she learnt to ski. She delighted in their house in Kongseteren, a mountain chalet, built in traditional Norwegian style, which their subjects had given them as a welcoming gift.

As a condition of acceptance of the throne, King Haakon had stipulated that his wife must be allowed to spend a certain period of each year in England. In that way, Maud was not deprived of those autumn months at Appleton.

Away from the intimidating eyes of strangers, Queen Maud was at her best: cheerful, warm-hearted, easily amused. She retained her keen sense of the ridiculous. She was never stuffy, never disapproving. Fridtjof Nansen, the celebrated explorer and great friend of the royal family, gives an account of a reception in the little town of Vadsø, in Norway's arctic north, which illustrates the Queen's well-known appreciation of a comic situation. Indeed, it is all reminiscent of one of her own practical jokes.

After a luncheon, at which the Queen's table companion, a self-important local dignitary, had been so engrossed in his food that he had not bothered to address one word to her, the royal party was solemnly conducted to a stairway which was to lead them to the reception on the floor above. To the consternation of the hosts, the stairs were found to be chock-a-block with half-empty beer bottles. They had been left there by the members of the band, in their hurry to get away at the approach of the official party. A frantic scramble to get the bottles cleared away resulted in the beer coursing down the stairs like a river. By now the Queen was battling to keep a straight face. The way finally cleared, the royalties were ushered up the wet and pungent staircase, to be met, on the landing, by a singular sight. There, presumably open for use during the coming reception, and taking up most of the space, stood an old-fashioned commode. Solemnly, in single file, the party was obliged to skirt it and make their way into the room in which the local ladies stood waiting to be presented. It was the sort of situation in which the irrepressible Maud delighted; only by exercising the utmost control could she prevent herself from exploding with laughter.

One imagines that the reaction of her grandmother, Queen Victoria, to such a situation would have been very different.

On 22 June 1906, seven months after their arrival in the country, King Haakon and Queen Maud were crowned. The Coronation took place in the old Gothic Cathedral at Trondheim, a straggling little city half-way up Norway's rugged western coastline. It was here that the old kings of Norway had been crowned. The royal party travelled to Trondheim through the heart of the country: by rail as far as they could and then by carriage to Andalsnes on the coast. From here they sailed to Trondheim. The coronation journey – this act, as it were, of 'taking possession' of their kingdom, introduced the King and Queen to some of Norway's most spectacular scenery. For the first time they saw the towering, snow-capped mountains, the wild, desolate countryside, the plummeting white waterfalls, the glaciers, the lakes, the fjords. For both Haakon and Maud, with their strong feeling for the outdoors, it was all enchantment. 'I have never seen a landscape with dimensions like this,' enthused the King. After each overnight stop, he would be up at six to take in his fill of this natural grandeur.

Trondheim had been transformed. The streets were gay with flags, stands had been built outside the old Cathedral, and at anchor in the harbour rode the yachts belonging to the various royal guests attending the Coronation. As the city had no palace, a special wooden building, the Stiftsgaarden, had been renovated for the use of the royal family. The rest of the royalties, including Maud's brother Prince George and his wife Princess May, were obliged to live on their yachts.

The Coronation ceremony was an unpretentious affair. It was as though the government was determined to stress the democratic spirit of the régime. Although, in theory (because the Norwegian constitution was not altered until 1908 and Haakon thus inherited the 1814 constitution) the King possessed more personal power than any sovereign in Europe other than the Tsar, in practice he was very much a constitutional monarch. To underline this, he was crowned jointly by the Bishop of Bergen and the Prime Minister. He was declared duly crowned by the President of the Storting. And when, two years later, the constitution was altered, the symbolic crowning was abolished for future kings.

'A *revolutionary* Coronation! such a *farce*,' wrote the unresigned Grand Duchess of Mecklenburg-Strelitz to Princess May. '*I* don't like your being there for it, it looks like *sanctioning* all that nasty Revolution . . . .'

But for all that, the ceremony was not unimpressive. King Haakon VII, so tall, erect and wearing an ermine-trimmed mantle, played his part with ease and authority. Queen Maud, in a dress of embroidered white satin, looked suitably regal. The watching Princess May considered it all 'fine and impressive – very well done and both Charles and Maud did it all in a dignified manner and both looked very well with the Crowns on their heads'.

But Princess May's Aunt Augusta was not to be won over. 'How can a future King and Queen of England go to witness a Coronation "*par la grâce du Peuple de la Revolution*"!!! makes me sick and I should say, *you too.*'

To this, the always tactful Princess May replied that 'The whole thing seems curious, but we live in *very* modern days.'

CHAPTER SEVENTEEN

Ena of Spain

I

In October 1887, the year of Queen Victoria's Golden Jubilee, her youngest child, Princess Beatrice of Battenberg, had given birth to a daughter. The girl had been christened Victoria Eugenie: Victoria after the Queen, and Eugenie after the ex-Empress of the French, who was living in exile in England. Throughout her long and often turbulent life, however, Victoria Eugenie was always known as Ena.

Princess Ena had been the second of the four children of Prince Henry and Princess Beatrice of Battenberg; the only girl amongst three boys. Of all Queen Victoria's granddaughters, not one had been more closely associated with the daily life of the Queen. Ena's mother, the shy Princess Beatrice, had been the Queen's constant companion. It was a position which had in no way been altered by Beatrice's marriage, at the relatively late age of twenty-eight, to the dashing Prince Henry of Battenberg. The Queen, determined to keep at least one of her children always by her side, had insisted that Prince Henry and Princess Beatrice make their home with her. Thus, as Queen Victoria had moved, with unvarying regularity, between Windsor, Osborne, Balmoral and Cimiez in the South of France, so had the Battenbergs moved with her. The death of Prince Henry (he had died, somewhat unheroically, from fever while taking part in the Ashanti campaign, in 1896) had made very little difference to this pattern of life. For Princess Beatrice, it had meant that she must spend even more time in her mother's company; for her four children, it meant that their lives became still more closely involved with that of the Queen.

They spent part of every day with their grandmother. Rising early, the young Battenbergs would breakfast with the Queen; on the lawns, under her parasol tent if it were fine, and indoors if it were not. They would devote the morning to study, join the Queen after luncheon for dessert, spend the afternoon out of doors and then rejoin the Queen for tea. To them, she was 'Gangan': a softly-spoken, loving, understanding grandmother, the fount of all 'treats'. To her, they were like a touch of spring, bringing to her old age a wonderful warmth and radiance. That the Queen's last years were distinctly less gloomy than her middle ones was in no small measure due to the constant presence of the four high-spirited, affectionate and endearing Battenberg children. 'I love these darling children so, almost as much as their own parents,' she exclaimed on one occasion.

Ena, who was eight years old at the time of her father's death in 1896, looked the perfect English princess: golden-haired, blue-eyed, fresh-complexioned. As the only girl amongst three lively brothers, she tended to share their interests and pastimes. She could ride a horse, row a boat or handle a fishing rod as well as any of them. She adored the open air. Like her older cousin, Princess Maud, there was something tomboyish about Ena. She glowed with good health and had a frank, somewhat outspoken manner.

Yet under this honest-to-goodness veneer lay a deeply sensitive nature. Even in childhood there was a vulnerability, a certain *tristesse* about Princess Ena of Battenberg. 'Ena has a charming disposition, so affectionate and full of feeling,' the Empress Frederick had once written, with some perspicacity, to her daughter Sophie. 'She is so sensitive that I fear she will never find life easy.'

The death of Queen Victoria brought considerable change to the life of the widowed Princess Beatrice and her children. Overnight, they slipped down the scale of importance. With the royal centre of gravity swinging to her brother, King Edward VII, Princess Beatrice – who had been the Queen's right hand – became simply another relatively un-important member of the family. Osborne House, which, more than any other of the royal residences, had meant home to the Battenbergs, was handed over to the Navy and Princess Beatrice was obliged to move into Osborne Cottage. Ill at ease in her brother's dazzling circle, the un-sophisticated Princess Beatrice spent very little time at the new court.

None the less, she still had a role to play. There were bazaars to open and hospitals to visit and functions to attend. And always with Princess Beatrice was her daughter, the fair-haired Princess Ena. In 1904, soon after her seventeenth birthday, Ena was officially presented at her uncle's court. By now, the somewhat rough-and-tumble girl had developed into an accomplished and dignified young princess. Only amongst her inti-mates did she reveal her warmth of heart and depth of feeling.

One of these intimates was her godmother, the Empress Eugenie. Ever since the collapse of the French Second Empire in 1870, the Empress Eugenie had lived in England. Regarded as the 'Tragic Empress' because of the loss of first, her throne, then her husband, the Emperor Napoleon III, and finally her only child, the Prince Imperial, the Empress Eugenie lived in a vast, rambling mansion known as Farnborough Hill in Hamp-shire. At the time of the death of Queen Victoria, with whom she had been very friendly, the Empress had been in her mid-seventies.

A woman of boundless energy, forthright views, considerable charm and enduring beauty, the Empress had always taken an interest in Princess Beatrice. Indeed, it had at one time been rumoured that this youngest daughter of Queen Victoria was to marry the Prince Imperial. His death, fighting for the British army in South Africa in 1879, had put an end to any such speculation, but the Empress had remained on the friendliest terms with Princess Beatrice and her family. It was some measure of the strength of this friendship with the British royal family that the sternly Protestant Queen Victoria had allowed the unquestioningly Catholic Empress to become godmother to the baby Princess Ena. Not many weeks went by without a visit by Princess Beatrice and her daughter Princess Ena to the fascinating old Empress at Farnborough Hill.

As Eugenie had been born a Spaniard, and as she adored young people, Princess Ena often met young Spanish noblemen at Farnborough Hill. Among them were friends of the young unmarried King of Spain, Alfonso XIII. An inveterate matchmaker, the Empress had always been interested in the future marriage of the young Spanish King. She had also, of course, given a great deal of thought to the matrimonial prospects of her goddaughter, Princess Ena. In her opinion, Alfonso and Ena would be very well suited. And what a brilliant match it would be for this relatively obscure English princess. The proposed state visit to England by the nineteen-year-old King Alfonso, in the summer of 1905, would see if she were right.

Alfonso XIII had been born a king. His father, the debonair young King Alfonso XII, had died six months before his birth. His mother, the reserved Queen Maria Cristina (she had been born an archduchess of Austria) had acted as Regent until his official coming of age, at sixteen, in 1902. That this young monarch should marry and start a family as soon as possible was the dearest wish of his Ministers. The history of Spain during the nineteenth century had been one of continuous and bloody strife: a succession of assassinations, uprisings and wars. The monarchy had been repeatedly threatened and even overthrown – sometimes by revolution, sometimes by the rival branch of the royal family, more recently by anarchists. Only in Russia did royalty live so constantly under the threat of an assassin's bomb. A royal visit to Spain was always looked upon as an extremely hazardous undertaking; King Edward VII stoutly refused to venture any further into the country than San Sebastian, the royal seaside home lying so reassuringly close to France. It was small wonder that Spanish politicians considered that the sooner their young monarch secured the succession, the better.

Nor were Alfonso XIII's Ministers the only ones anxious that he should marry. The other sovereigns of Europe were hardly less impatient. Not for years had so eligible a bridegroom come onto the market. Young Alfonso might not have been conventionally handsome but for a king – and a Spanish Bourbon at that – he was not at all bad. Slightly above average height, he was lean, lithe and athletic. His skin glowed with good health. His beak-like Bourbon nose jutted proudly from his long head; his eyes were alive with youth and high spirits. His smile was dazzling; his expression alert.

The same animation marked his personality. He was quick-witted, precocious, something of a prodigy. His charm was exceptional. Only on closer acquaintance did one come up against his failings: his wilfulness, his imperiousness, his determination to get his own way.

Still, whatever his faults, it was not every day that a princess of one's house had the opportunity of becoming the Queen of Spain. With Germany chock-a-block with marriageable princesses, some of them Catholic, Kaiser Wilhelm II wasted no time. Brushing aside a nice point as to whether Alfonso should not, in fact, have visited him first, the Kaiser descended on Vigo and there reviewed the Spanish fleet. King Edward VII, no less anxious but rather less impulsive, confined his attentions to sending his brother, the Duke of Connaught, to bestow the Order of the Garter on the young King. As the Duke of Connaught had an eligible daughter, Princess Patricia, King Edward VII hoped that the gesture would draw Alfonso's attention to his niece. The idea of an English alliance was eagerly taken up by Liberal politicians in Spain. Photographs of Princess Patricia began to appear in Spanish journals with embarrassing frequency.

However, Alfonso was not going to be hustled into a political marriage. He would never, he assured a friend, choose his bride by photograph; he would see her for himself. The proposed state visits to Paris and London in 1905, soon after his nineteenth birthday, promised him just such an opportunity.

In republican France, of course, there was no hope of being offered a royal bride. At the opulent court of King Edward VII, on the other hand, there was every likelihood. Throughout a week of magnificent ceremonial during all those sumptuous banquets and glittering receptions, Alfonso kept his eyes open for a suitable princess. With Princess Patricia he seemed to make no headway at all. At the supper table at Londonderry House the chair beside his was empty while Princess Patricia chatted upstairs. At luncheon the following day he turned from Princess Patricia on his right to the Duchess of Westminster on his left with the remark that he must be very ugly as he did not seem to please the lady on his right.

There were, however, plenty of other ladies and one of them was Princess Ena. Alfonso first met the seventeen-year-old Princess at a family dinner party at Buckingham Palace on the night of his arrival. As the hopes of a match between himself and Princess Patricia faded, so did Princess Ena find herself more and more the object of his attentions. At first, amongst that bewildering galaxy of princesses, Alfonso could never remember her name. He would refer to her as 'the fair one'. But within a few days he came to know it very well. He danced with her at Buckingham Palace, he sat beside her at Covent Garden, he sought her out at every reception. As predicted by the Empress Eugenie, the two young people were falling in love. By the time Alfonso's week in England was up, there was little doubt that Ena would be his choice.

One evening a few months later, when the court was at Windsor, Princess Beatrice asked her brother the King if she could speak to him on an urgent matter. 'I have heard from Queen Cristina,' she told him, 'and she says that Alfonso is set on marrying Ena.'

The King was astounded. He had always assumed that Alfonso would want to marry Princess Patricia.

'No,' said his sister, 'Ena. It has been Ena all the time.'

Edward was delighted. Unlike his mother, Queen Victoria, he had no objections to crowns and titles. With one nephew as the German Kaiser, a niece as the Empress of Russia, a daughter about to become the Queen of Norway, two more nieces due to become the Queens of Greece and Romania, how gratifying to have yet another niece as the Queen of Spain. Thus far, in the spread of Coburg influence through Europe, Spain had remained immune. There were Coburgs in Portugal, but not Spain. Indeed, during the past half-century, the British royal family had had very little to do with Spain. Queen Victoria had visited it only once. This had been in 1889, when she had been holidaying in Biarritz. She had driven over to nearby San Sebastian to visit Queen Maria Cristina, who had at that time been Regent for her three-year-old son Alfonso. Victoria's most memorable comment on the day's visit concerned the undrinkability of the tea provided for her. 'I only touched it,' she noted in her Journal.

On the subject of the Spanish national sport of bull-fighting, Queen Victoria, in marked contrast to the majority of her subjects, had always proved surprisingly tolerant. She once remarked that she considered Sir Henry Layard very prejudiced 'to object to this sport which the Spaniards love more than we love our foxhunting here'.

Inevitably, there were some objections to the match. Amongst certain Spanish reactionaries, the choice of an English princess represented a triumph for liberalism. A Hapsburg bride would have been far more acceptable. In some royal circles, too, Princess Ena of Battenberg was looked upon as unsuitable. Ena's father, Prince Henry of Battenberg, had been one of the sons of a morganatic marriage, and not all the royalties of Europe were as sensible as Queen Victoria had been on the subject of morganatic blood. At the time of the marriage of Prince Henry to Princess Beatrice, certain Prussian royalties had had the temerity to write to the Queen expressing their reservations about the suitability of the match. Victoria had been furious. How *dare* they address her in that tone? It would never do to inquire too deeply into the history of the royal families of Europe, had been her pointed reply; one would discover many 'black spots'.

However, all these years later, the prejudice still persisted. 'So Ena is to become Spanish Queen!' wrote the astounded Grand Duchess of Mecklenburg-Strelitz to her niece, Princess May, 'a Battenberg, good gracious!'

But the main obstacle to the marriage was the religious one. It was said that Ena had always been attracted to her godmother, the Empress Eugenie's, religion but how could a British princess possibly forswear her Protestantism? No sooner had the news of a possible engagement become known than there was an uproar. 'Beatrice,' wrote the Prince to the Princess of Wales, 'is advised . . . to keep Ena quiet somewhere, at Osborne, and not to bring her to London as the feeling is so strong.' In letters to the Press, by way of public protests and private appeals, staunch churchmen voiced their disapproval.

It was all to no effect. The Coburgs had seldom hesitated to barter faith for a crown and in this King Edward VII proved no exception. He side-stepped the issue by robustly declaring that Ena was a Battenberg princess, not a British one. That her father, Prince Henry, had become a naturalized Englishman on his marriage to Princess Beatrice, the King blithely ignored. As a German princess, Ena could adopt any religion she liked. However, to play down the controversial business of her conversion, Edward suggested that Ena undertake her religious instruction out of England. The Empress Eugenie had offered Princess Beatrice the use of her villa in the South of France but it was decided that mother and daughter would go to Versailles instead.

On 7 March 1906, while visiting Queen Cristina at San Sebastian, Ena was received into the Catholic Church. That done, she returned to England where King Edward insisted that, as a Catholic, she sign away her rights of succession to the British throne. As these rights were, to say the least, remote, it was not much of a sacrifice. Knowing something of the uncertainties of the Spanish throne, King Edward warned his niece not to come whining back to England if things went wrong.

With this somewhat unnerving piece of advice ringing in her ears, Princess Ena, accompanied by her mother and an imposing suite, arrived in Spain for her wedding in May 1906.

2

From all over Europe, royalties were coming to Madrid for the royal wedding. The scene at the Spanish frontier town of Irun, at which a Spanish *train de luxe* was waiting to convey this host of royal guests to the capital, was said to be one of 'indescribable confusion'. Onto the dimly-lit platform, on a night of almost unbearable heat, assorted princes and princesses, together with their chamberlains, equerries, ladies-in-waiting, valets, maids and portmanteaux, alighted from one set of trains and, after milling about for an hour, boarded the waiting Spanish *train de luxe*. The coaches were like ovens. 'At midnight,' reports one of the guests, 'we all met in the dining-car and tried to refresh ourselves with cooling drinks.' Not until three the following afternoon, exhausted, dusty and dishevelled, did they reach Madrid.

Immediately they were plunged into the stiff and colourful ceremonial for which the Spanish court was renowned. While brass bands blared appropriate national anthems, the guests stepped onto the red-carpeted platform into a dazzlement of national flags, potted palms, guards of honour, gold-embroidered uniforms and bemedalled officials. They were welcomed by the King's older sister, the Infanta Maria Thérèsa, and her husband. In strict order of precendence, entailing an agonizing wait for the less important, the royalties entered the waiting carriages and drove off.

Through the hot, noisy streets and surrounded by their jogging escorts, they were driven to the Palacio Real. In its vast forecourt they faced still more pageantry. Drums rolled, trumpets shrilled, uniforms glittered, and again the various national anthems rang out as each carriage-load alighted at the main entrance. Between rows of magnificently uniformed halberdiers armed with pikes, the guests moved forward to greet the young King, his mother Queen Maria Cristina and the rest of the Spanish royal family. From here, and this time between rows of ladies-in-waiting in evening dress, they were conducted to the magnificent reception rooms. 'The heat,' says one of the royalties, 'was indescribable.'

The wedding day itself – 31 May 1906 – was no less hot. In forty state coaches, each drawn by either six white or six black horses with pink and orange ostrich feathers on their heads, the guests drove to the Church of San Jeronimo. The streets were bright with the red and yellow banners of Spain. From every window along the royal route fluttered silks and tapestries. Flowers blazed from every balcony. As Princess Ena, in white satin shimmering with silver, drove to the church, the great crowd roared its approval. To the Spaniards, Ena was the beau-ideal of English womanhood. Her conventional prettiness – the corn-coloured hair, the sky-blue eyes, the milk-and-roses complexion – fitted their picture-book conception of an English princess exactly. '*La Reina hermosa*' – the beautiful Queen – they called her.

The wedding ceremony lasted for almost three hours. Not until after two o'clock in the afternoon did the procession again set off, still in brilliant sunshine and to the sea-like roar of the crowd, for the Palacio Real.

At snail's pace it wound its way through the clamorous streets. In their coach, surmounted by a golden crown and drawn by eight lavishly plumed horses, sat Alfonso and Ena. They passed through the Puerta del Sol and on along the Calle Mayor, the narrow old high street of Madrid. Two-thirds of the way down the Calle Mayor, and a few hundred yards from their journey's end, the coach stopped. Upon Ena asking why, Alfonso answered that there was possibly some delay caused by those ahead alighting at the palace. 'In five minutes,' he said cheerfully, 'we shall be home.'

It was as well that they had paused, for just then a large bouquet of flowers was thrown from the window of one of the narrow houses opposite. It landed in front of the carriage to the right of the horses. A second later, an explosion rocked the coach. There was a flash of flame, a sickening smell, the scream of wounded horses, and a cloud of smoke so black and thick that the King could not see his bride. The carriage, dragged by the rearing, terrified horses, plunged forward and then came to a dead stop.

Ena was lying with her head back and her eyes closed. For a moment the King thought she was dead. After he had made certain that she was all right, he leaned out of the window and was told that it would be impossible to go on. One of the horses was dead and the others wounded. Alfonso remained calm. He commanded that the door of his coach be opened, that his mother and Princess Beatrice be told that they were safe and that the *coche de respeto* be brought. While the *coche de respeto* – the customary empty coach preceding the royal carriage – was made ready, Alfonso helped his Queen out of their coach. Her shoes and the train of her dress were soon red with blood. Trying to shield her from the sight of the torn and bleeding bodies of men and horses sprawled across the road, he led her to the waiting carriage. Then, in a loud, clear, deliberate voice, for all that stunned crowd to hear, he ordered the coachman to drive on very slowly to the palace.

The procession moved on, leaving behind it in the street twelve dead and over a hundred wounded. If the royal coach had not been delayed for those few seconds before the bomb was thrown, the King and Queen would have been among the dead.

A young man by the name of Mateo Morales was responsible for the outrage. He appears to have been a disciple of a well-known anarchist from Barcelona. Only on being unable to get into the Church of San Jeronimo with his bomb (and what a death toll amongst the royal guests would there have been if he had) had Morales made for the Calle Mayor. Having thrown the bomb, he escaped and was not arrested until two days later. As he was being led to prison, he shot both his guard and himself.

But bomb or no bomb, the day's ceremonial had to continue. No sooner had the King and Queen arrived at the palace ('I saw a man without any legs! I saw a man without any legs!' the horrified Ena kept repeating) than they had to preside at a state luncheon. It was an anything but convivial affair. 'I proposed their healths,' wrote Ena's cousin, the

Prince of Wales, 'not easy after the emotions caused by this terrible affair.' The already overwrought atmosphere was hardly improved by the Russian-born Duchess of Edinburgh, who kept assuring everyone that she was 'so accustomed to this sort of thing'. She was indeed, having had both her father and her brother blown to bits by anarchists.

The luncheon over, the newly-married couple were obliged to expose themselves to the crowd once more and then, while the King visited the wounded in hospital, the Queen made ready for the state banquet. The banquet was no more successful than the luncheon had been. For all the artificially induced gaiety, a vein of hysteria lay very near the surface. It must have been with relief that the royal couple, whose day had lasted for something like seventeen hours, took leave of their guests and went to bed.

Such a day was unlikely to inaugurate a peaceful reign or a happy marriage. For Queen Ena, it inaugurated neither.

CHAPTER EIGHTEEN

The Royal Disease

I

With this gradual spread of Queen Victoria's descendants throughout the courts of Europe, so was something more sinister being passed on. Haemophilia, the dreaded bleeding disease, was being introduced into the royal families of the Continent.

Queen Victoria had always been worried about the quality of the blood of the British royal family. Both she and the Prince Consort had felt strongly about the necessity of revitalizing what the Queen called the 'lymphatic' blood of their house. 'I do *wish* one could find some more black eyed Princes and Princesses for our children!' she had once written to her daughter Vicky. 'I can't help thinking what dear Papa said – that it was in fact a blessing when there was some little *imperfection* in the *pure Royal* descent and that some fresh blood was infused . . . For that constant fair hair and blue eyes makes the blood so lymphatic . . . it is *not* as *trivial* as you may think, for darling Papa – *often* with vehemence said: "*We must have some strong dark blood*".'

At the time of writing this letter, it is doubtful whether the Queen knew exactly what was wrong with her family's blood. Later, she had learnt rather more. Haemophilia was rife in her family.

The disease was, and is, a strange and frightening one. The blood of a haemophiliac lacks the qualities necessary to cause it to coagulate and so stop the flow of blood: clotting takes place either slowly or not at all. Any wound suffered by a haemophiliac can be fatal. Even an apparently harmless bump, causing internal haemorrhage, often leads to death.

A peculiarity of the disease is that it occurs exclusively in males and is carried by females. However, not every male in a family will automatically suffer from it; nor will every female in the family be a carrier. Not until a woman has children will it be known whether or not she is a transmitter; not until a son first bleeds will it be known whether or not he has haemophilia.

The disease first manifested itself in Queen Victoria's family in her fourth son, Prince Leopold, Duke of Albany. From childhood, Leopold had been described as 'very delicate' and throughout his short life he had suffered severe haemorrhages. As any cut, or bump, could lead to death, he could not lead the life of a normal youngster. It had been necessary to keep him always under strict surveillance. Once, when a Prime Minister suggested that he go to Australia to open an exhibition, the Queen had been adamant in her refusal. 'She cannot bring herself to consent to send her very delicate son who has been *four or five times at death's door* and who is *never* hardly a *few months* without being laid up . . .' she protested.

Prince Leopold died, at the age of thirty-one, in 1884, as the result of a minor fall.

Anguished and bewildered by the fact that this mysterious disease had appeared in one of her sons, the Queen could only protest that it did not come from *her* side – the Hanoverian side – of the family.

She was right. But then nor did it come from her husband's side. It appears that the disease had originated in Victoria herself; that a spontaneous mutation had occurred in her genes. It was she who had transmitted the disease to her son. Worse still, she had transmitted it to two of her daughters: Princess Alice and Princess Beatrice. They, in turn, transmitted it to their children and so carried it into the royal houses of Europe.

Of the fact that she herself had originated the disease, the Queen was never aware. Indeed, neither she, nor the members of her family, understood much about it. The disease was rarely mentioned, and certainly never openly discussed, in public. Royal policy was to hush it up; to treat it simply as another risk to be faced by royal parents. It certainly never restrained royalties from marrying one another. Its causes and pattern were shrouded in mystery; it might as well have been something visited on the family by God.

The more gullible whispered in terms of 'the curse of the Coburgs'. This curse was supposed to have dated from the early nineteenth century, when a Coburg prince had married a Hungarian princess named Antoinette de Kohary. As she was an only child, her rich and doting father (having made legal arrangements for her to receive the benefits due to a son) left her everything. The Coburg husband was delighted. Distinctly less delighted at having been thus deprived of their inheritance were the male members of the Kohary family. So incensed was one of them – a monk with an eye to the things of this world – that, having studied up his *Manuale Exorcisorum*, he positioned himself in a churchyard at midnight and there pronounced a curse.

'Then verily shall I pray to the Lord Almighty to visit the sins of the fathers upon the children to the third and fourth generation of the Coburg line,' intoned the irate monk.

To be cursed because one of one's predecessors had been fortunate enough to marry a rich wife seems unfair, but in the spread of haemophilia from generation to generation, the Coburg family certainly seemed cursed.

It was through Queen Victoria's second daughter, Princess Alice, that the disease passed into the German and Russian imperial families. By her marriage to the Grand Duke of Hesse, Alice had six children. Of these, three were tainted with haemophilia. At the age of three, their son Frederick, known as Frittie, bled for three agonizing days from a cut on the ear. Eventually, the flow of blood was staunched. But a few months later, while romping wildly in his mother's room, little Frittie charged headlong through an open window and fell to the terrace below. At first it was thought that he had simply bruised himself. But he was bleeding internally and by the evening he was dead.

Two of Princess Alice's daughters were carriers of the disease: Princess Irene and Princess Alix. Princess Irene married her first cousin, Kaiser Wilhelm II's brother, the bumptious Prince Henry of Prussia. They had three sons, two of them haemophiliacs. Every attempt was made to conceal the fact that the dreaded disease had shown itself in the German imperial family but, at the age of four, the youngest of the princes bled to death. The other prince died, in 1945, at the age of fifty-six. He had had no children.

Had Princess Alix, the other transmitter, accepted that offer of marriage from Prince Eddy and, after his untimely death, married (as Princess May had done) his brother George, haemophilia would have been introduced into the reigning branch of the British royal family. But Alicky married Tsar Nicolas II instead and so carried the disease into the Russian imperial family.

Queen Victoria's youngest daughter, Princess Beatrice of Battenberg, was also a transmitter. Two of her three sons were haemophiliacs and her daughter, Ena, was a carrier. When Ena married King Alfonso XIII of Spain, the disease spread to the Spanish royal family.

Thus, of Queen Victoria's children, grandchildren and great-grandchildren, sixteen were definitely sufferers from, or transmitters of, the disease. Another twenty princesses might well have been carriers. Present in the royal families of Britain, Germany, Russia and Spain, haemophilia came to be known as 'the royal disease'.

The Grandmama of Europe, who had bequeathed this frightening affliction to her widely scattered descendants, could only cry out that 'Our poor family seems persecuted by this awful disease, the worst I know.'

2

The unalloyed joy of Nicky and Alicky at the birth of an heir to the Russian Empire was short-lived. Within a few months of Alexis's birth, his parents realized that he had haemophilia.

The first sign had been some unexpected bleeding from the navel. After a few days this had stopped. Much more serious, however, were the dark swellings that appeared each time the child bumped an arm or a leg. The blood, failing to clot, was flowing unchecked to form painful swellings. And worst of all was the bleeding into the joints. This meant, as well as excruciating pain, a crippling of the affected limbs. As the boy grew older, he was often obliged to spend weeks in bed and, after he was up, to wear a heavy iron brace. For his affliction there was no cure.

All this meant that the Tsarevich had to be ceaselessly watched. Throughout his infancy, nurses kept guard and, as he grew older, their places were taken by two sailors. As Alexis was, in all other respects, a normal boy – mischievous, adventurous and high-spirited – the task of watching his every move was an all but impossible one. Inevitably he slipped and fell. This could be followed by days or weeks of the most frightful pain, from which the only escape was fainting.

From the beginning, it was decided that the Tsarevich's affliction must be kept secret. Russia must know nothing of the heir's illness. Rightly or wrongly, Nicholas and Alexandra decided that the dynasty would never withstand the pressures if the Russian people were to find out that the Tsar's only son could die at any moment.

The keeping of this imperial secret was not quite as difficult as might have been imagined. For one thing, to the majority of the Russian people, the Tsar was a distant, god-like figure about whose private life they knew, and expected to know, very little. In addition to this, Nicholas and Alexandra had always led a self-contained life. They were almost as remote from St Petersburg society as they were from the masses. Moreover, since the revolutionary upheavals in 1905, the imperial family had lived in even greater seclusion; it was simply not safe for them to leave the confines of Tsarskoe Selo. Within the Alexander Palace itself there were many who did not appreciate the exact nature of the boy's illness. They knew that he had to be watched, that he had to spend long periods in bed, that he was often in pain or temporarily crippled. And those – the doctors and the intimate members of the household – who did know what was wrong, were sworn to secrecy.

On the Empress Alexandra, her son's illness had a devastating effect. She might not have known a great deal about the disease but she knew that it was hereditary and that she had passed it on to her son. It was her fault, therefore, that he had to suffer such terrible agonies. As a result, she became over-solicitous and over-protective. She lavished him with attention and could not bear to be parted from him. When he was ill, she would spend hours, days, even weeks by his bedside; soothing him, reassuring him, caressing him. Never knowing when the disease would strike, she could not relax. Not for one moment of his waking day was she free from anxiety.

Always withdrawn and anti-social, Alicky became increasingly so; she lost all capacity for enjoying herself. As a result, her own health began to fail. She was always tired, she breathed with difficulty, she worried about her heart. She spent more and more time in bed or in a wheelchair. For days on end she lay stretched out on her mauve chaise-longue. She almost never appeared in public, not even to take meals with her husband and family. All her energies were needed to cope with her son's illness.

'One morning I found the mother at her son's bedside,' writes Alexis's tutor, Pierre Gilliard, during one of his attacks. 'He had had a very bad night. Dr Derevenko was anxious as the haemorrhage had not stopped and his temperature was rising. The inflammation had spread and the pain was worse than the day before. The Tsarevich lay in bed groaning piteously. His head rested on his mother's arm and his small, deadly white face was unrecognizable. At times the groans ceased and he murmured the one word, "Mummy". His mother kissed him on the hair, forehead, and eyes as if the touch of her lips would relieve him of his pain and restore some of the life which was leaving him. Think of the torture of that mother, an impotent witness of her son's martyrdom in those hours of anguish – a mother who knew that she herself was the cause of those sufferings, that she had transmitted the terrible disease against which human science was powerless. Now I understood the secret tragedy of her life. How easy it was to reconstruct the stages of that long Calvary.'

As there was nothing that the doctors could do to alleviate, let alone cure, her son's illness, the Empress turned, more and more, to God. A miracle was what was needed. She prayed for hours on end; she sought the advice of various holy men. In her anguish, and with her ardent, introspective nature, Alicky was particularly susceptible to the mysticism of the Orthodox religion. She responded, not only to the sensuous splendours of its ceremonial, but to the aura of the supernatural diffusing its fringe.

In Russia, the line between faith and superstition was blurred. The air was thick with talk of miracles, of weeping statues, of unaccountably glowing icons, of unexplained voices; across the vast spaces of the Empire tramped pilgrims, faith healers and so-called 'fools of the Lord'. The *starets* – the Man of God – was a familiar figure in most Russian villages; poor, unkempt, saintly, he took upon himself the sufferings of others. And it was not only the illiterate and superstitious peasants who so readily embraced the supernatural. The aristocracy was no less ready. For them the Orthodox ritual, no matter how colourful, was not enough. They dabbled in the occult, they consulted clairvoyants, they discussed miracles.

Into this twilight world – half-pagan, mysterious, ecstatic – the un-happy Empress Alexandra flung herself with characteristic fervour. Within it, she was certain that she would find what she sought: the way to God, who would cure her son and make him, in time, the autocratic Tsar of Holy Russia.

And in the autumn of 1905, when Alexis was just over a year old, the Empress Alexandra first met the man whom she came to believe to be her link with God. 'We have got to know a man of God, Gregory, from Tobolsk Province,' wrote Nicholas in his diary, on the fateful day that he and Alexandra met Gregory Rasputin.

In the year 1905, Rasputin was thirty-three years old; a dirty, untidy, uncouth, tangle-bearded, lank-haired, evil-smelling peasant with a pair of extraordinary eyes. These eyes were large, blue-grey, brilliant, piercing and hypnotic. It was due, as much as anything, to the power of his gaze that Rasputin gained ascendancy over so many people. Few could resist the fascination of those probing eyes.

As a youth, born in Siberia, Rasputin had been notable for his licen-tiousness; indeed, the name Rasputin meant 'debauchee'. It was only later, after he had married, that he became a Holy Man and began his wanderings through Russia. In time, he gained a reputation as a *starets*, a miracle worker, blessed with supernatural powers. Arriving in St Peters-burg, he was taken up, first by various eminent priests, who were im-pressed by his apparent fervour and sincerity, and then by St Petersburg society, who thrilled to his more flamboyant qualities: his burning eyes, his unpolished speech, his earthiness.

It was one of the leading members of St Petersburg society, the Grand Duchess Militsa, wife of one of the Tsar's cousins, who introduced the *starets* to the Emperor and Empress. This first meeting seems to have been little different from those with other holy men; a year was to go by before they met again. By their second meeting, however, the Empress had heard considerably more about Rasputin's powers of healing. She was told how he he had stood praying at the bedside of the Prime Minister's dying daughter and how the girl had made a miraculous recovery. When the *starets* came to Tsarskoe Selo in October 1906, the Empress introduced him to her children. From then on, he came more and more frequently to the palace.

There was a good deal about Rasputin, other than his aura of mysticism, that the Empress found appealing: his unaffectedness, his frankness, his simplicity. She warmed to the way he addressed her, not as 'Your

Majesty', but in the peasant fashion, as *Matushka*. He was never syco-phantic, never grovelling. Here, she felt, was her link with the real Russia. To her, this plain-speaking *moujik* – this peasant – represented the Russian people; he personified the loyal, devout, unchanging Russia of her imaginings.

The Empress's relationship with this uncouth man was not quite so extraordinary when one remembered that her grandmother, Queen Victoria, had established similar relationships in her time. Throughout Alicky's girlhood, the Queen had been very close, and had allowed every liberty, to that rough-mannered and bluntly-spoken Highlander, John Brown. As Rasputin called the Empress *Matushka*, so had Brown called the Queen 'Woman'. And after Brown's death, Alicky had seen the Queen give her confidence to yet another humbly-born creature – the Munshi. Thus, in befriending this man of the people, the Empress was following her grandmother's example.

But to Alicky, Rasputin was more than a confidant and a support. Gradually, she came to look upon him as her longed-for link with God. For not only did he seem to be a man of simple piety but he was the one person who was able to relieve the Tsarevich's sufferings. How he managed to do this is uncertain. A likely explanation is that Rasputin, with his hypnotic eyes and his self-confident presence, was able to create the aura of tranquillity necessary to slow the flow of blood through the boy's veins. Where the demented mother and the dithering doctors merely in-creased the tenseness of the atmosphere around the suffering child, Rasputin calmed him and sent him to sleep. And even more miraculous was the fact that it sometimes needed only a telegram, in which the *starets* assured the Empress that he was praying for her son's recovery, for the boy's condition to improve.

It was no wonder, then, that the Empress Alexandra developed an implicit faith in Rasputin's powers. Through him she was joined, not only to the Russian people, but to God. He had been sent by God to alleviate her son's sufferings and to ensure that he would one day become *Batiushka* – the autocratic father of the Russian peasants. If she wished Alexis to live, she must be guided by God – speaking through Rasputin or, as she called him, 'Our Friend' – in all things.

In *The Brothers Karamasov*, Dostoevsky writes that 'The *starets* is he who takes your soul and will and makes them his. When you select your *starets*, you surrender your will. You give it to him in utter submission, in full renunciation.'

And this, in effect, is what the Empress Alexandra did. In the twentieth century, in the age of electricity, the telephone, the motor car and the aeroplane, this half-English princess, granddaughter of the eminently practical Queen Victoria, put herself – and the fate of imperial Russia – into the hands of a coarse and ambitious faith healer who was able to bring a measure of relief to her little son.

3

The eighteen-year-old Queen Ena of Spain faced a formidable task. Overnight, one of the least important of Queen Victoria's thirty-two grandchildren had been transformed into one of Europe's leading queens. A shy, straightforward, unsophisticated girl from a secure background, Ena suddenly found herself mistress of the most formal and flamboyant court in Europe. It was a position that called out for someone of exceptional qualities: perhaps a Marie of Romania – passionate and theatrical, or an Alix of Russia – grave and burningly devout. But Spain had had queens like Marie and Alix before, and the capricious Spaniards had still not really approved of them. What hope, then, did the unaffected, uncomplicated Ena have?

In spite of the first impression she made on the Spaniards, she was not a great beauty. What beauty she had was of colouring and complexion rather than of feature and expression. There was something a little stolid about Ena's face. A contemporary speaks of her 'set' expression, and her subjects complained that she did not smile enough. Her bearing was considered too stiff and her manner too wooden. Nor were her clothes especially elegant. In her large, lavishly trimmed hats and richly detailed dresses, she looked matronly, older than her age.

In time, of course, all this would change. The years would bring greater poise and Queen Ena would one day be known as the best-dressed Queen in Europe. But in these early days of her reign, her immaturity, coupled with her shyness, made her appear ill at ease in public.

There were so many things, other than being always the centre of attention, to which Queen Ena had to accustom herself. Life in the grandiose palaces of Spain – the Palacio Real, El Pardo, Aranjuez, La Granja – was a far cry from what she had known before: the almost *bourgeois* simplicity of Windsor, Osborne and Balmoral in Queen Victoria's day. In Spain, royal etiquette had changed little since the sixteenth century. Everything was solemn, pompous and hedged about with protocol; court ritual was elaborate and complicated; the sovereigns moved as in a well-rehearsed pageant. At the time of Ena's wedding, Princess May had been fascinated by the ceremonial at the Spanish court. Each time the Prince and Princess of Wales left their apartments (and it was never without a Duke in attendance) an official would clap his hands and the superbly uniformed halberdier at their door would present arms, crying out '*Arriba Princesa! Arriba Principe!*' The cry would be taken up by the next halberdier and, as the royal couple passed along, so would the cry echo and re-echo down the long, gleaming, colonnaded corridors.

For the duration of a visit, such colourful ceremonial was indeed fascinating; to live with it every day of one's life could be very inhibiting.

Different too, from those homely Sunday sermons in Crathie Church at Balmoral or Whippingham Church on the Isle of Wight, was the ritual surrounding the Queen's new faith. Spanish Catholicism was emotional, fervent and ostentatious. The lives of the soveriegns were closely interwoven with the faith of their country. Cross and Crown were inextricably linked. The King and Queen were expected to play their part in all the pageantry of the Church. They assisted at elaborately staged masses, they walked in great religious processions. At Easter, with the King in full uniform and the Queen in some opulently embroidered dress, they knelt to wash and kiss the feet of twelve old men and women. On meeting a priest carrying the last sacrament through the streets to some dying subject, the King would be obliged to offer his coach to the cleric and continue on his own way on foot.

The character of the countryside, too, was alien. For Ena, who had spent most of her life amidst the soft green beauties of southern England, the landscape of Spain was strangely harsh, dry, unsympathetic. The summer was burningly hot and the winter bitterly cold. Instead of the leafy, informal parks that had surrounded Queen Victoria's homes, she was faced with the artificially created and mathematically laid out gardens of the various royal palaces: the flamboyant statuary, the pleached avenues, the arrow-straight paths, the ornamental waterways.

Something of this harshness, only just tamed, seemed to characterize the people as well. A violence lurked beneath the formal manner, the proud bearing, the grave demeanour. The bomb on Ena's wedding-day was but the first of the many to explode during her husband's reign. In the roar of the bullring, too, did this violence reveal itself. Queen Ena hated bullfighting. Yet she was forced to sit in the royal box, with a mantilla over her head, pretending to enjoy what to her must always have been a cruel and distasteful spectacle.

Within the intimate circle of the royal family she likewise faced problems. Not only did the Queen have to accustom herself to things like the extraordinary Spanish mealtimes – luncheon at three and dinner at ten – but she had to learn to live on close terms with her mother-in-law, Queen Marie Cristina. Although, in many ways, an admirable woman (her sixteen-year-long regency had been surprisingly successful) Maria Cristina lacked warmth. Her manner, although unpretentious, was withdrawn, formal, dignified. In time, by virtue of her self-effacement and innate goodness of heart, Queen Maria Cristina came to live in complete harmony with her daughter-in-law, but for Ena the constant presence of this cool, pious and stiff-backed Queen, the idol of her son Alfonso, could hardly have been comforting.

During the first years of marriage, Ena and Alfonso were happy enough. In some ways, they were not unalike. They were neither of them intellectuals; their taste was conventional; they shared a love of sport and the outdoors. For relaxation they played golf and tennis, they danced, they swam and they went motoring – a sport for which Alfonso had a passion. The differences which would eventually undermine their marriage were not yet apparent.

The first blow to their happiness fell with the birth of a son in May 1907. He was haemophilic. The realization marked merely the start of their parental tragedies. Their second son, born the following year, was a deaf-mute. Another of their off-spring was stillborn. Their two daughters and their third son were healthy enough, but their last son, like the first, suffered from haemophilia. Thus, of their four sons, only one was sound.

The realization that their sons were haemophiliacs could not have been entirely unexpected for Ena and Alfonso. Two of the Queen's brothers, Prince Leopold and Prince Maurice of Battenberg, suffered from the disease. It was thus not unlikely that Ena, like her mother, Princess Beatrice, should prove to be a transmitter. The Spanish Embassy in London seems to have been fully aware of this danger inherent in Ena's blood and King Alfonso had been warned. But as it did not follow that every female was a transmitter, and as Ena looked the very picture of health and vitality, Alfonso had decided to take the risk. He was always a man for risks.

Disappointment, within the royal family, was acute. And by no one, of course, was it more deeply felt than by Queen Ena. Overriding her sense of failure was her sense of dread. No amount of hushing up or of making light could minimize the seriousness of her sons' afflictions; no amount of rationalization could stifle her feelings of pity, responsibility and fear. Like her cousin, the Tsaritsa, Ena had started out on her 'long Calvary'. Indeed the position of the two women, apart from their both being the mothers of haemophilic sons, was strangely similar. Once again the disease had struck in a court where the atmosphere was formal, flamboyant, religious and superstitious. While the country seethed with speculation on the nature of the illness, the royal family felt incapable of taking the people into its confidence. In Spain, no less than in Russia, the reigning family lived always under the threat of assassination; with the possibility of the sovereign being killed at any time, it was imperative that the succession be secure. Revolution was never far away.

But whereas Alicky would always have the support of an adoring and sympathetic husband, Ena would not. Alfonso XIII had many sterling qualities, but constancy, patience and tenderness were not among them. While, with the passing years, he would remain virile, high-spirited, perennially boyish, she would gradually become sadder, quieter, more fatalistic.

As her aunt, the Empress Frederick, had once predicted, Ena would never find life easy.

CHAPTER NINETEEN

A Family of Kings

Never had the myth that the destinies of Europe were controlled by a family of kings appeared to have more substance than during the first decade of the twentieth century. This was the Indian summer of monarchy. By their exchange of spectacular state visits, these sovereigns gave the impression that they were making history: that its tides ebbed and flowed to their commands. Who could doubt, as they watched some magnificently beplumed and bemedalled emperor in earnest conversation with some equally lavishly uniformed king, that they were settling matters of international importance? Who, on seeing some monarch being piped aboard a luxurious royal yacht or arriving at a palace in a glittering cavalcade, could suspect that it was not an occasion of great moment? Surely these sovereigns – so gorgeously dressed, so self-confidently mannered, so surrounded by pomp and deference – were as powerful as they looked?

Few monarchs, of course, were more addicted to such state visits than King Edward VII. Delighting in travel, movement, change, ceremonial, dressing up and the creation of a harmonious atmosphere, he was forever setting out, by land or by sea, for yet another royal meeting. By doing so, he gave the impression that he was a political force; that by the authority and diplomacy of his manner he was manipulating the affairs of Europe.

During his short reign, he managed to pay state visits to almost every sovereign on the Continent. Of these sovereigns, only the Austrian Emperor and the King of Italy were not closely related to him; he had family connections in Berlin, St Petersburg, Vienna, Madrid, Brussels, The Hague, Stockholm, Oslo, Copenhagen, Bucharest, Sofia, Athens and Lisbon. This kinship appeared to render his visits more significant still. Few doubted that Uncle Bertie was making use of his position as the doyen of the great royal clan to guide European policy.

To his credit, King Edward himself did not believe this. There were times, admittedly, when his enthusiasm for foreign affairs caused him to strain the limits of constitutional monarchy to the utmost but usually he merely eased the way for his Ministers. 'I have no wish to play the part of the German Emperor who always meddles in other people's business,' he once protested. Indeed, with his nephew, Kaiser Wilhelm II, King Edward usually refused to discuss politics at all. But there is no doubt that his Ministers found him extremely useful when it came to making the initial advance and creating a sympathetic atmosphere. 'The greatest diplomatic victories are gained by doing nothing,' Sir Harold Nicolson once wrote when contrasting the methods of the King and the Kaiser, 'and King Edward, although too superficial to be a statesman, was a supreme diplomatist.'

If these visits to his relations were not always politically productive, they were invariably packed with incident. The King's obsession with such things as the correct choice of clothes, the number of decorations conferred and the value of gifts presented, caused his suite endless difficulties. In the matter of dress, the King could be tyrannical. Nothing would put him out of temper as much as to see an order incorrectly worn or an outfit wrongly chosen. The sight of a Cabinet Minister in a white instead of a black tie could ruin his meal.

His own taste was impeccable. To Frederick Ponsonby, who was about to set out before luncheon to an exhibition of pictures in a tail coat, the King remarked, 'I thought everyone must know that a *short* jacket is always worn with a silk hat at a private view in the morning.' And a Minister in attendance during a cruise up the British coast was once very amused to hear the King, as they approached the shores of Scotland, say to his valet, 'Something a little more Scottish tomorrow.'

In the spring of 1906, having in previous years paid official visits to the sovereigns of Portugal, Italy, Austria and Germany, the King sailed to Greece. In Athens, of course, he would once more be among relations. King George I of the Hellenes was Queen Alexandra's brother and the Crown Princess Sophie was King Edward's niece. The first five days of the visit were spent on the beautiful island of Corfu. 'It is interesting to note the remains of the British occupation more than fifty years before,' observed one chauvinistic member of the King's suite, 'which even the want of care and slovenliness of the Greeks had been unable to destroy.' While on Corfu, King Edward and Queen Alexandra were reunited with their son and daughter-in-law, the Prince and Princess of Wales, who were on their way home from an official tour of India. Together, the royal party sailed on to Athens for the official part of the visit.

Queen Alexandra enjoyed the Greek visit immensely. She was devoted to her brother, King George, and the recent death of their father, old King Christian IX of Denmark, brought brother and sister closer still. King Edward's stay was somewhat spoiled by the fact that Lord Charles Beresford, commanding the battleship squadron of the British Mediterranean Fleet, neglected to change into full-dress uniform to receive the

Greek King. The normally easy-going King George complained to the King about the implied insult and King Edward (who anyway disliked Beresford) lost no time in reporting him to the Board of Admiralty.

Crown Princess Sophie was delighted to welcome her English relations. Displaying almost as much enthusiasm as her late mother, the Empress Frederick, Sophie took them sightseeing: to the Acropolis, the British School of Archaeology, the Athens Museum, the Theatre of Dionysus, the Theseus Temple and the Olympic Games Stadium. There were dinners, *en famille*, for eighteen, and a state banquet for a hundred and eighty.

One day the party drove out to the royal home at Tatoi where they all lunched in the garden. The Greek royal family, says Ponsonby, 'were all delightful', with the Crown Princess Sophie the most delightful of them all. Although, with the years, Sophie had become more assured and dignified, she had none of the conceit of her brother, the Kaiser. Indeed, she was quite ready to laugh with Sir Charles Hardinge, the Minister in attendance on King Edward, about 'the pompous airs of the Kaiser, comparing them with the dignity of King Edward'. She asked Hardinge if he did not find her brother 'absurd'. It was not, says the disconcerted Hardinge, 'an easy question to answer'.

During his Mediterranean cruise the following year – the spring of 1907 – King Edward met yet another of his relations: King Alfonso XIII of Spain, the husband of his niece Ena. King Alfonso had invited King Edward to pay a state visit to Madrid, but with the memory of his niece's wedding-day fresh in his mind, the British King refused the invitation. They met, instead, at the Spanish port of Cartagena; or rather, off the port, as the King's well-founded fear of anarchists prevented him from setting foot in the town itself. The meeting was a great success. King Edward was fond of the Spanish King: Alfonso XIII was exactly the sort of charming, amusing, animated, daredevil, unintellectual young man with whom King Edward felt at ease. They shared a passion for uniforms. 'Alfonso has created me a Captain-General in his Army and I wore the uniform at dinner last night,' reported the delighted King Edward to his son, Prince George. 'He appeared as a 16th Lancer, which suited him very well.'

Again the question of a uniform soured the King's visit to Spain no less than it had to Greece. This time the offender was Sir Maurice de Bunsen, the British Ambassador at Madrid. Uncertain as to what he should wear to board the *Victoria and Albert* on its arrival off Cartagena at ten in the morning, de Bunsen plumped for white knee breeches and stockings. The King was furious. 'Trousers are always worn on board ship!' he spluttered.

If sartorially the visit had its disasters, politically it was highly satisfactory. After protracted negotiations and by a secret exchange of notes, England, France and Spain agreed to guarantee each other's possessions in the Mediterranean. That accomplished, the King sailed on to Gaeta where he met the King of Italy. On this occasion, there were no political discussions.

Continuing the royal round, Edward and Alexandra went to Scandinavia in the spring of 1908. Again, the series of visits was very much of a family affair, for the King had relations in Denmark, Norway and Sweden. With the death of old King Christian IX of Denmark in 1906, Queen Alexandra's brother had become King Frederick VIII of Denmark. His second son (Queen Alexandra's nephew) was now King Haakon of Norway and married, of course, to King Edward's daughter Maud. In Sweden, too, there was a family connection: for in 1905, Princess Margaret of Connaught (the daughter of one of King Edward's brothers) had married Gustaf Adolf, the eldest son of the Swedish Crown Prince.

Only in the Swedish capital of Stockholm was there some show of pomp. In Denmark, the new King was as unpretentious as the old; and King Haakon of Norway was less pretentious than either. Indeed, King Haakon shocked King Edward's entourage by announcing his intention of travelling about the streets of his capital by tram. Only by moving amongst his subjects with the utmost simplicity would he be able, he reckoned, to win popularity and combat republicanism. Against any such notion, the British argued hotly. 'I told him,' claims Ponsonby, 'that he must get up on a pedestal and remain there.'

Queen Maud, although overjoyed to welcome her parents to her new home, experienced considerable difficulty in entertaining them adequately. The vast royal palace, still in the process of renovation, was said to be 'very uncomfortable' and lacked enough bathrooms and furniture. The state banquet, complained one of the guests, 'was very indifferently done, as the suite were new to the game and the staff had never done a big dinner'. The visit, never the less, was very enjoyable, assuming, as Sir Charles Hardinge put it, 'the character of a family rather than an official visit'.

'The Norwegians,' he added blandly, 'are a very simple race, though not without culture. There was little scope for political conversations with them.'

However, it was as a result of political conversations between Britain and Russia, that King Edward paid his next visit: to Tsar Nicholas II, in the summer of 1908. An Anglo-Russian convention had been signed the year before. This convention, whose existence was rather more significant than its text, was looked upon as 'the triumph of King Edward's policy of which the Anglo-French entente [of 1904] was the first step'. In other words, Britain was now loosely allied to both France and Russia.

As Russia was regarded as being even more dangerous to crowned heads than Spain, the sovereigns arranged to meet at sea. They would anchor off Reval (now Tallin) in the Gulf of Finland. The passage of the *Victoria and Albert* through the North Sea was extremely rough. Even Queen Alexandra, who was a very good sailor (she always appeared on deck, it was said, looking as elegant as though she had just emerged from a bandbox) experienced a nasty moment. This was when, at the tea table, a sudden lurch of the ship flung her to the floor and sent everything – tea-urn, teapot, china, cakes, biscuits, bread and sugar – tumbling into her lap. Characteristically, she treated it as a great joke.

At Reval were waiting the imperial yachts *Standart* and *Polar Star*, escorted by such remnants of the Russian Imperial Navy as had survived the naval disaster of Tsushima during the recent Russo-Japanese War. By now the weather had cleared and the two days spent off Reval were delightful. While the Ministers talked, the royalties exchanged visits. The two families were doubly related: Tsar Nicholas II was Queen Alexandra's nephew (her sister, the Dowager Empress Marie, was there as well) and the Tsaritsa Alexandra was, of course, King Edward's niece. 'There was no disguising the fact,' claims Hardinge, 'that the Emperor and Empress were extraordinarily happy in the company of their uncle and aunt, and the visit had largely a family character.'

The King, almost bursting out of his uniform of the Kiev Dragoons, boarded the *Standart* and delighted the guard of honour of Russian sailors by saying to them, according to the Russian custom and in Russian, 'Good morning my children'. To this they answered, 'God save the King'. This quaint exchange was followed by another Russian tradition: a snack of caviar sandwiches and kirsch; the liquor tasting, thought the British visitors, 'like boot varnish'.

Somewhat less satisfactory was the King's reception of his Ambassador to St Petersburg, Sir Arthur Nicolson. Again it was a question of dress. Throughout the interview, at which King Edward seemed quite uninterested in Nicolson's answers to his disconnected questions, the King's eyes never left the Ambassador's decorations.

'What is that bauble?' he finally asked.

With some pride Nicolson explained that it was the 'badge of Nova Scotia Baronetcy', the only hereditary order in England, conferred on his ancestors in 1637.

The King was not impressed. 'Never wear that bauble again,' he said.

For the Empress Alexandra, the visit of her 'dear Uncle Bertie' was a blessed break from both the public and the private trials of her life. The King and Queen were so kind; they brought, to Alicky's tortured mind, a breath of another, more light-hearted, more honest-to-goodness world. If life aboard the imperial yacht was safer and more relaxed than life ashore, then how much more so was it aboard the *Victoria and Albert*. To the British visitors, the security measures aboard the Russian yachts seemed extraordinary. Even the women members of a choral society, singing from a boat anchored near the *Polar Star*, were stripped and searched before their concert. 'What,' wondered Ponsonby, 'would be said if, when the Russian Emperor came to England, and some ladies' choral society asked leave to serenade him, our police insisted on stripping and searching them?'

But even now, in the comforting atmosphere of King Edward's visit to Reval, the Tsaritsa's latent hysteria was never far from the surface. On the last night of the King's visit, the British party dined on board the superbly appointed *Standart*. Both King and Emperor made reassuring speeches and, after dinner, there was a dance on deck. As the sun, so far north, did not set until almost half-past eleven at night, the sky above the gently heaving yacht was a weird and beautiful red. In this strange half-light, Sir Charles Hardinge left the company dancing under the paper lanterns and wandered around to the other, deserted, side of the deck. Suddenly, he heard sobbing. Following the sound, he discovered the Tsaritsa, sitting alone and in floods of tears. He asked if there was anything that he could do to help. No, she answered, nothing. She merely wished to be left alone.

Could it have been that this contact with her English relations had brought back to Alicky, all too poignantly, memories of the tranquil, trouble-free days of her English-style girlhood?

The following morning, the *Victoria and Albert* sailed back to England.

Because of his state visits to France, Russia, Germany, Austria, Spain, Italy, Greece, Portugal, Denmark, Norway and Sweden, King Edward VII earned his reputation as a supreme royal diplomat: the 'Peacemaker of Europe'. And all the while, as he spread what many considered to be his propitiatory influence, the stage was being set for the great conflict of 1914–1918.

2

By not every sovereign in Europe was King Edward VII looked upon as an angel of peace. To his nephew, Kaiser Wilhelm II, King Edward appeared in a very different guise. He was 'the Encircler': a satanic schemer intent on ringing Germany with enemies. King Edward's main purpose, imagined his nephew, was the isolating of the Second Reich in a hostile Europe.

There had never, of course, been much love lost between uncle and nephew. They met, officially and unofficially, several times during the King's reign, and the occasions were anything but harmonious. 'There was always a feeling of thunder in the air whenever the King and the Emperor were together,' noted Ponsonby. To the King, the Kaiser was a vulgar, unpredictable, mischief-making megalomaniac; to the Kaiser, the

King was a corrupt and double-dealing old roué. King Edward always tried to keep their meetings as short as possible and to avoid all contentious subjects.

One of the most contentious was the expansion of the German navy. Germany, anxious to become a world power and jealous of British naval might, was determined to build up her own fleet. This Britain, as Mistress of the Seas, hotly resented. As a result, a frantic and expensive naval race had developed between the two nations. It was a race in which the emotions of both King and Kaiser were deeply involved.

Yet the Kaiser dismissed his uncle's assumption that Germany was planning a naval invasion of Britain as 'sheer nonsense'. In this, he was probably quite sincere. Wilhelm's motives in building up the German fleet were not necessarily belligerent. A powerful navy would deter any would-be aggressor and would establish the Reich as a great maritime power. It would be a symbol of national greatness. It might even, the Kaiser had once imagined, encourage Britain to turn her back on France and Russia and join the Triple Alliance of Germany, Austria and Italy.

His Chancellor, Bernhard von Bülow, was not far wrong when he claimed that the Kaiser's aims were not really aggressive. 'What Wilhelm II most desired . . .' he wrote, 'was to see himself, at the head of a glorious German fleet, starting out on a peaceful visit to England. The English sovereign, with his fleet, would meet the German Kaiser in Portsmouth. The two fleets would file past each other, the two monarchs, each wearing the naval uniform of the other's country . . . would then stand on the bridge of their flagships. Then, after they had embraced in the prescribed manner, a gala dinner with lovely speeches would be held in Cowes.'

Be that as it may, the shipbuilding continued. And so did Wilhelm's conviction that Uncle Bertie was pursuing a nefarious anti-German policy. To each of King Edward's Continental visits, the German Press was quick to attribute some sinister, Machiavellian motive. It was a conviction which not even the King's state visit to Berlin, in February 1909, was able to refute.

This three-day stay in the German capital was to be the last of King Edward's state visits. The occasion, which the Kaiser was determined should be one of unparalleled magnificence, opened with several farcical incidents. A sudden lurch of the train carrying the royal party to Berlin scattered a trayful of quails over the accident-prone Queen Alexandra, leaving one perched on her *toupet*. She would arrive in Berlin, she assured her amused companions, *coiffée de cailles*.

On reaching the Brandenburg frontier the following morning, the King (having mistaken the time) was not yet dressed in his German Field-Marshal's uniform for the inspection of the guard of honour. While he scrambled into his clothes, the entire company stood to attention on the platform for ten minutes while the band thumped out 'God save the King' over and over again.

At Berlin it was worse. On the red-carpeted platform of the Lehrter Bahnhof, the German imperial family was solemnly waiting opposite the spot where the King's carriage was destined to draw up. However, the King, having moved into the Queen's carriage, suddenly alighted a good hundred yards farther down the platform. With an undignified clanking of swords, clinking of medals, fluttering of plumes, clutching of feather boas and hitching up of skirts, the German royalties came dashing down the platform to receive him.

And finally, as the procession moved pompously through the acclaiming streets, the second carriage – carrying the Queen and the German Empress – stopped dead. The horses refused to move. This meant that the entire procession was held up while the royal ladies and several others were obliged to change carriages, in full view of the public. Quite unaware that his was the only carriage moving forward, the Kaiser, with the King by his side, drove on to the Royal Schloss. On hearing about the fracas, Wilhelm was furious. That it should happen in front of the horse-conscious British was doubly infuriating.

The rest of the visit was suitably impressive. The imperial court might have been showy but it was not without a certain brilliance. The luncheons, the gala dinners, the receptions and the balls were all superbly done. The Kaiser was on his best behaviour. In the ordinary way, King Edward would have enjoyed the pageantry, but he was feeling far from well. He felt puffed and fretful; he tired easily. One day, after a luncheon at the British Embassy, he suddenly collapsed. His doctor, Dr James Reid, was summoned immediately, but once the tight collar of his Prussian uniform was unfastened, the King recovered. According to his doctor, King Edward had suffered a bronchial attack.

As a result, some of the King's less important duties were taken over by Queen Alexandra. As always, she looked lovely. Although Alexandra was old enough to have been the German Empress's mother, she was said to be looking more like her daughter. During the *entr'acte* at the opera, Alexandra moved amongst the audience, saying a few words here and there. Despite the fact that she could not hear a word that was being said in reply, she charmed everyone by her grace and beauty. 'I have never seen anything better done,' says Ponsonby.

The visit ended, as it had begun, on a note of farce. One of the stars at the Kaiser's court was the English-born Princess Daisy of Pless. Seeing in her own, decidedly attractive, person, the embodiment of a *rapprochement* between Britain and Germany, the Princess was determined to play her part to the full during the English King's visit. Surely the King, with his well-known weakness for beautiful young women, would not fail to be impressed by her? He was not impressed; and he very soon tired of her efforts to monopolize him.

However, it was while chatting to her after the British Embassy luncheon that the King had his bronchial attack. Here was her opportunity.

She would win his confidence by recommending a German throat specialist. That very afternoon she dropped a line to Frederick Ponsonby, suggesting that her specialist visit the King immediately. Ponsonby referred the matter to the King's doctor, Sir James Reid; Reid referred it to the Kaiser's physician; the Kaiser's physician referred it to the Kaiser; the Kaiser threatened to have the man flung out of the palace if ever he dared set foot in it. Ponsonby thus wrote to the Princess, declining her offer.

But she was not to be put off. If the Kaiser would not allow her man into the palace, she must arrange for him to meet the King elsewhere. She wrote again to Ponsonby, outlining a new plan: on leaving Berlin at the end of the state visit, the King was to order his train to halt at the nearby station of Spandau, where it would be boarded by Princess Daisy and her throat specialist. Unbeknown to Ponsonby, the Princess wrote to Sir Charles Hardinge as well. Again she suggested that the royal train stop at Spandau. This time, however, she made no mention of the throat specialist; suspecting, by now, that the King was simply not interested in having her protégé forced, so to speak, down his throat, she merely indicated that she wished to take leave of the King. When Hardinge consulted King Edward about it, the King refused to have anything more to do with Princess Daisy.

And so, as the royal train steamed through Spandau station, the King, peeping through the curtains of his saloon, was diverted by the spectacle of the beautiful Princess Daisy of Pless, swathed in furs from head to foot, standing alone and disconsolate on the dark and snow-strewn platform.

Politically, the royal visit to Berlin was of no consequence whatsoever. 'I derived the impression,' says Ponsonby, 'that [the Germans] hated us. The Germans never forgave the King for having, as they imagined, isolated them from the rest of Europe. They attributed to him the fact that Germany practically stood alone in the councils of Europe. The Emperor for his part seemed to do all he could to make the visit a success, but he was never at his ease with the King. There were always forced jokes, and the whole atmosphere when the two were together seemed charged with dangerous electricity.'

But, of course, this hostility between King and Kaiser was not the cause of the hostility between their two countries. It merely happened to epitomize the rivalry between Britain and Germany. King Edward's dislike of his nephew was no more a cause of the First World War than his love of Paris had been responsible for the *entente cordiale*. By now, both King and Kaiser were anachronisms; much more important than their personal relationship was the fact that the countries in which they happened to reign were rival power-blocs.

One of the main reasons for the First World War was that Europe had developed into a series of just such competing power-blocs, all striving to be larger, stronger, more magnificent than each other. Each wanted a bigger navy, a stronger army, a greater empire, a more extensive market than the others; each was anxious to score diplomatic victories over its neighbours. Germany's misfortune was that her diplomats had isolated her in a hostile world and that, like her Kaiser, she had become too self-confident, too boastful and too militant.

Against such forces, the quality of the relationship between King and Kaiser mattered very little. That the blood of Queen Victoria ran in the veins of both mattered even less.

3

'The monarchy,' King Edward VII once said in a disgruntled moment, 'will not last much longer. I believe my son will stay on the throne, as the people are fond of him, but certainly not my grandson.'

This uncharacteristic pessimism on the part of the King was due to several factors. He was feeling old and ill; he was worried about such things as the maintenance of peace in Europe, the stirrings of change in the Empire and the possibility of social upheaval at home. Especially disturbing was the conflict which was developing between the House of Commons and the House of Lords; a conflict which directly involved the sovereign. With the Liberal government determined to curtail the powers of the House of Lords and the Lords just as determined to reject any such legislation, the King was being forced into a difficult position. There was a strong possibility that he would have to use his Royal Prerogative to create new peers to ensure the passing of the projected legislation. King Edward was extremely loath to do any such thing. He tried hard to find a compromise solution. He even talked, in moments of despair, of abdicating. In fact, the dilemma was not to be resolved until after his death.

As far as the durability of the monarchy was concerned, he need have had no cause for apprehension. Certainly the succession had seldom been more assured than it was in 1910. Things had been much shakier a generation before when, on the death of the lethargic Prince Eddy, the sickly and unmarried Prince George had been the heir presumptive. Prince George was now a robust forty-five-year-old, married to a woman of great strength of character and the father of no fewer than four sons and a daughter, with ages ranging from sixteen to eight.

King Edward was correct, of course, in prophesying that his eldest grandson, Edward (known as David) would not stay on the throne; for, as King Edward VIII, David abdicated to marry Mrs Wallis Simpson in

1936. But the monarchy, although shaken, did not fall, and the crown passed to David's more dependable brother, Bertie, who became King George VI.

Many of the thrones occupied by Queen Victoria's descendants were to topple but her own was to remain secure.

King Edward VII's nature was such, however, that his moods of dejection never lasted long. Although in his late sixties by the year 1909, and far from well, he remained as restless, as impatient and as energetic as he had ever been. His appetite for enjoyment was as enormous as ever. He still paid his little visits to Paris, he still spent March at Biarritz and April cruising the Mediterranean. The visits to various country houses continued. So too, did the nights at the theatre and the suppers with Mrs Keppel. To her children he was 'Kingy', an indulgent and warm-hearted old gentleman who allowed them to race slices of toast, buttered side down, along his immaculately tailored trousers. He shot, he skated, he urged his chauffeurs to drive his gleaming, maroon-coloured cars faster and faster. At Epsom, in May 1909, his horse 'Minoru' won the Derby. The victory brought forth an almost hysterical reaction from the crowd. As the portly and pleasure-loving monarch led in his horse, the acclaim was deafening. It was one of the happiest moments of his life.

But not all the activity in the world could hide the fact that his health was failing rapidly. His bronchial attacks became more frequent, his movements were slower, his moods of depression lasted longer. The problem of the House of Lords pressed upon him more and more heavily. No sooner had the King arrived at Biarritz in the spring of 1910 for his annual holiday than he collapsed. Although he refused to remain in bed, he was obliged to keep to his rooms. Queen Alexandra, who was about to embark on a Mediterranean cruise, begged him to leave what she called 'that horrid Biarritz' and join her. He refused. With the constitutional crisis still simmering, he had to be ready to return home at any moment. This proved unnecessary and it was not until 27 April that the King arrived back at Buckingham Palace.

During the following nine days, despite increasing tiredness, he insisted on carrying on as usual. He granted audiences, he worked at his papers, he attended the theatre, he supervised alterations at Sandringham, he played bridge, he dined with friends. His doctor, by now, was seriously alarmed and the Queen was urged to return home as soon as possible. She arrived on the evening of 5 May. No sooner had the King greeted her than he sent for his secretary, Frederick Ponsonby. He had work to do.

'I found the King sitting at his writing table with a rug round his legs, and I was rather shocked with his appearance,' writes Ponsonby. 'His colour was grey and he appeared unable to sit upright and to be shrunken.' Never the less, the King attended to such business as Ponsonby handed him and afterwards discussed a meeting which had been held that afternoon. As Ponsonby, with forced cheerfulness, wished him a speedy recovery, the King replied, 'I feel wretchedly ill. I can't sleep. I can't eat. They really must do something for me.'

There was nothing that they could do. Although, the following morning, he rejected the informal clothes which his valet had laid out for him and insisted on wearing a frock-coat, he spent most of the day in an armchair, fighting for breath. In the afternoon, he suffered a series of heart attacks. He was clearly dying. Among the people whom Queen Alexandra allowed in to take leave of him was Mrs Keppel. Finally, just before midnight on 6 May 1910, King Edward died. He was in his sixty-ninth year.

His funeral was every bit as impressive as he would have wished it to be. For three days his body lay in state in Westminster Hall; on 20 May it was borne in procession through the streets of London on its way for burial at Windsor. Of the many cavalcades which had marked King Edward VII's reign, this final one was the most spectacular. The weather was superb; the crowds were enormous. Because of the King's dislike of black, the funeral route was draped in purple. Amidst a sea of brilliantly uniformed troops, on a gun-carriage draped in purple, red and white, the coffin passed slowly through the streets. Whenever the military bands paused in their solemn thumping, one could hear the tramp of feet and the scrunching of wheels. Behind the coffin was led the King's horse, with empty saddle and boots reversed in the stirrups, and then – a more poignant sight still – came his wire-haired terrier, Caesar.

But the most impressive sight by far was the parade of royalties that followed after. Three by three, in tunics of red and blue and green and purple and white, rode the kings, the heirs apparent, the imperial and royal highnesses. On and on they came, plumes fluttering, orders flashing, gold braid glinting, top-boots gleaming, the jingling of harness enlivening the steady clip-clop of their horses' hooves. There were nine kings in the procession and each of them was related to King Edward. The new King of England, George V, was his son; Kaiser Wilhelm II was his nephew; King Frederick VIII of Denmark and King George I of the Hellenes were his brothers-in-law; King Haakon VII of Norway was his son-in-law; King Alfonso XIII of Spain was his niece's husband; King Manuel II of Portugal, King Ferdinand I of Bulgaria and King Albert I of the Belgians were all Coburg cousins, at various removes.

There were relations too, among the forty-five princes that came after; and among the seven queens and countless princesses – their faces smudgy behind their mourning veils – that followed in twelve gleaming coaches.

Never again was the world to see quite so immense a cavalcade of inter-related royalties. For, unsuspected by the majority of overawed observers, this swaggering parade marked, not a royal high noon, but a royal sunset.

CHAPTER TWENTY

'Our Friend'

I

In the autumn of 1912 the Russian imperial family spent several weeks in their hunting lodge at Spala, in Poland. This unpretentious house, set in the middle of a vast forest, was to be the scene of a drama whose effect, on the highly-strung Empress Alexandra, was to be catastrophic.

Things started happily enough. At Spala, far from critical St Petersburg, the Tsaritsa could lead the simple, secluded life she preferred. While the Tsar spent his days hunting, she devoted herself to her children. Her four daughters, whose ages now ranged from eleven to sixteen, were all pretty, unaffected girls who gave their parents very little trouble. Constant vigilance, however, was needed for the eight-year-old, haemophilic Alexis. The Tsaritsa seldom let him out of her sight. Yet not even the most devoted care could protect the high-spirited boy from every bump or fall.

One such tumble had occurred a week or two before the family's arrival at Spala. The boy had bruised his thigh. After spending a few days in bed he seemed to have recovered. But at Spala, during the course of a jolting carriage drive, Alexis complained of pains in his leg and abdomen. He was rushed home and put to bed. Soon, he was in agony. Unchecked, the blood was flowing into his groin to cause an enormous swelling. He had never experienced a more violent attack. Every few minutes he was racked by the most excruciating pain. His screams filled the house. Specialists and doctors, summoned by telegram, came hurrying to Spala. There was nothing that they could do. That the remorseless flow of blood would cease was doubtful. The child could obviously not survive many days of this torture. Death could come at any moment.

Throughout the nightmarish days that followed, Alicky hardly ever left her son's bedside. Sometimes she would fall into a short, exhausted sleep on a sofa beside his bed; for the greater part of the time she sat comforting him. 'Mama, help me. Won't you help me?' the little boy would cry, and she, torn by his suffering and certain that he was dying, could only pray.

Yet, such was the artificiality of the atmosphere in which the family lived, the Empress was obliged to play her official role as though nothing were wrong. The exact nature, even the seriousness, of the heir's illness, must be kept from the public. The members of the household (some with their ears plugged to shut out the horrifying sound of the boy's screams) carried on with their duties; the house was full of guests. Alicky, beautifully dressed, would briefly act the hostess, 'smiling and talking gaily to her neighbours'. Pierre Gilliard, the boy's tutor, once came across her running down a corridor to her son's sickroom, her long, cumbersome train clutched in her hands, a 'distracted and terror-stricken look' on her face. Yet within a few minutes she was back with her guests, behaving as though nothing was happening.

But the secret could not be kept forever. Expecting death at any time, the doctors began issuing bulletins. Still no mention was made, however, of the cause of the illness. By 10 October it was agreed that the end was near. The last sacrament was administered to the pale, wasted figure on the bed and a bulletin, so worded that the following one would announce the Tsarevich's death, was sent out.

That night, the Empress telegraphed Rasputin for help.

He answered immediately. 'God has seen your tears and heard your prayers. Do not grieve. The Little One will not die. Do not allow the doctors to bother him too much.'

From the moment that she received the telegram, Alicky ceased to worry. Although the doctors could see no improvement in Alexis's condition, she felt completely reassured. As far as she was concerned, the danger was over. Alexis would live. Serene and smiling, she came down from the sickroom to assure the company that all would be well.

She was right. A day later the haemorrhage finally stopped and the boy began to improve. Within a month, he was able to be moved back to Tsarskoe Selo.

How had this come about? There are several possible explanations. The bleeding might have stopped, as sometimes happens, of its own accord. Then Rasputin's advice, that the doctors should cease to bother the patient, was extremely valuable. What Alexis needed to help stop the bleeding was an atmosphere of calm. This could hardly have been provided by a group of anxious and bewildered doctors. Nor could it have emanated from the desperately worried Empress. But once she had been reassured by Rasputin's message, she may, in some fashion, have transmitted her newly-found feeling of tranquillity and confidence to her son. This suddenly relaxed and optimistic atmosphere, coinciding with a natural easing of the flow of blood, may well have saved Alexis's life.

That a miracle had occurred, the Tsaritsa had no doubt. More than ever she was convinced that Rasputin had been sent by God to ensure that her son would live to be Tsar. From now on the staret's word, as far as Alicky was concerned, was law. Her faith in him was unshakable. To survive, to become stronger, to reach the heights of glory, the dynasty must be guided by this simple Man of God.

It would not be an exaggeration to say that, from the time of Spala, Rasputin – through the fervent Empress and her weak-willed husband – controlled the destinies of Russia.

2

As Rasputin's influence over the Empress Alexandra waxed, so did his reputation in St Petersburg wane. Success, by now, was going to Rasputin's head. No longer did he act the humble *moujik*, a raggedly dressed, disinterested, a-political *starets*, ill at ease among an artificially-mannered society. He clothed himself in rich fabrics, he moved with confidence in the highest circles, he concerned himself with affairs of state. His conversation was more outspoken, his manners more outrageous, his drinking heavier. Seemingly irresistible to women (there was still enough earthiness about his looks and manner to attract jaded society ladies, and his eyes were no less hypnotic) he became more sexually ambitious than ever. His method of seduction had always been successful. Redemption from sin, he would explain huskily to some fluttering young matron, could not come about unless one had sinned first; therefore by committing adultery with him – so patently a man of God – one could achieve sin and redemption at, so to speak, the same stroke.

But not quite every aristocratic lady was prepared to follow this facile line of reasoning and subject herself to Rasputin's rough caresses. As his behaviour became more openly lascivious, his former patrons began to bar him from their homes.

It was inevitable, with Rasputin's well-founded reputation for licentiousness, that there should be speculation on the nature of his association with the Tsaritsa. Many believed that they were lovers. A series of letters, said to have been written by Alicky to the *starets*, passed from hand to hand. Their fulsome phrases ('I only wish one thing: to fall asleep, to fall asleep, for ever on your shoulders and in your arms . . . Come quickly, I am waiting for you and I am tormenting myself for you') gave strength to the rumours. Scurrilous pamphlets were secretly printed and circulated. Obscenities were scrawled on walls. Smutty rhymes were repeated. Outrageous stories were told. It was claimed that Rasputin, after ordering the Tsar to pull off his boots, would push him out of the room and climb into bed with the Tsaritsa. The *starets* had raped all four of the young grand duchesses with the result that the girls, in a fever of sexual desire, now fought for his attentions.

Nor was disapproval of Rasputin's behaviour confined to talk or surreptitious scribblings. Newspapers openly attacked the favourite on his debauchery. The Church, beginning to have second thoughts on the saintliness of this Holy Man, formally investigated his activities. Peter Stolypin, an energetic Prime Minister of the period, presented the Tsar with a frank report on Rasputin's behaviour. He even commanded the *starets* to leave St Petersburg for a time. Rasputin's growing influence in the country's affairs was hinted at and then openly discussed in the Duma. The President of the Duma drew up another report on the subject. Yet another Prime Minister, Stolypin's successor, Vladimir Kokovtsov, spoke openly to the Tsar.

It was all to no purpose. The Empress would not hear a word against Rasputin. When told of his debauchery, she explained that saints were always calumniated. The apostles, she explained, had greeted everyone with kisses; so why should this latter-day apostle not do the same? When the Grand Duchess Militsa, who had been responsible for introducing the *starets* to the Tsaritsa, admitted that she had been deceived by this Man of God, Alicky refused to listen. Even the revelations of the Empress's sister Ella, the Grand Duchess Elizabeth, on Rasputin's true nature, made no impression.

When the Press began its attack on the *starets*, Alicky talked her husband into ordering a ban on any mention of his name. When the Duma debated his activities, she insisted that the Prime Minister forbid it. If anyone complained to the Tsar about Rasputin, she engineered their downfall. A governesss, demanding that the leering peasant be barred from the young grand duchesses' bedrooms, was dismissed. Two bishops, who had dared to question Rasputin's sincerity, found themselves speedily transferred. A monk, whose criticism was distinctly more outspoken (it was he who had set in circulation the Empress's letters to Rasputin) was secularized. Even Kokovtsov, the Prime Minister, was dismissed because he had drawn up a report on the favourite.

The *starets* had only to drop a hint in the Empress's ear for her to act. 'Our Friend's' advice was always sacrosanct. Alicky would not rest until she had talked her complaisant husband into carrying out Rasputin's wishes.

And, as Rasputin became steadily more unpopular, so, too, did the Empress. She had always been considered cold, stiff and bigoted; soon she would be accused of being a heartless, power-hungry virago, determined to rule the Tsar and, through him, Russia, along the lines laid down by the 'Holy Devil'.

CHAPTER TWENTY-ONE

Moments of Glory

I

With the opening of the second decade of the century, life for Crown Princess Sophie of Greece suddenly began to brighten. In a matter of months, almost, she was to be raised to a position of greatness.

Until then, Sophie's career had not been especially rewarding. The early years of her marriage to Crown Prince Constantine had been fraught with personal problems. She had been shy, bored, lonely and easily depressed. She had had to battle against such things as ill health, inadequate accommodation and a disheartening lack of response to her various charitable enterprises. Later years had brought more serious troubles. The disastrous war against Turkey had embittered her, not only against the Great Powers that had refused to help Greece, but against certain Greeks themselves who, after their defeat, had suddenly turned against the royal family.

Within the family, too, there had been dissension, with her father-in-law, King George I, refusing to concede that his sons were grown men, worthy of trust and responsibility. Her husband's tireless work towards the reorganization of the Greek army after its defeat had been unappreciated. When, in 1909, a group of young army officers calling themselves the 'Military League' seized power, they forced Crown Prince Constantine to resign as Commander-in-Chief. For someone with as Teutonic and orderly an upbringing as Sophie's, these caprices of Greek political life were all but incomprehensible.

Although the claim by the Crown Prince's secretary, George Mélas, that Crown Princess Sophie 'never had any love for Greece' and that 'she never missed an opportunity of saying anything offensive' about the Greeks was grossly exaggerated, she may well have felt periodic disenchantment with her adopted country. To Maurice de Bunsen, at one time First Secretary at the British Embassy in Constantinople, she admitted that her life in Athens was 'a great trial'.

Yet, with her kind heart, Sophie continued to concern herself with the sick and underprivileged. The Union of Greek Women, which dedicated itself to welfare work, was her inspiration. And, having inherited an interest in her surroundings from her mother, the Empress Frederick, Sophie applied herself to the improvement of the Greek capital.

Giving weight to the belief that the Crown Princess had become somewhat embittered was the fact that, with the passing years, she had developed from a mercurial young girl into a woman of considerable force of character. By the year 1913, in which she turned forty-three, Crown Princess Sophie had been married for twenty-four years. Whereas the forty-five-year-old Crown Prince remained the frank, open-hearted, headstrong man he had always been, she had become something of a martinet. As softly spoken, as unaffected and as fair-minded as ever, Crown Princess Sophie could none the less give the impression of a woman of iron resolve.

With her high-piled hair, her erect carriage and her ropes of waist-long pearls, she had an undeniably regal air. Her bearing was dignified; her public manner reserved. This royal reserve, allied to the shyness which she shared with her cousins Alicky, Maud and Ena, made her appear almost unapproachable. She was, says one who knew her well, 'extra-ordinarily distant in her manner'.

The celebrated hostess, Roma Lister, meeting the Crown Princess for the first time at the home of Baroness Mathilde Rothschild, wrote of Sophie's somewhat imperious air: 'This Princess was certainly made to play a part in a wider horizon and a greater position than the little kingdom of Greece. I noticed, even in this short hour, a stronger personality than exists in most feminine royalties. She was friendly and gracious to all the party, but there was a latent power hidden in her, as in her brother [Kaiser Wilhelm II] – a reversion to the medieval type of sovereign that pierced through the banalities of life.

'Even in this informal gathering a certain etiquette was observed and all our conversation was carried on in low voices, almost in whispers . . . I have never been with royalty when the natural deference has been so much asked for and conceded.'

Yet there were occasions when, even in public, Sophie could forget her reserve and talk with great spirit and unexpected knowledge. An observer once noticed her in animated conversation with Jean Valaority, a director of the Banque Nationale. When the Princess had passed on, Valaority 'expressed great admiration for her, and observed that he had been positively taken aback by her extensive acquaintance with matters of which he would never have suspected her of knowing anything.'

With the years Sophie had developed something of the methodicalness of the Empress Frederick. It was said that she 'simply worshipped order. The internal arrangements of her palace were perfection itself, and, excellent housewife that she was, she gave her personal attention to the ordering of every detail. This same orderly spirit, this same practical instinct for organization and discipline was applied by her in connection with all the various charitable undertakings on which she conferred her patronage.'

In the upbringing of her children, too, Sophie exercised a great deal of discipline. She was never unkind but she could be firm. Into them she attempted to instil – mainly by example – self-control, good manners and a sense of their duties towards others. Although Mélas's accusation that 'none of her children had a real affection for her, and she, on her side, often exhibited great *sécheresse de coeur*' is nonsense, Crown Princess Sophie was a strict and conscientious mother.

But, like any mother, she could not help talking about her children. She delighted in repeating their more amusing prattle. She would tell of the occasion when, on her way to a ball, all a-dazzle in jewels and satins, she came to the nursery to say good night to the children.

'Mama is just like a fairy Queen,' enthused one of them.

'No,' exclaimed another. 'She is like God's wife!'

To improve the characters of her children still more, the Crown Princess sent them to English schools. In common with her mother, Sophie had great faith in the character-building qualities of British boarding-schools. They encouraged independence, unselfishness and a sense of fair play. In her determination to have her children educated in England, the Crown Princess came up against the opposition of old King George. If a Greek education had been good enough for his children, argued the King, why should it not be for his grandchildren? But Sophie held firm and a compromise was reached. George, the heir presumptive, would be educated in Greece but his brothers and sisters could spend some time at schools in England. Eastbourne was chosen as the most suitable centre for the Greek royal brood and on summer Sundays Sophie would travel from Windsor to see them. Usually she would put up at the Grand Hotel; sometimes, during the school holidays, she might rent a house at Seaford.

That Crown Princess Sophie loved and admired her grandmother's country there is no doubt. 'The most beloved country in the world,' she would call it. The irrepressible Princess Daisy of Pless once met her at a children's party at Buckingham Palace. As an Englishwoman living in Germany, Princess Daisy spoke of the difficulties of her life. The German-born Princess Sophie was all sympathy. 'She said she loved England,' writes Daisy, 'and how easy and happy it all was compared with Germany. The true motto of England, she said, was "live and let live", but in Germany it seemed to be: "you must do and think as I do, or die".'

Sophie was referring, of course, to the megalomania of her brother, Kaiser Wilhelm II. It might almost have been her mother, the Empress Frederick, speaking.

Sophie's husband, Crown Prince Constantine, Princess Daisy mentioned only briefly. He was, she wrote, 'a dear; a big, fair man'.

A more telling description of the Crown Prince at this time comes from his great friend Princess Paola of Saxe-Weimar. He was 'tall, fair, with an active figure and with soft blue eyes like those of his aunt, Queen Alexandra, eyes in which a quizzical smile constantly appeared even when his face was grave . . . there was a sweetness in his face and a charm in his smile which were reflections of his mind'. In short, Crown Prince Constantine was an attractive and good-natured man.

Not until the years just prior to the First World War, however, did Constantine and Sophie have the chance of putting their undoubted talents to good use. Suddenly, opportunity, for which they had waited so long, opened up before them.

2

In the year 1910 the 'Military League', considering its task of the reorganization of Greek affairs accomplished, retired from the political scene. Its withdrawal was followed by a general election. The election brought to power, as Prime Minister, a politician by the name of Eleftherios Venizelos. An astute, ambitious and patriotic man, Venizelos set himself the task of rehabilitating the Greek nation. He was determined that the humiliating defeat by Turkey be avenged and Greece restored to greatness.

One of Venizelos's first moves was to reinstate Crown Prince Constantine as Commander-in-Chief of the army. Venizelos fully realized how well fitted was Constantine for the post. Not only was he a man of considerable military ability but he was extremely popular with the troops. Constantine's bluntness, his simplicity, even his occasional bursts of temper, were something which the men appreciated. And then, as *Diadoch*, or heir, he was endowed with an almost mystical prestige. The country could not have wished for a more inspiring Commander-in-Chief.

While Constantine devoted himself to the military preparations, Venizelos applied himself to the diplomatic. In this he had the unqualified backing of King George. Before she could again face Turkey, Greece must come to an understanding with her fellow Christian neighbours, Bulgaria and Serbia. By the summer of 1912, Venizelos had arranged military alliances between the three Balkan states. By October they were at war with Turkey. The First Balkan War was under way.

The campaign, this time, was glorious. Assuming personal command of the reorganized Greek army, Constantine gained one victory after another. Everywhere the Turks were forced back. After four hundred years of Turkish rule, the Macedonian capital of Salonika was liberated. King George, followed by his heir, rode in triumph through the streets to celebrate the great victory with a *Te Deum* in the Byzantine Cathedral. Four months later, in February 1913, Janina, the capital of Epirus, fell to the Greeks. Turkey, soundly beaten, was obliged to withdraw almost entirely from Europe. Constantinople and its outskirts remained its only European possession.

For the sixty-eight-year-old King George these were rewarding days. He was to celebrate the golden jubilee of his reign that year. After that, he planned to abdicate. 'I shall have reigned fifty years in November, and it's long enough for any king,' he told his sons. 'I think I'm entitled to a little rest in my old age. Besides, Tino will be able to do far more with the country than I ever could. He has been born and bred here, while I am always a foreigner.'

Ever since his triumphal entry into Salonika, King George had been living in the Macedonian capital. On the afternoon of 18 March 1913 he went for his usual walk. As always, he was accompanied only by an equerry. On their way towards the harbour they passed a squalid café outside which sat a raggedly dressed man who looked closely at them as they passed. When they returned that way a couple of hours later, the man was still there. As they passed him, the man drew out a revolver and shot the King in the back. Within seconds, King George was dead.

The assassin turned out to be mentally deranged. While awaiting trial, he committed suicide.

Crown Prince Constantine was at Janina when he heard the news of his father's death. Immediately he set out for Athens to assume the crown.

Crown Princess Sophie, then expecting her sixth and last child, was resting on a settee in her writing room on the evening of the fateful day. There was a knock at the door and the Marshal of the Court entered.

'Your Royal Highness,' he said, 'I bring very bad news.'

Princess Sophie's first thought was of her husband. But the Marshal went on to tell her that the King had been seriously injured.

'You mean . . .' asked Sophie, guessing the truth, 'he is dead?'

'An hour ago,' answered the Marshal, 'he was shot by an assassin in the streets of Salonika, and died immediately.'

At once Sophie hurried across to the Old Palace to comfort her mother-in-law, Queen Olga. 'It is the will of God,' murmured the heartbroken old Queen.

King George's body was brought back to Athens by sea from Salonika and lay in state in the Metropolitan Cathedral. Then it was buried under the fragrant pine trees on a hillock on the family estate at Tatoi. Below shimmered the hot plain of Attica but here, on the hilltop from which the King had often admired the view, it was always cool.

Tino and Sophie were now the King and Queen of the Hellenes. There was very little time, however, for them to accustom themselves to their new status. Constantine had hardly sworn allegiance to the constitution before war broke out once more. Bulgaria, dissatisfied with her share of the spoils from the recent war, now turned on her former allies, Greece and Serbia. Romania, hitherto neutral, decided that she might as well get what she could and promptly declared war on Bulgaria as well. By the summer of 1913, the Second Balkan War was under way.

For King Constantine, this campaign was no less successful than the last. Under his personal command, the Greeks soundly beat the Bulgarians. From the peace conference which followed, Greece, led by Venizelos, emerged triumphant. She now controlled most of Macedonia, Thrace, and the Epirus, the Aegean Archipelago and Crete. The size of the country had more than doubled. It was, indeed, a moment of national glory.

On 5 August 1913, King Constantine returned to Athens. Now the idol of his people, he was given a stupendous welcome. Escorted by the entire Greek fleet, his battle cruiser, *Averoff*, steamed into Phaleron Bay. On the quayside, in dazzling sunshine, stood Queen Sophie. Together, in an open landau, the King and Queen drove through hysterically cheering crowds into the capital. At the sight of the two of them – he so tall and soldierly and she so erect and proud – it was not difficult to believe that the old prophecy was being fulfilled. Throughout the centuries of Turkish domination, the flame of Hellenism had been kept flickering by the legend that Byzantium would rise again when another Constantine and Sophie sat upon the Greek throne. This new Constantine would reconquer Constantinople and make it once more the capital of a great Hellenic Empire. The 'Great Idea' would be realized.

Already, there existed between the Soldier-King and his men an almost mystical relationship. The troops were devoted to this honest, unaffected giant who had led them to such magnificent victories and won for them such widespread territory. To them, he was known as 'Son of the Eagle'. At the end of the Balkan wars, the King had given each soldier who had served under him a photograph of himself. It showed him in a plain khaki uniform and dusty boots, smoking a cigarette. Each picture carried the handwritten inscription: 'To my gallant fellow soldiers of two glorious wars.' It was signed CONSTANTINE B. (The B, meaning King, always followed the royal name.) Yet, to many of its enraptured recipients, this scrawled B looked more like IB, which in Greek numerals stood for XII. The last Emperor of Byzantium had been Constantine XI; had the new King, inadvertently or intentionally, signed himself Constantine XII? Was he destined to lead his people back to Constantinople and there, under the great dome of St Sofia, to wear again the imperial crown of Byzantium? Would Queen Victoria's granddaughter Sophie become Empress of Byzantium?

King Constantine and Queen Sophie were indeed living, in the words of one of Constantine's brothers, through 'glorious moments'.

During the early months of 1914, there was talk of a marriage between two of Queen Victoria's great-grandchildren: Olga, the eldest daughter of the Empress and Emperor of Russia, and Carol, the eldest son of the Crown Prince and Princess of Romania. The Grand Duchess Olga turned eighteen that year and Prince Carol twenty.

The reasons for the proposed match were political. Romania, ruled by the Hohenzollern King Carol I, had long been allied to Germany and Austria-Hungary. But with a considerable section of Romania's population being violently anti-Hungarian and with many Romanians being pro-French, Russia was hoping to attract Romania towards the Entente Powers – Russia, France and Great Britain. When old King Carol I eventually died, he would be succeeded by his nephew, the ineffectual Nando, who would, in turn, be ruled – there was no doubt – by his energetic wife, Marie. And as one of Crown Princess Marie of Romania's grandparents had been Queen Victoria and another Tsar Alexander II, there seemed every reason to believe that Romania would one day come over to the Entente camp.

What better way of ensuring this than by marrying the Tsar's daughter to Princess Marie's son, Romania's future King?

Nicholas and Alexandra, steeling themselves to the idea that their daughters would have to marry sooner or later, favoured the suggestion. Marie was not so well disposed. Although flattered by the proposal that her son marry the Tsar's daughter, she was afraid that Olga might be a transmitter of haemophilia. She did not want the dreaded disease carried into the Romanian royal family. Still, not wanting to refuse the imperial invitation to Russia, the Crown Prince and Princess, with their son Carol in tow, arrived at Tsarskoe Selo in the spring of 1914.

The visit was not a great success. The always perceptive Marie found the atmosphere at Tsarskoe Selo unreal and, at the same time, deadly dull. The imperial family lived as in a dream, cut off, not only from the grim realities of life in Russia but from all society, even their relations. Although the Tsar was as gentle and charming as ever, he appeared remote; he seemed to live, says Marie, 'in a sort of imperial mist'. And of course, one could never get close to the Tsaritsa.

One of the troubles was that Alicky and Marie were as unlike as chalk and cheese. Where the one cousin was frank, charming and socially accomplished, the other was reserved, inarticulate and *gauche*. 'She managed to put an insuperable distance between her world and yours,' wrote the disapproving Marie, 'between her experiences and yours, her thoughts, her opinions, her principles, rights and privileges. She made you, in fact, feel an intruding outsider, which is of all sensations the most chilling and uncomfortable . . . .

'The pinched, unwilling, patronizing smile with which she received all you said as if it were not worth while answering, was one of the most disheartening impressions I ever received. When she talked, it was almost in a whisper and hardly moving her lips as though it were too much trouble to pronounce a word aloud. Although there was little difference in age between us, she had a way of making me feel as though I were not even grown up!'

The girls Marie liked better. She found them natural and gay and pleasant; more so when their mother was not in the room. They regarded her, Marie was quick to point out, as 'a good sport'. Olga she did not find especially pretty. Nor, it seems, did Carol. Indeed, neither of the young people showed the slightest desire to get to know the other better. As the object of the visit – a possible match between Olga and Carol – was never mentioned by Nicholas and Alexandra, Marie took it upon herself to broach the subject.

One day before luncheon she asked to see Alicky alone. The Empress invited her into her famous mauve boudoir and there the two cousins spoke with, on Alicky's part, unusual candour about the project. Both agreed that the children must decide for themselves; it would never do to force a marriage. All that the parents could do was to 'create occasions' on which the two could meet. 'Smilingly we agreed that we felt entirely incapable of influencing Fate, that, in fact, we had no idea how such things were done. At that moment we were simply two mothers, mutually relieved that we "had had it out". I felt that I had done my duty, the rest was in the hands of Fate.'

It was without regret that Marie, Nando and Carol left Tsarskoe Selo to spend a few days in St Petersburg. In the home of one of her aunts, Marie was able to see 'all those who had not dared approach Tsarskoe's solitude, had not dared intrude into that mysterious centre where somewhere in the shade Rasputin held his fatal sway'. She did not see Rasputin.

That summer the Russian imperial family created one of the occasions on which Olga and Carol were able to meet. They paid a formal, day-long visit to the Romanian Black Sea port of Constanza. It was a day of brilliant sunshine. On the gaily beflagged pier to greet them were old King Carol, his Queen Carmen Sylva ('in a too long, flowing gown, whiter than the foam of the sea'), Ferdinand, Marie and their six children. Whatever else the imperial visit might have achieved (the day's ceremonial was glittering) it brought the young couple no nearer to marriage. Olga would not even contemplate it and Carol was not interested enough to take things any further.

That Carol had nothing against the institution of marriage itself was to become only too apparent in later years; it was simply that he had no wish to marry Olga.

That night with, according to the effusive Marie, 'the heavens a mighty map of stars', the imperial family sailed back to Russia. Marie was never to see them again.

Her parents were not unduly upset by the fact that Olga had decided against marrying Carol. They would never have dreamed of forcing one of their daughters into marriage. 'You know how difficult marriages are in reigning families,' the Empress once explained to a Russian Foreign Minister. 'I know it by experience, although I was never in the position my daughters occupy, being [only] the daughter of the Grand Duke of Hesse, and running little risk of being obliged to make a political match. Still, I was once threatened with the danger of marrying without love or even affection, and I vividly remember the torments when . . . [the Empress named a member of one of the German reigning houses] arrived in Darmstadt and I was informed that he intended to marry me. I did not know him at all and I shall never forget what I suffered when I met him for the first time. My Grandmother, Queen Victoria, took pity on me, and I was left in peace. God disposed otherwise of my fate, and granted me undreamed of happiness.'

CHAPTER TWENTY-TWO

The Balkan Queens

I

The outbreak of the First World War, on 4 August 1914, proved, if proof of it had been necessary, the irrelevance of the family ties between the various royal houses of Europe. That the majority of European sovereigns were members of Queen Victoria's family made not the slightest difference to the course of events. Although, during the hectic days before the fighting began, telegrams flew between the closely related sovereigns of Germany, Russia and Great Britain – Willy, Nicky and Georgie – their urgent phrases affected the outcome not at all. War found the various grandchildren of Queen Victoria in firmly opposed camps. Germany, headed by the Queen's eldest grandson, Kaiser Wilhelm II, was chock-a-block with Victoria's relations. Against them were ranged the families of her British grandson, King George V and her Russian granddaughter, the Empress Alexandra. Still neutral at the outbreak of war were the countries in which lived her other granddaughters, Queen Ena of Spain, Queen Maud of Norway, Queen Sophie of the Hellenes and Crown Princess Marie of Romania. But they, too, were to suffer the agonies of divided family loyalties. For all Queen Victoria's descendants, the next four years were to be a heart-breaking time.

Yet Wilhelm II, ever wont to over-estimate the powers of reigning sovereigns, simply could not admit that the war had been caused by anything other than the duplicity of his relations. He accused King George V of conspiring with Tsar Nicholas II to complete the nefarious policy of encirclement begun by King Edward VII. To think, he exclaimed, that George and Nicky should have played him false; if his grandmother had been alive, she would never have allowed it.

It was ironic that at the moment when Queen Victoria's matriarchy reached its zenith – when her direct descendants sat on the thrones of no fewer than seven European countries – Europe should be ravaged by the greatest war that it had ever known.

In few countries was the problem of opposing loyalties more acute than in Romania. King Carol I, *der Onkel*, and Queen Elisabeth, Carmen Sylva, were staunchly pro-German. Crown Prince Ferdinand, as always, kept his own counsel, but Queen Victoria's granddaughter, the volatile Crown Princess Marie, was unhesitatingly pro-Entente. As a result, feelings in the royal household ran high. King Carol, old and broken in health, tried to be tactful and not to air, too often, his belief in the invincibility of the German Army. But there was no hiding Carmen Sylva. Overnight, she found herself, says Marie, '*die Rheintochter* (daughter of the Rhine) with a vengeance; it was *Deutschland über Alles, Gott mit uns,* and all the rest of it'. In her ringing voice the Queen would proclaim that Germany's day had come; that the Germans must, for the good of humanity, become lords of the earth; and, more obscurely, that England must fall because of the immorality of her women. This last might, or might not, have been a shaft aimed at the flirtatious Marie.

In less heroic moments the Queen would cry out against the horrors of war. If only, she would declaim, they could all 'join hands in a mighty circle and sail up to Heaven, away from the miseries of this darkened sphere'.

To this effusion the King would grunt an eminently sensible answer. 'That is rubbish, Elisabeth.'

On the day after France and Germany had opened hostilities, King Carol convoked a crown council to decide on Romania's attitude to the war. Although the country's treaty with the Central Powers was merely a defensive one, the King was anxious for Romania to join Austria and Germany in the field. He had no doubt that Romania, as Germany's ally, would reap enormous benefits from a quick German victory. In this he came up against the implacable opposition of his council. The result of the conference was that Romania would remain neutral.

So upset were the King and Queen by what they considered to be the country's rejection of them, that they began to talk of abdication. If King Carol abdicated, would Crown Prince Ferdinand, who was said to share his uncle's pro-German sympathies, do the same? Marie was appalled at the idea. She had no intention of giving up her rights to a crown which was almost within her grasp. Yet when she tackled Nando on his intentions, he refused, as always, to commit himself.

Nor was Marie the only one to be alarmed at the prospect of the dynasty's wholesale withdrawal from the scene. The politicians were no less anxious. One day a leading Liberal member came to implore her not to think of leaving the country. 'Even if the Prince, your husband, feels bound to follow his uncle into self-imposed exile, promise that you will remain with us with your son Carol, if possible with all your children, remain to carry on the work begun by the old King; it is not possible nor fair that you should forsake us at this crisis when we know you are with us with all your heart . . . .'

That, indeed, was the core of the matter. Marie was undoubtedly with them with all her heart. Not only would she not think of deserting the Romanian people but she was in complete harmony with them. With public opinion swinging away from the Central Powers towards the Entente Powers, she was becoming the symbol of the nation's new allegiances. The egocentric Marie was not slow to appreciate her position. 'I,' she exclaimed in her histrionic fashion, 'was becoming their hope . . . at the Great Hour my country and I were one.'

'I felt prepared,' she continues, 'for all that would be asked of me, equipped for the battle that lay before me; I was not afraid – on the contrary, a strange elation possessed me and with it the certainty that I was ready for the great call that was coming, for it *was* coming; I felt it in every drop of my blood; only, I did not know that it was to come so soon!'

It came, that 'great call', on 10 October 1914, just over two months after the outbreak of war. King Carol, disheartened by his country's ingratitude and the German retreat on the Marne, died in his sleep. Early the following morning the news was telephoned to Princess Marie. Her husband was now King Ferdinand of Romania and she Queen.

Whatever else the momentous news might have done, it did not strike Marie dumb. On the contrary, she has recorded her reactions vividly and at great length. Her moment had arrived and she responded to it, she assures us, unhesitatingly. Lest her ineffectual husband respond to it with rather less enthusiasm, she presented him with a golden bowl which she had obviously been keeping in readiness against this day. 'Tomorrow may be thine,' ran its somewhat hectoring inscription, 'if thy hand be strong enough to grasp it.'

The same note of doubt about her husband's capabilities permeates her description of him taking the oath before Parliament on the day of their accession. 'He was neither loved nor unloved,' she wrote, 'he was a closed book; no one knew his thoughts, but he might be as the dawn of something greater, might become the fulfiller of a long-dreamed-of dream.'

She leaves one in no doubt whatsoever about her country's appreciation of her abilities.

'I stood somewhat apart, with my children around me, a long black mourning veil covering my face. My heart-beats were as the feet of Fate.

'I hardly heard the King's voice, nor his words, but I heard how they acclaimed him, their King of tomorrow, a long thunder of applause rolled round the walls.

'Then suddenly my name ran through space:

' "Regina Maria . . ."

'And there was something in the way they called out my name that had within it a sound of hope.

' "Regina Maria . . ."

'I suddenly felt that I must bare my face before the whole house, that I must turn towards them with no veil of mourning between them and myself.

'A great clamour mounted to the vault above, something long drawn out and tremendous that came irresistibly from many hearts!

" 'Regina Maria . . ."

'And we faced each other then, my people and I.

'And that was *my* hour – mine – an hour it is not given to many to live; for at that moment it was not only an idea, not only a tradition or a symbol they were acclaiming, but a woman; a woman they loved.

'And at that hour I knew that I had won, that the stranger, the girl who had come from over the seas, was a stranger no more; I was theirs with every drop of my blood!

'Disappointment, sorrow, misfortune might follow, for are we not all in the hands of God? But that hour when we stood looking into each other's eyes, all their many faces turned towards my face, was my hour . . . my people turning towards me as though I were their supremest hope . . . .'

Of false modesty, Queen Marie of Romania could never be accused.

2

Queen Sophie of the Hellenes was on her way back from her usual summer holiday in England when war broke out. After ensuring that her cousin, King George V, would see that two of her children still at Eastbourne were sent after her, she returned to Athens. Here she found her husband, King Constantine, determined that Greece should remain neutral. The conflict did not directly concern Greece; the country had no reason to side with any of the belligerents. Moreover, the recent successful Balkan wars had left Greece exhausted and depleted. To consolidate her gains, she needed a long period of peace. These were the views, not only of the King, but of the General Staff and the majority of the Greek people.

They were not, however, the views of the Prime Minister, Venizelos. He, and his adherents, were all for Greece joining the Entente Powers immediately. Only by throwing in their lot with France and England could the Greeks hope to realize their great dream of a new Byzantium. With Turkey allied to Germany, there seemed no reason why Greece could not, by joining the Entente, finally win Constantinople from the Turks.

This conflict between King and Prime Minister came to a climax early in 1915. The British were about to attack the Dardanelles. Here, reckoned Venizelos, was Greece's golden opportunity. She must join the attack. But the General Staff could not agree. Militarily, it would be too risky an adventure. In protest at the scheme, the Chief of the General Staff resigned. His assessment of the situation was supported by the King. At this, Venizelos also resigned.

The country was now divided into two irreconcilable camps. The fiery Venizelos, encouraged by Britain and France, came to symbolize 'The Great Idea' of an aggrandized Hellenic Empire, while the realistic Constantine, in clinging to neutrality, seemed suddenly to have become a stumbling-block to national aspirations.

It was a situation of which the Entente Powers, anxious for Greek support, took immediate advantage. From now on Britain and, particularly, France, lost no opportunity of denouncing King Constantine. That he commanded the loyalty of the majority of his subjects was a fact they conveniently ignored. The most obvious way of blackening him was to accuse him of being pro-German. To support this contention, they cited his visit to Germany in the autumn of 1913. At a banquet given in Constantine's honour by Wilhelm II, the ebullient Kaiser had unexpectedly presented the King with a Field-Marshal's baton. Taken by surprise, Constantine had blurted out an impromptu speech of thanks in which he had made mention of the fact that he had received his military training in Germany. The Kaiser, in drawing up a draft of the Greek King's reply for publication, slightly altered the emphasis. Constantine, out of politeness, made no objection. The subsequent publication of the speech, together with a photograph of Constantine in his German Field-Marshal's uniform, caused a furore, especially in France. Constantine was astounded. When chided by his secretary for having agreed to the Kaiser's version, the King's answer was typically artless. 'How was I supposed to know that the thing would be telegraphed all over Europe?'

Now, two years later, the King's speech was being cited as 'irrefutable proof' of his pro-German leanings. Not only in the French and British Press but in Greek newspapers sympathetic to Venizelos, Constantine was constantly under attack. He was accused of 'using a veil of treacherous neutrality to hide his pro-German sympathies'. He was, they claimed, an autocrat acting in defiance of the popular will as epitomized by Venizelos – 'the voice of the people'. With funds provided by the intelligence sections set up in the French and British legations in Athens, local propagandists became more and more virulent in their abuse.

Nothing that Constantine could say in his defence carried any weight. He could protest that King George V was also a German Field-Marshal, and that Kaiser Wilhelm II was a British one. He could claim that he was neither pro-German nor pro-Allies but pro-Greek; that to admire the German army made him no more a German sympathizer than to admire the British Navy made him pro-British. He could prove that he had held firm in the face of the Kaiser's threats to attack Greece unless she joined the Central Powers. (To Constantine's reasons for neutrality, Wilhelm II had answered 'Rubbish'.) He could point out that Germany's allies, Turkey and Bulgaria, were his enemies.

It was all to no effect. His justifications were never even given an airing by the Allied censors. 'We wanted to run into the streets and cry out that the things they said about my father were not true,' exclaimed one of his daughters afterwards.

Yet King Constantine was spared the worst of the vilification; that was aimed at Queen Sophie.

As the sister of Kaiser Wilhelm II, Sophie was in an invidious position. Once before, after the disastrous war against Turkey in 1897, she had experienced the sudden and unreasoning hatred of a certain section of the Greek people. But that had been as nothing compared with the accusations now flung at her. In the eyes of her critics she was a fanatically pro-German, hard-hearted virago, determined to force her weak-willed husband into fighting for the Kaiser.

No story about her was too bizarre to be believed. She would only speak German, they said, not Greek; after Lord Kitchener had visited the King she forced her way into the room to counteract 'whatever impression favourable to the Entente might have been left' on her husband's irresolute mind; she had a private cable installed at Tatoi by which she could communicate with German submarines; Constantine's near-fatal illness of 1915 was due to the fact that, during the course of a disagreement between them on the question of Greece joining Germany, Sophie had grabbed a dagger and stabbed him in the chest.

One of her most virulent critics was George Mélas, the secretary who, because of his disapproval of King Constantine's policy of neutrality, left his service to become an ardent supporter of Venizelos. In a book published after the war, Mélas vilified the royal couple in no uncertain terms. According to his somewhat implausible theory, the outbreak of hostilities changed Sophie from the a-political Queen of the Hellenes into a power-hungry German princess. 'I never forget,' he quotes her as saying before the war, 'that I am Queen of Greece first and a German princess next.' But how profound, he exclaims, was the change that followed. 'Queen Sophie completely forgot that she was Queen of the Greeks. She bethought herself only of the fact that she was a German, and the Kaiser's sister into the bargain. She remembered her duty as a princess of Germany, she forgot her duty as a Queen.'

Yet even Mélas was forced to admit that the widely believed rumour that Sophie, in the course of a pro-German tirade, had stabbed her husband in the chest, was nonsense. Throughout the King's long illness (which was pleurisy) she nursed him devotedly. But having admitted that, Mélas goes on to accuse the Queen of several lesser offences. Only those favourable to the German cause were allowed to see the King; only

German doctors ('emissaries of the Kaiser') could attend him. Because of his pro-Allied sympathies, she refused to admit the King's brother, Prince George, who had come all the way from Paris, to the sickroom. She so enjoyed wielding power that she minimized the seriousness of her husband's illness and discouraged any talk of their eldest son, the twenty-five-year-old Crown Prince, acting as Regent.

As Sophie's mother, the Empress Frederick, had been unjustly reviled in Germany during her husband's tragic illness thirty years before, so was Sophie suffering from the slanders of those sympathetic to the Entente cause.

But if Queen Sophie had ever shown a bias towards any country other than Greece, then that country was undoubtedly England. Her homes looked like English country houses, her home language was English, her children had attended English schools. Time and again she had voiced her admiration for English institutions and English ways. Of all Queen Victoria's continental granddaughters, none moved in a more English atmosphere than she. England, not Germany, had been her second home. 'My beloved England,' she once exclaimed, 'is the one place I love to be in most.'

On the other hand, between Sophie and her brother the Kaiser there had never been much *rapport*; they had quarrelled incessantly. So un-affected herself, she had always considered him insufferably ostentatious and ludicrously conceited. Why then, should she suddenly be champion-ing him against England?

King Constantine's convalescence was slow. For three years after his illness he carried a tube in his back through which a poisonous discharge passed from an incision in his lung. Gradually, this suppurating wound weakened his once powerful physique. According to his brother, Prince Christopher, he 'lost much of his vigour and the capacity for crisp decision that had carried him through so many difficulties in the past. He was no longer master of the situation.' Once so dynamic and impatient, King Constantine became dispirited and lethargic.

While the King was still in this weakened state, an attempt was made on his life – and on the lives of some of his family.

The court was living almost continuously at Tatoi at that time. One day, as the royal party was driving out through the trees surrounding the palace to inspect a distant pall of smoke, they suddenly found them-selves trapped in a raging, roaring, wind-driven forest fire. With no room to turn the car, they scrambled out and began running back home. However, the King, realizing that some other members of the party who had gone on ahead would be in danger, left the Queen and one of their daughters to make their own way home, and hurried off to help. He was too late. Seventeen members of the court had been burnt to death. With the swiftly spreading flames blazing all about him, he stumbled back to the palace. Here he found the Queen and the princess. He at once packed them off to Athens lest the palace catch fire. The building was saved from the flames, however, by a belt of green trees surrounding it.

That the fire had been started with the intention of burning the royal family to death there was very little doubt. On the following day the police discovered, to windward of the palace, a row of empty petrol cans.

With the King having survived the attempt of his life, Venizelos now attempted to undermine his authority. Working hand in glove with the French, the Prime Minister staged a rising in Salonika and set up a Government of National Defence, or Provisional Government, in opposition to the King's government in Athens. On 24 November 1916 Venizelos formally declared war on the Central Powers. With the King still stubbornly refusing to abandon his neutrality, the French attitude became more menacing. The French fleet had been anchored off Athens for some months; now a contingent of troops landed at Pireaus and marched on the capital. When the Greek troops, loyal to the King, resisted, the French ships began bombarding the city. When even these bullying tactics failed to coerce the Greeks into joining them, the Allies applied another method. They imposed a strict blockade. For the following eight months the Greeks all but starved.

Small wonder that Queen Sophie's cousin, King George V of England, could ask his Prime Minister whether they were 'justified in interfering to this extent in the internal Government of a neutral and friendly country?' He declared himself astonished at the way the French were treating those Greek soldiers who, in refusing to join Venizelos's revolutionary movement, were remaining loyal to their King and government.

But King Constantine, by now, was little better than a prisoner of the French. 'How weary I am of all these dirty politics!' he wrote to a friend at the time. 'I have periods of disgust and lassitude which almost bring tears to my eyes . . . .'

Queen Sophie had become even more embittered. To see all her husband's work for Greece ruined and their people hounded and starving for no other reason than they they had wished to remain neutral, appalled her. 'Can Belgium have suffered more at German hands?' she would ask.

3

While Queen Sophie of the Hellenes was being denounced by the
Western Allies, her cousin Queen Marie of Romania was being acclaimed.
For two years after the outbreak of the war Romania, like Greece,
remained neutral. But whereas neutral Greece was being reigned over by
a king whose wife was suspected of harbouring pro-German sympathies,
King Ferdinand of Romania was known to have a wife who was passionately pro-British. And while King Constantine was merely accused of
being influenced by his wife, it was generally accepted that Queen Marie
of Romania led her husband by the nose.

She herself always denied this. It was simply not in her nature, she
protests blandly, to dominate others. Her husband, she none the less
forces herself to admit, was of a retiring disposition, slow to make up his
mind and not fond of asserting himself. She, on the other hand, was quite
different. He therefore turned to her for encouragement and advice.
'Owing to having been too long subjected and oppressed [by the late
King Carol]' she explains, 'King Ferdinand needed to be continually
stimulated and upheld; my attitude gave him courage and hope. In the
hour of doubt he found in me a steel-like assurance which he did not find
in himself. Hand in hand we were strongest; life did not appal me, for I
had about me something of the joyful warrior who never shuns a fight.'

The particular fight which she was determined not to shun was, of
course, a war against the Central Powers; especially now that they had
been joined by Romania's old enemy, Bulgaria. As she so candidly puts it,
Marie 'loathed neutrality'. King Ferdinand was not showing anything
like the same eagerness. For one thing he could not help feeling sympathetic towards Germany. He was a Hohenzollern, German-born and
with brothers fighting for Germany. For another, little Romania was in
no position to wage war against the Central Powers. Like a bent finger,
Ferdinand's country poked into the territories of the Central Powers:
along the north-western borders lay Austria-Hungary; along the southern
borders, Bulgaria. It was true that Romania shared its far, north-eastern
border with Russia, but the Russians were already heavily engaged along
their extended frontiers facing Germany and Austria-Hungary.

On the other hand, a great many Romanians shared the Queen's
anxiety to get into the fight. Not only were the majority of Romanians
favourably disposed towards the French but they were violently anti-
Hungarian. For years they had had their eyes on Transylvania, an area

of Hungary considered to be the heartland of Romania. Territorially, an Entente victory would benefit Romania tremendously; she could win what she considered to be Romanian lands from both Austria-Hungary and Bulgaria. Queen Marie could then become, as she assures us her soldiers were longing for her to become: 'Empress of all the Romanians'.

But for two years Romania remained neutral. While the Queen dashed off reassuring letters to her cousins Nicky and Georgie and flirted with emissaries of the warring countries (the most handsome man in Germany, claims Princess Daisy of Pless, was dispatched to the Romanian court) her husband heeded the arguments of the pro-German faction. The death, in the spring of 1915, of the inimitable old Queen, Carmen Sylva, removed one strong proponent of the German cause from the King's circle. It was not until the summer of 1916, however, that King Ferdinand was finally prevailed upon to throw in his lot with the Entente. He did so with a heavy heart. On 27 August 1916, Romania declared war against the Central Powers.

With the outbreak of hostilities, Queen Marie of Romania came into her own. The war brought out the best in her; she could live to the very limits of her abilities. Showy and self-opinionated Queen Marie might have been, but she was neither frivolous nor foolish. All her great qualities – and she had many – were now brought into play: her courage, her compassion, her skill, her verve, her sense of duty, even her appreciation of the dramatic. 'I have health and vigour which God has given me for a purpose,' she would exclaim. 'It must not be wasted. Because I can't help but feel strong, I must work to win.' And she did. She was tireless. Invariably dressed in a nurse's white uniform, she spent her days organizing, inspecting, encouraging and visiting the wounded. Though sometimes ill and exhausted, she never spared herself. She became, in a way, the symbol of Romania's will to fight.

It certainly needed a symbol. From the outset, the war was a disaster. The Romanians, who had crossed so bravely into Transylvania, were beaten back almost immediately. Within a month of the declaration of war, the country had been invaded by the Germans from the north and the Bulgarians from the south. Everywhere the army fell back in confusion. One town after another went to the invading armies; hospitals, weapons and provisions had to be abandoned as the troops retreated helter-skelter towards the north-east. Munitions, promised by the equally hard-pressed Entente Powers, never materialized. The Black Sea port of Constanza, so recently the scene of the Tsar's brilliant state visit, fell in October. By the end of the month Bucharest itself was threatened. Early in November it was decided to evacuate the capital.

At this moment of extreme national despair, with Bucharest about to be abandoned, fate dealt Queen Marie a terrible personal blow. Her youngest child, a three-year-old boy named Mircea, contracted typhoid fever. For day after day the mother watched the little boy become weaker. Every moment that she was able to spare from visiting hospitals was devoted to nursing him. To sit by his bedside, to see his glazed eyes and to hear his anguished cries almost broke her indomitable spirit. By the morning of 2 November 1916 he was clearly sinking. That night he died.

They buried him in the church at Cotroceni Palace. No sooner had this been done than Bucharest, and the Palace, had to be evacuated. In the scramble to get away, the Queen found time to scribble a note to be handed to the commander of the occupying forces. 'I do not know who will inhabit this house that I have loved,' she wrote. 'The only prayer I ask is that they should not take away the flowers from the new little grave in the church.'

In what the Queen calls 'panic, disorder and confusion', the Romanians fell back before the enemy until only a fraction of the country remained in their hands. The royal family established itself at Jassy, a provincial town not far from the Russian frontier. With Russia finally coming to their assistance, the Romanians were able to check the enemy advance and hold the line around Jassy. Behind the front, however, all was chaos. The winter of 1916–17 was the coldest for fifty years. There was not enough food. There were too few doctors and too few beds. With typhus raging throughout the army, conditions in the hospitals were deplorable. At one stage it was thought that the army would have to retreat into Russia; at another that Queen Marie should personally plead Romania's cause with her cousin, Tsar Nicholas II. Both suggestions – the first which Marie hated and the second which she rather fancied – were abandoned. She remained at Jassy, giving advice, encouragement and consolation.

It was a heart-breaking task. The Romanians, she complained, 'are more or less fatalists; they always imagine that God, or Fate or Chance will step in at the last hour and save them! But being of English origin my motto is: Help yourself and God will help you'.

She certainly never gave way to despair. Like her grandmother, Queen Victoria, during an earlier war, Marie would countenance no talk of defeat. Her courage was an inspiration to them all. Always smiling, always calm, always beautiful, she travelled across nightmare roads to visit indescribably squalid hospitals and to bring comfort to appallingly wounded men. Everywhere her white uniform, with it red cross on the armband, served as a spur and a solace to her people. As an Englishman in one of the Allied missions put it, 'She was a flame of resistance that no storm could put out.'

CHAPTER TWENTY-THREE

'The German Woman'

Yet another of Queen Victoria's granddaughters to be accused of dominating her husband during the First World War was the Empress Alexandra of Russia. About the validity of this charge there was no doubt whatsoever.

During the first few months of the fighting Alicky had been content to play the traditional role of a royal consort in wartime: she devoted herself to hospital work. Forgetting her own ailments, she converted several palaces into hospitals. To nursing the often cruelly mangled men, she gave herself unstintingly. Her dedication, her courage and her compassion could not be faulted. At last, in practice as well as in theory, the Empress had become the *Matushka* of these loyal and simple Russian soldiers.

Not until the spring of 1915, when the Russians began to fall back before the Germans, did the Tsaritsa actively concern herself with the Tsar's affairs. The army, up to that time, had been under the supreme command of one of the Tsar's relations, Grand Duke Nicholas. The Tsar himself, although often at the front, controlled affairs of state. The Emperor was not very happy with this situation. He would much rather have been acting the warrior-Tsar at the front. Even less happy about it was the Empress. With her high-flown ideas on autocracy, she firmly believed that her husband's place was at the head of his soldiers. It was quite wrong that someone else should hold that all-powerful position; particularly the popular and physically impressive Grand Duke Nicholas. Might he not, in time, overshadow the small and mild-mannered Tsar?

Encouraging Alicky in her thinking was Rasputin. His motives, however, were not anything like as elevated as hers. Hating Grand Duke Nicholas (he had once threatened to hang the *starets*) Rasputin wanted him removed. While the Russian army was successful this was almost impossible, but once it began to retreat, the *starets* worked up the Empress's feelings against the Grand Duke. And she, in turn, harried the Emperor.

After the fall of Warsaw in August, the Tsar made up his mind. Grand Duke Nicholas was dismissed and, against the violently expressed advice of his Ministers, the Emperor took personal command of the army.

Alicky was overjoyed. 'You have fought this great fight for your country and throne – alone and with bravery and decision,' ran her impassioned phrases. 'Never have they seen such firmness in you before... I know what it costs you . . . forgive me, I beseech you, my Angel, for having left you no peace and worried you so much, but I too well know your marvellously gentle character and you had to shake it off this time, had to win your fight alone against all. It will be a glorious page in your reign and Russian history, the story of these weeks and days . . . God anointed you at your coronation, he placed you where you stand and you have done your duty, be sure, quite sure of that and He forsaketh not his anointed. Our Friend's prayers arise day and night for you to Heaven and God will hear them . . . It is the beginning of the great glory of your reign. He said so and I absolutely believe it . . . .'

That was all very fine but it was going to need more than Our Friend's continuous prayers to ensure victory at the front and contentment at home. Not only had the control of the army passed from the strong hands of the Grand Duke Nicholas into the weak ones of Tsar Nicholas II but the disappearance of the autocratic Head of State to the battlefield had left a vacuum in the capital. It was a vacuum which was to be filled, with increasing assurance, by the Empress Alexandra. While the Tsar attended to the army, she would attend to the government. Together, they would save Holy Russia and the autocracy for their son.

In what Alicky considered to be her divine mission she was backed up, indeed guided, by the wily Rasputin. Her faith in him remained absolute. And, lest she might develop any reservations about him, Rasputin never hesitated to remind her of his importance in her life. 'I need neither the Emperor or yourself,' he would say in his apparently artless fashion. 'If you abandon me to my enemies, it will not worry me. I am quite able to cope with them. But neither the Emperor nor you can do without me. If I am not here to protect you, you will lose your son and your crown in six months.'

And, believing him, Alicky carried out all his wishes. Together, and with disastrous results, they managed the affairs of the Empire. The Empress began by trying to chivvy her husband into being firmer, bolder, more autocratic. 'Be the master and lord, you are an autocrat,' she would write. All that was needed to secure victory on the battlefield and harmony in the country was a strong hand at the helm. 'Never forget that you are and must remain autocratic Emperor,' she commanded. 'We are not ready for constitutional government.' Loathing the Duma, the Empress simply ignored its existence. As Our Friend says, she assured her husband on another occasion, 'responsible government . . . would be the ruin of everything'.

Anyone advocating even a slight relaxation of autocracy had to be got rid of. The Ministers, reckoned the Empress, were simply there to carry out the Tsar's will. If they disagreed, they had to go. One by one, and always on the advice of Our Friend, competent Ministers were dismissed to be replaced by nonentities. But even Ministers of unquestioned loyalty to the autocratic ideal fell from power because of Rasputin's antipathy towards them. One word of criticism about the Man of God's dissolute way of life or dangerous influence in affairs of state was enough to end a career. The vacant places would be filled by almost anyone fortunate enough to have won Rasputin's approval. It was not that he was ambitious for power; he merely wanted to have his own way in everything. In letter after letter to the front, the Empress would urge the dismissal of one Minister or the appointment of another.

'Be firm,' she wrote after yet another of Rasputin's nominees had emerged triumphant, 'one wants to feel your hand – how long, years, people told me the same "Russia loves to feel the whip" – it's their nature – tender love and then the iron hand to punish and guide. How I wish I could pour my will into your veins . . . Be Peter the Great, Ivan the Terrible, Emperor Paul – crush them all under you . . . .'

Not content with controlling affairs in St Petersburg, the Empress and Rasputin turned their attention to the front. On the conduct of military affairs, the *starets* proved no less voluble. There was no aspect of the campaign on which he did not have, or did not give, an opinion. His instructions, coming from God and passed on via the Empress, reached the harassed Tsar in a steady stream. He told the Emperor when to advance, when to retreat and when to stay put. An order, given by the Tsar's Chief of Staff, would be countermanded after the Empress, primed by Rasputin, had buffeted her husband with contrary instructions.

By the year 1916, the Empress Alexandra's mauve boudoir at Tsarskoe Selo had become the nerve centre of the Russian Empire. Industrious, dedicated, convinced that everything she was doing was for the good of Holy Russia, the Empress forged ahead. Not an evil, nor a heartless, nor even an entirely foolish woman, the Empress Alexandra was a supremely misguided one. Serenely unaware of her limitations, obsessed by her inaccurate picture of Russia, she took upon her own shoulders the entire task of managing the Empire. With God's emissary to advise her, what need had she of anyone else?

By the autumn of 1916 the Empress, never popular, was loathed by all strata of Russian society. 'Their hatred of the Empress has reached a terrible pitch;' noted her cousin, Queen Marie of Romania after talking to a group of Russian officers, 'they consider her a misfortune to the country and there is no one today who would not gladly get rid of her by any means.'

Few doubted that the Tsaritsa was Rasputin's mistress. For what other reason would she be so intimate with this coarse-mannered *moujik* whom even the Church had rejected and whose chief characteristic was his lecherousness? And not only were they accused of being lovers; many believed them to be working together for a German victory. The charge of treason was one to which the German-born Empress was especially vulnerable. Ignoring the fact that she had been raised by her grandmother, Queen Victoria, her critics harped on her German connections. Was not her brother, the Grand Duke of Hesse, fighting for the German army? Was not one of her sisters married to the Kaiser's brother? Indeed, was the Kaiser not her cousin?

The capital was full of a story about a general who, while walking down a corridor in the Winter Palace, came across the Tsarevich in tears. 'What is wrong, my little man?' asked the general. In bewilderment the boy answered: 'When the Russians are beaten, Papa cries. When the Germans are beaten, Mama cries. When am I to cry?'

The Russian military disasters could only be explained, it was said, in terms of betrayal. Alexandra and Rasputin, aided by the puppets that they had put into power, were working against Russia. The Empress, having badgered her weak-willed husband into entrusting her with secret military information, passed it on to Rasputin who, in turn, gave it or sold it to the Germans. Just as Alicky's cousin, Sophie, was being accused of being in direct touch with the Kaiser, so was Alicky. The Alexander Palace at Tsarskoe Selo was said to be fitted with secret wireless sets by which the traitors communicated with the enemy. There was talk of a direct telephone line to the Kaiser and about an incognito visit of the Empress's German brother to Tsarskoe Selo. On her, and on Rasputin, was blamed the chaotic economic situation: the rising food prices, the shortage of flour and butter, the blatant profiteering. The shortages, it was claimed, were being contrived. With the country starving, it could be handed over, all the more easily, to the Germans.

No one was to know, nor would it have been believed, that Alexandra – in her honest, if inexpert, fashion – was trying to do something about these overwhelming economic problems. Even Rasputin was applying himself to the alleviation of the serious shortages. In a vision, reported the Empress to her husband, Our Friend had seen a solution to the problem. Alexandra was to speak 'earnestly, severely even' to the Tsar about it. For three days no trains other than those carrying flour, butter and sugar must be allowed to pass.

As for the charge that the Empress harboured pro-German sympathies, nothing, according to those who knew her well, could have been more ridiculous. 'The Empress was very English in her feelings,' wrote one of her ladies. 'Her upbringing and her long visits to Queen Victoria had all fostered her love for her mother's country. English was the language which came easiest to her. The Allies' cause was hers. All her recorded conversations and published correspondence show this clearly, and she rejoiced at the Allies' successes nearly as much as at the Russian ones.'

Beyond the walls of Tsarskoe Selo, however, none of this was known. As hunger and dissatisfaction spread, so did the cry against 'the traitoress' become louder. On the streets, they were openly calling the Empress *Nemka* – 'the German woman', or more graphically, 'the German whore'. A mob had rioted in Moscow, demanding her arrest. Warming to their task, they had attacked the convent in which lived the Empress's sister, the saintly Grand Duchess Elizabeth. 'Away with the German woman!' they had yelled.

Things could obviously not go on like this much longer. If the dynasty were to survive, there would have to be some drastic changes. Queen Marie of Romania, on being visited by her sister Ducky (now married to Grand Duke Cyril) was told something of the situation in Russia. It was, says Marie, 'very dangerous because of the prevailing great hatred of the Empress'. Even the Emperor was becoming the object of widespread contempt; 'there is actually talk,' continues Marie, 'about suppressing them one way or another'.

2

On the first day of January 1917, Rasputin's corpse was found under the ice of one of the tributaries of the frozen River Neva in the capital. Its discovery confirmed the rumours that had been circulating for the past two days. During the course of a gathering at the palace of young Prince Yussoupov, the *starets* had been murdered.

The manner of his death had proved to be no less bizarre than that of his life. Prince Yussoupov, having decided that the survival of the monarchy depended on the removal of the *starets*, had invited Rasputin to visit him in a cellar of his palace. Here, while his fellow conspirators huddled at the head of the stairs, the Prince had fed his guest a plate of cakes liberally sprinkled with cyanide. They had no effect on Rasputin whatsoever. Yussoupov then gave him two glasses of wine, similarly poisoned. These too, seemed to affect the *starets* not at all. The Prince, by now considerably unnerved, next tried a revolver. He shot Rasputin in the back. The *starets* fell to the floor, apparently dead. But a few minutes later he leapt to his feet and grabbed his opponent by the throat. The terrified Prince dashed helter-skelter up the stairs. Behind, on all fours, followed the bellowing Rasputin. With Yussoupov having locked himself in his parents' apartments, Rasputin decided to get away. In spite of a stomach full of cyanide and a bullet in his back, he ran 'quickly' across the snow-covered courtyard towards the gate. Twice more he was shot by one of the other conspirators. When he fell, he was savagely kicked on the head. At this stage Yussoupov reappeared. Taking a club, he pounded the prostrate form. When, at last, there was no more movement, they roped the body in a curtain and carried it to the frozen river where they stuffed it through a hole in the ice.

But, incredibly, Rasputin was not yet dead. When his corpse was brought up three days later, it was discovered that he had still had enough strength to free one of his roped hands and that he had actually died from drowning.

At first, the Empress Alexandra could simply not believe that the Man of God had been murdered. Until his body was found, she convinced herself that he had temporarily disappeared, that he would soon return. 'God have mercy,' she wrote distractedly to the Tsar. 'Such utter anguish (am calm and can't believe it) Come quickly . . . .' When she learnt the truth she was devastated. Rasputin, to her mind, was a martyr, the victim of that corrupt and effete society that she had always abhorred. She had him buried in the great park at Tsarskoe Selo. Around his grave, in deep mourning, stood the Tsar and his family.

With the hated Rasputin out of the way, attention was focused on the equally hated Empress. Those who had imagined that the death of Rasputin would put an end to her political influence were proved quite wrong: she played a more active part than ever. To any suggestion that she withdraw from the political scene, the Tsar turned a deaf ear. Nor would he listen to any talk of choosing a government more acceptable to the Duma. Time and again he was warned – by members of the imperial family, by ambassadors, by politicians – that the Empress's attitude was leading, not only the dynasty, but all Russia, to disaster.

But the usually irresolute Nicholas remained firm. Completely in tune with the Empress, he was determined that the autocracy be passed on, untainted by democracy, to his heir.

With the Emperor refusing to listen to reason, there were mutterings about more drastic methods of getting rid of Alexandra. The talk was loudest within the imperial family itself. The Tsar's grand-ducal relations planned a palace revolution: the Empress would be arrested, the Emperor forced to abdicate in favour of his son and Grand Duke Nicholas proclaimed Regent. It all sounded brave enough but nothing ever came of it. In the spring of 1917 the Tsar went back to the front and the Tsaritsa continued to rule through her utterly incompetent Ministers.

There was no way, now, of averting the storm.

It started on 8 March 1917. That day the Empress heard that there had been some disturbances in the streets of the capital. The mob, cold and hungry, had broken into several bakeries. During the following few days she was told that rioting had become more serious and that workers were out on strike. Worried by the turn of events, the Empress was not nearly as worried as she should have been. For one thing she had no real appreciation of the seriousness of the situation. The Prime Minister, one of Rasputin's ineffectual nominees, was playing down the danger. Everything, he assured the Empress, was under control. Street disturbances were hardly anything new.

And then Alexandra had problems closer at hand. On the very day that the first riots broke out, the eldest and youngest of her five children – Olga and Alexis – went down with measles. They were followed by her second daughter Tatiana and her friend Anna Vyrubova. Busy nursing the invalids herself, Alicky could not give all her attention to the trouble in the streets. Only on hearing, on 12 March, that the soldiers in the capital were joining the mob did she come to a full realization of the danger. Immediately she wired the Tsar. He had already heard about the troubles. He wired back that he would be arriving at Tsarskoe Selo two days later, 14 March.

By 13 March almost the entire capital was in the hands of the revolutionaries. The imperial government had collapsed and power had passed to the Duma. On the following day the Tsar's last bastion, the Imperial Guard, pledged allegiance to the Duma. The revolution had triumphed.

That morning the desperately worried Alicky was up early to welcome her husband home. But no train arrived at Tsarskoe Selo station. Nor was there any message from the Emperor. Later she heard that his train had been stopped. Why, she did not know. Throughout the day she received news of the defection of hitherto loyal troops. Already discipline among the men guarding the palace was beginning to slacken. The servants were slipping away. The vast palace was emptying.

By the following morning Marie and Anastasia had caught measles as well. Still there was no word from the Tsar. Several times during the day, telephone calls were put through to the capital, asking for news of the Emperor. There was none. The water was cut off; then the electricity. The silence was unnerving. In the huge, dark, cold rooms, the little band of faithful huddled together apprehensively. They could only wait. 'No one,' claims the admiring Gilliard, 'can have any idea of what the Tsaritsa suffered during those days when she was despairing at her son's bedside and had no news of the Tsar. She reached the extreme limit of human resistance in this last trial . . . .'

Yet, outwardly, she remained calm. She knew how important it was for the others to see her going about her duties as though nothing were wrong. In the presence of her sick children she appeared cheerful. When the remaining members of the household moved into the imperial wing, she helped the ladies make their beds: 'You Russian ladies don't know how to be useful,' she chided. 'When I was a girl, my grandmother, Queen Victoria, showed me how to make a bed. I'll teach you . . . .' She dared not panic. She dared not let them see that she was worried to death about her children, her husband, the appalling situation in which they found themselves. What was happening? What was going to happen?

Not until the evening of 16 March did the Empress hear any news of the Tsar. His uncle, Grand Duke Paul, came to Tsarskoe Selo to see her. He told her that her husband had abdicated the day before. In the drawing-room car of the imperial train, drawn up at Pskov, the Tsar had renounced not only his own rights to the throne, but those of his invalid son. There had been nothing else that he could do. Not only the political leaders in the capital but the generals commanding the various fronts had urged him to abdicate. Without the support of either of these groups, he had had no choice. Having signed his act of abdication, he had travelled back to headquarters for a few days to take leave of the army.

Betraying as little emotion as possible, the Empress heard the Grand Duke out. Only after he had gone did that steely self-control break down. With, according to one witness, her face 'distorted with agony' and her eyes 'full of tears', she tottered towards the windows. Leaning heavily against a writing table she uttered the word '*Abdiqué!*' Her next words were scarcely audible. 'The poor dear . . .' she whispered, 'all alone down there . . . what he has gone through, oh my God, what he has gone through . . . And I was not there to console him . . . .'

She was the first of Queen Victoria's grandchildren to lose her throne.

3

The loss of the throne brought forth an immediate reaction from yet another of Queen Victoris's grandchildren, King George V of England. The British King was doubly related to the Russian imperial family: both Nicholas and Alexandra were his first cousins. King George's father. King Edward VII, had been the brother of Alexandra's mother, while King George's mother, Queen Alexandra, was the sister of Nicholas's mother – the Dowager Empress Marie. And not only were George and Nicky first cousins; they looked extraordinarily alike and were very similar in taste and temperament. It was thus with considerable alarm that King George heard of his cousin's abdication.

'Events of last week have deeply distressed me,' he wired to Nicholas on 19 March 1917. 'My thoughts are constantly with you and I shall always remain your true and devoted friend, as you know I have been in the past.'

Nicholas never received the telegram. By the time it reached Russia, he and his family were already under arrest. This step had been taken by the Provisional Government with the sincere intention of ensuring the Tsar's safety; a murder would not be the way to inaugurate a new and enlightened régime. But as not everyone in Russia was inclined to show the same concern for the Tsar's life, the Provisional Government decided to withhold the telegram. Despite its uncontroversial tone, the telegram could be interpreted as evidence of a British plot to rescue the Tsar. Any such suspicion could jeopardize the Tsar's position. The Soviet – a fiery assembly of soldiers' and workers' deputies sitting side by side with the more moderate Duma – was determined that the imperial family be kept imprisoned in Russia. Therefore the Provisional Government, which was hoping that the family could be spirited away to safety, had to move cautiously. Any attempt to get the Tsar out of the country could be foiled by the Soviet: it would simply instruct its workers to halt the train carrying the imperial party.

So, while the Tsar, his family and his band of loyal attendants remained under guard in the echoing rooms of the Alexander Palace at Tsarskoe Selo, the Provisional Government considered how best to get them away to safety.

King George V's telegram, although not delivered to the Tsar by the new Russian Foreign Minister, strengthened the Minister's conviction that it must be to England that the imperial family should go. He therefore asked the British Ambassador, Sir George Buchanan, to approach the British Government on the matter. Buchanan wired the request. Somewhat reluctantly, the British Government agreed to grant asylum to the Tsar. Lloyd George, the Liberal Prime Minister, had the highest regard for the new revolutionary government and it was only because the request had come from them, and not from the Tsar himself, that he granted it.

The decision created a furore. In British left-wing circles, there was an outraged reaction. To many Englishmen, Nicholas II was simply a blood-stained tyrant, whose fall from power had been richly deserved. Why, they wanted to know, should this reactionary autocrat be given asylum in freedom-loving Britain? Even Sir George Buchanan was beginning to have second thoughts. By receiving the Tsar, Britain might alienate the extreme left wing of her Russian ally, he warned.

As the opposition mounted, so did the suspicion grow that the proposal had originated with King George V. It was only too easy to believe that he was behind this scheme to grant asylum to his cousins. This would not be the first time that his close relationship to foreign royalties had landed him in trouble. Already he had been accused of being too well-disposed towards that other controversial pair of first cousins: King Constantine and Queen Sophie of the Hellenes. Strong exception had been taken to the fact that the King had recently entertained two of King Constantine's brothers. Within days of the proposal to grant the Tsar asylum becoming public, the King was receiving abusive letters.

The truth was quite different. From the start the King had doubted the wisdom of his Cabinet's invitation. He was fully alive to the delicacy of the situation. It would be much better, he thought, for the imperial family to take refuge in some neutral country, such as Denmark or Switzerland. His reservations, passed on to his government at the end of March, were politely waved aside. His second letter, ten days later, was more sympathetically received. By now the British government, heeding the public clamour, was changing its mind. Might not France, it wondered, be a more suitable place of refuge? To this suggestion, the British Ambassador in Paris replied in no uncertain terms. 'I do not think that the ex-Emperor and his family would be welcome in France,' he wrote. 'The Empress is not only a Boche by birth but in sentiment. She did all she could to bring about an understanding with Germany. She is regarded as a criminal or a criminal lunatic and the ex-Emperor as a criminal from his weakness and submission to her promptings.'

From that time on, the plan to offer asylum to the imperial family began to die a slow death. The British government could not risk offending the public and the Russian government could not risk offending the Soviet. After the murder of the imperial family, each side denied responsibility for the collapse of the plan. A member of the Provisional government accused the British of withdrawing their offer; the British contradicted the statement.

But whatever the reason, the imperial family remained shut up at Tsarskoe Selo. How much longer they could remain there was another matter. The Provisional government's grip on affairs in Russia was becoming progressively shakier (Lenin had by now arrived back from exile) and once that grip was lost, the imperial family would be in real danger. By August it was decided that they must be secretly moved away from the capital as soon as possible. The Tsar wanted to go to Livadia, his summer residence on the Black Sea (his mother, the Dowager Empress, was there) but the journey was considered too hazardous. Instead, the Minister of Justice, Alexander Kerensky, chose the provincial town of Tobolsk, in western Siberia.

If, during the early days of the revolution, Kerensky had protected the imperial family because he had regarded any show of vengeance unworthy of the new Russia, by now he had developed considerable respect for them. Their behaviour during their captivity had been exemplary. They had had so much to contend with: physical discomfort, humiliation, the loutishness and antagonism of their guards, the frightening uncertainty of their fate. One day had seen them at the pinnacle of power, the next at the mercy of the crude soldiery surrounding their palace. Yet they had remained dignified, uncomplaining, courteous. The children, with the resilience of youth, had to some extent adapted themselves to the changed circumstances, but for the Empress it had not been easy. Convinced of the correctness of her attitude, she had been very embittered by the turn of events. To strangers she appeared haughty and unreconciled.

'I don't understand why people speak ill of me,' she once exclaimed to Kerensky. 'I have always loved Russia from the time I first came here. I have always sympathized with Russia. Why do people think that I am siding with Germany and our enemies? There is nothing German about me. I am English by education and English is my language.'

Only gradually did she adjust herself to the new situation. But adjust herself she did. 'Did you know, Alexandra Fedorovna, I had quite a different idea of you,' admitted a common soldier after he had talked to her in the garden, 'I was mistaken about you.'

Nicholas's behaviour, on the other hand, had been impressive from the start. Everyone, companions and visitors alike, were struck by his calm, his simplicity, his resignation and his charm. Those who had expected to find either a hard-hearted autocrat or a simple-minded weakling were astonished to find an unassuming and sensible gentleman.

It was with considerable relief, therefore, that Kerensky got the family aboard a train bound for Tobolsk on 14 April 1917. How long they would remain there, no one knew. By now, however, the Tsar had come to respect Kerensky as much as Kerensky respected him. 'I have no fear,' said Nicholas on hearing that they were to be sent away. 'We trust you. If you say we must move, it must be. We trust you.'

Others were not quite so sanguine. 'News has reached us that the Tsar and his family have been transported to Tobolsk, no one knows why,' wrote Queen Marie of Romania. 'What are they going to do with my poor Nicky? I am so anxious . . . .'

CHAPTER TWENTY-FOUR

The Fall of Kings

I

The next one to lose her throne was Queen Sophie of the Hellenes.

If, during the first two years of the war, the accusations of pro-Germanism made against Sophie had been groundless, by the beginning of 1917 there was something more to them. Her attitude is understandable. Neutral Greece had suffered no harm at the hands of Germany. On the other hand, she had suffered nothing but harm at the hands of the Entente Powers. The Allies had intentionally and consistently undermined King Constantine's position, they had encouraged Venizelos in his rebellious stand, they had bombed Athens and, when their belligerent tactics had still not forced Greece to abandon her neutrality, they had blockaded the country. In addition they had heaped abuse on the heads of both the King and Queen.

All this had incensed Queen Sophie to the point where she was ready to forget past disagreements with her brother, Kaiser Wilhelm II, and call upon him for help. It was not so much that she had become pro-German as that she had become anti-Entente. Nor was she alone in her attitude. Many Greeks, suffering under the Allied blockade, felt the same way. As Sophie's cousin, King George V of England, so rightly pointed out to his government, a 'kindly' instead of a 'bullying' attitude would probably have induced Greece to join the Allies voluntarily.

But the bullying attitude persisted and by the spring of the year 1917 the Greeks could no longer resist the Allied pressure. They were ready, at last, to abandon their neutrality.

They were not ready, however, to abandon their King. 'The Greeks,' as the Russian Minister informed his government in April, 'are ready for any capitulation, provided that the King is left untouched.'

But the Entente Powers had other ideas. In June a French warship, carrying Senator Charles Jonnart, 'High Commissioner of the Protecting Powers of Greece', dropped anchor off Athens. Summoning the Greek Prime Minister aboard, Jonnart presented him with an ultimatum. It demanded the abdication of King Constantine. The King could choose a successor from among his sons, provided it was not Crown Prince George, who was considered to be too closely identified with his father's and mother's 'pro-German' views. Failure to comply with this ultimatum would lead to a full-scale military occupation of Greece and to a second bombardment of Athens.

The King had no choice. Unhappy, disheartened, sick to death of the atmosphere of intrigue and duplicity in which he had been forced to live since the outbreak of war, Constantine agreed to the demand. He was determined that no more blood should be spilt for his sake. To one of his daughters, who begged him not to give way, he answered quietly, 'It is out of the question that I should cause more bloodshed. Don't you understand the meaning of sacrifice?'

At a meeting of the crown council, the King explained that he, Queen Sophie and their children had decided to leave the country. While neither he nor Crown Prince George would sign any act of abdication, the royal power would go to his second son, the twenty-three-year-old Prince Alexander. That same afternoon, the new King took the oath of allegiance at a sad little ceremony in the ballroom of the palace. Just over four years had passed since King Constantine, at the height of his popularity and surrounded by gorgeously robed clergy and beaming Ministers had taken his oath; now only four people – Constantine, Alexander, the Prime Minister and the Archbishop of Athens, who had been smuggled in by a back door – were present.

The ceremony concluded, King Constantine and his family prepared to leave. But an extraordinary thing happened to prevent them from doing so.

The news (which was meant to have been secret) that the King was to leave Greece had spread rapidly through the city. In their thousands the people had trooped to the palace. The building was now surrounded by a vast multitude, determined that the King should not go. 'One by one they took up the cry,' reports the King's brother, Prince Christopher, 'that age-old lament in a minor key with which the Greeks proclaim death or disaster.' Nothing would disperse the mob. Closer and closer to the palace they pressed, all the time shouting, 'He shall not go! He shall not go!' When, at length, King Constantine, Queen Sophie and their children emerged to enter the waiting cars, people flung themselves to the road to prevent the cars from moving forward. The royal party was obliged to return indoors. Each time they made for the cars the same thing happened.

All night the crowd surged about the palace. In the morning they were still there, as vociferous as ever. In desperation King Constantine issued a proclamation. 'Bowing to necessity, and fulfilling my duty towards Greece, I am leaving my beloved country . . .' it explained. 'I appeal to you, if you love God, your country and myself, to submit without disturbance.'

But the crowd would not listen. Under the blaze of the summer sun, their lamentations were turning to hysteria; there were cries that it would be better to kill the King than to let him leave Greece. Finally, the desperately worried family decided on a ruse to get away. Word was spread among the crowd that the King was going to leave by an obscure back gate and the cars were driven round there. In the meantime, other cars were drawn up in the thickly wooded grounds of the Old Palace, which stood alongside. With the attention of the crowd focused on the back of the palace, the royal family slipped out of the front entrance, dashed across a road, pushed through a gate in the railings surrounding the Old Palace grounds and flung themselves into the waiting cars. Queen Sophie, falling behind, was lifted under the arms by two of her brothers-in-law and dumped unceremoniously into her seat. They were only just in time for, as the cars pulled away, the crowd came thundering into the grounds.

The family drove to Tatoi where things took on a less frenetic tone. But even here the King and Queen were besieged by loyalists, all begging them not to leave. Bewildered and tearful, the new King, Alexander I, came to take leave of his family. Alexander was a handsome young man, tall, well-built and dashing, but he was not especially bright nor in any way equipped for the task which had been thrust upon him. This, indeed, is why Venizelos and the Allies had insisted that Crown Prince George be excluded from the succession. Not only had Prince George been trained for kingship but he was a young man of considerable ability; as such, he might prove too independent for Venizelos's liking. Alexander, on the other hand, would be a puppet king.

King Constantine gave Alexander what advice he could, impressing on the young man that he was merely an interim king and that the throne rightly belonged to his father and then his elder brother. To all this Alexander listened and agreed.

When King Constantine had finished, King Alexander broached a more intimate subject. It concerned his secret engagement. Women, and fast cars, were Alexander's passion and he had fallen deeply in love with Aspasia Manos, the daughter of one of his father's equerries. He now asked for permission to marry her. King Constantine was not unsympathetic but he made his son promise that he would not do so until after the war. To this the complaisant Alexander agreed.

Switzerland had been decided upon as the place of exile (King George V had 'strongly disapproved' of the choice of the Isle of Wight) and the royal family left Greece the following day. Despite the fact that they sailed from a small fishing port, the scenes were hardly less feverish than they had been in Athens. Again the royal party had to fight their way through a great crowd and, as they were ferried out to their yacht, *Sphakteria*, scores of people waded into the water, shouting, 'You will come back!'

'Yes,' shouted the King in return, 'be sure I shall come!'

'The whole bank,' says Prince Christopher, 'was lined with men and women waving frantically to that solitary figure standing alone in the stern of the boat with his eyes fixed on the shores of his beloved Greece. And when at length the yacht carried him out of sight and their voices calling to him to come back could no longer be heard across the water, they turned away and went sorrowfully home to Athens.'

The scene on the *Sphakteria* was no less sorrowful. The King was visibly dejected, the children in tears. Only Queen Sophie, who in her youth had given way so readily to tears, kept her emotions under control. 'As gold tried in the fire comes out brighter and purer still,' her mother, the Empress Frederick, had said to her twenty years before, 'so those who are noble show their grandest qualities in misfortune.' Dry-eyed and straight-backed, this cruelly misunderstood daughter of a cruelly misunderstood mother watched the shores of her husband's kingdom fade and disappear from sight.

2

King Ferdinand and Queen Marie of Romania were deeply disturbed by the news of the Russian revolution. With the greater part of Romania in enemy hands, the little Romanian army was utterly dependent on Russian support; without it, Romania's brave resistance would crumble in a day. Its other allies, Britain and France, were in no position to help; heavily engaged on the Western Front, they were not even able to send the promised munitions to their embattled Romanian ally. It was thus with considerable foreboding that the Romanian sovereigns followed the course of the Russian upheaval.

But for the moment, all was well. Russia fought on. And, lest a similar revolutionary spirit manifest itself in Romania, King Ferdinand, egged on by the astute Queen Marie, made his troops a promise: after the war, Romanian land was to be more fairly divided among all its peoples. The aristocratic landowners might have been incensed but this timely declaration may well have kept the troops loyal to their sovereigns in the difficult months ahead.

For suddenly, difficulties came thick and fast. In July 1917 Russia, spurred on by huge loans from its anxious allies, launched another offensive. Initially successful, it developed into a *débâcle*. By the middle of the month, the Russians were falling back everywhere. It was not known how much longer the Romanians, fighting bravely on Russia's disintegrating flank, could hold out. At Romanian headquarters, everything was confusion. There was talk of evacuating Jassy, of falling back into Russia, everyone was packing. Queen Marie, usually so buoyant, so optimistic, was plunged into black despair. Yet she would not hear of moving to safety. 'The King has sworn to me,' she wrote, 'that whatever happens I shall be allowed to remain with him in the army on Romanian ground to its last possible limit. Nothing will induce me to go off as many are trying to persuade me to do.'

Outwardly confident, she continued her manifold duties. In the searing heat of summer, she went jolting over dusty roads to spend hours in the hospitals, on the parade grounds and in the trenches. Within sound of the guns and sometimes within sight of the enemy, she moved encouragingly among the men. 'Looking into the eyes of their Queen,' she says, 'they had sworn to stand up like a wall to defend the last scrap of Romanian territory which was still ours. Many a dying soldier whispered to me with his last breath that it was for me that he was fighting, for was I not his home, his mother, his belief and his hope?'

Be that as it may, it was going to take more than the soldiers' admiration for their indomitable Queen to save the situation. The Romanians were staunch enough but the Russians were becoming daily more unreliable. In their hundreds of thousands, they were deserting from the front. Before the year was out the Russian Provisional Government had fallen and power had passed to the Bolsheviks. To consolidate his still precarious hold on the country, Lenin, the Bolshevik leader, needed peace at any price. By the middle of December 1917, an armistice had been signed between Russia and Germany.

A telegram from Marie's cousin, King George V, offering her family asylum in Britain, merely underlined the desperateness of the Romanian situation. Emphasizing it still more vividly was the visit of her other cousin, Kaiser Wilhelm II, to the conquered part of Romania. In a gesture at once triumphant and respectful, the Kaiser laid wreaths on the tombs of his Hohenzollern relations, King Carol and Queen Elizabeth. It was ironic, thought Nando, that *der Onkel*, who had always longed for a visit from the illustrious Kaiser, should receive one only after he was dead and his country invaded. 'I have always imagined,' wrote Marie sourly, 'that the imperial wreath must have lain heavily on Uncle's tomb.'

All about her now, the air was thick with talk of the hopelessness of continued resistance. She refused to listen. Onto the head of some poor British general who dared suggest that Romania give up the fight, she poured a torrent of abuse. How could he, an Englishman, tell her, an Englishwoman 'and into the bargain a queen', that her country must surrender? 'I am English,' she hurled at yet another dumbfounded general, 'a race that cannot give up.' She could not bear the thought of submission. Heroic schemes chased each other through her fevered mind. She ached to make *le grand geste*. With part of the army, the sovereigns must cut their way through the 'Russian traitors' to link up with the 'still faithful

Cossacks'. There must be *la guerre à outrance*, with the King and Queen, encircled by their loyal troops, fighting to the very last. Alone, if necessary, like some medieval heroine, she would face the oncoming German hordes.

'Oh God, if only I were a man, with a man's rights and the spirit I have in my woman's body!' she exclaimed, 'I would fire them to desperate, glorious resistance, *coûte que coûte*!'

It was magnificent but it was hardly practical politics. In January 1918, the Germans sent King Ferdinand an ultimatum. The Romanians were to come and treat with them. They were given four days in which to reply. The government resigned and a new government, headed by one of the generals, decided to sue for peace. There was nothing else that they could do. Queen Marie was appalled. 'I *cannot* resign myself to it, I cannot;' she cried out, 'it breaks my heart, it kills my soul, it is too, too unfair.'

She was more appalled still on hearing the peace terms. To her, they were quite unacceptable. Yet, if they were not accepted, Romania was to be totally erased from the map of Europe. The country would be divided up among Germany, Austria, Bulgaria and Turkey.

Poor King Ferdinand, faced with a resolute enemy on one hand and a no less resolute wife on the other, was in a terrible state. Throughout the agonizing days of decision, he tried to have as little as possible to do with Marie. He simply could not face another of her impassioned harangues. Moreover, neither he, nor anyone else at Jassy, was in any doubt whatsoever about her views. But, of course, a blazing, climactic row was bound to come.

On the day that the King was to preside over the Crown Council specially assembled to accept or reject the peace terms (it was the day on which the peace of Brest-Litovsk was signed between Germany and Russia) things came to a head between husband and wife. 'Woman-like,' says Marie, in what must be the understatement of her life, 'I had my say.' Have her say she certainly did, and even she admits that she might have said too much. 'If we are to die,' runs her subsequent, and no doubt refined, version of her arguments, 'let us die with our heads high, without soiling our souls by putting our names to our death warrant. Let us die protestingly, crying out to the whole world our indignation against the infamy which is expected of us.'

But soil his soul by putting his name to his death warrant King Ferdinand did. The German peace terms were agreed to. To the anguished Marie, the capitulation marked one of the bitterest and most tragic hours of her life; 'dark,' she wails, 'as death'.

Before going out to meet what she somewhat over-dramatically called 'a fate almost too dark to be conceived', Marie wrote a last letter to her cousin, King George V. She was not too distraught to remember to draw his attention to the sacrifices made by the Romanians and to explain that their defeat was due to the betrayal of their Russian allies and the overwhelming might of their German enemies. She ('for have I not English blood in my veins?') would rather have fought on to the bitter end. As he, however, would fight on and win, she hoped – and here was the core of her letter – that he would not forget Romania in the hour of victory.

Her fate at the hands of the victors was not nearly as dark as she seems to have imagined it was going to be. Kaiser Wilhelm II was not one for dethroning kings. A new government, sympathetic to the Germans, managed the country's affairs and the royal family remained at Jassy.

But there was no consoling Marie. Far worse, perhaps, than the anguish of defeat and the shame of capitulation was her feeling of personal failure, of a destiny unfulfilled. In a revealing passage, written in those black days after the surrender, she makes mention of her shattered hopes. 'I thought I was destined to be a happy, brilliant, successful queen;' she wrote, 'all within me seemed to promise this, and I seemed made for that part. But perhaps, on the contrary, my lot is to be a tragic, vanquished queen, ever so much more tragic than Carmen Sylva ever was with all her talk of a martyr's crown. I had no vocation for a martyr's part and yet it looks as though God had singled out Nando and myself to bear a cross which at times seems almost too heavy.'

3

The peace of Brest-Litovsk, signed between Russia and Germany on 3 March 1918, had an almost immediate effect on the Russian imperial family. Since late August the year before, the Tsar, the Tsaritsa and their five children had been living in comparative comfort at Tobolsk in Siberia. Even the Bolshevik revolution had not unduly worsened their lot. The troops guarding them had become more truculent and their allowance had been cut down, but their way of life had been little altered. The Tsar kept himself busy by sawing wood, the Tsaritsa by doing handwork and the children by acting and doing lessons.

They remained a devoted family. Nicholas and the children behaved as simply and as charmingly as always while Alexandra revealed herself as a woman of real nobility of spirit. Her piety, her integrity and her sincerity remained unaltered and to them were added an almost sublime humility and resignation. She never complained, she never felt sorry for herself, she was never bitter. She hoped, as they all did, that they would be released or rescued and that they would live to see better days but she wasted no time railing against fate or regretting past glories. Sustained by her faith in God and her love of her husband and children, she bore her long martyrdom with dignity and calm.

Her chief worry, now as always, was for the health of her thirteen-year-old son Alexis. During the last few months he had been quite well but in the spring of 1918 he had a fall. The resulting haemorrhage was the worst since the terrible attack at Spala in 1912. With no Rasputin to help her, Alicky was forced to face the trial alone.

It was at this stage, with the Treaty of Brest-Litovsk recently signed, that a new commissar arrived at Tobolsk. His name was Yakovlev. He appears to have had orders to take the imperial prisoners to Moscow. Why they should be wanted there is uncertain. The Tsar imagined that he was going to be forced to sign the Peace Treaty; Kaiser Wilhelm II would far rather have dealings with a fellow monarch than a revolutionary government. But whatever the reasons for the move from Tobolsk it soon became obvious to Commissar Yakovlev that young Alexis was in no state to be transported. He therefore decided that the Tsar alone must accompany him. This flung the Empress into an agonizing dilemma. Without her support, she felt that her husband might be forced into some shameful action. Yet her heart was torn at the thought of leaving Alexis. After a searing period of indecision, she decided to accompany her husband. Alexis was getting better and he would be left in the devoted care of three of his sisters and the tutor Gilliard. The Empress and her daughter Marie would go with the Tsar.

At dead of night, on 25 April 1918, they set out. After a nightmarish journey in carts through the snow and slush of the spring thaw, they reached Tyumen, where they boarded a train. As the line from Tyumen to Moscow ran through Ekaterinburg, where the local Soviet (the Ural Regional Soviet) was known to be violently antagonistic towards the Tsar, Yakovlev appears to have decided to take another route.

But the Ural Regional Soviet got wind of his plan. On nearing Omsk, the train was stopped and diverted to Ekaterinburg. The Tsar was now delivered into the hands of a group of hostile and ruthless men. Whether it was by accident or part of an elaborate plan by the Central government to get rid of the Tsar is uncertain. What is certain is that everyone now washed their hands of responsibility for the imperial family; everyone, that is, other than the Ural Regional Soviet, who loathed them.

The Tsar and his party were put into a two-storeyed house in the centre of the town. Within a month they had been joined by the rest of the family from Tobolsk. Gilliard and some of the others were set free. In contrast to their earlier treatment, the imprisonment at Ekaterinburg was both severe and humiliating. The family was closely guarded and allowed only short periods of exercise in the walled-in yard. They were subjected to petty cruelties and lewd indignities. Not even in the lavatory were the young grand duchesses safe from the crudities of their captors: the door had to be left open and on the walls were scrawled obscene drawings of the Empress and Rasputin.

In July 1918 the Ural Soviet, having all along intended to execute the Tsar, was hurried into taking action. Civil war had broken out in Russia and a strong anti-Bolshevik force was already sweeping westward towards Ekaterinburg. By 12 July it was feared that the town might fall at any day. It was therefore decided that the imperial family must be shot as soon as possible and their remains totally destroyed. Already their ill-disciplined guards had been replaced by an alarmingly efficient force of secret police under the command of a Commissar Yurovsky. It was he who was to organize the mass killing.

Towards midnight on 16 July, the imperial family was awakened. They were told to dress and hurry downstairs as they were to be moved once more. With the sleepy Alexis in his arms and the rest of the family trailing behind, Nicholas came down. They were ordered into an unfurnished cellar and told to wait. The Tsar asked for chairs for his wife and son. Three chairs were brought in. The Tsar, the Tsaritsa and Alexis sat down. The rest of the little party, including the four grand duchesses, stood behind. Suddenly Commissar Yurovsky and his armed squad entered the cellar. He announced that they were all to be shot. With that the men opened fire. They did not stop until the entire party of eleven people had been massacred. The second last one to die was the young Tsarevich. The last one was his sister Anastasia.

The bodies were piled onto a lorry and driven some fifteen miles out of Ekaterinburg. Here they were cut to pieces and burned. When they had been reduced to little more than ashes they were flung down a disused mine-shaft. Five days later Ekaterinburg fell to the anti-Bolshevik forces. Of the imperial family they had come to save, there was no trace.

It was not quite twenty-five years since that morning in Darmstadt when Queen Victoria's breakfast had been disturbed by the news that Alicky and Nicky had become engaged. Hand in hand the flushed and radiant young couple had come to her for her blessing. It had seemed impossible to the old Queen that 'gentle simple Alicky should be the great Empress of Russia'.

4

The end of the First World War, in November 1918, saw a wholesale collapse of European monarchy. Throughout Central and Eastern Europe, sovereigns tumbled like skittles. In Germany, the flight of the dethroned Wilhelm II to Holland precipitated the overthrow of a host of lesser kings and reigning princes. In Russia the Tsar had already been murdered. In Austria the old Emperor Franz Josef had died and his successor, the Emperor Karl, deposed. In Bulgaria King Ferdinand, 'Foxy Ferdie', having proved himself not quite foxy enough by joining the Central Powers, was forced to abdicate. In Greece, King Constantine had been driven from his throne. Two pre-war monarchs only withstood the hurricane that swept through the eastern half of Europe: King Peter I of Serbia and King Ferdinand of Romania.

This meant, of course, that Queen Marie of Romania had been triumphantly and gloriously vindicated.

Never once, in the dark days of defeat, had she lost faith in ultimate victory. She might have been depressed but she was never entirely without hope. 'For the moment I was beaten,' she wrote, 'this I had to recognize. Beaten yes, but not broken, oh, no, not broken! I was, in fact, biding my time, relentlessly attached to one steady ideal, though for the present it was quite impossible to see whence light might again come to us.'

Nor did she lose any opportunity of keeping alive Romania's spirit of resistance. She was constantly haranguing the King to stand up to his Germanophile government; Crown Council meetings were forever being interrupted by the arrival of yet another hectoring note from the Queen to the King. She encouraged anti-German talk, action and attitudes. She even, on one occasion, drove into neighbouring Austrian Transylvania with a car-load of supplies and there regaled the peasants with promises of a brighter, Romanian-controlled future.

And, gradually, things did indeed begin to look brighter. The tide of war had begun to turn. At first slowly, then more quickly, and finally in a rush, the Allied Powers moved towards victory. In a foam of mounting excitement Queen Marie followed these stirring events. Every day brought better news. The Germans were falling back on the Western Front. At the end of September Bulgaria capitulated to the Allied forces moving up from Greece. A month later Turkey dropped out of the war. Five days afterwards Austria capitulated. Revolution broke out in Germany. In Romania, the pro-German government fell. The Romanian army was once more mobilized.

Queen Marie, who during the last few months had been something of an embarrassment, suddenly found herself being acclaimed. Her flicker of resistance had developed into a great blaze of victory. One day, on returning to Jassy by train after a short holiday, she was given a totally unexpected and overwhelmingly vociferous reception. The station and the streets were packed with cheering people. In language as fulsome as her own, she was welcomed as 'The Guardian Angel of our Great National Dream: the one who through every adversity has never weakened or lost hope and who, like a beacon, has led us through darkness to the great hour of light.'

Indeed, the Great National Dream seemed to be coming true. For not only had the country been reconquered but territories previously part of the swiftly crumbling Austrian Empire were clamouring to join Romania. Bessarabia had already declared itself annexed to Romania; now deputations arrived from Transylvania and Bucovina asking to be part of the Romanian kingdom. 'The dream of *Romania Mare* seems to be becoming a reality,' wrote the exultant Marie. 'It is all so incredible that I hardly dare believe it.' She might yet be Empress of all the Romanians.

On 1 December 1918, King Ferdinand and Queen Marie re-entered Bucharest. It was an unforgettable day: a day of 'wild, delirious enthusiasm'. With the bands crashing and the troops marching and the people cheering, the King and Queen rode their horses through the beflagged streets of their capital. Both were in uniform; on her head Marie wore a grey astrakhan busby (it gave her the look, she says, of 'a healthy, chubby youth') and over her tunic, a long military cape with a fur collar. Through a hail of flowers they made their way towards the Cathedral. At one point they halted to kiss a great cross held up from an assembly of brightly robed priests; at another they were presented with the traditional gift of bread and salt by the mayor of the city. Before the *Te Deum*, Queen Marie changed out of her uniform into one of her glittering, trailing, diaphanous garments and, so dressed, kneeled in the light of a thousand flickering candles to give thanks for victory.

Her dream of being a 'happy, brilliant, successful queen' was coming true. Indeed, her most brilliant days still lay ahead.

PART THREE

1918 — 1969

CHAPTER TWENTY-FIVE

'Too Exuberant to Last'

I

The coming of peace found only three of Queen Victoria's grand-children on Continental thrones. Maud was the Queen of Norway, Ena was the Queen of Spain and Marie the Queen of Romania. Alicky, the Empress of Russia, was dead; Willie, the German Kaiser, was in exile in Holland; Sophie, the Queen of the Hellenes, was in exile in Switzerland. But the Coburgs were nothing if not resilient and gradually the old Queen's matriarchy began to burgeon once more. The first one to regain her throne was Queen Sophie.

Ever since the expulsion of King Constantine from Greece in 1917, the royal family had been in Switzerland. For a time they lived in the Villa Werli, belonging to the Dolder Hotel, in Zürich; later they moved to the National Hotel in Lucerne. Their exile, which was bitter enough, was rendered more bitter still by the insulting way in which they were being treated by the French and British living in Switzerland. French and British subjects were warned by their respective consuls against having any truck with the exiled family; old friends turned their backs as the King or Queen approached to greet them.

King Constantine, visibly depressed by the situation, would sit for hours on end, absently twiddling his thumbs. Queen Sophie, on the other hand, kept up a proud, unyielding front. Yet she was suffering as much as he. She was terribly hurt when the two British governesses, Miss St John and Miss Nicholls, were forced to leave her employment lest they lose their passports. She ached to hear from her adored son, Alexander, now King of the Hellenes, but he could not write directly to her. Any little scrap of news about him she cut out of the newspapers; she listened avidly to the reports of those who had seen him.

Once, on hearing that he was going to be in Paris, she decided to tele-phone him. For days, says her brother-in-law Prince Christopher, she could talk of nothing else. Her telephone call to her son's suite at his Paris hotel was answered by the Greek Minister in Paris. The Queen asked to speak to her son. For a moment or two the Minister waited. Then he said, 'His Majesty regrets he cannot come to the telephone.' King Alexander was never even told about the call.

'Queen Sophie went quietly from the telephone,' reports Prince Christopher. 'She said nothing, but the disappointment on her face wrung one's heart.'

No less distressing for the Queen than this enforced separation from her son was his determination to marry Aspasia Manos. Sophie was enough of a Hohenzollern to disapprove of this proposed match between her son and the daughter of one of King Constantine's equerries. Nor was she alone in her disapproval. Her enemy, the Greek Prime Minister Venizelos, was no less opposed to the idea; he knew that the Greek people would not approve of this marriage between a King and a commoner. He begged Alexander not to be too hasty.

But Alexander was determined. He became more determined still during the visit to Athens of the old Duke of Connaught, Queen Victoria's last surviving son. The Duke had come to deliver to King Alexander, on behalf of King George V, the Order of the Bath. Alexander, having heard that the Duke was going to make use of this opportunity to propose a marriage with King George V's only daughter Mary, the Princess Royal, was extremely apprehensive. But nothing was said and, on being introduced to Aspasia Manos, the old Duke made an appreciative comment to the effect that, had he been a few years younger, he would have fallen for her himself.

In November 1919, King Alexander and Aspasia Manos were secretly, and morganatically, married. King Constantine and Queen Sophie were considerably upset by the news.

Within less than a year, however, they recieved far more distressing news of their son. While trying to break up a fight between his dog and a pet monkey, King Alexander had been bitten in the leg by the monkey. The bites began festering and a specialist was called in. There was talk of amputating the leg. Desperately worried, Queen Sophie begged permission to be allowed to go to her son's bedside. It was refused. She arranged for King Constantine's mother, Dowager Queen Olga, who had joined them in Switzerland, to go in her stead. But Queen Olga arrived too late. In excruciating pain, the twenty-six-year old King Alexander died on 25 October 1920.

So Greece was without a king. Acting swiftly, Venizelos sent an emissary to the National Hotel in Lucerne to offer the crown to Alexander's younger brother, King Constantine's eighteen-year-old son, Paul. It was refused.

Prince Paul's refusal of the crown came at an awkward time for Venizelos. New elections were scheduled for the following month. Venizelos, fresh from his triumphs at the Peace Conference in Paris (by his untiring efforts he had fulfilled – on paper – almost all Greek national aspirations) was expecting a landslide victory for his Liberal Party. But with Prince Paul having refused the throne, the electoral contest rapidly developed into one between the supporters of Venizelos and those of King Constantine.

The result of the election, held on 14 November 1920, was a complete rejection of Venizelos. Even in his own constituency he was defeated. Disgusted, he left Greece and went into self-imposed exile.

The new government promptly appointed the Dowager Queen Olga as Regent and arranged for a plebiscite to be held on the question of King Constantine's return. The result of the plebiscite of 5 December 1920 exceeded King Constantine's wildest hopes: he gained over ninety-eight per cent of the votes.

On 19 December 1920, the train bringing back King Constantine and Queen Sophie steamed into the station at Athens. For hours the streets had been packed with a vast multitude, chanting *Erchetai*! *Erchetai*! – He is coming! He is coming! When the King stepped onto the beflagged platform, so tall and imposing in his bemedalled uniform and plumed helmet, they went wild with enthusiasm. For half an hour the royal family battled against the excited crowd in order to reach the open carriages drawn up outside the station. The drive to the Old Palace was a triumph. Church bells clashed, flowers rained down and cheer upon tumultuous cheer rang out. On reaching the Old Palace, the King was lifted shoulder-high by the crowd and carried indoors.

King Constantine was deeply moved by this riotous show of affection but Queen Sophie was less impressed. 'The level-headed Queen Sophie,' writes that champion of the Greek royal family, Arthur Gould-Lee, 'on whom the manner of her son's death and the unjust treatment of the war years had left a bitter imprint, remembered the demonstrations that had attended the Conqueror-King's triumphant entry into Athens in 1912, and she asked whether all this excitement was not too exuberant to last.'

She could hardly know, he continues, 'how quickly her doubts were to be confirmed'.

2

There was very little *rapport* between the two Balkan Queens, Sophie of the Hellenes and her cousin, Marie of Romania. Sophie, reserved, un-affected and soured by her experiences, was very different from the stagy and self-confident Marie. Where the Greek court was run along the most unpretentious lines, the post-war Romanian court was lush, formal and colourful. Meals, in the Greek royal household, were simple family gatherings; in the Romanian they were grand occasions, attended by equerries, ladies-in-waiting and numerous guests. The palace in Athens was hardly more than a large town house, and Tatoi not unlike a suburban villa, but Cotroceni and the royal homes at Sinaia were vast, ornate and opulently furnished. Athens was still a small provincial city; Bucharest was the Paris of the Balkans. And whereas Queen Sophie's family was still living under a cloud of Allied disapproval, Queen Marie's was basking in the sunshine of international acclaim.

Yet in 1921, the royal houses of Greece and Romania were doubly united. Sophie's eldest son, Crown Prince George, married Marie's eldest daughter Elizabeth, and Marie's eldest son, Crown Prince Carol, married Sophie's eldest daughter Helen. All four young people were, of course, great-grandchildren of Queen Victoria.

This was not Crown Prince Carol's first marriage. In 1918, at the age of twenty-four, the feckless young man had married a Romanian *mondaine* called Zizi Lambrino. Queen Marie was furious. Not for the world was she going to allow the marriage to stand. She insisted that it be annulled. Brushing aside her husband's uncertainties and Carol's protestations, she plunged into the problem of annulment. 'I have had many difficult battles to wage,' she asserts, 'but this was the most terrible of all, because it meant that we had to fight against one of our own, to save him against his own will.' When her husband's Ministers suggested that Carol be disinherited and that the succession pass to his brother Nicholas, she would not hear of it. Referring to herself, sometimes as a tigress and sometimes as a lioness, she tells how she fought for 'her son and her country'.

'Gentlemen,' ran her impassioned answer to their suggestion that Carol be passed over, 'that must not be, not for the country nor for Carol. It is Carol who was born the ruler of Romania . . . Carol is of royal blood. A marriage among the people is for him impossible. It is for a ruler to remain above the people, a demi-god. Carol was born the ruler of Romania. And it is his duty to be.'

As always, she had her way. An annulment was pushed through the Romanian Supreme Court. The 'demi-god' was packed off on an extended tour around the world and the heart-broken Zizi (with their baby Mircea) sent to Paris. She was not quite so heartbroken, however, as to refuse the generous sum of money granted her by the Romanian government.

With the somewhat tarnished Prince Carol once more on the market, Marie made sure that she did the choosing of a bride this time. Her choice of Princess Helen seemed eminently sensible: the Greek princess was an attractive, affectionate and lively young woman. 'She is sweet and she is a lady,' announced Marie. 'Besides, she's one of the family, since we're all descended from Grandmama Queen.' And, what was of even more importance to Queen Marie, she was the daughter of a reigning house.

For the same reason, Queen Marie had engineered the match between her daughter Elizabeth and Crown Prince George. After the death of King Constantine, George would be King of the Hellenes and Marie had no doubt that her classically beautiful Elizabeth would make a splendid Queen.

That neither of the marriages would be love matches, would not have bothered the ambitious Queen Marie unduly. Royalties had more important things to think about than love. But the more sensible Queen Sophie was not nearly so sanguine. She was particularly disturbed at the prospect of a marriage between the worldly Carol and the unspoilt Helen. She distrusted the hot-house atmosphere of the Romanian court and the decadent life of the Romanian capital. Her children had been raised along simple, 'English' lines; Queen Marie's in an aura of poetry and pageantry. Time and again Queen Sophie cautioned Helen against the match but Helen, attracted to Carol and anxious for a new life, insisted. 'Had I listened,' said Helen afterwards, 'I would have been spared years of misery.'

The two weddings were celebrated in March 1921. King Constantine and Queen Sophie did not attend Crown Prince George's wedding in Bucharest, but Queen Marie, all dazzling smiles and floating draperies, came to Athens for Carol's wedding to Helen on 10 March. King Ferdinand did not accompany his wife. Carol and Helen were married in the Metropolitan Cathedral and, after a honeymoon at Tatoi, left for Romania.

While Queen Marie was in Athens, King Constantine and Queen Sophie were one day subjected to an embarrassing and humiliating experience. A large royal party was walking at the foot of Mount Hymettus when Lord Granville, the new British Minister, approached. With the Allied Powers still refusing to recognize King Constantine, Granville had never paid an official call on the King. A meeting such as this, however, was different and as Granville was an old friend of the Greek royal couple, they prepared to give him a cordial greeting. But he ignored them. Going up to Queen Marie, he greeted her warmly. Then, without the slightest sign of recognition, he turned and left. Constantine and Sophie were appalled.

Yet to meet the royal couple was to appreciate the absurdity of the Allied attitude. Soon after the two weddings, Queen Sophie played hostess to Mrs Philip Martineau, an Englishwoman much in demand in royal circles for her expert knowledge of gardens. Having come on from the Romanian court, where all was glitter, Mrs Martineau was immediately struck by the simplicity of life in Athens. She was particularly struck, however, by Queen Sophie herself. In England, Sophie's reputation was such that the visitor had expected to meet an aggressive, masterful German *Hausfrau*; indeed, Mrs Martineau had at first refused the invitation to Athens because of Queen Sophie's reputation. She was thus astonished to find – in an extraordinarily English setting – a small, fragile and sad-eyed woman, dressed in deepest mourning for her son Alexander. She had an air of majesty but she was certainly not the virago of Allied propaganda.

'Could this be the belligerent German we had always read of, who was supposed to have taken a knife to her husband in order to make him throw over the Allies?' asked the bewildered Mrs Martineau. 'We found her gentle and quiet, full of thought and kindness for her guests, and the most feminine and charming lady, ever ready to efface herself and her own views.'

Of course, they discussed gardening: Sophie's own typically English garden surrounding her palace, and her schemes for the afforestation and landscaping of Athens. While at Tatoi, Mrs Martineau was shown where part of the forest had been set fire to during the war.

'Why should they do this, Ma'am?' she asked.

As though 'numb with pain', Sophie replied, 'They said I had a private wire to my brother concealed here.'

King Constantine, noted Mrs Martineau, looked ill and tired, with dark pouches under his eyes. He was 'very bitter about his treatment'.

During this period, Aspasia, the widow of Queen Sophie's son Alexander, gave birth to a daughter. It was Sophie's first grandchild. By now the Queen had overcome her earlier reservations about the match and she devoted herself to the mother and child. At her suggestion, King Constantine arranged for the title of Princess to be bestowed on his late son's morganatic wife. The baby girl was given the name of Alexandra.

Twenty-three years hence yet another link was forged between the royal houses of Greece and Romania when this granddaughter of Queen Sophie married the grandson of Queen Marie: the ill-fated King Peter II of Yugoslavia.

3

King Constantine had inherited a difficult political situation. Venizelos, in his stubborn pursuit of 'The Great Idea' – the aggrandizement of Greece – had landed a large army in Turkey and occupied the area around the old Greek city of Smyrna. This he had done with the blessing of the Allied Powers. Once King Constantine was restored to the throne, however, the Allies, only too glad of an excuse to wash their hands of what they now realized was a questionable scheme, withdrew their support. This placed King Constantine in an awkward position. Having had his fill of military adventures, Constantine would have liked nothing better than to bring the troops home. But he dared not. To give up the territory already won from Turkey and so expose Smyrna's large Greek population to the angry Turks would be to risk losing his crown. Yet to continue to fight the Turks without Allied support would mean almost certain defeat.

His position was further complicated by the fact that his General Staff was anxious to deal the enemy a quick, knockout blow before they had time to build up their army, and by the knowledge that it was his refusal to join battle during the First World War that had cost him his throne.

'They have arranged it,' he commented bitterly, 'to seem that it is only me who holds back Greece from recovery.' So he surrendered to pressure.

To inject some morale into the Greek forces, it was decided that King Constantine must take over supreme command. Towards the end of May 1921, after a *Te Deum* in the Cathedral in Athens, he set off for Turkey. But it was going to need more than a *Te Deum* to save the situation. The fifty-three year-old Constantine was no longer the 'Conqueror-King', the 'Son of the Eagle' of the Balkan Wars. He was ill and tired and dispirited. Assisted by Queen Sophie, who had established herself on a small yacht off the Turkish coast and who daily, and in burning heat, visited the hospitals ashore, he did what he could. It was not much. Within four months he collapsed and had to return to Athens.

By the summer of 1922 the Turks, under the inspiring leadership of Mustapha Kemal Pasha, were ready to attack the invader. With their lines of communication dangerously stretched, the Greeks could not hold their positions. In considerable disorder, they fell back on Smyrna. The city fell to the Turks on 9 September 1922. For the following five days it was savagely sacked. It is estimated that some 300,000 Greeks lost their lives during those five horrifying days.

The effect on King Constantine's position was immediate. A few days after the fall of Smyrna the defeated Greek army revolted. Again their King was made the scapegoat. His abdication was demanded. Constantine acceded. Once more he and Queen Sophie packed up and left the palace. This time, however, there was no frantic crowd flinging itself at the wheels of their car to prevent their departure. From the very same little port from which they had sailed into exile five years before, Constantine and Sophie once more quit Greece. On this occasion their eldest son remained behind, for he had just been sworn in as King George II of the Hellenes.

The second rejection finished Constantine. A few weeks later, in a hotel room in Palermo in Sicily, he died from a haemorrhage of the brain. In his hand was clutched a small leather pouch containing Greek soil.

Even now, Queen Sophie did not relax her self-control. Keeping in check her own grief, she consoled her heartbroken daughters. She let no one see her sorrow. But she had still more heartbreak to contend with: the Greek government refused to allow the body of her late husband to be brought back to Athens and buried with the honours due to a king. His coffin was therefore taken to Naples and placed in a chapel in the Orthodox Church. A year later, when Queen Sophie went to live in Florence, she brought the coffin to lie in the crypt of the Russian Orthodox Church. She did not doubt that, sooner or later, her son, King George II, would be in a position to give his father's remains a state funeral and that they would be buried on that quiet hill-top at Tatoi.

But in just over a year after King Constantine's death, King George II was also in exile. Convinced that he was in a plot to overthrow the government, extreme republican elements began agitating for his dethronement. New elections brought to power an even more unsympathetic National Assembly and on 25 March 1924, it passed a resolution abolishing the monarchy and declaring Greece a republic. The decision was ratified by a plebiscite the following year. The volatile Greeks, who four years before had voted nearly 100 to 1 for King Constantine's return, now agreed to a complete abolition of the monarchy.

Not without justification had Queen Sophie wondered whether all the excitement of their triumphant return had not been 'too exuberant to last'.

CHAPTER TWENTY-SIX

Marie of Yugoslavia

I

'I'll be a Queen all right,' Marie of Romania once said to King Alfonso XIII of Spain. 'And I'll be it splendidly. For that's the way I believe Queens ought to be.'

She was as good as her word. Of all the queens of post-war Europe, none was more brilliant than Queen Marie of Romania. Utterly free of the shyness that plagued so many of Queen Victoria's descendants, she played her royal role for all – and rather more than – it was worth. Not for her the reserve of Queen Sophie or the diffidence of Queen Maud or the naturalness of Queen Ena. To meet her was to be without the slightest doubt that one was in the presence of a queen.

Like her Uncle Bertie, the late King Edward VII of England, who used to say that if he knew nothing about art he knew something about arrangement, Marie knew exactly how to create the right setting. It might not have been conventionally regal but it was undoubtedly impressive. Gold, she maintained, was the colour for royalty; orange, the colour best suited to her personality. Therefore it was against a background of shades ranging from primrose to flame that she invariably presented herself. Guests, awaiting her arrival, would be ushered into one of her famous gold rooms. The architecture of these rooms would be Byzantine; their atmosphere sumptuous, Eastern, self-consciously Bohemian. Squat, elaborately carved columns would support shadowy, vaulted ceilings, all a-glimmer with gold leaf. Golden lamps would swing on golden chains. Great bronze and copper vases, filled with chrysanthemums, marigolds and orange dahlias, would stand on floors of intricate mosaic. Against the walls would hang panels, painted by the Queen herself, of tall-stemmed white lilies on a dull gold ground. Instead of conventional chairs there would be huge divans, covered with gold stuffs and piled high with cushions of yellow, apricot, orange and vermilion. In the warm half-light would glitter chains, crucifixes and exotically jewelled icons. It was all somewhat redolent of a scene from an Elinor Glyn novel or, as the traveller, Rosita Forbes, once put it, 'Hollywood-esque'.

A fanfare of trumpets, echoing down the arched corridors, would herald her arrival. Into the room, with a flutter of white draperies and a flash of golden embroideries, she would sweep. Beside her, the brilliance of the setting would fade. Queen Marie was forty-three at the end of the First World War and by all accounts she seems to have been as beautiful as ever. One guest talks of her rose-petal complexion which is said to have been washed in an extract of her favourite white lilies. Her hair, which many mistakenly assumed to be a wig, was a deep, vibrant gold, or as one breathless admirer put it, 'more of the tone of rich autumn leaves, with glints of sunshine'. Her clothes, which were designed with little regard for fashion but all for effect, were flamboyantly regal. 'So she made,' writes another dazzled guest, 'a splendid figure, oriental surely and almost barbaric in her beauty.'

Her vivacity was exceptional; her charm outstanding. There was an indefinable radiance about her. She might have been showy and self-satisfied but she was never unkind, never tactless, never haughty. Her air was warm and friendly; she was, says Rosita Forbes, 'the very spirit of enjoyment'. 'I defy anyone,' writes Mrs Philip Martineau, 'to meet that radiant personality and come away with anything but wonder and admiration in their heart.' Her manner was the same to all: to visiting royalties or to the thousands of peasants who so adored her. Dressed in her somewhat fanciful version of Romanian national costume, she would alight from her superbly appointed train at some small wayside station. She would step down onto embroidered carpets strewn with flowers to be given a riotous welcome by the assembled peasant women. She delighted in the warmth of their reception no less than they in the warmth of her manner.

'Why do you all like her so much?' a bemused visitor once asked the mayor of a mountain town. He looked at the inquirer 'as if I had questioned the divinity of Bethlehem's Mary', and replied simply, 'Because she is so good.'

With the troops Queen Marie was no less popular. Here the trailing draperies would be exchanged for a superbly tailored, if slightly theatrical, uniform and a tall fur busby. Mabel Draggett, accompanying the Queen on a military inspection, claims that 'in every man's face was worship and reverence and wonder at her. I watched their eyes. Those beautiful, dark Romanian eyes all followed her as if a magnet drew them. The devotion they offered Her Majesty was as to a goddess divine . . . .'

'That,' said Marie briskly when the inspection was over, 'is what I call a good day's work for the King. It is when you have the army with you that King and country are safe.'

Her interests were wide-ranging. She was an accomplished linguist, she was a talented painter, she was an imaginative gardener; she was forever designing, restoring and furnishing houses. Her golden rooms at Cotroceni near Bucharest and Pelishor at Sinaia, her romantic castle of Bran in the Carpathian mountains, her idyllic white villa at Balcic on the Black Sea all bore witness to her gifts as a decorator. She was a superb horsewoman. Her writing was fluent, vibrant and stylish. She somehow found the time to write dozens of children's books as well as her own monumental memoirs.

Her guests would always be treated to readings from her famous war diary. The time for this would be after dinner, in her boudoir. The scene, says one of her listeners, would be one of 'barbaric splendour'. They would sit in semi-darkness on low, massive pieces of furniture, especially 'antiqued' by charring wood and rubbing it with a wire brush. On the floor would be great jars of pink peonies. The Queen would be seated on a divan strewn with furs and cushions. She might be wearing a filmy dress with a heavy, antique girdle; over her shoulders would be flung a glittering cape of rose and flame, embroidered with gold. Her huge 'Book of Memories', bound in gold, would be unlocked and, in her beautiful voice, she would read about the sufferings of those war years: the death of little Mircea, the flight to Jassy, the privations, the hopelessness and the horrors. By the end of the evening, everyone – and the Queen not least of all – would be in tears.

But Queen Marie was more than simply a decorative, vivacious and accomplished woman with a flair for winning hearts. Very much a Coburg, she took her royal duties seriously and to them brought an energy, intelligence and acumen extremely rare in royalties. As the Count de St Aulaire, French Ambassador to the Court of St James's, once said, 'She has all the brain-power of a man, and all the allurement of a woman.' Her grandfather, the Prince Consort, had once claimed that his eldest daughter – Marie's aunt, the Empress Frederick – had a man's head on a woman's shoulders; the same could have been said of Queen Marie.

When King Ferdinand was due to open the first parliament after the war, Queen Marie insisted on her right to take her place beside him. 'I have given this country six children,' she said to the Ministers. 'I have been your inspiration and mainstay through the war. Now it seems no longer fitting that I sit in a box in the background at the opening of Parliament. I wish to stand side by side with the King when His Majesty assembles the government.'

And from then on, she actively involved herself in the running of the country. There was no aspect of Romania's affairs in which she was not keenly interested. She had, it was claimed, 'a positive genius for finance' and an organizing ability which left the Ministers 'gasping with admiration'. It was in no small measure due to her promptings that King Ferdinand introduced two revolutionary measures after the war: universal suffrage, and that agrarian reform which had already been promised to the troops. With her strong feeling for the peasants, Marie was especially insistent on this more equal redistribution of the land.

None of this, of course, is to claim that Queen Marie was fired with an egalitarian spirit. She was very much a child of the Victorian era. 'I do not believe in equality,' she would announce bluntly. 'God makes one class higher than another. Some of us have been born to high places. Mine happens to be the highest of all. And if I were to resign my job tomorrow, who could do it better?' Who, indeed?

One of her greatest triumphs was at the Peace Conference in Paris. With Romania having been on the winning side during the war, Marie felt that the country should be richly rewarded. At last the dream of a Greater Romania – *Romania Mare* – could become a reality. At last the Romanian people, a Latin enclave in a Slav world, could be united under one crown. Already Bessarabia, Transylvania and Bucovina had asked to be annexed to Romania; it remained for the victorious powers in Paris to agree to these annexations.

Suspecting that little Romania was being ignored at the conference table, Queen Marie decided to go to Paris herself. Arriving with sixty dresses, thirty-one coats, twenty-two fur pieces, twenty-nine hats and eighty-three pairs of shoes, she put up at the Ritz. 'I have come,' she announced imperiously, 'to give Romania a face in the affairs of nations.' It was a face not easily ignored.

Statesmen, politicians and diplomats flocked to her suite at the Ritz. 'I don't like your Prime Minister,' growled Clemenceau. 'Perhaps you will find me more agreeable,' answered Marie deftly. No one remained impervious to that blend of charm and determination. Whether or not her presence in Paris made any real difference, there is no denying that when she went back all sorts of concessions, financial as well as territorial, had been granted to Romania. Queen Marie had arrived in Paris as Queen of eight million subjects; she left as Queen of eighteen million. Romania had more than doubled its size. She had indeed become 'Empress of all the Romanians'.

So spectacular an achievement, decided Marie, should be marked by an equally spectacular ceremony. Why not a coronation? She and Nando had never been crowned. Now that all Romanians were united, the ceremony would have a deeper significance. Into the project, Queen Marie poured all her taste, imagination and energy. 'Do yourselves the honour to give me that which best represents your own ancient Romania,' she instructed the men assembled to stage the ceremony. 'I want nothing modern that another Queen might have. Let mine be all medieval.'

And medieval, more or less, it was. Alba Julia, the city in recently-won Transylvania where, over three centuries before, Michael the Brave had briefly united the Romanian people, was chosen as the most evocative site for the ceremony. 'To my country,' wrote one of Marie's daughters, 'my parents' Coronation at this shrine of Romanian independence was symbolic of their position as the embodiment, the inspirers, and the executors of an age-old dream.'

As Alba Julia had no cathedral, Queen Marie had one built. Its style, of course, was Byzantine; its walls dazzlingly white. Byzantine, too, in its splendour, was the Coronation ceremony. The date was 15 October, 1922. Poor King Ferdinand, fighting down his distaste for such public display, arrayed himself in conventionally regal robes of red velvet and ermine. On his head he wore the crown which had been fashioned for his uncle, King Carol. For Queen Marie, on the other hand, everything had been especially designed. Her dress was of gold tissue; her robe of gold lined with ermine. Her crown was a copy of a medieval crown. Worn fashionably low on the brow, it was a massive, ornate, barbaric concoction of solid gold set with chunky precious stones. While she knelt, for what must have been the one and only time in her life, before her husband, he placed this monumental crown upon her golden head.

'I am a winner in life,' she declared to someone when the Coronation was over. 'Somebody has to lose. But I am a winner . . . .'

And so, for a time, she was.

2

Having established her country, Queen Marie began to think in terms of establishing her dynasty. Already she was being referred to as 'the brains of the Balkans': could she not, by judicious marriages of her children, become the most influential figure in south-eastern Europe? Her eldest son, Carol, married to the daughter of the King of the Hellenes, would one day be the King of Romania. Her eldest daughter Elizabeth, married to King Constantine's eldest son George, would one day be Queen of the Hellenes. To her third child, her daughter Marie, the Queen now turned her attention.

Marie, known as Mignon, turned twenty-three in 1922. As a child, Mignon had been exceptionally pretty, with a Greuze-like face: china-blue eyes, fair hair and a pale complexion. Queen Marie, a talented photographer, had delighted in photographing this angelic-looking child against backgrounds of pastel peonies or hydrangeas. With Mignon's quiet prettiness went what Marie called a 'smiling, passive, docile, sweet, patient and indolent' nature; her daughter had, she said, 'a peasant endurance'. In other words, she had very little of her mother's sparkle and energy. Mignon's was a calm, steady temperament.

During the war years, Mignon's qualities of steadfastness and imperturbability had been of considerable value to her mother in her hospital work. 'She will do anything and has no wish to shine,' wrote Marie, 'she will just as readily wash the windows, sweep the floor, or serve up the meals, as hold a man's leg when it has to be cut off. Mignon has no pretensions.'

Mignon was happiest when doing something practical. Pretty, placid and unselfish she might have been, but through her nature ran an honest-to-goodness, no-nonsense, almost masculine streak. Marie complained that her daughter was not at all romantic and Mignon seems to have had very little time for conventionally feminine pursuits. She did not really care about her looks. Her prettiness did not last much longer than her girlhood. Too fond of food, she tended to put on weight; uninterested in clothes, she wore whatever she felt comfortable in. Her manner was tomboyish; her talk peppered with schoolboy slang. Although, like her mother, she painted and sculpted, Mignon seems to have been more interested in motor cars and tractors. More often than not, to the despair of her lady-in-waiting and dresser, she was to be found in a pair of dirty overalls with smudges on her face.

'Her driving,' one of her sons afterwards wrote, 'was excellent and very fast; I never knew a better woman driver.' When she rode, it was like the Romanian peasant women, with legs astride the saddle. Indeed, with each passing year, the name Mignon seemed less and less appropriate for this anything but daintily pretty young woman.

No less than most of Queen Victoria's continental grandchildren and great-grandchildren, Mignon had had an English-style upbringing. Queen Marie always spoke English to her children; an English nanny, Miss Green, had been followed by an English governess and English tutors; Mignon had completed her education by spending a year at Heathfield, the girls' school near Ascot in England.

It was through this easy-going daughter ('she fills the house with good cheer and sunshine,' reported Marie) that the Queen intended to expand her dynasty still further. She did not need to look far.

3

Romania's neighbour-in-arms during the First World War had been the kingdom of Serbia. Like Romania, Serbia's loyalty to the Allied cause had been richly rewarded. With the breakup of the Austro-Hungarian Empire after the war, the Croats and the Slovenes had been united with the Serbs under the Serbian King, Peter I. In time, this single Slav state was to be known as Yugoslavia.

King Peter I had been a member of the Karageorgeovitch family, the dynasty which had originally won Serbian independence from the Turks. During his eighteen-year-long reign, King Peter I had bestowed a certain respectability on the Serbian court at Belgrade. His task had not always been easy. The Serbs were a proud, rugged, turbulent people with a marked tendency towards assassinating their kings. Indeed, King Peter I's eldest son and heir, George Karageorgeovitch, could be counted amongst the most turbulent of them all. His brutal kicking of a valet while in an uncontrollable rage was merely one of his eccentricities. In 1909 George had been prudently declared unsuitable and struck off the line of succession.

With his removal from the scene, the succession had passed to his brother Alexander. In 1921, King Peter died. His thirty-two-year old bachelor son, Alexander, then became King Alexander II of Serbia.

King Alexander was an exceptional man. Small, spare and dark, with eyesight so bad that he had always to wear a pince-nez, Alexander had the look of an alert bantam cock. The army was his passion. It was not so much that he was militant (although his record in the Balkan and First World Wars had been outstanding) as that he enjoyed a military atmosphere. He liked the discipline, the orderliness and the simplicity of army life. Nothing pleased him more than to be talked of as 'the Soldier-King'. Other than smoking heavily, he followed a spartan régime: he ate and drank sparingly; he cared not a jot for his own comfort. While the palace in Belgrade stood empty, he lived in a modest stone house opposite, in conditions of almost barrack-like austerity. He was seldom out of uniform. Yet they were not the theatrical, superbly tailored uniforms of such monarchs as King Alfonso XIII of Spain; they were old, simple and quite often darned. Nor was there anything showy about his conduct on the battlefield. At the front he had always behaved with coolness, calmness and an utter disregard for danger. He seemed to have no fear of death whatsoever. This same imperturbability marked his peacetime behaviour. He was a quiet, simply-spoken man who kept his own counsel.

Loving the hard, masculine, almost monastic quality of military life, Alexander had very little interest in women. The death of his mother, Princess Zorka of Montenegro, when he was only a year old, meant that he had been raised by his austere old father, King Peter I. He had never known a woman's love. Nor does he appear to have sought it in later years. His name had never been coupled with that of any girl; his youth had been quite free of any sexual, or even amorous, scandal. His closest companion, and only confidant, was his cousin, Prince Paul, who shared his home with him. Not until the age of thirty-one did Alexander contemplate marriage, and then only because circumstances, and his anxious Ministers, demanded it. For the sake of the dynasty, it was essential that he marry. Having been forced into making the decision, the King looked for a suitable bride.

To link himself, matrimonially, with Romania, would be the most sensible thing to do. Serbia and Romania had been allies in the war. Romania belonged firmly to the West, as Alexander wished Greater Serbia to belong. Emphasizing the Western, as opposed to the Balkan, flavour of Romania still more was the fact that its royal family – through Queen Marie – was related to the British royal family. That her daughters were the great-granddaughters of Queen Victoria counted for a great deal with King Alexander.

What Queen Victoria herself would have thought of the proposed alliance was another matter. Victoria might have tolerated the Battenbergs (who were, after all, merely a morganatic branch of the royal and respectable Hesse family) but the Karageorgeovitchs were quite a different proposition. Alexander's family had only just attained respectability. Not many generations before, his ancestors had been pig farmers; indeed, to his enemies, King Alexander was still 'the gypsy'. By allying itself to a member of Queen Victoria's family, the Karageorgeovitch dynasty could finally rid itself of its brigandish and upstart air.

Between them, then, Queen Marie and King Alexander arranged the match: he would marry her daughter Mignon. Marie would have the satisfaction of seeing yet another of her daughters become a queen, and Alexander would move firmly into the charmed circle of long-established and generally accepted royalties. And to those countries in which the descendants of Grandmama Queen wore, or had worn, crowns, would be added yet another, somewhat improbable-seeming one: Greater Serbia, soon to be known as Yugoslavia. Alexander and Mignon were married in Belgrade, in the summer of 1922.

Although any of King Ferdinand's and Queen Marie's three daughters would have met King Alexander's political and dynastic requirements, he was fortunate that Mignon was the one who happened to be available. Theirs was no love match but a certain similarity of temperament ensured that the marriage developed into a happy one. When they were first married, Mignon, to Alexander, was simply a pleasant-natured girl with a gratifyingly 'English' air about her. With the years, he would come to appreciate her more valuable virtues – her calm, her bravery, her unpretentiousness and her ability to mind her own business. She had none of the coy, cloying femininity which he would have found unbearable. Nor did she have any of her mother's political interests. Unlike Queen Marie, Mignon would never interfere; she would never try to influence her husband's decisions. Her independent, practical, almost masculine qualities suited him admirably.

The couple were never crowned. Alexander (who had been King for less than a year at the time of his marriage) considered a coronation to be a waste of money; besides, he hated ceremonial. He did feel obliged, however, to provide his consort with a suitable home. Having decided that the existing palace in Belgrade was inadequate (and that his wife could not possibly move into his bachelor house) Alexander enlarged it. The completed palace was spacious but simply furnished. In it, King Alexander and Queen Marie lived all but separate lives. His apartments were austere; hers somewhat more comfortable. While he attended to affairs of state, she gardened or sculpted or drove about the countryside. Alexander was not a uxorious man but whenever he happend to be in his wife's company, especially if they were in the country, he was happy enough.

Their first child was born on 6 September 1923. It was a boy. With King Alexander too overcome to go into his wife's room, his close friend and cousin, Prince Paul, fetched the baby and showed it to the apprehensive father. In an anything but complimentary comparison, Alexander announced that the child looked exactly like its grandfather, King Ferdinand of Romania. The boy was then delivered into the hands of one of those compulsory English nannies, presiding in practically every royal nursery from the North Sea to the Black Sea – this time a Nurse Bell of Harrogate.

The baptism was a gala occasion. From Romania came King Ferdinand and Queen Marie (she resplendent in a towering pearl tiara and floating chiffon panels), from Greece came Marie's daughter Queen Elizabeth, and from England, as proxy-godfather for King George V, came the Duke of York with his Duchess – afterwards King George VI and Queen Elizabeth.

The child was given the first name of Peter. As King Peter II of Yugoslavia, he was to have an extraordinarily chequered career.

CHAPTER TWENTY-SEVEN

'La Reina! La Reina!'

'He tires of everything,' Queen Ena once said of her husband, King Alfonso XIII of Spain. 'Some day he will tire even of me.'

In this, she was being proved right. By the year 1921, the thirty-four-year-old Queen Ena had been married to King Alfonso for fifteen years. Their marriage, inaugurated by a bomb blast, had not really been a success. Although Ena shared, to a certain extent, her husband's love of sport and his taste in entertainment, she seemed to be losing his interest. But then it is doubtful whether any woman could have held the attention of this restless, mercurial, perennially young man for long. Each year saw them drifting farther apart. To the ebullient Alfonso, Ena might well have seemed too staid, too reserved, too *triste*. She could not match his boyish enthusiasms; she could not share his tremendous zest for life. So persistently English, she was never able to identify herself completely with Spain.

Their children, too, were a disappointment to Alfonso. For a man who set so much store by physical vigour, he could not help being distressed by the poor health of their family. Although their two daughters seemed healthy enough, only one of their four sons was bodily sound. Two of the others were haemophiliacs and the third deaf and all but dumb. And one never knew whether the daughters, like the mother, might be transmitters of the 'royal disease'. The Spanish sovereigns, like the late Russian Emperor and Empress, endured constant anxiety and took every precaution with their haemophilic sons. But not all the care in the world (even the trees in the royal parks were padded) could prevent some mishap. Nor was there anything to alleviate the days or weeks or months of agony that could follow some apparently harmless tumble. And whereas, in Queen Ena, these marital trials led to an ever-deepening melancholy, in Alfonso they led to an even more frenetic search for distraction. He was rumoured to be seeking more congenial female company; Europe, by the 1920s, was abuzz with stories about the King's amorous adventures.

Yet, both as a sovereign and a woman, Queen Ena was charming. 'She was by far the most human representative of her kind in spite of the long period of years spent at the stiffest court in Europe,' wrote Grand Duchess Marie of Russia. 'She achieved perfect balance between ease and simplicity on one side and the obligations of her rank on the other.'

With the years this tomboyish, high-spirited, badly dressed English princess had developed into a graceful and *soignée* woman, the most elegant Queen in Europe. She had lost neither the radiance of her complexion nor the lustre of her fair hair. Her figure was still slender. Into the Spain of the mantilla, the voluminous petticoat and the long black dress, she introduced the pastel colours, the luxurious fur trimmings and the short skirts of London and Paris. 'I can think of none who possesses the "clothes sense" to a greater degree than the Queen of Spain,' wrote Lady Duff-Gordon. 'Had she been born into another position she would have made a fortune as a *grande couturière*.'

Her bearing, on formal state occasions, was faultless. She wore her clothes – her diamond coronet, her white lace mantilla, her gold and silver dresses – with ease and always moved with dignity. During the round of sumptuous and exacting ceremonial at Easter time, she never faltered. At the symbolic washing of the feet of the poor, she would cover her lavishly embroidered dress with a white towel and kneel to wash and kiss the feet of the twelve old women. While the King would slither on his knees from one old man to the next, the Queen, because of her long train, would have to kneel and rise and kneel again as she worked her way down the line. Her duty done, she would wash her hands in a gold basin and then move to the table to serve the ceremonial meal.

King Alfonso, who always turned the ceremonial meal into a game, would purposely embarrass his gentlemen-in-waiting by the speed and vigour with which he snatched the plates from their hands. If, in his enthusiasm, one of the round cheeses rolled off the plate, he would run after it and, like a goal-keeper, stop it with his foot. He would always finish long before the Queen and would stand at the altar, with helmet, sword and gloves, waiting for her to join him. Walking at the end of a magnificent procession, they would leave the hall, pausing just before they passed through the great double doors for the King to bow and the Queen to make a sweeping court curtsy.

When the novelist Elinor Glyn visited Spain in 1923, the account she gave of the royal pair, with whom she stayed, was ecstatic to the point of delirium. The King she compared to a perfectly bred Derby winner ('the same look of race and self-confidence and *dauntlessness*') but it was for Queen Ena that she reserved her most fulsome praise. 'She really looked like a fairy queen, so young and fresh and lovely,' she writes. In those silver, turquoise and aquamarine lamé dresses, she looked 'a dream of beauty all the time'. For Queen Ena's charm and beauty and dignity, Miss Glyn was almost – but not quite – at a loss for words. One night the royal party paid an unexpected visit to a fiesta to see the Spanish dancers; the crowd, says Miss Glyn, pressed about the Queen in adoration. '*La Reina! La Reina!*' they murmured ecstatically.

It is not altogether unexpected that King Alfonso's aunt, the Infanta Eulalia, should compare Queen Ena to Queen Marie of Romania. 'The two cousins – Queens – sprung from this extraordinary [Coburg] stock,' she writes, 'are curiously alike in features, build, and expression. The Queen of Romania is some years older than the Queen of Spain, and, like her cousin, she is beautiful; but whereas the younger woman loves her beauty because it represents much of the joy of life, the other Queen depends largely on a *mise-en-scène*, and she is often the slave of her artistic temperament. To the one – Queen Ena – her palace embodies a home, just as she embodies the ideal of beautiful English womanhood. To the other – Queen Marie – a palace represents a temple, a stage, or *un coin du temps du Paganisme*! Both Queens love colour, jewels, beautiful clothes – and in this the Orientalism of the Coburgs is strikingly apparent, which has probably developed since their marriages, since the countries of their adoption throb with life, and differ absolutely from the soft greens and greys of England.'

But the similarity between the cousins began and ended with their appearance. Marie had none of Ena's naturalness nor her preference for the simple things of life. Indeed, it was away from the splendours of the court that Queen Ena was at her best. At the country palaces of El Pardo, La Granja, Aranjeuz and particularly at the seaside palace at San Sebastian, she could relax and indulge her taste for active, open-air living. She played golf, she played tennis, she danced. She was often seen drinking tea with her ladies in a public teashop on the sea front at San Sebastian.

Queen Ena was one of the first women in Spain to wear a tight-fitting bathing costume and her daring scandalized a great many of her subjects. The Duke of Sutherland once saw her bathing at San Sebastian. Two soldiers, in uniform and fully armed, stood guard, one on either side of her. The deeper the Queen went into the water, the deeper the soldiers followed her. They were finally to be seen, still staring impassively ahead, up to their necks in the waves.

The one sport for which the Queen could never acquire a taste was the national sport of the country – the bullfight. 'I long for the day when the horses will be left out of the displays,' she confided to a friend. 'Already their fate is less cruel as they are now shielded from the bull's horns.' Such squeamish, Anglo-Saxon sentiments she had to keep from her subjects, however. Little did any of them guess, as their Queen raised her glasses to her eyes to watch the *coup de grâce* in the ring below, that the glasses were opaque and that she could see nothing of the savage and bloody climax.

But if, on public occasions, Queen Ena did her best to identify herself with her husband's country, in private she made no bones about her preference for all things English. She not only looked the English rose, she acted it. Queen Ena remained unremittingly English, claimed the Infanta Eulalia, not only in her passion for sport and the outdoors, but in 'her love of home comforts, her admiration for law and order, and in her flair for domesticity, chintzes and interior decorations'. She insisted that afternoon tea be a private family occasion, and managed to get the time of the evening meal advanced to what, in Spain, was the extraordinarily early hour of nine o'clock. English ideas on hygiene, English ideas on diet and the English maxim of 'Plenty of fresh air and early to bed' held good in the nursery. Christmas was always celebrated as an English Christmas, with a decorated tree, a traditional Christmas dinner and a plum pudding sent out by Ena's mother, Princess Beatrice of Battenberg.

The Queen greatly enjoyed her visits to her mother at Kensington Palace. On her journeys to England (which she always regarded as 'home') she would be met, at Dover, by the Spanish Ambassador, and at Victoria by a member of the royal family, often by her cousin, King George V, himself. In London she would spend her time shopping, going to the theatre, visiting friends or giving little luncheon parties at Claridge's. It was always with regret that she took leave of her old mother and exchanged the freedom and security of her native land for the formality and uncertainties of her life in Spain.

English in all things, it was only in her chic, comments the Infanta Eulalia, that Queen Ena differed from her countrywomen. 'Her taste in dress is certainly not a heritage of her English ancestors . . . .'

2

He had immense faith, King Alfonso XIII once declared, in the future of Spain. If she had been great in the days of Charles V, she would, he felt certain, become greater still in the not too distant future.

The main thing which, in the King's estimation, was keeping Spain back from the realization of this potential greatness, was the state of her political life. The workings of Spanish democracy were chaotic. There were no large, clearly defined political parties; with real power lying in the hands of the political bosses, or *caciques*, elections were shamelessly rigged. One crisis followed another; governments fell with incredible speed and regularity; every few months yet another Prime Minister was in office. As a result, few political programmes were ever launched and fewer still seen through to their conclusion. Everything was dissipated in talk.

On the King, this political turmoil had a significant effect. As each change of government meant a complete change of governmental machinery, the King would remain in sole charge until the change had been effected. More and more, as the years went by, did King Alfonso seem to be the one constant factor in the continually shifting political scene. It was no wonder that he came to regard the comings and goings of various politicians with at first, cynicism, then impatience. And as his contempt for these political manoeuvrings increased, so did his faith in his own abilities gather strength. He had never lacked confidence in his own judgement and, naturally imperious, he began to rely on it more and more frequently.

The qualities which might have helped him through his difficulties – patience, prudence and tolerance – he lacked almost completely. He suffered those whom he considered fools very badly. He was, perhaps, too much of a politician himself to preside over other politicians; he was not sufficiently a statesman. When faced with opposition or indecision, Alfonso's tendency was to answer it with a show of strength. He relied on force rather than reason.

There was plenty of temptation to use force during those years. The rise and fall of various governments were not the only upheavals with which the King had to contend. Hardly a week went by without an eruption of violence somewhere in the country. With this explosive situation, no government seemed able to cope.

Running parallel with King Alfonso's growing disenchantment with Spain's parliamentary system was his craving for the Spanish army to prove itself by some glorious feat of arms. For many years, under the high, bright African sky, the Spaniards had been carrying on a desultory war against the Moorish tribesmen in Spanish Morocco. The campaign, conducted with extraordinary inefficiency against a shrewd and dashing enemy, had cost Spain very dearly in men and money. It was also the cause of mounting dissatisfaction at home. What was needed, both to put an end to this drain on the country's resources and to enhance the army's somewhat tarnished reputation, was a spectacular victory.

Such a victory would also strengthen Alfonso's position *vis-à-vis* the politicians considerably. He had always considered the army to be his special province. He delighted in reviews and uniforms and his speeches to the army were his most heartfelt. Immortality, glory, sacrifice, he would cry, were the words to be engraved on the hearts of soldiers. He longed for Spain – the Spain which he loved so sincerely – to shake herself free of sordid political squabbling and to emerge as a great Catholic military state with himself at its head. And a victory in Morocco could well be the first step towards the realization of his somewhat medieval ideal.

Perhaps to prepare public opinion for whatever future move he might need to make, King Alfonso delivered a speech at Cordoba in May 1921, denouncing the parliamentary system of Spain. He followed this up with a fervent address at the tomb of El Cid – that warrior who had fought against the Moors – in which he spoke of the past greatness of Spain. 'Spain,' he cried, 'is great enough still to realize her destiny; and apart from that, with what Spain is in the Peninsula, and with what belongs to us on the other side of the Strait, we have enough to figure among the first nations in Europe.'

It was on this other side of the Strait, on the very day that the King was making his rousing speech before the tomb of El Cid, that there occurred a military disaster of the most appalling magnitude. A general by the name of Sylvestre, determined to win a great victory over the tribesmen, marched ten thousand men to a place called Anual. They were invested in a narrow ravine and the entire force annihilated. The bulk of Spain's Moroccan army, as well as an incalculable amount of guns and equipment, had been lost.

The news of the Anual disaster first stunned, then infuriated Spain. Who was responsible for this shocking waste of life? Although the government collapsed, there was a feeling that it was not they who had encouraged Sylvestre in his rash move. The republicans were not slow to point a finger at the King. So anxious for a great victory, he might well have urged Sylvestre forward.

Then, among the dead general's papers were found two telegrams from the King. The first read, 'On the 15th I expect good news'; the second, '*Holá hombres*, I'm waiting.' They proved nothing but the suspicion that Alfonso's ambition had sent ten thousand Spaniards to their death persisted. The word Anual became a stick with which to beat the King.

The disaster in Morocco not only robbed Alfonso of his anticipated victory but threw the country into a state of even greater unrest. Spain, wrote the new British Ambassador, Sir Esmé Howard, was like 'a stage in a state of chaotic welter . . . awaiting the advent of some wise strong man . . . to hurl all the tragi-comedians into their right places and allow the play to proceed'.

Just such a man seemed to have settled the similar confusion in Italy. In 1922 Mussolini overthrew the parliamentary government and set himself up as a dictator. Could not the same thing, it was wondered, be done for Spain? There was, in fact, a willing person to hand: General Primo de Rivera, Captain General of Barcelona. The King, in a somewhat equivocal speech made to the garrison in Barcelona, had hinted that although *he* was not able to dislodge his parliament, there was no reason why the army could not force his hand. It was a task which General Primo de Rivera was more than ready to undertake. How much King Alfonso knew of the General's plans is uncertain, but in planning his *coup d'état* for 14 September 1923, the General must have known that he would meet with very little opposition from the King. It has been suggested, in fact, that since the commission to examine the responsibilities for Anual was to open on 21 September, a *coup d'état* the week before would be welcomed by the King.

On 11 September 1923 a riot in Barcelona gave the General his opportunity. He declared a state of martial law and signalled his fellow military commanders to do likewise. When the government tried to dismiss him for his rebellious act, he answered by issuing a manifesto, calling upon the King to dismiss parliament and rule the country with the help of the army. Then, amidst general acclamation, the General took the train to Madrid.

King Alfonso was at San Sebastian when he heard of the *coup*. Refusing to be hurried, he returned to the capital on 14 September. At the station he was met by his apprehensive Ministers. The choice seemed to be between civil war and the acceptance of General Primo's military dictatorship. When the Prime Minister offered his resignation, Alfonso accepted it. At noon he asked General Primo de Rivera to form a government. Spain, in other words, had become a dictatorship. King Alfonso had broken his constitutional oath.

Throughout all this upheaval, Queen Ena played no part. It is doubtful that Alfonso would have consulted her or that she would have expressed any opinion. Her role, in the political life of the country, had always been a negative one. Unlike her cousins, the late Empress of Russia or Queen Marie of Romania, Queen Ena did not interfere, either directly or indirectly, in affairs of state. She never discussed politics with anyone, says one of her daughters. Queen Ena always confined herself to such nonpartisan duties as nursing services. Her pioneer work on behalf of Spain's backward hospitals would one day be regarded, it was claimed, as her most lasting memorial. Her Red Cross Hospital in Madrid, to which she devoted so much time and energy, was in many ways a model institution.

'How this English princess feels,' wrote the famous novelist and political exile, Blasco-Ibanez, 'now that the constitution has been torn up like a scrap of paper and a military tyranny rivalling that of the former Czars inflicted on the country of her adoption, it would be hard to describe.'

It would not only be hard; it would be almost impossible. One could merely speculate. That the Spanish were a fiery, unstable, capricious people, Ena needed no convincing. The bomb on her wedding-day had left its mark. Nor had it been the only one. There had been at least half a dozen attempts on the King's life and countless abortive plots. The Peninsula was in a permanent state of eruption. It was no wonder that when Queen Ena drove in procession through the streets of Madrid and Barcelona she looked anxious and unsmiling. But whether she would agree that the only way to manage this difficult people was by force is another matter. Was this very English Queen too imbued with British concepts of constitutional government to approve of her husband's easy acceptance of dictatorship? One does not know. In this matter, as in everything, Queen Ena behaved with tact, dignity and discretion.

CHAPTER TWENTY-EIGHT

Louise of Sweden

I

Queen Victoria, with her *penchant* for the handsome Battenberg princes, had sanctioned the marriages of two of them into her own family. Prince Henry of Battenberg had married the Queen's youngest daughter Princess Beatrice (and had fathered the future Queen Ena of Spain) while his elder brother, Prince Louis of Battenberg, had married one of the Queen's granddaughters: Princess Victoria of Hesse.

Princess Victoria of Hesse was a daughter of Queen Victoria's third child, Princess Alice. The early death of Princess Alice in 1878 meant that Princess Victoria, like her sister Princess Alix of Hesse (later the Empress Alexandra of Russia) grew to womanhood under the eye of her grandmother, Queen Victoria. That eye, which could be so devastatingly disapproving, could also be surprisingly understanding. Thus, when Princess Victoria fell in love with the dashing but relatively unimportant Prince Louis of Battenberg (the Battenbergs were a morganatic branch of the Hesse family) Queen Victoria was all approval. Other royalties – and the Prussian chief amongst them – might declare themselves horrified at Prince Louis's morganatic blood but the Queen dismissed their objections as nonsensical bigotry. She considered Prince Louis of Battenberg to be an eminently suitable husband for her granddaughter. Not only, with his coal-black hair and beard, would he supply the family with that 'strong dark blood' after which the Queen was always hankering, but he was an Englishman.

This had come about by registration. As a youngster, the German-born Prince Louis of Battenberg had changed his nationality in order to join the British Navy. Developing into a man of considerable ability and charm Prince Louis had won rapid promotion. By the time he was in his late twenties he regarded himself, and was generally regarded, as a British naval officer rather than a German prince. Indeed, in describing his future wife, Princess Victoria of Hesse, to a friend, Prince Louis assured him that she was 'more English than German' and that they always spoke English to each other.

Louis and Victoria were married, at Darmstadt, in the spring of 1884. He was thirty, she twenty-one. Their life together was happy and Princess Victoria bore her husband four children. As a family, they were forever on the move. Heiligenberg Castle in Hesse was their permanent home but with Prince Louis so often away at sea, his wife and children spent long periods with relations all over Europe. There were holidays with Queen Victoria at Osborne, there were visits to various Continental palaces, there were stays in different houses throughout England. For several periods, they lived on Malta.

As both Prince Louis and Princess Victoria were people of culture and intelligence, their children were brought up in a lively and enlightened fashion. Two of the children, George and Alice (she was to become the mother of the Duke of Edinburgh, husband of Queen Elizabeth II) were somewhat contemplative by nature; the other two were brighter. They were Louis, who later became Earl Mountbatten of Burma, and Louise, who became the Queen of Sweden.

Princess Louise of Battenberg was born on 13 July 1889, the second of the four children. Although her parents' constant moves and widespread continental relationships gave her early life a somewhat cosmopolitan flavour, it was essentially as an English princess that Louise grew up. Two things ensured this: Queen Victoria's position as head of the family and Prince Louis's career in the British Navy. In 1889 he was Assistant Director of Naval Intelligence; within ten years he was Commander-in-Chief of the Atlantic Fleet. Heiligenberg Castle might have been regarded as their permanent home but it was in or near British naval stations that Princess Louise spent the greater part of her time. She loved England. The thought that marriage might one day compel her to leave the country always appalled her.

In the year 1907, Princess Louise turned eighteen. She was by no means a beauty. The features which made the men in her family so good-looking were too strong for a woman. Her face was too thin, her nose too long, her mouth too wide. She was toothy, angular, gaunt. For clothes, she cared hardly at all. Only her eyes – dark, expressive, heavy-lidded – saved her from ugliness. When that indefatigable painter of late nineteenth and early twentieth-century royalties, Philip Laszlo, arrived to paint a portrait of Princess Louise, even he seems to have been at a loss to make something of his gawky and unsuitably dressed sitter. First he caught up a bright yellow shawl and draped it round her shoulders. Then, catching sight of an old gardening hat hanging on the wall, he turned it inside out and tilted it across her upswept hair. Finally, still not satisfied, he found two curling ostrich plumes and pinned them to the hat. But not even all these romantic and frothily brushed-in accessories could soften the sitter's angularity. Nor, on the other hand, could they disguise the character in her face. For what Princess Louise of Battenberg might have lacked in prettiness, she more than made up for in personality.

Hers was a strong character. She was intelligent, sharp-witted, know-ledgeable; she suffered fools badly. Yet she was without a trace of malice. Her manner was warm, affectionate, kindly; her aunt, the Empress Alexandra, used to speak of her 'self-sacrificing nature'. Although, like so many of Queen Victoria's descendants, Louise was shy in public, among friends and relations she was known for her quickness, her gaiety, her vivacity and her ready laughter. She had a strong sense of humour; sharper, more subtle than the knockabout variety of so many of her cousins. Of those less endearing but honest Battenberg characteristics, she had her share as well: a quick temper, a certain outspokenness, strong likes and dislikes. All these, however, stopped well short of arrogance, and were invariably kept under control.

It may have been this combination of plainness of feature and force-fulness of character that kept Princess Louise of Battenberg single for so long. It was true that in 1909, when Louise was twenty, King Manuel of Portugal asked for her hand. She refused. Not only was she not attracted to him but she had no desire to become a queen. She did not relish the limelight. That opportunity lost, she seems not to have had another for well over a decade. The First World War might have had something to do with this. For one thing, Princess Louise threw herself, with character-istic verve, into nursing services; for another, the Battenbergs suddenly found themselves out of public favour.

In 1912, Louise's father, the handsome and bearded Prince Louis of Battenberg, became First Sea Lord. The appointment marked the apex of his brilliant career: he was now in supreme operational command of the British Navy. The family moved into the splendours of Mall House in Admiralty Arch. With the outbreak of war, however, Britain was swept by a strong and unreasoning hatred of all things German. Everything, from dachshunds to Wagnerian operas, came under attack. And one of the first people to be agitated against was Prince Louis. Despite the fact that Battenberg princes (Louis's sons and nephews) were fighting for England, it was alleged that a Battenberg could not be trusted as First Sea Lord. In the Press, an increasingly frenzied campaign was launched against Prince Louis. Finally, on 28 October 1914, after a particularly vicious attack, Prince Louis handed in his resignation.

'I feel deeply with him,' wrote King George V, Prince Louis's wife's cousin, that evening, 'there is no more loyal man in this country.' For the fifty-eight-year-old Prince Louis, who had devoted his whole life to the British Navy, it was a tragic moment. For his devoted daughter, it was hardly less tragic.

'Our father's resignation cut up Louise very, very much,' wrote her brother Louis, afterwards Lord Mountbatten. 'She knew what the Navy meant to her father, she knew that from 1868 to 1914, almost half a century, he had given up his entire life to the Navy. It was his one passion and his one joy, his one pride.'

But she was not one to brood on misfortune. Early in 1915, deciding that her work for the Soldiers and Sailors Families' Association was not enough, Princess Louise joined the V.A.D. – the Voluntary Aid Detachments – as a nurse. Having completed her training, she was sent to a French military hospital at Nevers. For the following three years she worked as hard, and in conditions as difficult and horrifying, as any other nurse behind the front line. Although frail, she never spared herself. Her experience of the sufferings of the wounded matured her and brought to full flower her concern for others. From this time on, unselfishness became her most notable quality. Louise would go to any lengths to help anyone in trouble. 'She was the kind of person,' says Lady Zia Wernher, 'who would give her last crust to help someone in need.'

In 1917, with anti-German feeling running as high as ever in England, Lloyd George suggested to King George V that those branches of the British royal family bearing German names and titles should change them for English ones. The proposal would no doubt have shocked Queen Victoria; the 'German element', she used to say, was the one which she wanted fostered in the family. Now, a mere sixteen years after her death, her grandson changed the name of her beloved Prince Albert's dynasty of Saxe-Coburg and Gotha to Windsor. Queen Mary's relations changed from Teck to Cambridge and the Battenbergs anglicized their name to Mountbatten. Prince Louis of Battenberg became the Marquess of Milford Haven; his daughter, Princess Louise, became Lady Louise Mountbatten.

The change took place on 17 July, 1917. Prince Louis, having lost his family name, seems to have retained his family sense of humour. Arriving to spend a few days at the home of his eldest son two days before the change, and leaving three days after, he wrote, in the visitors' book, 'arrived Prince Jekyll . . . departed Lord Hyde'.

Louise returned from the war to face a bleak period. The year 1918 had seen the murder of her Russian relations (the Empress Alexandra was her aunt; her five children were her cousins) and the collapse of the thrones of her German relations. Her family lost considerable sums of money after the war and were forced to economize. Many of the young men whom Louise had known before the war had been killed in battle; the young women were married, with families of their own. In September 1921, her father, still bitter at his forced resignation from the Navy, died suddenly at the age of sixty-seven. On his death, his widow and unmarried daughter were obliged to move into an apartment in Kensington Palace.

Louise was now thirty-two, a plain, thin, frail, somewhat awkward woman; 'figuratively and almost literally,' as she put it, 'in no man's land'. With her keenly developed sense of social responsibility, she dedicated herself to welfare work and, with relations all over the Continent, she travelled. But for someone of her undeniable qualities – her spirit, her warmth, her compassion, her intelligence – this could hardly be enough. Was she destined to lead the purposeless and circumscribed life of a royal old maid?

2

'I will never marry a king or a widower,' Louise Mountbatten used to say. Yet in 1923 she married the widowed Crown Prince Gustaf Adolf who became, in time, the King of Sweden.

In 1923 Prince Gustaf Adolf of Sweden turned forty-one. He had been a widower for three years. His wife had been Princess Margaret of Connaught, a daughter of Queen Victoria's son Arthur, Duke of Connaught. The couple had had five children, the eldest of whom was seventeen and the youngest seven, in 1923. Crown Prince Gustaf Adolf was a tall, not unattractive man, gentle by nature with a kindly, somewhat studious air. Having done his obligatory military service as a young man, he gave military matters very little further thought; his interests lay in quite different directions. He was a highly civilized and cultured prince, interested in history, art, music and gardening. Archaeology was his passion; he developed into an authority on Chinese antiquities. With this feeling for the past was allied an interest in contemporary affairs: he was a student of politics, a progressive thinker and an ardent democrat. Calm, modest and well-mannered, Crown Prince Gustaf Adolf struck one as being more like a professor than a future king.

As such, he suited Louise admirably. Herself a woman of culture and intelligence, unaffected and forward-looking, she would never have been satisfied with some royal nonentity. Indeed, shortly before his death in 1921, Louise's father had said, 'There is only one person in the world who would suit Louise, and that is Gustaf of Sweden; and the only person who would suit Gustaf is Louise.'

Yet, at first, the thought of marrying Gustaf Adolf terrified Louise. They had known each other for some years but when, on a visit to England in the summer of 1923, Prince Gustaf Adolf began paying court to her, she did all she could to avoid being left alone with him. She liked him well enough but she could not face the thought of leaving England, of living in a strange country and of one day being a queen. She had no taste for ceremonial, she had no interest in clothes, she had no talent for small talk. And how would the children take to her? To become the stepmother of five young children was a daunting prospect. In mounting panic Louise consulted her friends and relations. They all urged her to accept.

Accept she finally did. Yet she remained full of doubts and self-depreciating comments. She was too old and thin, she protested, to be a bride. And how could she think of wearing white?

In Sweden too, there were some signs of apprehension. To the majority of the Swedish people, the name of Lady Louise Mountbatten meant nothing. Even the government knew very little about her. With the Swedish constitution expressly forbidding the marriage of the heir to a commoner, the government wanted to know if this mere 'Lady' was of royal blood. The query, which would probably have earned the Swedes one of Queen Victoria's most withering replies, was answered by the sending of the list of precedence at the Court of St James's. The Mountbattens, despite their war-time changes of title, remained listed among the members of the British royal family.

Yet the Swedish royal family was hardly in a position to demand proofs of unsullied royal blood. The dynasty, by now respectably royal, had distinctly plebeian origins. The founder had been that Napoleonic soldier, Jean Baptiste Bernadotte; his wife, whom Napoleon himself had once considered marrying, had been a silk merchant's daughter named Désirée Clary. To strengthen still more the Napoleonic flavour of the dynasty, Bernadotte's son, King Oscar I of Sweden and Norway, had married the daughter of Napoleon's adopted son, Eugène Beauharnais. Only with the nineteenth century well under way did the Bernadottes begin marrying into less exotic but more firmly established royal houses.

As a result, perhaps, of these parvenu origins, the court at Stockholm was now the most formal and lavish of the three Scandinavian courts. There was no talk here of riding on trams. The Royal Palace, the Stockholm *Slott*, situated on one of the fourteen islands which make up this beautiful water city, was sumptuously furnished. King Edward VII of England, visiting the Crown Prince's father, King Gustaf V, delighted in the ornate, somewhat Frenchified atmosphere of the Palace; even the soldiers lining the main staircase wore the 'uniform and bearskins of the Old Guard of Napoleon'. Things were not quite so French, however, as to prevent the King's suite from enjoying a hearty English breakfast. Drottningholm, the palace outside Stockholm, was no less lavishly decorated and furnished.

As Louise's future mother-in-law, Queen Victoria of Sweden, was never well enough to play a public role, many of her duties would devolve on Louise. In other words, the relatively unimportant Lady Louise Mountbatten would overnight become the leading female figure at this elegant Swedish court. For someone of her retiring nature, it was a frightening prospect.

Louise and Gustaf Adolf were married on 3 November 1923. The ceremony took place in the Chapel Royal at St James's Palace. The Crown Prince looked uncharacteristically military in the uniform of a Swedish general. Louise's dress was of silvery silk. A tiara, worn low on the forehead in that particularly unbecoming style of the early 1920s, held her lace veil. Her bouquet was of lilies-of-the-valley. Compared with the grey mistiness of the day outside, the scene within the Chapel Royal was rich, warm and colourful.

The reception was held in the splendid Round Room in Kensington Palace. It was not inappropriate that from here, where one summer morning in 1837 the young Victoria had heard that she had become the Queen of England, her great-granddaughter should set out to add Sweden to those other countries – Germany, Russia, Greece, Spain, Norway, Romania and Yugoslavia – in which her descendants had worn crowns.

CHAPTER TWENTY-NINE

Ruritania

Hardly had Queen Marie of Romania experienced, quite literally, the crowning moment of her life – the Coronation at Alba Julia – than her glittering world began to fall apart.

Her eldest daughter, Elizabeth, who, on the abdication of King Constantine in 1922, had become Queen of the Hellenes, did not long enjoy her new position. Within eighteen months her husband, King George II, had been deposed and Greece declared a republic. The couple came to live in Romania. The collapse of one of her dynastic dreams upset the ambitious Marie considerably. 'George should never have left Greece;' she would declare, 'once you leave a country you are forgotten. The great thing is to stay in the capital . . . .' He was, she would complain, 'a good man wasted'.

Distressing her still further was the fact that the marriage between George and Elizabeth was breaking up. Exile was emphasising their differences: Elizabeth, like her mother Queen Marie, was romantic, temperamental, gifted, while George had a great deal of the realism, honesty and simplicity of his mother, Queen Sophie. 'My daughter and he don't get on,' sighed Queen Marie, 'it is a pity but they are both rather obstinate. That is quite a good quality in a king, but not in a queen.'

Much more worrying for the Queen, however, was the behaviour of her son, Crown Prince Carol. His marriage to another of Queen Sophie's children, Princess Helen of Greece, was breaking up even more rapidly than that of George and Elizabeth. They, too, were very different types. None the less, on 25 October 1921, Helen had given birth to a son. The boy had been christened Michael, in honour of that Romanian national hero, Michael the Brave, the first man to unite the Romanian people. For Queen Marie, this was a gratifying moment: the succession had been secured.

Hardly had his son been born, however, before twenty-nine-year-old Crown Prince Carol resumed his old feckless and dissolute ways. Drawn again to that easygoing society in which he had found his first wife, Zizi Lambrino, Carol took up with the wife of an army officer. Her married name was Tampeanu, but she had been born Elena Wolf, a surname which was later Latinized to Lupescu. Plump, pale-skinned and titian-haired, Elena was hardly a beauty but she had a certain quality, part-voluptuous, part-sophisticated, which appealed to Crown Prince Carol. In fact, he was soon besotted by her. Having caught the Prince's interest, Elena quickly rid herself of her husband. On the divorce being granted, she reverted to her maiden name of Lupescu.

The romance, which was to be the talk of Europe for almost two decades, was under way. For such a colourful, Ruritanian, highly romantic affair, Carol and Lupescu hardly looked the part. He was already showing signs of developing into the chinless, jelly-jowled and watery-eyed creature that he was to be in middle age while she, with her heavy body and mouthful of outsize teeth, was no heart-melting *ingénue*. None the less, to the bewilderment and humiliation of his wife Helen, and to the titillation of the world, Carol threw himself into the role of princely lover with gusto.

No less bewildered and humiliated was Queen Marie. At first she had blamed Crown Princess Helen for not being able to hold her husband's interest. But once the full extent of her son's feelings for Elena Lupescu became apparent, Marie was seriously alarmed. The scandal could do the dynasty untold harm. King Ferdinand, hoping that the affair would work itself out, advised patience. But this was not Marie's way. Although Carol was now too old to take any notice of her dictates, there were other ways of bringing him to heel. She let him know, in an indirect fashion, that the King and his government were about to take the sternest measures unless he immediately ended his liaison with Madame Lupescu. Faced with this threat, Carol decided to get Elena out of the country. She applied for a passport. The government decided to grant it. They had an idea that Lupescu, fired by some finer feeling, had decided to end the affair by leaving Romania. Marie was more sceptical. She felt sure that if Elena went, Carol would follow her. The government, however, was confident that they would be able to keep him in the country.

This they were unable to do. In November 1925, Queen Alexandra, the widow of King Edward VII, died in London. It was imperative that, as Crown Prince, Carol should represent his father at the funeral. No sooner had Carol set out for London than Elena, after a series of comic-opera ruses to throw the Romanian police off her scent, crossed the border into Hungary. The funeral over, the lovers were reunited in Milan. From here, in letters to his wife, his father and the Romanian government, Crown Prince Carol announced that he had no intention of returning home. This time even the long-suffering King Ferdinand lost patience with his son. Rejecting Princess Helen's offer to go to Milan to plead with her husband, the King sent the Marshal of the Court with an order for Prince Carol to end the affair and return immediately. Carol refused. He declared that he was severing all connections with the Romanian royal family and that he was renouncing his rights to the throne.

On the last day of the year 1925, a government communiqué announced King Ferdinand's acceptance of Prince Carol's 'irrevocable renunciation of the succession to the Throne and of all the prerogatives appertaining to that rank, including membership of the Royal family'.

The heir to the throne was now Carol's only son, the four-year-old Prince Michael.

Prince Carol's dramatic and much publicized disappearance from the scene turned an even brighter spotlight on to Queen Marie. As Princess Helen was no longer Crown Princess (she was granted the title of Princess Helen of Romania, Princess Mother) she appeared less often in public. This meant that Queen Marie appeared more. And lest the world begin to sympathize a little too much with the Prince who had given up a throne for love, Marie decided to draw some attention to the Queen who had retained her throne through a devotion to duty. She arranged to be invited to pay an official visit to the United States. In the spring of 1927, with her two youngest children in tow, she set out on her spectacular and much criticized tour.

Acting with that characteristic blend of charm and majesty, trailing her flamboyant dresses, making endless speeches, granting innumerable interviews, 'selling', as one critic puts it, 'rights to Queen Marie this and Queen Marie that', she moved across the States in a blaze of publicity. 'We take off out best Sunday hat to Queen Marie . . .' wrote the jaundiced Edward H. Packard. 'We take off our hats, here in America, to anyone who successfully "puts over" their proposition. If they are smart enough to separate us from our money, we like them so much the better. We are fond of being humbugged . . . We exploit everything and we love being exploited.' Queen Marie might talk about 'love, brotherhood and peace' but what she was after, claims Packard, was dollars. She was hoping for the cancellation of European debts to the United States, an American loan to Romania and 'to make an honest, albeit undignified dollar selling rights to the various deals she pulls off'.

Such criticism infuriated Marie. 'There are those,' she would say scathingly, 'who tried to turn my visit into ridicule and accuse me later on of having come to try and get money out of America. This was an ugly and ill-natured calumny . . . there are some who do not understand my sincerity and try to make of me an actress full of tricks.'

Her triumphant tour was cut short by the news that King Ferdinand was dying. She sailed at once for Europe. Nando, his spirit broken by his son's behaviour, was suffering from cancer. So hesitant and pessimistic in wartime, King Ferdinand, in the years that followed, had revealed himself as a somewhat endearing figure: modest, gentle and scholarly. His chief interest was botany. Yet, no less than his wife, he had a highly developed sense of duty, although his was of an altogether less showy variety. 'It was this innate sense of duty,' writes his daughter Ileana, 'that made him overcome his personal shyness and gave him an air of royal dignity which made him stand out among other men, in spite of his retiring nature.'

During the last two weeks of his life, Queen Marie seldom left her husband's bedside. She had often lost patience with him in the past but during the last few years their shared concern over their son's transgressions had brought them closer together. A few hours before Nando died, he spoke to her of Carol. Their son, he murmured in his wry fashion, was like a Swiss cheese: excellent for what it was but so full of holes. The King died, with his tired head on his wife's shoulder, on 27 July 1927.

His grandson, the five-year-old Michael, was now the King of Romania.

2

But of course, Queen Marie remained the most notable figure in the land. Sporting mourning clothes which from the front made her look like a nun but with trains so long that those coming behind nearly tripped over them, she continued to play her special part. 'If you're going to Romania,' said Princess Ghyka to the celebrated travel writer Rosita Forbes, 'of course you must meet the Queen. Whatever you think, she is a very significant part of the country.'

Rosita Forbes went and, like everyone, was impressed by this 'beautiful, warm-hearted, preposterous woman who delighted in being a Queen'. While the silver teapot (in the shape of a partridge) stood untouched and cooling on the laden tray, Queen Marie held forth on every subject under the sun. 'It is customary now,' wrote the visitor afterwards, 'to criticize this English-and-Russian-born Balkan Queen for her love of display and her love of being admired, for her extravagance, her political ambitions, her business deals, and her plain speaking.' But Rosita Forbes could not join in that criticism; she thought Queen Marie admirable, a real force for good in Romania.

But in spite of appearances, the widowed Queen Marie was no longer quite the force she had once been. With the proclamation of her little grandson as King, a Regency had been set up. As the Romanian constitution excluded women from acting as regents, neither Queen Marie nor Princess Helen could fill the role; therefore three somewhat ineffectual regents were appointed. Real power, however, lay with the long-standing Liberal Prime Minister, Ion Bratianu. As Queen Marie and Bratianu had always been allies, matters, for a few months after King Ferdinand's death, remained much as before. But in November 1927 Bratianu died and his much less authoritative brother, Vintila Bratianu, became Prime Minister.

With Vintila Bratianu's accession to power coinciding with a worsening of the country's economic state, a rival party – the Peasant Party – began gaining ground. The Peasant Party, led by Juliu Maniu, tended to champion the absent Prince Carol, for no stronger reason than that the late Ion Bratianu and his Liberal Party had opposed him. Therefore they started agitating for Carol's return.

In November 1928, a year after Ion Bratianu's death, the Liberal government resigned and the Peasant Party came to power. On their installation, Queen Marie's influence waned considerably.

With her grandson, the little King Michael, her influence was also not as strong as she would have liked. Although Queen Marie and her daughter-in-law were on friendly enough terms, Princess Helen's ideas on the raising of her son were very different from Queen Marie's. Helen, very much Queen Sophie's daughter, wanted him brought up strictly, quietly and as privately as possible; Marie wanted him to be the centre of a wide, colourful and varied circle. As a result, Helen kept the boy away from his grandmother's flamboyant court. The inevitable English nanny, Miss St John, took him to see Queen Marie every morning, but that was all. This Queen Marie resented.

In the meantime, Prince Carol had been nagging Princess Helen for a divorce. At first, she had refused to consider it but finally, as a result of various pressures, she agreed. The marriage was dissolved on 21 June 1928.

Maniu, the new Prime Minister, who had been so vocal in opposition, was proving to have rather less to say now that he was in power. The country continued to flounder in its economic difficulties. Anxious to provide some sort of panacea for Romania's ills, Maniu decided to recall Prince Carol. It was generally known, by now, that Carol was eager to come back. Maniu's condition for Carol's return was that he leave Madame Lupescu behind. With this proposal, Queen Marie is said to have been in agreement. She had a strong sense of dynastic continuity and, as much as anyone, realized that Romania needed a stronger national symbol than that of a weak-kneed regency and a little boy. She probably hoped that Carol, having had his fling with Elena Lupescu, would be ready to leave her and to come to some sort of arrangement with Princess Helen and their son. Secret negotiations were opened with Carol.

Somewhat surprisingly, Prince Carol agreed to the proposed conditions. Madame Lupescu would be left behind. On 6 June 1930, four and a half years after his flight from Romania, Carol flew in to Bucharest.

There followed an extraordinarily confused series of events. Amidst scenes of frenzied acclamation, Carol was proclaimed King. ('How can Papa be King when I am King?' asked Michael, not unreasonably.) Within a month Elena Lupescu was back in the country and luxuriously installed in a house at Sinaia. Princess Helen was all but placed under arrest and her son, once again Crown Prince, encouraged to spend more and more time with his father. In an effort to get her to leave the country, Helen was subjected to every sort of pressure. Finally, tried beyond endurance, she fled. Michael was not allowed to go with her. After spending a few weeks in England, the heartbroken Helen joined her mother, the exiled Queen Sophie, in Florence.

To Queen Marie, with her clear ideas on royal obligation and discipline and her conviction that royalties should behave like demi-gods, these sordid and highly publicized domestic manoeuvrings were extremely painful. Nor had even she escaped her son's high-handedness. Jealous of her still considerable reputation at home and abroad and of the devotion she inspired in the hearts of most Romanians, he moved against her as well. He dismissed several of the officials in her service, including the Marshal of her Household, and forbade her to see certain of her close friends. His wishes, he warned her, were always to be loyally respected.

And, because of her concern for the dynasty and the country, Marie acquiesced. Carol must be given every opportunity to lead Romania out of its difficulties. Revealing an uncharacteristic humility, she effaced herself and withdrew from the court. Indeed, with Madame Lupescu's influence now all-powerful, there was not much else that she could do. She spent more and more time away from Bucharest; in her romantic castle of Bran or in her blazing white villa at Balcic on the Black Sea. In public, she never complained. Nor did she ever speak bitterly. 'I have had such a lot of happiness,' she would say, 'and battles too, of course, but that is all part of living.'

3

When the distraught Helen joined her mother in Florence in the autumn of 1931, Queen Sophie had been living there for almost eight years. Her home was a rented house, the Villa Bobolina on the Via Bolognese. With the sixty-one-year-old Queen Sophie lived her two youngest daughters, Irene and Katherine. In behaviour and appearance, Sophie was still very much the Queen. Her bearing was stately, her manners exquisite. The black, mauve and silvery grey of the mourning which she always wore for King Constantine suited her elaborately dressed white hair. But although Queen Sophie might look as regal as ever, her attitudes had mellowed during her long period of exile from Greece. No longer was she that stiff-backed, icily controlled woman of the war years; 'suffering,' according to her daughter Helen, 'had given her a tolerance and understanding of human frailty.'

'Poor misjudged Queen Sophie is one of the best of women;' wrote the Infanta Eulalia, 'her patience in adversity was wonderful, and her stoical philosophy enabled her to regard her life entirely as a state of *omnia vanitas*, in which nothing was lasting.'

One day, at a royal wedding reception, Queen Sophie was placed beside King Ferdinand of Bulgaria, the enemy against whom her husband, King Constantine, had fought during the Second Balkan War. Apprehensively, her family watched the two of them in conversation. Their fears proved groundless: Sophie and Ferdinand got on so well that they could hardly be separated after the luncheon.

'But what did you find to talk about?' asked one of Sophie's brothers-in-law.

In surprise, but with no trace of 'bitterness in her voice or on her face', she answered briskly, 'Why, old times, of course.'

All reservations too, about the morganatic marriage of her dead son, King Alexander of the Hellenes, to Aspasia Manos, had long since faded. She doted on their only child, the little Princess Alexandra. For a while this granddaughter and her mother lived in Florence and each day the little Princess would be brought to visit Queen Sophie. 'I had a wonderful time with Amama [the Queen] who adored and spoiled me outrageously,' remembered Alexandra. When she was older she was sent, as Queen Sophie's daughters had been sent, to boarding-school in England. She hated it. Only a visit from her grandmother ('looking lovely as ever') could brighten her days.

If Queen Sophie had come to accept one morganatic marriage, she was still conscious enough of the status of the dynasty not to countenance another. As her eldest son, ex-King George II, and his wife, Elizabeth of Romania, had no children, the heir to the Greek throne was now George's brother, Queen Sophie's third son Paul. Prince Paul, who turned twenty-nine in 1930, had been living in London for some years. From here, Queen Sophie heard rumours that her son had fallen in love with an English girl and that he intended marrying her. The Queen hurried to London. Tactfully but firmly she explained to Prince Paul that it would never do. Not only were morganatic marriages to be avoided at all costs but any such marriage – by the heir to the throne – would be interpreted as an acceptance of the fact that the monarchy was unlikely to be restored in Greece. This would be a blow to the hopes of King George II and the monarchists. Prince Paul, impressed by his mother's reasoning and anxious to avoid causing her any further distress, agreed to postpone the matter. Queen Sophie returned to Florence and the affair died a death.

It was, perhaps, this possibility of a restoration (for Sophie, better than anyone, appreciated the capriciousness of the Greeks) which prevented the Queen from buying a permanent home in Florence. Yet she had her eye on a likely property. Near Fiesole, on the wooded hill of San Domenico overlooking the city, lay a charming fifteenth-century villa. On Helen's arrival from Bucharest, Queen Sophie took her to see the house. 'If we had to stay here permanently,' she said, 'that is where I should like to live.'

But Queen Sophie did not live long enough; not to decide to buy the villa nor to see the restoration of the monarchy in Greece. Towards the end of 1931 she went into a hospital in Frankfurt for an operation. During the course of the operation, it was discovered that she had cancer. Both her parents, the Emperor and Empress Frederick, had died of the same disease. She lived for a few weeks more, surrounded by all her children, and died, peacefully, on 13 January 1932.

Her body lay in state in the great hall at Friedrichshof, the home which her mother, the Empress Frederick, had built near Frankfurt, and in which her own body had lain thirty years before. Queen Sophie's body was then taken to Florence to lie beside the remains of King Constantine and of his mother, Queen Olga (who had died in 1926) in the crypt of the Orthodox Church.

The villa, which Queen Sophie had loved so much, was bought by her daughter Helen and turned into a family home for the late Queen's exiled sons and daughters. It was renamed the Villa Sparta. After long and complicated negotiations between Helen and Carol, it was arranged that their son Michael would live in Romania and spend one month, twice a year, with his mother at the Villa Sparta. With this, Helen had to be content.

Within less than four years of Queen Sophie's death, the monarchy was restored in Greece. One of those inevitable plebiscites recalled her eldest son, King George II, to the throne. This time the restoration would last for almost forty years, until the declaration of yet another republic in 1973. In November 1936, King George II had the bodies of his parents King Constantine and Queen Sophie, and of his grandmother, Queen Olga, brought back to Athens. The funeral was a magnificently staged affair. Through silent crowds, the three flag-draped coffins were drawn on gun-carriages to the Cathedral. For six days they lay in state while the people filed by in their tens of thousands to pay homage. On the seventh day they were buried with all possible pomp. 'Eighty bishops,' writes Constantine's brother Christopher, 'gathered from every town in Greece, lined the steps of the high altar, making in their jewelled robes a symphony of light and colour against the sombre background of the Cathedral.'

The ostentatious ceremony over, the coffins were taken to that simple family cemetery at Tatoi for final interment. Queen Sophie, the honest, dignified, unpretentious and much maligned granddaughter of Queen Victoria, had come back to Greece for the last time.

CHAPTER THIRTY

'I thought I had done well'

I

'And who, after all, can tell . . .' Queen Ena of Spain once said to the Grand Duchess Marie of Russia, who was living in exile in Paris. 'In a very few years I might join you here.'

For Queen Ena's apprehensions, there was considerable justification. The situation in Spain, by the end of the 1920s, was as uncertain as it had ever been. For a period, after the establishment of General Primo de Rivera's dictatorship in 1923, things had looked fairly secure. A well-meaning and somewhat genial dictator, General Primo had applied his energies to the reorganization of the country. Having restored order, he set about improving and constructing roads, railways, hotels, hospitals, dams and schools. By allying herself with France, Spain finally subdued Morocco, and the King was able to pay a truimphant visit to the pacified territory. When a plebiscite on the question of the dictatorship was submitted to the Spanish people, a large majority pronounced in its favour. In the autumn of 1925, the dictatorship was re-established as a civil institution.

Nor did the régime neglect the showier side of national life. Spain, although shorn of her once-mighty Empire, was still the mother country of much of South America and, in an effort to renew kinship, Primo's Directory staged two great exhibitions. One was held at Barcelona, the other at Seville. Both were dedicated to the achievements of the Spanish-speaking world. The International Exhibition at Barcelona concentrated on industry; that of Seville, where each South American state had a pavilion, was the more romantic. A semicircle of Moorish arches, flanked by slender towers, had been built in a beautiful park; from the elegant centrepiece, one could stroll through the trees to the various pavilions. Painting, sculpture, tapestry, jewellery, armour, furniture, embroidery, brocades – all these bore witness to the taste and genius of Spain. And at night, when the floodlit fountains flung their water high into the warm air, and golden balls, lit from within, glowed on the orange trees, it was like fairyland.

King Alfonso and Queen Ena showed themselves frequently during this memorable season. They made a handsome couple: he so dark and lithe and splendidly uniformed, she so fair and elegant. One could almost believe, as one moved about these magnificent exhibitions and heard the tumultuous ovations for the royal couple, that Alfonso had indeed brought greatness back to Spain and that no monarchs were more popular than they.

The façade might be impressive but the walls were cracking. 'How long,' the French journalist Tharaud once asked King Alfonso, 'do you think this régime will last?' The King protested that he would like nothing better than to return to parliamentary rule but that the old party leaders, the *caciques*, had shown no sign that they had mended their ways. 'If one reopened the Cortes,' he said, 'one would see the old parties which led the country to its own undoing begin their disputes again and recommence their chatter at the point where General Primo interrupted it. We should be back into anarchy.' Spain, he assured his listener, had at most six thousand politicians as against twenty million people who cared nothing whatsoever for politics. 'To please six thousand people must we sacrifice twenty million?' he asked. 'I leave the answer to you.'

Those six thousand, however, were becoming increasingly restive. Although the King had never intended the Directory to be permanent, neither he nor Primo seemed able to make up their minds as to what sort of government should replace it. The years of strict censorship, the banishment of critical intellectuals, the worsening economic situation (this was a problem which Primo never mastered), an indefinable craving for change – all these things led to a growing discontent. And to them was added a vague irritation with the King himself.

Although over forty years of age, Alfonso had never acquired the gravity and serious-mindedness so dear to the Spaniard. In his well-cut suits, with one hand holding a cigarette and the other caressing his jaunty moustache, he looked and behaved like a young man-about-town. He still drove his cars at breakneck speed, he still galloped his horse across the polo field, he still joked and gossiped with dangerous indiscretion. With the intellectual life of the country he had no contact at all. Whenever he visited a school or a university, his equerries would see to it that he spoke only to the sportsmen or the aristocrats, never to the thinkers. This chronic adolescence, grumbled his critics, was distinctly out of place in a ruler.

His home life, too, gave cause for discontent. He was said to neglect Queen Ena; his amorous adventures were widely discussed. There was disappointment, and much ill-informed gossip, about the poor health of his sons. It was known that his haemophilic heir, the Prince of the Asturias, who turned twenty-three in 1930, was obliged to spend long periods in bed. There was a macabre rumour prevalent among the simpler-minded Spanish peasants, which no number of official denials could stamp out, that a young soldier had to be sacrificed every day in order that his warm blood might be used to keep the heir apparent alive. The Prince of the Asturias played almost no part in public life; what sort of King would he make? King Alfonso's second son, the deaf and nearly dumb Don Jaime, would be no better; nor his youngest son, the haemophilic Don Gonzalo. To only one life, that of the third son, Don Juan, could the succession be entrusted.

It was no wonder that the habitual expression of the once lively Queen Ena was now one of melancholy.

By the end of the 1920s, the old charges of the King having broken his constitutional oath and of his being responsible for the disaster of Anual were being raised once more. And Primo de Rivero was in no position to silence them now.

For the General himself had fallen from power. By the beginning of 1930 he was feeling so conscious of his loss of prestige that he sent a circular letter to the captains-general asking for their confidence. Their replies, when they bothered to reply, were noncommittal. None of them came out in full support of the dictator. The King, who learned of this move, not from Primo but from the newspapers, was furious. He summoned the General to the palace and demanded to know why he, the King, supreme representative of the people and head of the armed forces, had not first been consulted. Primo attempted to explain his motives but when, a day or two later, he offered his resignation, Alfonso accepted it. The ex-Dictator, dispirited and ill, left for Paris. He died there two months later.

His body was brought back to Madrid where, as *El Salvador de España*, he was given a hero's funeral. Notable by his absence from the impressive ceremony was the man whom the Saviour of Spain had tried to save – King Alfonso XIII. Quick to dissociate himself from Primo's failure, the King by his adroitness earned nothing but contempt. If he could not remain true to his friends, to whom then, it was argued, would he ever remain true?

As the Queen had said, he tired of everything.

2

In January 1931, Queen Ena had a telephone call from London to tell her that her mother, Queen Victoria's youngest daughter Princess Beatrice, was seriously ill. She had broken her arm in a fall at Kensington Palace and had then developed bronchial trouble. She was not expected to live. Queen Ena hurried to London. Although her mother recovered, the recovery was slow and painful and Queen Ena was obliged to spend several weeks by her bedside. She did not return to Spain until February.

While she was away, the political situation in Spain worsened considerably. To fill the gap left by General Primo de Rivera, the King and his advisers had chosen another dictator, General Berenguer, ex-High Commissioner of Morocco. The appointment of this somewhat milder man was looked upon as a temporary measure only: his task was to prepare Spain for immediate elections. The news threw the Republicans into a flurry of preparations. With the relaxation of censorship of the Press, anti-monarchical propaganda flooded the cities of Spain. But apprehensive lest these new elections, like the old, be managed by the *caciques*, the Republicans looked for additional ways to undermine the King's position. With the Socialists and the separatist Catalans, they entered into an anti-dynastic pact. Only a republic, it was declared, could cure the kills of Spain. '*Fuera el Rey!*' – Away with the King – became the cry, to which Alfonso, in his flippant fashion, remarked that he seemed to have gone out of fashion.

However, towards the end of February 1931, he seemed suddenly to have come back into fashion. A totally unexpected incident gave him a resurgence of confidence.

Her mother recovered, Queen Ena left London to return home. She was seen off at Victoria station by King George V and Queen Mary, both of them urging her, with encouraging little pats on the back, to get Alfonso to act constitutionally. Queen Ena, bracing herself to face a revolution, entered Spain at Irun on 28 February and travelled down to Madrid. At each station her welcome was more vociferous than at the last and, by the time she reached the capital, she was overwhelmed by the fervour of the crowd. As she stepped down from the train, so chic in her pale, fur-trimmed coat, she was almost deafened by the shouts of '*Viva la Reina!*' She drove beside the King through a roaring sea of people to the Palacio Real where, time and again, they were obliged to appear on the balcony to show themselves to the hysterically applauding crowds.

Convinced by this apparently spontaneous demonstration that his position was as secure as ever, the King set about preparing for the promised elections. Municipal elections were to be held on 12 April; those for the Cortes in June. Alfonso, cool as always, went off to England for a short holiday. He returned late in March.

The day of the municipal elections was a Sunday. The people voted quietly. There were no demonstrations, either in the streets or at the polling booths. The first returns, the urban returns, were overwhelmingly Republican. Even the revolutionaries were amazed at the extent of their success. And although, in the final count, the Monarchists gained a majority, these urban results gave the Republicans all the encouragement they needed. The revolution could begin.

Toward sunset the following Tuesday evening a great crowd, waving red flags and screaming *'Viva la Republica!'* converged on the Palacio Real. Inside, with the exception of the Infante Don Juan, the King's third son, was gathered the entire royal family. The Prince of the Asturias was in bed, too weak to move. The King was calm. He was determined, at all costs, to avoid bloodshed. He could not allow civil strife for his sake. If a republic was what Spain wanted, then a republic he must let her have. Confident, however, that this republican fervour would burn itself out, he decided that the best thing to do was to leave Spain for a while. He would agree to a suspension of his powers but, like King Constantine of Greece in a similar situation, he would not abdicate. In a moving manifesto to the nation, Alfonso made this clear. 'I renounce nothing of my rights,' he wrote, 'because rather than my own, they are a deposit accumulated by history . . . .'

Having written his manifesto, Alfonso took leave of his family. It was decided that he would set out at once for France, with the Queen and the children following the next day. As the Prince of the Asturias could not leave his bed, the King went up to his room to say good-bye. He then took leave of the Queen and the other children. A small convoy of cars was waiting in the darkness below the garden terrace. Having said a last good-bye to the hushed group of well-wishers, the King stepped into the leading car and disappeared into the night.

The dawn was just beginning to silver the sea when he arrived at Cartagena. Here a cruiser was waiting to take him into exile. To shouts of *'Viva la Republica!'* from the crowd on the quayside, he climbed aboard and set sail for Marseilles. When he asked why the royal standard was not being flown at the masthead, he was told that it was being cut up by the ship's tailor in order to make the new Republican flag.

Queen Ena and her children remained in the vast, echoing Palacio Real. All night the mob howled about the palace, filling the great rooms with the threatening sound of their voices. Sleep, even rest, was impossible. It was as though the nightmare would never end. As Queen Ena sat by the bedside of her haemophilic son, it seemed like an echo of the time when her cousin Alicky had sat with Alexis at Tsarskoe Selo after the abdication of the Tsar. A sudden heightening of the noise, while the family was eating an informal meal around the sickbed, sent them rushing to the windows. Peeping through the blinds, they saw a truck being driven at full force against one of the palace doors in the hope of breaking it down. Time and again, to the encouraging shouts of the crowd, it reversed and recharged. Was the palace about to be invaded? Already some youths had scrambled up the façade and attached a Republican flag to one of the balconies. Fortunately for the family, a squadron of Hussars cleared away the mob. But the howling went on.

To the accompaniment of this frightening clamour, the royal family gathered a few things together, borrowed some money and said their arewells. They left, just after dawn, by the garden entrance. They were to drive to the Escorial and from there take a train to Paris. The Queen had hoped to keep her departure as quiet as possible but as a small crowd of devotees had gathered by the roadside in the Casa de Campo, she stopped the car and alighted. Sitting on a rock, with the white walls of the Palacio Real glittering in the distance behind her, she took leave of them.

Queen Ena, wrote a witness of this moving scene, 'had held many Courts in the Palace on the horizon, received foreign sovereigns, been the brilliant central figure in many spendid and sumptuous ceremonials. At not one of them had she been more queenly, more royally self-controlled, more splendidly a woman than on this sun-drenched morning with a rock for her throne, the high blue sky for her canopy and the unfailing love of a few of her truest friends and servants as her only solace and support'.

At Escorial they entered the train. The Prince of the Asturias, too weak to move, had to be carried aboard. When the very last of the agonizing farewells had been said, the blinds of the royal saloon carriage were drawn and, in almost complete silence, the train slid out of the station.

Almost twenty-five years after becoming Queen, Ena was taking the road to exile. Her comment of this rejection by the Spanish people was poignant: 'I thought I had done well,' she said quietly.

CHAPTER THIRTY-ONE

Murder in Marseilles

I

At the other end of Europe, in the Balkan peninsula, the austere King Alexander of Yugoslavia was battling with a no less difficult situation. That conglomeration of states, united under the Serbian crown after the war to form a single Slav state, was showing no signs of doing so. The country was a hotch-potch of different peoples, different nationalities, different religions, different languages and different alphabets. Where some states, like Serbia, had considerable experience of parliamentary democracy, others, like Bosnia and Herzegovina, had almost none. The result was that the central parliament, sitting in Belgrade, was simply a collection of bickering minorities. The plans of one section would invariably be defeated by the other sections voting together. No one co-operated; no one compromised. Serbs argued against Croats, Croats against Slovenes; the Orthodox Church against the Catholic Church, the Catholic Church against the Moslems. Insult was heaped upon insult; crisis followed crisis. Every government had to be a coalition; no coalition lasted very long. Cabinets had to be reconstructed several times a year. The first Minister for Agriculture lasted one month; the second for four; the third for two weeks; the fourth for four months; the fifth for three months. Everyone had plenty to say but very few seemed prepared to do anything.

Least co-operative of all were the Croats. Catholic Croatia, which before the war had been part of the Austrian Empire, had joined the new state rather unwillingly. Since then she had resolutely refused to pull together with the Orthodox Serbs. That democracy could not work in Yugoslavia was in no small measure due to this intractability on the part of the Croats. The dream of many Croatians was autonomy for their country. To achieve this, they would first have to destroy the newly established state.

All this King Alexander found exasperating. So self-controlled and undemonstrative a man, he could not understand these parliamentary rantings. Accustomed to the ordered ways, the *esprit de corps*, the unity of purpose and, it must be admitted, the unquestioning obedience of the army, he had no patience with these squabbling politicians. As Rebecca West has so succinctly put it, he 'suffered at all times from the professional soldier's inability to distinguish between an argument and a mutiny'. King Alexander was, in many ways, too straightforward and incorrupt to make his way through the labyrinth of Balkan politics. And then, although no fool, he did not like to be surrounded by clever men. Regrettably, he valued good character above brain. Honest, simple men who did their job he appreciated; he did not really have much faith in democracy.

Yet, in the beginning, King Alexander did what he could to make parliamentary democracy work. Elections were free. On the rare occasions that the politicians came to some agreement, he never tampered with their decisions. Determined to unify the various nationalities (there were no fewer than nine different groups in the new state) he showed admirable impartiality. He never favoured his own Serbs above the others. Orthodox himself, he showed every consideration for the Catholics. The British Minister at Belgrade claimed that the King was the only real Yugoslav that he had ever met. To prove that he was as much King of the Slovenes as the Serbs, Alexander established a summer residence at Bled, in the mountainous, far-western corner of Slovenia. To please the fractious Croats, he named his second son – born on 19 January 1928 – Tomislav, after the legendary King of Croatia. Going further still, he gave a cabinet post to Stephan Raditch, the hitherto persecuted leader of the Croat Peasant Party.

But not all King Alexander's moves were quite so statesmanlike. The régime had its share of bannings, censorship, imprisonments and arbitrary actions by the police. These, in turn, simply led to further upheavals. Indeed, ten years after the founding of the new state, the situation was more chaotic than ever. National unity was still no more than a word; little was being inaugurated, let alone accomplished.

By 1928 even Raditch, the Croat leader, was advising a temporary dictatorship as the only solution to the country's troubles. The King should sweep away the wrangling politicians and appoint a military government. To Alexander, the idea had considerable appeal but he hesitated to take so bold a step. But Raditch persisted, and in parliament delivered an impassioned harangue in favour of a royal dictatorship. 'What is more natural,' he cried, 'than that the King, who is the glory of the monarchy, should become the arbiter of our destinies?'

His answer came from a wild-eyed Montenegrin deputy. On 20 June 1928, he shot Raditch, who died six weeks later.

For a few months longer Alexander grappled with the situation. Since the murder of Raditch, the Croat deputies had refused to sit in parliament. This emasculated body had become, in the King's words, simply a negative force causing dissension in the land. Thus on 6 January 1929, he dismissed it and appointed a general as Prime Minister, thereby infringing the constitution. In a statement to the nation, the King declared that his greatest aim was the unity of the country. Although parliamentarianism remained his ideal, it had failed and he was being forced to try another method. He was now a dictator.

'The Queen,' King Alexander once said of his wife Mignon, 'has no part in affairs of state. I admire her because she is devoted to her children and seeks no other sphere of interest.'

This was true. 'I really don't know much about politics,' the Queen would say. 'I have the children to look after and the houses and the vines.'

This is not to say that Queen Marie of Yugoslavia was an excessively maternal creature, interested in nothing other than her children. On the contrary, she had a brusque, somewhat unmotherly manner. With the passing years, she had developed into something very like an English country gentlewoman: plainly dressed, plainly spoken, practical and unflurried. She had been brought up, she would say, in the English fashion – never 'to make a fuss'. Of the theatrical aura of her mother, Queen Marie of Romania, Mignon had nothing. 'I shall never be as good a Queen as she is,' she once declared. 'You see, I don't really like clothes.' That was all too obvious. She was very little interested in her appearance. She wore no make-up; her hair, cut short, was often kept in place by a hairnet; she was happiest in flannel suits and brogues. Yet her air, if blunt, was never gruff. Her smile was attractive, her manner friendly and her nature unexpectedly gentle.

Her interests, as she said, were her children, her houses and her vines. The royal couple had three sons, Peter, Tomislav and Andrej. All three were healthy, lively, attractive boys. For most of the time they lived separately from their parents: with their nurses or governesses in cottages in the grounds of the various royal homes. There were several royal residences. The official palace was the main one in Belgrade, which Alexander had enlarged on his marriage. But the couple had never really enjoyed living there. It was too public. All day the trams hurtled past the front door; all night the crowds jabbered at the pavement café on the corner. In 1929, after assuming dictatorial powers, Alexander moved his family out to a new palace, on a hilltop at Dedinje, a few miles from the capital. In a way, this was a mistake. Alexander was simply removing himself still farther from his people. Already considered somewhat aloof, undemocratic and un-Serbian, the King seemed to be emphasizing his remoteness from his subjects by moving away from their midst.

As far as the family was concerned, however, the great white, arcaded palace at Dedinje was a delight. The estate was quite self-contained. The King, an ardent bibliophile, devoted himself to his books. Often, late at night, he would be found in dressing-gown and slippers on a small step-ladder, peering through his pince-nez at some rare and beautifully bound volume. He allowed no one to touch his books. With him, said the Queen, the pleasure of acquisition was greater than the pleasure of reading. His poor eyesight might have had something to do with this. 'You are happy,' he once said to her. 'You can always find something to do with your hands in your spare time, whereas I can only read.' Indeed, Mignon was never at a loss for something to do. Interested in practical things, farming in particular, she busied herself with the garden, the horses, the cows, the poultry, even the carpenter's and machine shop.

In the summer the family moved to their home at Bled, in the Julian Alps. Here they spent some of their happiest times. The house was beau-tifully situated. The King could go shooting and fishing, the Queen could go careering along the mountain roads. Wedged between Austria and Italy, the countryside around Bled was quite different from the rest of the Balkans. Its flavour was Austrian, German, Western. The royal family, however, lived in an almost exclusively English atmosphere. The King's cousin, Prince Paul, now married to Princess Olga of Greece, lived twelve miles from Bled. The aesthetic Paul, having been to Oxford, was some-thing of an Anglophile; his household spoke English. In fact, it was at his home near Bled that his wife's sister, Princess Marina, became engaged to Prince George, the youngest son of King George V of England.

Into this British enclave, the Queen fitted very happily. Although she usually spoke French to the King, she preferred using English. Her sons were being educated in English. Nurse Bell had given way to Miss Crowther (called, inevitably, 'Crowdy') and a Mr Parrot arrived as tutor. Plans were being made to send Crown Prince Peter to school in England. In time, all three boys went to British schools.

And, of course, whenever Queen Marie of Romania descended on the royal household, its tone became more British still. That, King Alexander never minded; what he did mind about his mother-in-law's visits was the atmosphere she engendered. She was far too ebullient for his taste. Once, towards the end of a particularly long and exhausting stay, he was heard to mutter, 'It's enough.'

An enthusiastic traveller, Queen Marie of Yugoslavia loved to visit Miločer, on the Adriatic coast. She adored the sea. Leaving the King in Belgrade, she and her sons would make the two-day train journey to the coast. Here they would revel in the informality of seaside life – the picnicking, the boating, the fishing and the bathing. In time, Mignon had a house built at Miločer.

Another of the royal houses was at Topola, some fifty miles from the capital. It had been built by King Alexander's father, King Peter I. For the taste of the royal family, however, it was far too ornate, and they had built a much less pretentious home for themselves nearby. It was, says Rebecca West, 'a cottage planned by the Queen, where she and Alexander and the children lived the kind of home life, uncultured but civilized and amiable, that Queen Victoria made common form for European royalty.' One of the chief glories of Topola was its vineyards. In these, the Queen took an active interest. It was here, at Topola, that Mignon was visited by Rosita Forbes, at that time touring the Balkans.

Miss Forbes had just come on from a hair-raising visit to King Alexander in southern Serbia. By now the royal dictator lived under the constant threat of assassination. Where southern Serbia bordered on the revolutionary province of Macedonia, the threat was particularly serious. His entourage expected the King to be blown to bits at any moment. Yet Alexander never showed the slightest flicker of nervousness; he was utterly without fear. 'It is a waste of time to be afraid,' he would say in his quiet fashion.

But if Alexander was without fear, Rosita Forbes was not, and it had been with considerable trepidation that she had accepted the King's invitation to join him in a cup of coffee at an ill-lit café, well known as a meeting place of the very Macedonian Comitadjis who were planning to kill him. Throughout the nerve-racking visit the King had remained quite calm. 'I doubt if they would shoot me here,' he said ruminatively. Miss Forbes was not quite so certain.

Her interview with the Queen would be, she imagined, much more relaxing.

The house at Topola was hardly more than a villa, and Miss Forbes was received in a room furnished with wickerwork and English chintzes. She found the Queen disarmingly matter-of-fact. When Miss Forbes apologized for being late, explaining that her driver had assumed that the royal family lived in the grandiose building on the hill opposite, Queen Marie laughed heartily. 'We probably shall be soon,' she said. 'It's the morgue.' On the visitor thanking her hostess for agreeing to receive her, the Queen's reply was no less to the point. 'Well, my mother told me that I must,' she said.

Inevitably, the talk turned to the assassination attempts on the King's life. Queen Marie treated the subject, says her guest, as though it were influenza. They were always trying to shoot the King, grumbled the Queen. 'He doesn't mind, but sometimes it does interrupt his work.'

Tea over (there were none of Queen Marie of Romania's silver, bird-shaped teapots here; merely a china one), Queen Marie took her visitor to see the vines. They passed the cottage in which lived the little princes;

a fully armed guard stood at every window. A few minutes later, as they strolled up a slope, there was a sudden, ear-splitting explosion. Part of a hillside was flung up into the air and came crashing down to within a few yards of their feet. Rosita Forbes stood rooted to the ground in terror. Queen Marie did not turn a hair. In fact, she went on speaking as though nothing had happened. Only on finishing her sentence did she remark on the violent crash. 'I wonder if they are dynamiting for my vineyard – or it might be a bomb,' she said briskly. 'I'll ask.'

At that moment a breathless aide-de-camp dashed up to reassure them it had indeed been a charge of dynamite for the vineyard. By some mis-calculation, it had been much too large. 'Well, I don't see how we're going to get the vines planted now,' complained the Queen, peering into the dust-filled chasm. 'It's too steep.'

The last sight that Miss Forbes had of this unaffected Queen that day was running down the steps of the villa after they had already said good-bye.

'Wait! Wait!' called the Queen. 'It's late and you'll be cold driving back to Belgrade. Look, I've brought you a coat.'

She handed it over and then strode back across the darkening garden to her closely guarded house.

3

A soldier and a dictator, King Alexander of Yugoslavia was dedicated to peace. Unlike those other European dictators, Hitler and Mussolini, he had no dreams of military conquest and national aggrandizement. His dreams were all of Yugoslav unity. But if this elusive ideal could be realized in no other way, then it must be imposed by the throne.

One of Alexander's first moves after becoming dictator was the geo-graphical reorganization of his country. The old names of the various states – Serbia, Croatia, Slovenia, Montenegro, Herzegovina, Bosnia, Macedonia and the Voivodina – were swept away, and a set of new provinces, making up a single country – Yugoslavia – were proclaimed. At an impressive military ceremony in Belgrade the various national regiments gave up their flags and adopted the new Yugoslavian flag. To conciliate the Croats, the Cyrillic script, so dear to the Serbs, was abolished to be replaced by the Latin script. A new constitution, vesting the King and his cabinet with absolute power, was introduced. A parliament, consisting of supporters of the government only, merely confirmed new laws. The Press was rigidly controlled. The police were all-powerful.

By none of these well-intentioned but draconian moves, however, could King Alexander impose unification or stamp out opposition. The country remained divided; its various groups remained dissatisfied. Agitation among Croats and Slovenes continued; terrorism increased. Arrests, bombings and political murders became daily occurrences. Acts of sabotage, designed to undermine confidence in the régime, multiplied. And, vigorously heaping fuel onto these political fires was Mussolini's Italy. Anxious to gain for his country the Dalmatian coast of Yugoslavia, Mussolini encouraged the Croats in their fight against a united Yugoslavia. A weak, divided Yugoslavia would suit Mussolini very well. The removal of King Alexander from the scene would suit him even better.

Fully alive to this international intrigue, Alexander remained cool. But there were further dangers. With Italy threatening him on one side, and Germany, under Hitler, beginning to rise to the north, King Alexander realized that not only the peoples of Yugoslavia, but all the Balkan countries, should stand together. Not again must the Western Powers be allowed to meddle in the Balkans. War in the Balkans would undo all his work for Yugoslavia. A pact must be signed between the various Balkan Powers. With this in mind, King Alexander and Queen Marie set off on a tour of the peninsula in the autumn of 1933. They visited Marie's brother, King Carol, in Bucharest; King Boris of Bulgaria at Varna on the Black Sea; Kemal Pasha in Constantinople and members of the Greek government on Corfu. In November 1933, shortly before Alexander's forty-fifth birthday, the Balkan Pact was signed. For the King, it was a great personal triumph. From now on, he was spoken of as a 'man of peace'.

The following year, King Alexander and Queen Marie were invited to pay a state visit to Paris. They were delighted. On discussing how they should travel to France, Alexander announced that he would like to go by sea. There were several reasons for this. He would avoid crossing unfriendly Italy; in a Yugoslav destroyer, he would be on Yugoslav territory until he reached France; his arrival on a warship would confirm Yugoslavia's claim to be a naval power; landing at Marseilles, he would be able to lay a wreath on the monument to those French troops who had sailed from there to help the Serbian army during the war.

Mignon was less enthusiastic. She was a very bad sailor and in October the Mediterranean could be stormy. Between them, then, they agreed that he should go by sea and she by rail. She would see him off on the *Dubrovnik* and then take her train.

They left Belgrade together early in October 1934. With them went the King's cousin, Prince Paul. Some time before setting out, the King had arranged for Prince Paul to act as Regent for his son Peter in the event of his own death. Assassination was very much in the air these days. There had been a plan to kill the King in the Croatian capital Zagreb the year before. Hitler had had Roehm murdered that year and the Austrian

Nazis had killed Dolfuss. Recently, the Queen had noticed that even her normally imperturbable husband was beginning to glance behind him as he walked. It was as well, therefore, that he had made some provision for the future of his régime.

Was it, perhaps, a premonition of death that made the King decide to revisit some of the scenes of his youth before sailing for France? In streaming rain, the royal party travelled again across the bleak, rocky countryside that had seen the Serbian retreat in the worst days of the First World War. Through these mountains, some twenty years before, the King had accompanied the broken army in its flight to the sea. Now, as Alexander passed by, the peasants, carrying the traditional bread and salt, came out to welcome their King. In Cettinje, the mist-shrouded old capital of Montenegro, Alexander showed his wife the unpretentious stone cottage in which he had been born. In the same room, a year later, his mother, Princess Zorka of Montenegro, had died. At Zelenika, from where he was to sail, the King insisted on revisiting the old monastery of Savina.

In her straightforward fashion, the Queen afterwards described this last excursion. 'The monastery was locked,' she remembered. 'We could not find anyone, either priest or monk, to open for us. We had not announced our visit and so were not expected. My husband said to Paul, "I must show you the cross; come on, let's wake them up." Then the boys did something they shouldn't have done. Of course it was very wrong. They found two ropes and rang the monastery bells. The bell my husband rang was very rarely sounded. It had a peculiar tone and must have greatly surprised those who heard it. A priest appeared as from nowhere running over the flagstone paving towards us and he was greatly surprised to see who it was had arrived . . . But afterwards we heard a curious story about this visit. I am not superstitious. I consider it rather a legend. We heard that the bells the boys had rung each had a name. The bell my husband had rung was called "Death" and the bell Paul had rung was called "Life". '

They returned to the port and the King boarded the *Dubrovnik*. Husband and wife kissed each other good-bye. Mignon had a feeling that this was no ordinary farewell. She felt vaguely troubled. As she drove back to the station she admitted to Prince Paul her feeling that all was not well. That night she boarded the train for France.

As it would not have done for the King and Queen to arrive separately in Paris, it had been arranged that they should meet at Dijon. By then Alexander would have paid his visit to Marseilles, and the two of them would travel on together to the French capital. But on the afternoon of 9 October, 1934, with the Queen already travelling through France, the Prefet of Doubs, a M. Peretti de la Rocca, boarded her train. He warned her that he had bad news. The King had been assassinated in Marseilles.

Immediately her train was diverted to Marseilles. The Queen arrived there at five on the morning of 10 October. Her husband's body lay in a small candle-lit chapel. He was wearing his Admiral's uniform. His hands were folded on his sword, his body was covered to the waist by the Yugoslav flag, at his feet were massed flowers.

The Queen was told the full story. King Alexander had been driving through the streets of the city in an open car. Beside him sat Louis Barthou, the French Minister of Foreign Affairs; opposite sat General Georges. The King was smiling his faint smile at the cheering crowds. Suddenly a man leapt onto the running-board of the car. He fired a revolver, first at the King, then at Louis Barthou and General Georges. After that, all was confusion; a confusion caught by a photographer and preserved for posterity. The King, slumped in his seat, was quickly driven away from the milling crowd of horse guards, police, photographers and spectators, and along the processional route to the Prefecture. Here his body was laid out on a sofa. The doctors examining him pronounced him dead. He had been shot twice; the first bullet had killed him. Louis Barthou had also died. General Georges recovered. Had Queen Marie been with him, she would probably have been shot as well.

The King had been murdered by a hired assassin named Velučko Kerin. The murder had been planned by a Croat organisation, supported and instructed by Italians. Its purpose had been the break-up of Yugoslavia, the creation of an autonomous Croatian state and the taking over of Yugoslavian Dalmatia by Italy. None of these results followed the murder; Yugoslavia remained quiet and intact. Kerin, wounded in the mêlée, died a few hours later.

Queen Marie having seen her husband's dead body, it was put aboard the *Dubrovnik* and carried back to Split, in Yugoslavia. Mignon then travelled on to Paris. As her eldest son, the eleven-year-old Peter, was at school in England, arrangements had been made for the boy to come over to Paris to meet her.

Peter had been woken early in his dormitory on the morning of 10 October and told that he must leave the school at once. Imagining that he was being punished for some misdemeanour, he dressed, took leave of the headmaster and was driven to London. Only on arriving at the Yugoslav Embassy was he told the truth. The normally impassive Ambassador was in tears. 'They have killed our King,' he cried. 'Long live Your Majesty.' The boy – Queen Victoria's great-great-grandson – was now King Peter II of Yugoslavia.

Luckily Peter's grandmother, Queen Marie of Romania, was in London at the time and she accompanied the little King to Paris. They arrived there late that same night. Not until the following morning was Peter taken to the Yugoslav Legation to meet his mother. Mignon, dressed in black and heavily veiled, was waiting for him in the main reception room. 'We embraced and wept together,' says Peter. 'I was terribly upset.'

For mother and son, the next few days were an ordeal. The train journey back to Yugoslavia was unbearably mournful. At Belgrade station they faced a formidable reception committee. The boy King, with a black band on his overcoat sleeve, was obliged to shake the hands of innumerable Ministers, generals and officials. Every eye was on him. Finally, overcome by emotion, he turned to the dark, veiled figure behind him. 'Mama,' he begged, 'please let's get home as soon as we can.'

But there was still more to be gone through. That afternoon the King, his mother and Queen Marie of Romania went to the Old Palace where King Alexander's coffin, now arrived from France, lay in state. During the following two days they had to welcome the guests arriving for the funeral and on the third day they attended the grandiose ceremony in Belgrade Cathedral. That over, they travelled in the funeral train to Topola. Not until King Alexander's body had been laid to rest in the crypt of the ornate family mausoleum at Oplanac, could they retreat from the public gaze.

'What I require,' King Alexander had said shortly before his death, 'is forty years of peace in which to build up a tradition of honest administration.' His far from peaceful reign had lasted for little more than a dozen. Within half a dozen years more, even this uneasy peace would have collapsed and his dynasty – the Queen, the boy King and the Regent Paul – would be grappling with a situation far more serious than King Alexander had ever known.

CHAPTER THIRTY-TWO

Ingrid of Denmark

I

One of the characteristics of the Kings of Sweden was, and still is, their longevity. For a Swedish king to die at eighty is for him to die young. Thus, when the apprehensive Louise Mountbatten became the Crown Princess of Sweden on her marriage to Crown Prince Gustaf Adolf in 1923, she need have had no fears of becoming Queen before she was ready. Ten years after her marriage, her seventy-five-year-old father-in-law, King Gustaf V, was still very much alive. He lived, in fact, to be ninety-two.

In 1930, however, Queen Victoria of Sweden had died. Although the Queen had never played a very active public role, her death meant that Crown Princess Louise was obliged to take on some additional duties. To those honorary posts, previously held by the Queen, Louise was able to bring her considerable energy, expertise and open-mindedness. Her years of nursing experience in the First World War proved particularly valuable. 'I find it difficult to be only a patron,' she would say, 'as I've been used to practical work of my own, like an ordinary person, before I married.'

Of the late Queen's deeply ingrained sense of royal exclusiveness, Louise had almost nothing. She was far too natural and democratic for that. Raised in an enlightened home, she brought this same enlightenment to her duties. And she was gratified to see it being applied to the political life of the country as well. To her, the workings of Swedish democracy seemed as near-perfect a political system as could be imagined.

'Look at Sweden,' she would say in her quick, emphatic fashion. 'No slums, no unemployment.'

The rise of European fascism during the 1930s filled her with alarm. It was contrary to everything she believed in. 'I boil internally with indignation and helpless rage,' was her comment on one of Mussolini's more outrageous political moves. Indeed, it would be almost impossible to imagine the progressively-minded and outspoken Louise in any Continental country other than a Scandinavian one.

With each passing year Crown Princess Louise identified herself more closely with the life of her new country. She still loved England and had great difficulty in tearing herself away after a visit, but Sweden was now her home. Although she and her husband usually spoke to each other in English, her voice began to take on that slightly lilting quality of the Swedish language. In her letters too, her phrasing became less English. 'Can one be anything but grateful,' she once exclaimed, 'for being able to live in a country like Sweden and to have a husband like mine?'

The royal couple had four homes. Their town residence was the northwest wing of the Royal Palace on the island of Gamla Stan in Stockholm. Outside the capital was Drottningholm, a splendid seventeenth-century palace set in formal gardens and surrounded by water. In the spring and autumn they went to Ulriksdal, but their favourite home was undoubtedly Sofiero. Here they spent the summer. Both passionately interested in gardening, the couple delighted in planning, planting and walking through their grounds. The rose garden and the orchard were their particular joys. At Sofiero they could get away from the cares of their position and lead a relaxed, cheerful and unpretentious family life. Louise was a born organiser and her households were run with care and efficiency. She left nothing unsupervised. Generous to those in need, she would tolerate no extravagance in the running of her homes. She was often heard exclaiming at the prices of things in the shops.

On herself, she spent very little. She was not particularly interested in her appearance. She always looked neat but she found the whole business of choosing and fitting clothes irksome. Yet, on those great state occasions which she so disliked, she always looked impressive. Her state robes – a dark velvet dress and train trimmed with ermine – were particularly elegant; the Swedish royal jewels, some of which had belonged to Napoleon's Josephine, were extremely fine. With her thin-faced, long-nosed, essentially aristocratic features, Louise might never have looked beautiful but she always looked unmistakably royal.

She and Gustaf Adolf had no children of their own. In 1925 Louise had given birth to a stillborn girl. She felt the loss of this child, and the lack of others, keenly, for she was very fond of children. However, she did have five stepchildren. There had been talk, soon after Louise first arrived in Sweden, that she could not be bothered with her stepchildren, that she did not seem motherly enough. For this latter claim, there were some grounds: so angular, so sharp-witted and quick-tempered, Louise cut an anything but conventionally motherly figure. Her look was spinsterish. But for the accusation that she could not be bothered with her stepchildren there was no justification whatsoever. She was devoted to them and they quickly established a happy relationship.

Like Louise herself, these five stepchildren were all great-grandchildren of Queen Victoria. Their late mother had been, of course, Princess Margaret of Connaught, the daughter of Queen Victoria's son Arthur,

Duke of Connaught. Therefore, when the only girl amongst them, Princess Ingrid, married the heir to the King of Denmark, yet another throne was in time to be added to those already occupied by Victoria's direct descendants.

Princess Ingrid of Sweden had been born in 1910, nine years after the death of Queen Victoria. Thus of all the direct descendants of Victoria who had first become queens of the various Continental countries, Ingrid was the only one not to have been born in the old Queen's lifetime. Yet her ties with her great-grandmother's country were strong. Her mother, Princess Margaret of Connaught, was usually described as being 'typically English'. To the court at Stockholm she had brought, says the Infanta Eulalia, 'just a touch of the elegance of the Court of St James's'. Princess Ingrid had thus been raised along English lines: in looks, attitudes and interests she was very like a British princess. In praising Ingrid's love of horses, one patriotic English society columnist pronounced it as perfectly understandable, 'for her English mother, Princess Margaret of Connaught, insisted on educating her according to the best of English traditions'. From her mother, too, continued the columnist smugly, came Princess Ingrid's 'truly British love of dogs'.

The death of Ingrid's mother, in 1920, by no means weakened the girl's ties with her mother's country. She paid long and frequent visits to her grandfather, the old Duke of Connaught, either at Clarence House or Bagshot Park. Her father's remarriage, to Lady Louise Mountbatten, merely strengthened the association. Speaking perfect English, fond of dancing, tennis, riding and gardening, Princess Ingrid was thoroughly at home in English society. And the British public was equally fond of her. In England, the pretty, cheerful and unassuming Princess Ingrid was always very popular. In fact, in 1932, when the Princess was twenty-two, there was a rumour that she would marry King George V's youngest son, Prince George, afterwards Duke of Kent. But the affair came to nothing and, two years later, Prince George married the Greek Princess, Marina.

There was more to Princess Ingrid, however, than met the eye. She was not merely the bright, attractive, sports-loving county girl that she seemed. For one thing, she was extremely practical. She could turn her hand to almost all household duties. There was a natural, sensible, honest-to-goodness quality about her; she had a very strong sense of proportion. And if, from her English mother, she had inherited her love of the out-doors, from her father, Crown Prince Gustaf Adolf, came her enthusiasm for the arts. She had a decidedly un-English passion for opera; she was interested in books and furniture. Exceptional, too, was her highly developed dress sense. In time she would become one of the best-dressed royalties in Europe, but even in her early twenties Ingrid dressed with style and simplicity. At an age when most girls looked overdressed or frumpish, Princess Ingrid of Sweden always appeared poised and elegant.

Not until she was twenty-four, in March 1935, did Ingrid become engaged. Her fiancé was the thirty-five-year-old Crown Prince Frederik, the eldest son of King Christian X of Denmark.

A better-looking prince, Ingrid could not have hoped to find. Crown Prince Frederik was six foot three inches tall, handsome, well-built and superbly fit. With those splendid looks went an easy, informal, demo-cratic manner. He was without a trace of arrogance or conceit. Having joined the Danish Navy as a cadet at the age of fourteen, Frederik had worked his way through every rank to that of Rear-Admiral. He was widely travelled and, during the course of these travels, had been all but covered with tattoos.

Other than for the Navy, his enthusiasms were for two widely different subjects: mechanics and music. He had a passion for all mechanical things and was an accomplished musician. One of Frederik's joys was to conduct the Royal Danish Symphony orchestra.

The popular and attractive couple were married in Stockholm on 24 May 1935. The wedding marked the greatest gathering of royalty since before the War: three kings and more than sixty princes and princesses attended the ceremony. It was as if the halcyon days of King Edward VII and Kaiser Wilhelm II had come back. The water city looked its glittering best. For days, the ornate royal barge, all flashing gilt and fluttering fringes, ferried royal guests from the yachts to the Royal Palace. Medals glinted, feathers fluttered, furs gleamed. Everything looked confident and secure. Yet, in four years' time, the majority of these happily beaming royalties would once again be subjected to conditions of danger, hardship and humiliation.

The day of the wedding was one of brilliant sunshine. It was celebrated in the old Storkyrkan Church beside the Royal Palace. The bridegroom was in naval uniform; the bride in a slim-fitting, classically severe white satin dress with a lace veil falling from a single wreath of orange blossom.

'That indescribable summer light of the far north . . .' wrote one enraptured witness, 'glowed on the golden copes of the three bishops at the altar and flashed on the steel breastplates of the Palace Guards standing with drawn swords the whole length of the aisle . . . The choir sang shrilly hymns both Swedish and Danish, the organ thundered, and jewelled orders, the Swedish blue and Danish scarlet of the Kings and Princes, the diamonds and pale gleaming gowns of the Queens and Princesses standing near the altar steps made a mass of colour as dramatic as a bed of glowing flowers.

'White and still in the heart of so much brilliance, Princess Ingrid looked as pale as one of her own lilies.'

Only on emerging into the dazzling sunshine outside the church did Ingrid break into a smile. Holding high her bouquet of madonna lilies, she waved it with a gesture so warm and spontaneous that it was answered with a roar of acclamation from the normally undemonstrative Swedish crowd.

That afternoon, escorted by squadrons of cavalry, the couple drove in an open carriage through the streets of the capital. The cheering was vociferous. Later, when they had changed their clothes, the royal barge carried them to the waiting *Dannebrog* and they set sail for Copenhagen.

CHAPTER THIRTY-THREE

Marie, Maud and Mignon

I

The assassination of her son-in-law, King Alexander of Yugoslavia, was merely one of the sorrows to cloud the last years of Queen Marie of Romania's life. By now, she had come to count for almost nothing in Romania. Her son, King Carol, theatrically uniformed and increasingly bombastic, saw to it that she played no part is the country's affairs. His mistress, Elena Lupescu, was the power at court. Looking slimmer and more soignée by the year, Madame Lupescu had become the fount of all honours, the channel through which men sought promotion and favours. No one consulted Queen Marie any more. She was not even allowed any say in the upbringing of her grandson, Crown Prince Michael. Twice a year, and each time for a period of a month only, the youngster was allowed to visit his mother, Carol's ex-wife Helen, in Florence. For the rest of the time he was kept under his father's eye. To Marie's disappointment, this unnatural régime was turning Michael into an exceptionally undemonstrative, almost sullen-looking youth; so different from the open and vivacious sort of person she preferred. Disappointing, also, was the marriage of Marie's second son, Nicholas, to a commoner and a divorcee; a woman whom Marie called 'a hardhearted, painted little hussy'. The court, which in Queen Marie's time had always been the brilliant centre of national life, was now rather tawdry; throughout the country, there was strong disapproval of King Carol's irregular life.

Politically, too, things were in a sorry state. Although Carol's intentions, and some of his achievements, were admirable, he was battling with a difficult situation. Romania, like so many Continental countries during the 1930s, had strong communist and fascist elements. With the rise of Nazi Germany, the Romanian fascists, calling themselves Iron Guard Legionaries, became increasingly powerful. With the *Anschluss* – the absorption of Austria by Germany early in 1938 – the Iron Guard became bolder still. In an effort to keep out of Germany's tentacles, King Carol assumed dictatorial powers. It did no good. It was too late now to check German aggression or to contain Romania's own green-shirted, bullying, pro-Nazi Iron Guard.

To Queen Marie, all this was extremely distressing. In a mere twenty years, the Germany against which she had made such a valiant, defiant stand was once again all-powerful. Was it for nothing that she had made so many sacrifices, suffered so much heartbreak and fought such desperate battles? And Romania, too, which she had seen so gloriously aggrandized after the First World War, was now an unstable, cruelly divided country, dictatorially ruled by a self-indulgent sovereign who had lost the respect of his people. Was another war about to ravage the Continent? 'If the instinct of destruction wins the upper hand,' she wrote, 'then Europe will go down and all the horror of Russia will sweep over everything that was beautiful and worthwhile living for. This thought is so frightful that my only prayer is not to have to live to see it.' Withdrawn from public life, the Queen devoted herself to writing her memoirs and tending her magnificent gardens. 'I know nothing,' she would say, when asked about Romanian affairs.

But, of course, Queen Marie was still a woman of exceptional style and personality. Nothing could ever alter that. Her guests would be no less impressed by her setting: the gold walls, the panels of Madonna lilies, the great bowls of orange flowers. Although she had turned sixty in 1935, she was still a striking-looking woman. Her hair, fashionably short and sleekly waved, was now silvery-gold, but her eyes were clear, her smile radiant and her figure supple. In her long dresses of gold or flame or salmon, she still moved with extreme grace. She had the litheness, it was said, of a girl of twenty. Her conversation was as colourful as it had ever been. Talking to Beverley Nichols of her love for her famous terraced garden at Balcic on the Black Sea, she said, 'I behave disgracefully. I break important engagements because of it. And the only excuse I can make is the true one. "I can't come because . . . *because I have a rendezvous with a rose"*.'

What would she have liked to have been, asked her visitor, if she had not been a queen. 'I should have been a painter,' answered Marie. 'All my emotions are visual. If there is anything good in my books, it comes from that. I see things so clearly that it almost hurts . . . and, let me tell you, I have seen a lot!'

In the spring of 1937 Queen Marie fell ill. By the summer she seemed to have recovered but that October, at Balcic, she suffered a severe haemorrhage and had to be moved to Bucharest. From then on, although from time to time she rallied, she was never really well. For most of her days she was bedridden. Yet her gaiety and her interest in things remained unimpaired. Once, leafing through a fashion magazine, she saw a picture of an evening wrap made by Revillon of Paris; it was a floor-length cape of ermine, lavishly bordered with Canadian red fox. 'How I should love to have this if I were well!' she exclaimed. 'But I shall never wear anything of that kind again.' Hoping that the possession of the cape might help her mother to fight her illness, Marie's daughter Ileana bought it for her for Christmas. Queen Marie was delighted. But she was never able to wear it; the cape lay always across her bed.

In the spring of 1938 she went again to Balcic. Here she lay in the pale sunshine on the terrace overlooking the Black Sea, surrounded by those tall-stemmed white lilies that she loved so much. She had long ago decided that although, after her death, her body would lie among the other members of the dynasty in the church at Curtea de Arges, her heart must be removed, placed in a jewelled casket and buried in the chapel she had built at Balcic. She had always looked upon the little town of Balcic, won from Bulgaria in the First World War, as her own. Here, her heart would be more accessible to her people than it would be in the royal mausoleum. During her lifetime, her subjects had been able 'to bring their sorrows and their wishes to her heart'; 'she wanted it to be so even after her death.'

From Balcic she travelled to a sanitorium at Dresden. Once again, she seemed to be picking up, but the improvement did not last long. Indeed, the entire course of Marie's illness was not only erratic but somewhat mysterious. At Dresden it was finally diagnosed as esophageal varices (dilated blood vessels) resulting from complications caused by alcoholic poisoning. Yet the Queen had never touched liquor and had always followed a strict regimen. How could this poisoning of the liver have come about? The fact that the illness had been wrongly treated until Marie's arrival at Dresden gave rise to rumours that its causes had been unnatural; the suspicions were strengthened by the fact that no autopsy was performed after her death. At Dresden the doctors did what they could, by way of blood transfusions, to repair the neglect, but it was too late. The Queen was clearly dying. Yet even now her thoughts were for the happiness of others. 'Poor doctor! I am so sorry for him,' she sighed. 'He is so disappointed,' And when someone who had at one stage caused the Queen much distress, came to visit her in hospital, Marie received her 'with open arms'. 'You see,' she explained to her astonished daughter Ileana, 'there is so little left to me except to be kind.'

In July 1938, she had a sudden relapse. Realizing that she was dying, she asked to be taken back to Romania. On the journey home, her train was forced to halt for almost fourteen hours while the Queen suffered another haemorrhage. She died at her palace of Pelishor, at Sinaia on 18 July 1938, a day after arriving home. She was sixty-three.

It was as well perhaps, that she died then. Had she lived another ten years, Queen Marie would have witnessed the total collapse of every-thing to which she had devoted her life. She was spared so many tragedies: the outbreak of the Second World War, the abdication of her son Carol in 1940, the unhappy reign of her grandson Michael – first as the tool of the fascists and then of the communists, the loss of part of

Transylvania to Hungary and of Dobrudja (including her house at Balcic) to Bulgaria, the Germano-Romanian campaign against Russia, the horrors of the Russian advance and occupation of the country, the abdication of King Michael, the fall of the monarchy and the conversion of Romania into a communist satellite state. All this would have broken her heart.

That same heart, buried in her chapel at Balcic, was hurriedly removed by a faithful aide-de-camp a few hours before the Bulgarians took possession of the territory. In its jewelled casket, it was carried to the late Queen's castle of Bran. Here her daughter, Princess Ileana, placed it in a chapel carved out of the rock in the hillside. 'There it stood apart and alone,' she says, 'a shrine easily accessible to all.'

With the death of this indomitable granddaughter of Queen Victoria, it seemed, said one contemporary, as though 'a light has gone out of the world'. It did, indeed. Affected and maddeningly self-satisfied Queen Marie might have been, but she was never mean, never unkind, never vindictive. Her aim was to spread joy, light and colour; in this, she never failed. She would have been, writes someone who knew her, 'an outstanding figure into whatever rank of life she had been born. A woman who has lived fully and loved deeply, who has braved the crowd, and commanded it. And though life has brought her many days in which her crown lay heavily upon her, she has worn it always with grace.'

Meriel Buchanan, the daughter of Sir George Buchanan, British Ambassador at St Petersburg during the First World War, tells a curiously touching anecdote concerning Queen Marie. Lady Buchanan, Meriel's mother, would often bring home to her young daughter the slips of paper on which, in one of those artless parlour games of the period, guests would be asked to write a suitable epitaph for each of the others present. On one of these slips was an inscription which Meriel had never forgotten. A young Russian grand duke had written his epitaph for Marie of Romania.

'A star danced when she was born.'

2

For year after year, always on the fringe of the turmoil in central Europe, Queen Maud of Norway had been living her simple, quiet, well-ordered life. By the year 1938 she and her husband, King Haakon, had reigned in Norway for thirty-three years. She was sixty-seven that year, he sixty-four. Their only son, Crown Prince Olav, was in his mid-thirties, married to a Swedish princess, and the father of three children.

Life in the palaces of Norway was extremely unpretentious. This was due as much to the personal preference of the King and Queen as it was to the character of Norway itself. King Haakon, tall, thin and hawk-faced, was a man of democratic habits and simple tastes. It was this democratic bearing, plus the fairness, conscientiousness and intelligence with which he carried out his duties, that made King Haakon such an ideal constitutional monarch. He had long ago stilled the republican sentiments of some of his subjects. Monarchist Norway was a contented and well-run democratic, socialist state.

Natural and unassuming, the King moved among his subjects with the minimum of fuss. Once, on arriving at the British Broadcasting Corporation in London to record a message to the British people, the King announced himself to the receptionist. While she was telephoning through to the person whom he had come to see, the girl turned round to ask, '*Where* was it you said you were the king of?'

Haakon's answer would have come without a flicker of irritation or pomposity.

Queen Maud was no different. Of the ostentatious and luxury-loving characteristics of her father, King Edward VII, she had nothing. Nor did she have Queen Alexandra's obsession with clothes. Queen Maud was a small, shy, simply dressed woman with no taste for ceremonial. 'I am so glad that I am Queen of a country in which everybody loves simplicity,' she once exclaimed to the visiting Infanta Eulalia. Her life in Oslo, says one of her friends, was 'far less pretentious than that of many well-to-do women in other countries'. Accompanied only by a lady-in-waiting, she would move freely about the streets of the city, doing her own shopping. 'It's easier,' she would say, 'and, in any case, I've no one to send.'

The same informality marked her life at home. Meals in the Royal Palace in Oslo were plain and frugal. No hordes of liveried servants hovered about the dining-room. Parties and receptions were kept to a minimum. Only a small section of the royal garden was reserved for the family's use; the public could wander about the palace grounds at will. Indeed, so accessible was the Palace that it was quite possible to peer up at the ground floor windows.

The Queen had never conquered her fear of public appearances. She would stand for minutes fiddling with her long white gloves before forcing herself to enter a reception room or the royal box at a gala performance. On great public occasions she usually looked stiff, almost disgruntled. Those who did not know Queen Maud found her somewhat forbidding.

Yet, in an intimate circle, she was charming and full of fun; one Norwegian Prime Minister spoke of her 'warm and generous personality'. Age had obliged her to give up riding and ski-ing for more sedentary pastimes, such as chess, photography, book-binding and leatherwork. But she was still a passionate gardener and she greatly enjoyed fishing.

To get away from Oslo to the family's wooden chalet in Kongseteren was one of her delights.

Over forty years of life in Scandinavia had made Maud no less English. Her tastes were still those of her English girlhood. She spoke English without a trace of Norwegian accent. The royal family's private apartments were furnished in English country house style. Her greatest joy was still her annual winter holiday at Appleton, her home at Sandringham There, says one contemporary, 'she indulged her love of English country ' life, which had gained that hold over her heart that no subsequent affections or experiences can entirely supersede'.

It was while Queen Maud was on her usual holiday to Norfolk in November 1938 that she was suddenly taken ill while shopping. She was rushed to hospital for an operation. King Haakon came over from Norway at once. The operation successfully carried out, the Queen seemed to be improving, but very early on the morning of 20 November, she died of heart failure. It was thirty-three years, to the very day, since she had become Queen of Norway.

A private funeral service was held in her childhood home, Marlborough House. Then, in bitter cold and driving rain, her coffin was borne in procession through the streets of London. A train carried it to Portsmouth where it was put aboard H.M.S. *Royal Oak*. Still in stormy weather, it was taken across the North Sea to Norway. The Queen was buried in the chapel of Akerhus Castle, which was henceforth to be the royal mausoleum.

One wonders whether Queen Maud, like her cousin Queen Marie of Romania, would have liked her heart to have been buried elsewhere. In England, at her beloved Sandringham, perhaps?

3

Since the assassination of her husband, King Alexander of Yugoslavia, in 1934, his wife Mignon – Queen Marie – had all but retired from public life. Her husband's cousin, the aesthetic Prince Paul, was now Regent for her young son, King Peter. Until the boy turned eighteen in 1941, he was expected to play no part in national life. He was still in the hands of his tutors.

This cessation of her public duties (for which the Queen had never had the slightest taste) allowed Mignon to live the sort of life she preferred. By 1938, having established her two younger sons, Tomislav and Andrej, at Sandroyd Preparatory School in England (from where they went on to Oundle and then Cambridge) the Queen was spending a great deal of her time in Britain. She found herself a cottage – the Old Mill House in Grandsden near Cambridge – and there settled down to a life of relative obscurity. Sharing her home was her inseparable friend, Mrs Rosemary Creswell; a woman whom King Peter calls his mother's 'old school friend'. Away from the public gaze, and not always in the best of health, Queen Marie paid less attention to her appearance then ever. She became increasingly stout and untidy. Her greying hair was cropped short, her bulky body was usually enveloped in a tent-like 'gown-cum-wrap'. She seldom wore dresses; her feet were usually stuffed into moccasins. Of the transcendentally beautiful child whom Queen Marie of Romania used to photograph against massed peonies or hydrangeas, only the intense blue eyes gave evidence.

The Queen's routine became as casual as her clothes. She woke late and, having breakfasted in bed, remained there throughout the day, dozing, reading the papers, writing letters and smoking innumerable cigarettes. Not until half past seven in the evening did she appear downstairs, wearing one of her voluminous 'tents' and slippers. Dinner over, she would settle down – always with a huge box of cigarettes beside her – for an evening's bridge or talk. She was skilled at both. 'Her conversation,' wrote one long-suffering listener, 'would get more and more animated as the night wore on. By midnight she would be in full voice . . .' Her talk, delivered in that blunt, emphatic fashion, could be fascinating. Queen Marie might have had little of her mother's poetic turn of phrase but, in her own way, she could be just as interesting. Utterly without affectation, she preferred, for some obscure reason, to be called 'Paiky' by her friends.

Mignon was on one of her visits to Yugoslavia when Germany attacked Poland in September 1939. 'What do you think will happen now?' her son, the fifteen-year-old King Peter asked her on hearing the news. Yugoslavia would wait and see, she said, what Britain and France did. But even when Britain and France declared war on Germany, Yugoslavia did nothing. There was not much that she could do. The Regent, Prince Paul, might have had British sympathies but his country lay at the mercy of Germany and Italy. His only hope was to sit tight. Yugoslavia declared its neutrality. Assuming that the country's neutrality would be respected, the Queen returned to England in November 1939.

She was still there when, in the spring of 1941, Yugoslavia became the scene of an extraordinary series of events. France, by now, had fallen and Italy was at war with Greece. Everywhere, except against embattled Britain, Hitler was victorious. The Yugoslav Regent and his government, unable to withstand German pressure any longer, signed an agreement with the Axis Powers in March that year. The move sparked off a revolution in Belgrade. On 27 March, a group of officers overthrew Prince Paul and his government and assumed control in the name of the seventeen-year-old King Peter II. The young King, who approved of the *coup* but who had been told nothing about it, was astonished to hear a voice, not unlike his own, broadcasting a proclamation to the people of Yugoslavia to the effect that he was party to the revolution. The rebels, unable to gain access to the young King, had been obliged to fake the broadcast by using a young officer with a voice similar to the King's.

The Yugoslav *coup* infuriated Hitler. He was determined to put defiant Yugoslavia in its place. Postponing his planned assault on Russia by four weeks (the delay was to prove fatal to the Third Reich) he attacked Yugoslavia on 6 April 1941. Within a week, and with unbelievable ferocity, he had crushed it. King Peter and his government were forced to flee. They escaped, first to Greece, which was also on the point of collapse, and then to England.

Queen Marie met her son at an airfield close to Grandsden where she lived. They had not seen each other for almost two years. Together, they returned to Old Mill House. For the first few weeks after his arrival, the house was the scene of considerable activity as Peter conferred with his government-in-exile. But gradually, as is the way with exiled sovereigns, there was less and less for him to confer about. The underground resistance to the Germans which was springing up in Yugoslavia was doing so quite independently of him. Indeed, of the two resistance groups – the Cetniks and the Partisans – the latter, as communists, were determinedly anti-monarchical. News of the exploits of the Partisan leader, Tito, which first came to Peter's ears during these early months of exile, could not have brought him much comfort.

To keep her son occupied, Mignon decided that he must continue his studies. After all, he was only just eighteen. For his coming of age, the British government had arranged a special service in St Paul's Cathedral. That scrap of ceremonial over, the boy was packed off to Cambridge. His mother arranged a room for him above the garage of her cottage and here he spent the occasional weekend.

It soon became apparent to Queen Marie that her son's mind was not entirely on his studies. Before he had been at Cambridge for many months, he asked her to come up to London to meet a young woman with whom he had become friendly.

The girl was the twenty-one-year-old Princess Alexandra of Greece. Her father had been Queen Sophie's son, that short-lived King Alexander of the Hellenes who had died from a monkey bite in 1920. Her mother, whom her father had married morganatically, had been Aspasia Manos, now known as Princess Aspasia. Exiled from Greece with the rest of the royal family during the years between the wars, Princess Aspasia and her daughter had lived in various Continental countries. The Second World War had deposited them, along with numerous other exiled royalties, in England. The attractive Princess Alexandra was now doing a course in nursing at Cambridge. She had met the slight, dark, eighteen-year-old

King Peter at a tea party given by the Allied Officers' Club at Grosvenor House. Within days, the two of them had fallen in love.

King Peter II and Princess Alexandra were related. 'My dear Sandra,' Princess Alexandra's mother had exclaimed in amused exasperation as the girl sat puzzling over the Almanach de Gotha to find out exactly how closely she was related to King Peter, 'if you start looking at Queen Victoria you'll find how practically everybody, in all the European Royal Houses, is related.' In fact, King Peter II and Princess Alexandra were both great-great-grandchildren of Queen Victoria: he, through his mother and his grandmother, Queen Marie of Romania; she, through her father and her grandmother, Queen Sophie of Greece.

Exchanging her dressing-gown for a dress, Queen Marie of Yugoslavia went up to London to meet Princess Alexandra. When the apprehensive Alexandra asked Peter what she should talk to his mother about, he assured her that 'anything under the sun' would do. The Queen had a 'reputation as a conversationalist'; she was also, he added for good measure, the best and fastest woman driver that he knew.

The meeting passed off successfully but Queen Marie was not happy about the situation. There were several probable objections to the match between Peter and Alexandra. He was only eighteen; his future was uncertain; marriage to a Greek princess with German blood could be unpopular in Yugoslavia; he might be able, at some later stage, to make a more politically, dynastically and financially advantageous match; with his country so cruelly occupied, his mind should be on more serious things than his own happiness; there was a strong superstition against Serbs marrying in wartime. Marie's reservations were backed up by the Yugoslav government-in-exile in England; the King, they insisted, should remain unfettered until he had regained his throne.

But young Peter, hopelessly in love, was blind to all objections. He asked Alexandra to marry him.

The engagement decided upon, Queen Marie was obliged to make the best of it. She invited Princess Alexandra and her mother, Princess Aspasia, to Grandsden to dine. Peter by now had explained something of his own and his mother's financial position to his fiancée. In addition to being a millionaire in her own right, Queen Marie owned jewellery worth £250,000 and received £3,500 a month from the Yugoslavian Civil List. But Alexandra would find this hard to believe, warned Peter, when she saw his mother at home.

Alexandra not only found it hard, she found it all but impossible. Old Mill House was simply a five-bedroomed cottage furnished in the most spartan fashion. The manservant's announcement of 'Your Majesty – Their Royal Highnesses Princess Aspasia and Princess Alexandra of Greece' sounded incongruous in these modest surroundings. For this significant occasion Queen Marie – or 'Paiky' as she insisted that they call her – was wearing a plain green woollen dress. The meal was simple to the point of frugality. Princess Alexandra was later to learn that for his room above the garage, Peter had to pay his mother £10 a week.

The group, which included Queen Marie's great friend Rosemary Creswell, spent a pleasant enough evening. Although forthright, Queen Marie could be charming. Not until after coffee did she bring up the question of the engagement. She gave the couple her blessing but asked them, in view of various factors, to keep the betrothal secret for the moment. This they agreed to do.

Alexandra assumed that all was well. Her more experienced mother, though, sensed that something was wrong. She suspected that Queen Marie was implacably opposed to the projected marriage.

She was soon proved right. Marie, assuming that her young son's feeling for Alexandra would turn out to be no more than a passing infatuation, had been prepared to let the affair run its course. But when she realized that he was determined to marry Alexandra, she did everything she could to prevent it. All Alexandra's attempts to concern herself in the affairs of her future husband's country were firmly discouraged by his mother. Backed up by the government-in-exile, Queen Marie kept the girl at arm's length.

In the meantime, the situation of Yugoslavia, as far as the dynasty was concerned, was deteriorating rapidly. The two groups of resistance fighters, Cetniks under Mihailović and Partisans under Tito, were almost as opposed to each other as they were to the occupying Germans. And whereas King Peter favoured Mihailović, the Allied governments were beginning to favour Tito. The Allies suspected Mihailović of collaborating with the enemy; of Tito's anti-Nazism, they had no doubt. Time and again they urged King Peter to abandon Mihailović and throw in his lot with the more aggressive Tito. The Partisans, they argued, were not nearly as dedicated to communism as the young King supposed. Peter steadfastly refused.

Finally, at the Conference of the three Allied Powers – Britain, America and Russia – at Teheran, towards the end of 1943, the Allies officially recognized Tito and his Partisans as the true National Liberation Army of Yugoslavia. It was to him they would give their support. (Over a year later, their decision was confirmed at Yalta: Britain and America agreed that the Balkans should be a Russian zone of influence.) Highly gratified, Tito assembled a National Parliament, made up of members of his movement, and founded a temporary government. Amongst its resolutions was one depriving the Yugoslav government-in-exile of all powers, and another forbidding the return of King Peter to Yugoslavia. The question of whether the country was to be a monarchy or a republic would not be decided until after the war.

With the ground thus cut from under his feet, King Peter, who had spent several frustrating months in Cairo in order to be nearer his country, returned to Britain. He was determined that at least one of his hopes – his marriage to Princess Alexandra – should materialize.

His mother was equally determined that it should not. More than ever did she feel that her son must not jeopardize his chances by making an ill-advised marriage. In an effort to get the Queen to change her mind, Peter and Alexandra travelled down together to see her. By now Mignon had moved from Grandsden to a house near Leatherhead. It was here that an extraordinarily violent scene took place.

The Queen, as usual, was in bed. Without a word she watched the young couple come into her room. She gave Peter her cheek to kiss; Alexandra she merely motioned into a chair. The unnerving silence did not last long. No sooner had Peter informed his mother that they were to be married in a few days' time than a torrent of recrimination burst forth from the bloated figure on the bed. The next hour, says Alexandra, was a nightmare.

'Accusations, condemnations, hostile and punishing words were flaying, scouring, tearing their way through the faint fragile hope of an attempted reconciliation.

'Peter lost his self-control; his mother lost hers entirely, ringing all the bells in the house, demanding witnesses, people to take us out of the room, and then to bring us back again.'

Princess Alexandra was no less vehement in her arguments. At one stage during the storm raging about that crumpled bed, she snatched up the telephone and called her mother, Princess Aspasia. Begging her mother to speak to the demented Queen, she pushed the receiver against Marie's ear. The Queen simply continued her denunciations, this time into the mouthpiece.

Suddenly Peter had had enough. Above his mother's ranting voice, he shouted, 'We're getting out of here. It's finished, *finished.*'

With that the young couple ran out of the house and sped back to London.

Eight days later, on 20 March 1944, Peter and Alexandra were married at the Yugoslav Embassy in London. The ceremony was attended by a galaxy of exiled royalties, including Queen Wilhelmina of the Netherlands, King Haakon of Norway and King George II of Greece. The principal guests were the British sovereigns, King George VI and Queen Elizabeth. Some twenty-one years before, as the young Duke and Duchess of York, the British King and Queen had been present at King Peter's christening. Throughout the months of uncertainty concerning the marriage, they had always been sympathetic and encouraging. Indeed, on the morning after the violent quarrel with Queen Marie, the young couple had visited King George VI and Queen Elizabeth at Windsor. It had been due, in no small measure, to the renowned tact and charm of the British Queen that the distraught Alexandra had regained her calm. Now, by their presence at the wedding ceremony, the British sovereigns (he, in uniform, as best man; she, in pale pink, furs and feathers, superbly poised) endowed it with an importance which not even the conspicuous absence of the bridegroom's mother, Queen Marie of Yugoslavia, could deny. For Marie had refused to attend the ceremony. Her official excuse was that she had toothache.

Not until eight months later did Peter and Alexandra again see Queen Marie. By now Alexandra had discovered that she was pregnant. It was this fact that decided King Peter to present to her the famous family emeralds which belonged, by right, to the sovereign's wife. For Alexandra was now the Queen of Yugoslavia. 'You must have them before the baby is born,' he insisted.

The set of jewellery, consisting of a tiara, necklace and earrings, was kept in a British bank. Peter contacted his mother to tell her that he intended passing the jewels on to Alexandra and then withdrew the boxes containing them from the bank. As Queen Marie held the key to the boxes, Peter was obliged to ask her to open them. She agreed. The three of them – Marie, Peter and Alexandra – arranged to meet in London, at a place which Queen Marie used as an office. They had not met each other since that terrible afternoon before the wedding and it was with considerable trepidation that Alexandra accompanied her husband to see his mother.

They were shown into the room by the faithful Mrs Creswell. Queen Marie, whose mannish streak seems to have become more pronounced with the years, was sporting one of the self-designed khaki uniforms which, other than her 'tents', were now her normal wear. For some strange reason she had a Sam Browne belt, complete with revolver, slung around her heavy body.

The Queen had no word of greeting for the young couple. She merely nodded in reply to Peter's bow and Alexandra's curtsy. Turning her broad back on Alexandra, who had been left standing in the doorway, Mignon gave her attention to the boxes. The operation seemed to take for ever. The girl, nervous, overwrought and feeling sick from her pregnancy, imagined that she was about to faint. Yet without Queen Marie's permission, she dared not sit. Unable to master her dizziness any longer, she blurted out, 'Paiky, I'm going to have a baby and don't feel very well, please may I sit down?'

Queen Marie turned to look at her. As far as Alexandra knew, this was the first that the Queen had heard of the expected child. Marie then addressed her only one word of the day to her daughter-in-law.

'Sit,' she growled.

Eight months later, on 17 July 1945, the baby was born. It was a boy. In honour of its grandfather, Mignon's late husband, it was christened Alexander. But that this Crown Prince Alexander would ever become King of Yugoslavia was by now extremely doubtful. With the coming of peace in May that year, the various exiled monarchs had begun returning to their war-ravaged countries; only King Peter II of Yugoslavia remained in England. He had little hope of returning. In November his fears were borne out. Following a one-party election, Yugoslavia ceased to be a monarchy and became a communist republic. As a kingdom, Yugoslavia had lasted for less than thirty years.

Denied any active occupation, King Peter embarked on the rootless, hopeless, feckless and ultimately impoverished life of so many royal exiles. Perhaps his mother had not been so wrong in discouraging his marriage or in resenting the handing over of the family jewels. His marriage fell to pieces and the money gained from the sale of the famous emeralds was lost in ill-advised speculation. Both King Peter and Queen Alexandra published their memoirs. Throughout the world, magazines serialized their life stories, and newspapers reported their marital upheavals. Their names were seldom out of the news.

Far removed from these matrimonial and financial wranglings, Queen Marie of Yugoslavia continued to lead her own highly individual life. Soon after the war she moved yet again, this time to a 450-acre farm at Cranbrook in Kent. Here she was joined by her two younger sons, Tomislav and Andrej, both of whom were studying agriculture at Cambridge. Her home was a six-roomed, stone-floored cottage with no electricity. She cooked on an old-fashioned kitchen range and played bridge or chess by lamplight. Dressed in tweeds and brogues, she would go striding across the fields to supervise the farming. 'It has meant long hours and hard work getting this farm in working order,' she would claim.

To see this sturdy, mannishly dressed figure cheerfully stirring a saucepan on an old black stove in a cottage kitchen, one could hardly believe that she had been raised among the gold walls and the white lilies and the glittering draperies of her mother's rooms or that she had once lived, as Queen, in a vast, white-walled, many-pillared palace above the Danube. A great-granddaughter of Queen Victoria, Queen Marie of Yugoslavia had ended up leading the life of an English countrywoman.

CHAPTER THIRTY-FOUR

The Last of the First

Of all the descendants of Queen Victoria who first sat, or were to be the first to sit, on Continental thrones, four were still alive at the end of the Second World War. These were Queen Ena of Spain, Queen Marie of Yugoslavia, Crown Princess Louise of Sweden and Crown Princess Ingrid of Denmark.

Crown Princess Ingrid became Queen of Denmark in 1947. Throughout the war years she and her husband, the bluff Crown Prince Frederik, had been virtual prisoners of the Germans. With the occupation of Denmark in April 1940, the royal family had decided to remain in the country. Their continued presence had brought considerable comfort to the Danish people. Determined to keep alive his country's spirit of independence, old King Christian X (the father of Crown Prince Frederik) had each day ridden through the streets of Copenhagen on a white charger. In the Amelienborg Palace, the Crown Prince and Princess had lived a simple and secluded life. Their first child, Princess Margrethe, had been born a week after the German invasion; their second, Princess Benedikte, in 1944; and their third, Princess Anne-Marie, in 1946.

On 20 April 1947, with the country barely recovered from the occupation, King Christian X died and on the next day the new monarch was proclaimed from the balcony of the Christiansborg Palace as King Frederik IX. At the end of his speech, the King was joined on the balcony by Queen Ingrid. Hand in hand, this handsome couple turned to face the sea of people beneath them.

Denmark could not have wished for a more suitable royal pair. At forty-eight, King Frederik was a giant of a man with a ready smile and a relaxed manner. Queen Ingrid, at thirty-seven, was a woman of considerable presence and beauty. More valuable than their splendid looks, however, was the way in which they carried out their royal tasks. The Danes, as citizens of a welfare state, preferred a classless society, yet they looked upon the monarchy as a means of insuring against a complete and colourless egalitarianism. Provided the sovereigns remained approachable and unaffected, the Danes were royalist to the core. They wanted a king, but on the condition that he was a citizen-king. In this, King Frederik IX did not disappoint them. Informal, conscientious and unintellectual, he was the citizen-king *par excellence*. His habit of referring to the Queen and himself in public speeches as 'Mother and I' struck exactly the right note: he was the father of a great family. With this sort of sovereign on the throne, Danish republicanism, which had never been particularly strong, dwindled still more, and the Social Democratic Party unobtrusively dropped 'abolition of the monarchy' from its programme.

Although, with his great height and upright bearing, Frederik IX always looked splendidly royal, his tastes were simple and his behaviour natural. Music remained one of his passions: he conducted at private concerts, he made records, he followed the activities of the Royal Danish Ballet. The sea was another of his delights. King Frederik was seldom happier than when sailing in the royal yacht *Dannebrog* along his country's intricate coastline. Even when confined to the Amelienborg Palace, he was able to watch the ships sailing by at the end of the street. Sometimes at night, using a torch, he would signal greetings in Morse to the captains.

Stories about his informality are legion. An American tourist, strolling through Copenhagen's famous Tivoli Gardens, once started up a conversation with a father and his three daughters. 'I'm a storekeeper from Chicago,' announced the tourist. 'Who are you?'

'Oh, I'm a king,' answered Frederik.

Queen Ingrid was no less informal. Together with her husband, she would go walking along the waterfront on winter evenings. Often, while shopping in Copenhagen, she would wait quite happily in a queue to be served. Deeply interested in books, auction sales and art exhibitions, she was frequently to be seen in different parts of the city. Although she could dress with great elegance and panache, she was just as happy in the tweed suits and brogues which she wore at the country palace of Graasten in South Jutland.

Yet, for all her Scandinavian unpretentiousness, Queen Ingrid never quite lost that indefinable air of Englishness, inherited from her mother, Princess Margaret of Connaught. By middle age, Queen Ingrid had all the brisk, no-nonsense and self-confident qualities of an aristocratic Englishwoman. Her homes were efficiently run, her daughters simply brought up and her duties carried out with charm and dignity. Like most of Queen Victoria's Continental descendants, she had considerable faith in the blessings of an English education: her eldest daughter, Princess Margrethe, was packed off to spend a year at an English school. Each afternoon, in one of those airy, comfortable rooms in the Amelienborg Palace, the Queen presided over an elegantly set and well-laden tea tray. When, at some public ceremony, one of her daughters accidentally stepped on her train, Queen Ingrid turned round to exclaim, in best

British governessy fashion, 'Good heavens child! Watch where you are going!'

One of Queen Ingrid's chief characteristics was her unfeigned interest in everything around her. Her homes – Amelienborg Palace in winter, Fredensborg Castle in spring and autumn, and Graasten Palace in summer – all bore the imprint of her talent for decoration. She could spend hours in bookshops; she was an accomplished needlewoman; gardening, and orchid-growing in particular, was one of her passions. She delighted in royal tours; unlike other royalties, she never found them exhausting. 'You just cannot be tired when you enjoy yourself so much and see so many interesting things,' she would exclaim. 'I had to see everything.' She had the rare gift of projecting this enthusiasm to all around her: the most mundane occasion would be enlivened by her evident interest. Her charm was exceptional. 'Mother,' claimed one of her daughters, 'can charm anyone.' Queen Ingrid, in short, was a thorough-going professional.

The home life of the Danish royal family was enviably serene. Husband and wife were devoted to each other and no less devoted to their daughters. Even after the three girls had married (the youngest, Princess Anne-Marie, married King Constantine of the Hellenes – the grandson of Queen Sophie – and thus linked Queen Victoria's descendants yet again) the relationship between parents and daughters remained close. 'I have never found a four-leaf clover but with the years one has grown up in my home,' said the King, turning to the Queen during a public speech, 'you, my dear, and our three daughters. The four of you have been the clover-leaf that has brought happiness into my life and sunshine streaming into my heart. My deepest thanks, Ingrid, for the support you have given me and for all you have meant through the years. I shall never be able to tell you how much gratitude I owe you . . . .'

As, by the year 1953, King Frederik and Queen Ingrid had had no son, the Danish constitution, which had hitherto excluded women from succeeding to the throne, was altered. A new Succession Law was introduced, whereby Princess Margrethe became the heir apparent. Thus, on the death of King Frederik IX, this great-great-granddaughter of Queen Victoria would become Queen Margrethe, the first reigning Queen of Denmark.

2

On 29 October 1950, Crown Princess Louise became Queen of Sweden. Her father-in-law, King Gustaf V, had finally died in his ninety-third year and Louise's sixty-eight-year-old husband became King Gustaf VI Adolf. Queen Louise was sixty-one.

With the best will in the world, and unlike the Danish sovereigns, one could not call King Gustaf Adolf and Queen Louise a handsome couple. He, tall and bespectacled, had the look of an amiable Professor; she seemed thinner, toothier, and more sharp-featured than ever. But this lack of good looks was no more important now than it had ever been. Gustaf Adolf remained one of the most civilized and conscientious kings in Europe while Queen Louise, with so vital a personality, had no need of conventional beauty. Within minutes of meeting her, one would be struck by her vivacity, her enthusiasm, her quickness and her naturalness. She spoke at such a rate that, if excited, she missed out words altogether. Although unselfish and compassionate to a remarkable degree, she could be critical and quick-tempered; a marshal of the court once described her as 'a saint with temperament'.

Through the Swedish court, grown stale during the old King's long reign, the new Queen swept like a fresh breeze. Obsolete formalities were scrapped, the staff thinned out and reorganized, and court etiquette, unchanged for forty years, revised and modernized. The royal guest list was enlarged to include whoever might prove interesting. Moving with her quick, light tread, Louise inspected the hundreds of rooms in the Stockholm Palace and set in motion their alteration, modernization and redecoration. On everything she left her imprint. Her biographer, Margit Fjellman, calling on the Queen at the Stockholm Palace, was once obliged to wait in the Hall of Mirrors while Louise finished a telephone call. Through an *enfilade* of lovely rooms, the caller could see, in the distance, the bird-like Queen gesticulating energetically as she spoke into the mouthpiece. 'Her thin figure looked small and far away,' writes Margit Fjellman, 'but none the less she radiated vitality and it flew into my mind that here was the dynamo on the heart of the Palace, the centre of a great machine.'

That she was now Queen in no way altered Louise's naturalness. Although, on gala occasions, in flashing jewels and gleaming satins, she could look undeniably regal, the Queen was happier on informal occasions, wearing simple clothes. She still enjoyed being able to move about without fuss. In Sweden, fortunately, this was quite possible. She could go shopping, or even ride on the underground, without being mobbed or stared at. The public's eagerness to catch a glimpse of her on the day after she became Queen had seemed all but incomprehensible to Louise. 'People look at me as if I was something remarkable,' she complained with characteristic sharpness. 'I don't look any different from what I did yesterday, do I?'

Indeed, it took her some time to appreciate that she had become a queen. At the funeral of King George VI, some eighteen months after her husband's succession, Louise was waiting for the car in which she would drive in the procession, when a large Daimler drew up beside her. 'For me!' protested the Queen, drawing back. 'No, it must have come for a Queen.'

Yet even to be a queen was not something that unduly impressed her. Some time after the death of her mother, the Dowager Marchioness of Milford Haven, Queen Louise was discovered at Kensington Palace by one of her nieces, going through her late mother's books. The Queen was planning to give some of them away. Several of the books had been the gifts of Queen Victoria to Louise's mother and bore inscriptions such as 'To dearest Victoria from her affectionate Grandmother V.R.I.' Queen Louise's niece was astonished to see her aunt energetically ripping out the pages carrying these valuable inscriptions. When she protested that anyone would be delighted to own a book inscribed by Queen Victoria, Louise brushed the idea aside. 'Do you think I'd want to have a book in my personal library just because it had Queen Victoria's signature on the flyleaf?' she scoffed. 'That wouldn't make it any more interesting to read would it?' And out, with a vigorous tear, came another page.

Queen Louise's links with Britain remained close. She was devoted to her brother Louis, now Earl Mountbatten of Burma, and frequently visited Broadlands, his home in Hampshire. With his two daughters and their families she was especially friendly. The marriage of her nephew, Prince Philip – the son of her elder sister Alice – to Princess Elizabeth, the eldest daughter of King George VI, linked her with the reigning branch of the present British royal family. Indeed, by his marriage to the future Queen of England, Prince Philip added the most brilliant chapter to the annals of the talented Battenberg family. One feels certain that Queen Victoria, always a champion of the Battenbergs, would have approved of the match.

In common with all Queen Victoria's descendants living on the Continent, Louise loved the London shops. To go shopping alone in London gave her great pleasure. But even on these outings her well-known efficiency manifested itself. 'I like going out shopping by myself,' she explained to a friend who had called on her at the Hyde Park Hotel, '[but] it would be so inconvenient if I got run over and they couldn't find out who I was!' And with that she popped a card into her handbag, on which was written in bold capital letters: I AM THE QUEEN OF SWEDEN.

In all her royal duties, Queen Louise showed a more than conventional interest. Whether it was a state visit, a dinner party, a tour through a hospital or a call on an old villager, the Queen, through her genuine concern for, and interest in, the lives of others, won the hearts of her subjects. That she was so devoted and solicitous a wife made her even more popular. One of her chief concerns was to prevent her husband from overworking; she was forever urging him to cut down his engagements. 'Swedish women allied themselves to Queen Louise and I think I can tell you why,' said Countess Estelle Bernadotte to Margit Fjellman after the Queen's death. 'Instinctively they realized that she was absorbed in the care of her husband, and that was something they understood and approved of.'

Yet it was the Queen who died first. She had always been frail and, after a heart attack in 1951, she had been left weaker still. However, by the exercise of her extraordinary will-power, she kept up her exacting royal role. Not until the end of 1964, when she suffered a very severe attack, did she give in. She lived for another three months and died on 7 March 1965 at the age of seventy-six. A week later, on a still, grey, snowy day, she was buried. The funeral ceremony in the ancient church on Gamla Stan was extremely moving. But no funeral oration was preached over the coffin as it lay draped in the Swedish flag and the Union Jack. The Queen, who had drawn up the programme for her own funeral, had stipulated that no personal words were to be spoken during the ceremony. She had remained efficient, and modest, to the end.

3

For Queen Marie of Yugoslavia, an echo of the day on which her husband, King Alexander, was assassinated in the streets of Marseilles, came in October 1959. To mark the twenty-fifth anniversary of the King's death, a service was held at his statue, situated at the Rond Point de la Muette in Paris. With head bowed and leaning on a stick, the dowdily dressed Queen paid tribute to her long-dead husband. Now sixty years old and far from well, Queen Marie had aged considerably during the previous few years; she was no longer the stout, uniform-wearing, pistol-carrying woman who had once quarrelled so tempestuously with her son Peter and his wife Alexandra. She looked frail and ill.

In fact, Queen Marie did not long survive the twenty-fifth anniversary of her husband's death. Less than two years later, on 22 June 1961, she died in London at the age of sixty-two. Her funeral service was held in the Serbian Orthodox Church in Lancaster Road, London. The chief mourner was her son, King Peter II. For a brief space of time, in this ornate church with its elaborate ritual, its richly robed priests, its black-clad royalties and its host of Yugoslavian mourners – many in national dress – one could catch something of the flavour of those days when, in the company of her exotic, ambitious mother, the attractive young Mignon had first come to Belgrade as a bride.

4

Since the end of the Second World War, Queen Ena of Spain had been living quietly in Lausanne in Switzerland. Her marriage to King Alfonso XIII, which had deteriorated so badly during the last years of the reign, had not survived the shock of their flight from Spain in 1931. For the most part, the couple had lived apart since then. During the 1930s both their haemophilic sons had been killed in car accidents; and in 1941, the King himself had died in Rome. Their third son, Don Juan, had then become the Pretender to the Spanish throne.

Of all the royal pretenders thronging Europe after the Second World War, the Spanish seemed to have the best chance of regaining a throne. For, in theory, Spain was a monarchy once more. In 1947 General Franco (who since the Civil War had ruled Spain) introduced a Succession Law whereby Spain was declared to be 'a kingdom in accordance with tradition'. On the death or incapacity of Franco, his position as Head of State would be filled by 'a person of Royal Blood' who would have to be male, Spanish, Catholic and over thirty years of age. It was generally assumed that this monarch would be – not Don Juan of whose candidacy Franco did not seem to approve, but his son – Prince Juan Carlos. Consequently, with his father's somewhat reluctant permission, this personable young prince was groomed by Franco for his future role. As Queen Ena's grandson, the next monarch of Spain would therefore be the great-great-grandson of Queen Victoria.

Yet another link was forged between two branches of Queen Victoria's family when, in the spring of 1962, this future King of Spain was married to the Greek princess, Sophie. For as Prince Juan Carlos was the grandson of Queen Ena of Spain, so was Princess Sophie the granddaughter of Queen Sophie of the Hellenes. The couple were thus both great-great-grandchildren of Queen Victoria. Their wedding in Athens, stage-managed by the bride's redoubtable mother, Queen Frederika of the Hellenes, had all the glitter of a pre-war royal occasion. Notable amongst the galaxy of kings and queens was the imposing figure of Queen Ena of Spain.

Married, Juan Carlos and Sophie took up residence in the little palace of Zarzuela in Madrid. In 1968, having already had two daughters, Princess Sophie gave birth to a son.

For the christening of this little prince, Queen Ena returned to Spain for a few days. Not for thirty-seven years had she set foot in this country where she had reigned for quarter of a century. Queen Ena had turned eighty a few months before but she was still a handsome woman, erect, dignified and elegant. What, one wonders, were her thoughts on coming back to this violent and sun-scorched land? A bomb had marked the start of her life in Spain; a revolution had ended it. Was she gratified at having lived long enough to see the dynasty once more established?

Queen Ena lived on for only a short while after her visit to Spain. In April 1969, she died in Lausanne. She was in her eighty-second year. Born in the year of Queen Victoria's Golden Jubilee, before any of the Queen's descendants had come to occupy a throne, Queen Ena had lived to see the full flowering of her grandmother's matriarchy. During the course of Ena's long lifetime, the thrones of Great Britain, Germany, Russia, Spain, Norway, Sweden, Denmark, Romania, Yugoslavia and Greece had been occupied by Queen Victoria's children, grandchildren or great-grandchildren. And in that lifetime, too, more than half these thrones had fallen.

The Matriarchy Today

Today, there are seven monarchies in Europe. They are Great Britain, Belgium, the Netherlands, Norway, Sweden, Denmark and that kingdom without a king, Spain. In five of these seven monarchies, the ruling families are directly descended from Queen Victoria. The Queen's great-great-granddaughter, Queen Elizabeth II, reigns in Great Britain. Her great-grandson, King Olav IV (the son of Queen Maud) reigns in Norway. In Sweden, on the death of King Gustaf VI Adolf in 1973, Queen Victoria's great-great-grandson, Crown Prince Carl Gustaf (grandson of the Swedish King and his first wife, Princess Margaret of Connaught) became King. With the death of King Frederick IX of Denmark in 1972, Victoria's great-great-granddaughter Margrethe became the reigning Queen of Denmark. In Spain, her great-great-grandson Prince Juan Carlos has already been sworn in as the future monarch.

In one of the two monarchies in which the dynasties are not directly descended from Queen Victoria – the Netherlands and Belgium – the relationship to the Queen's family is close. The founder of the Belgian royal family was Queen Victoria's uncle, Leopold of Saxe-Coburg. Thus, of all the remaining reigning houses of Europe, only the Dutch is not closely related to Queen Victoria's family. If the old Queen's matriarchy has shrunk somewhat, it is, proportionately, no less all-pervading.

What, if any, are the advantages of this closely-woven dynastic web? Today, other than to the members of the dynasties themselves, they are negligible. To a greater or lesser degree, present-day monarchs have been stripped of all personal power, or even influence, in affairs of state. The fact that one monarch is a second cousin once removed to the monarch of a neighbouring country has not the slightest bearing on the political relationship between the two countries.

But then, this was hardly less true during the years that Queen Victoria's matriarchy was at its apogee. At one time seven of Queen Victoria's grandchildren sat on important European thrones: they were King George V of Great Britain, the German Kaiser Wilhelm II, the

Empress Alexandra of Russia, Queen Maud of Norway, Queen Sophie of the Hellenes, Queen Marie of Romania and Queen Ena of Spain. Ironically, the period during which all seven of these first cousins were enthroned at the same time was from 1915 to 1917; the middle years of the First World War. Nothing could more vividly illustrate the irrelevance of these close family relationships than this.

The unfortunate fact was that the spread of Queen Victoria's matriarchy coincided, almost exactly, with the growth of nationalism in Europe. During the second half of the nineteenth century the various countries of Europe became increasingly and aggressively nationalistic. The old Europe of little kingdoms and duchies and principalities, with their dynastic rather than their nationalistic allegiances, was replaced by half a dozen or so rigid power blocs. Men thought of themselves as Englishmen or Germans or Italians rather than as subjects of a reigning house. The state had become more important than the sovereign.

Queen Victoria's husband, Prince Albert, had at one time imagined that a great royal caste – a set of upright, enlightened and conscientious rulers – would ensure political, social and international stability. How much more effective would this not be if these model sovereigns were not only friends, but relations? Surely this would guarantee the peace of Europe? But, of course, not only could model princes not be made to order but, with the growth of ever more powerful national states, each competing with the other, the idea of a great royal clan became obsolete. By 1914 it did not much matter whether a king were good or bad; and it certainly did not matter that he was a first cousin to half the other kings of Europe.

Yet the fact that Queen Victoria's descendants occupied almost all the thrones of Europe was not entirely without significance. This flock of English and half-English princesses introduced more than just chintzes and nannies and rice puddings into the royal households of the Continent. They 'made their presence felt in every Court of Europe,' wrote the astute Infanta Eulalia, 'where English is talked freely, and where English influence, secret or otherwise, is never absent from the family life of the Royal Houses. In short, if the private history of the Courts and aristocracy of Europe were written, it would surprise many people to know the important parts played in both by certain English women.'

With the exception of the Empress Alexandra of Russia, they all brought an informality, a tolerance, a certain honest-to-goodness quality to the dynasties into which they married; they were free of the bigotry of so many Continental royalties. They introduced also the English language. Within a couple of generations, English had superseded French as the language of most Continental courts. Royal children were being educated in English, and in England, by the score.

Inevitably, something of the British ideas on such things as constitutional monarchy brushed off on some of these continental royalties. It is certainly the dynasties which adopted the Coburg ideals of a sovereign above politics that have lasted the course. The kings who have willingly yielded their powers have kept their thrones; those who have clung to, or extended them, have not. The horror of the Grand Duchess of Mecklenburg-Strelitz at the thought of Maud ascending the 'revolutionary' throne of Norway is still more absurd now that Queen Maud's son sits securely on that throne while the Mecklenburg-Strelitzes have long since disappeared from the public arena. A monarch such as the Emperor Franz Josef of Austria-Hungary would have been astonished at the idea of a sovereign reigning over a welfare state; Prince Albert would probably have been less surprised.

None of this is to claim that Queen Victoria's family introduced democracy on to the Continent. When the Empress Frederick tried to do so in Germany the results were lamentable; Queen Ena of Spain and Queen Marie of Yugoslavia were obliged to sit helplessly by while their husbands abolished democracy altogether; the Empress Alexandra of Russia actively discouraged the spread of democratic ideas.

But what they did introduce, and tried to pass on to their children, was a Coburg sense of royal duty; of obligation towards their subjects. Whatever the shortcomings of these various queens and empresses, they all applied themselves to their task with a great sense of responsibility. They were none of them lazy or frivolous or heartless. Misguided they sometimes might have been but they were always conscientious. Even the claim by the ineffable Queen Marie of Romania that it was one of her royal duties to remain beautiful for as long as possible reveals this sense of dedication.

'The crown has no meaning,' a Coburg queen once said, 'unless it is a symbol of service.' And a symbol of service is what Queen Victoria's descendants always tried to make of their own crowns.

Notes on Sources
and
Bibliography

Notes on Sources

Unless otherwise indicated, all quotations from Queen Victoria are taken from the Queen's Letters and Journals, both published and unpublished. The hitherto unpublished extracts are from the Royal Archives at Windsor and are published here by gracious permission of Her Majesty Queen Elizabeth II. The published extracts are taken from *The Letters of Queen Victoria; A Selection from Her Majesty's Correspondence*. First Series, 1837–61, edited by A. C. Benson and Viscount Esher; 3 vols. John Murray, London, 1907. Second Series, 1862–85, edited by G. E. Buckle, 3 vols, John Murray, London 1926. Third Series, 1886–1901, edited by G. E. Buckle, 3 vols, John Murray, London, 1930.

Prologue

Crown Prince Rudolf ('I am frightfully rushed . . .') Stephanie, *I was to be Empress*. Crown Prince Frederick's looks ('one of the legendary . . .') Duff, *Hessian Tapestry*. Princess Alexandra snubbed, Battiscombe, *Queen Alexandra*. Abbey service, *London Illustrated*. Coburgs ('the Coburgs gain throne . . .') Hyde, *Mexican Empire*. Victoria's prestige ('they spoke of her . . .') Marie of Romania, *The Story of my Life*. Visit to Victoria ('I have so much . . .') Pope-Hennessy, *Queen Mary*. ('Well-behaved little geese . . .') Marie of Romania, *Life*. ('Mind you curtsy . . .') Alice, *For my Grandchildren*. ('it was like passing . . .') Marie of Romania, *Life*. Victoria at table ('kind of dumb talk . . .') Alice, *For my Grandchildren*. At Balmoral ('I remember . . .') Alice. *For my Grandchildren*. ('There was a quite special thrill . . .') Marie of Romania, *Life*. Victoria's influence ('In a way . . .') Marie of Romania, *Life*. Cross-examinations ('I like Balmoral . . .') and pregnant girl, Pope-Hennessy, *Queen Mary*. Moretta's marriage, Victoria *Queen Victoria at Windsor and Balmoral*. Victoria on great marriages, and to Princess Alice ('I do not think . . .') Longford, *Victoria R.I.* Princess Alice's new home, Alice, *Letters*. Vicky ('The house would enchant you . . .') *The Empress Frederick writes to Sophie*. Ena of Battenberg, Sencourt, *King Alfonso*. Empress Alexandra, Kerensky, *Memoirs*. Marina, Wentworth Day, *H.R.H. Princess Marina*.

Chapter One

Vicky on Fritz ('he is not born . . .') Corti, *The English Empress*. Vicky wins heads 'rather than hearts', Gould-Lee in *Empress to Sophie*. Love of England and Victoria's instructions, Corti, *English Empress*. Vicky ('to be friends . . .') Corti, *English Empress*. Disraeli, Zetland, *Letters*. Prince Henry, *Letters of the Empress Frederick*. Wilhelm's education, Victoria *Dearest Mama*. Wilhelm on Bismarck, Wilhelm II, *Memoirs*.

Chapter Two

Bertie and practical jokes, Magnus, *King Edward the Seventh*. Crown Prince Rudolf, Jullian, *Edward and the Edwardians*. Bertie's education ('a man of calm . . .' and 'the great object . . .') Magnus, *King Edward*. Victoria on Bertie, Victoria, *Dearest Mama*. Albert ('the greatest pain . . .') Magnus, *King Edward*. Victoria to Vicky, ('I never can . . .') *Dearest Mama*. Victoria, Bertie and government, Magnus, *King Edward*. Victoria on Bertie's good qualities, *Dearest Mama*. Tutor on Eddy, Magnus, *King Edward*. Prince George ('I wonder who will have . . .') and Victoria's comment, Nicolson, *King George the Fifth*. Wales girls' conversation, Marie of Romania, *Life*. 'Whispering Wales girls', Duff, *Hessian Tapestry*.

Chapter Three

All quotations from Vicky are from Victoria, *Letters of the Empress Frederick*. Crown Prince and syphilis, Stevenson, *Famous Illnesses in History*.

Chapter Four

Unless otherwise indicated, all quotations from Vicky are from *Letters of the Empress Frederick*. Alexandra's looks ('To the very end . . .') Marie of Romania, *Life*. Alexandra on Bertie ('after all . . .') Battiscombe, *Queen Alexandra*. Fritz ('That is where . . .') Corti, *English Empress*. Bismarck on Fritz ('as dependent . . .') Ludwig, *Bismarck*. Swaine's report, *Letters of the Empress Frederick*. Interview with Bismarck, Queen Victoria's *Journal*, ('one could do business . . .') Bolitho, *Further Letters*. Hohenlohe, *Memoirs*.

Chapter Five

Victoria on Eddy ('that angular . . .') Pope-Hennessy, *Queen Mary*. Victoria's secretary ('who is it tells . . .') Magnus, *King Edward*. Bertie ('a good sensible wife . . .') Pope-Hennessy, *Queen Mary*. Vicky on Alicky's refusal, *Empress to Sophie*. Hélène on Eddy, Queen Victoria's *Journal*. Victoria on May, Pope-Hennessy, *Queen Mary*. Vicky on Eddy's engagement, *Empress to Sophie*. Victoria on George, Pope-Hennessy, *Queen Mary*. Alexandra ('Fancy my Georgie boy . . .') Nicolson, *King George*. Alexandra ('I must say . . .' and 'I only wish . . .') Battiscombe, *Queen Alexandra*. Vicky ('Aunt Mary Teck . . .') *Empress to Sophie*. Victoria ('Let me now say . . .') Nicolson, *King George*. Vicky ('No one . . .') *Empress to Sophie*. Duke of York on baby's name, Nicolson, *King George*.

Chapter Six

Vicky ('I am completely . . .') *Letters*. Friedrichshof ('not a Schloss . . .') Pope-Hennessy, *Queen Mary*. Vicky ('His spirit . . .') *Letters*. Vicky on Tino and brothers, *Letters*. Victoria on royal mob, Pope-Hennessy, *Queen Mary*. Vicky on Sophie's wedding, *Letters*. Royal ball in Athens ('Do you mind . . .') Christopher of Greece, *Memoirs*. Sophie ('I cannot tell you . . .') *Empress to Sophie*. Tatoi ('we children . . .') Christopher, *Memoirs*. Sophie's Englishness, Anon, *Recollections of Three Kaisers*. Wilhelm ('If my poor baby . . .') Corti, *English Empress*. Fuss over Sophie's conversion, *Empress to Sophie*. Sophie's telegram, Corti, *English Empress*.

Chapter Seven

Unless otherwise indicated, all quotations are from Marie of Romania, *The Story of my Life*. Princess of Wales ('they won't even know . . .') and Victoria on Marie's engagement, Pope-Hennessy, *Queen Mary*. Nando and breakfast rolls, Martineau, *Roumania and her Rulers*.

Chapter Eight

Victoria ('the same blood . . .') Longford, *Victoria R.I.* Vicky ('Aunt Marie . . .') *Empress to Sophie*. Ponsonby, A. Ponsonby, *Henry Ponsonby*. Hesse family ('The Grand Ducal family . . .') Buxhoeveden, *Life and Tragedy of Alexandra Feodorovna*. Alicky ('Have you not been . . .') Duff, *Hessian Tapestry*. Alicky's looks ('What a charming . . .') Eulalia, *Court Life from Within*. Nicky's looks ('Gentle charm . . .') Marie of Romania, *Life*. Nicky ('My dream . . .') Nicholas II, *Journal Intime*. Vicky ('could not help . . .') *Empress to Sophie*. Nicky (a 'marvellous . . .') Nicholas, *Journal*. Nicky to Empress Marie, Massie, *Nicholas and Alexandra*. Victoria and jewellery, Buxhoeveden, *Life and Tragedy*. Victoria on Nicky, Corti, *English Empress*. Nicky and Prince of Wales, Magnus, *King Edward*. Alicky ('I am yours . . .' and 'Be firm . . .') Nicholas, *Journal*. Nicky ('Sandro . . .') Massie, *Nicholas and Alexandra*. Funeral ('thirty-ninth . . .') Battiscombe, *Queen Alexandra*. George to May, Pope-Hennessy, *Queen Mary*. Tsar's face, Magnus, *King Edward*. Alicky ('now I wore . . .') Fülöp-Miller, *Rasputin*. George ('Nicky is very lucky . . .') Nicolson,

King George. Bertie on wedding night, Magnus, *King Edward*. Alicky in diary, Nicholas, *Journal*.

Chapter Nine

Unless otherwise indicated, all quotations are from Marie of Romania, *The Story of my Life*. Hardinge on Nando, *Old Diplomacy*. Alexandra on Playfair, Griscom, *Diplomatically Speaking*. Nicky and uncles, Massie, *Nicholas and Alexandra*. Coronation ('Wherever the eye . . .') Marie of Romania, *Life*. British Ambassador ('The Empress appeared . . .') Massie, *Nicholas and Alexandra*. Nicky on Victoria ('kinder and more amiable . . .') Magnus, *King Edward*. Alicky's sister ('on whom the blame . . .' and 'would have made . . .') Duff, *Hessian Tapestry*. Victoria ('all her own . . .') Longford, *Victoria R.I.* Alicky ('it has been such . . .' and 'I have a right . . .') Buxhoeveden, *Life and Tragedy*.

Chapter Ten

Secretary ('really only requires . . .') Magnus, *King Edward*. Beatrice ('apart from the most . . .') Pope-Hennessy, *Queen Mary*. Alexandra ('too pretty . . .') Battiscombe, *Queen Alexandra*. Alexandra ('a pretty sight . . .' and 'You my sweet May . . .') Pope-Hennessy, *Queen Mary*. Victoria and Maud ('like Juno's swans . . .') *Royalties of the World*. Vicky ('two such Ducks . . .') Pope-Hennessy, *Queen Mary*. ('Not at all stuck-up . . .') Mary Gladstone, *Diaries and Letters*. ('appeared so invariably . . .') *Royalties*. Vicky on princesses ('it would be . . .') Pope-Hennessy, *Queen Mary*. Victoria on princesses and 'just a glorified . . .' Battiscombe, *Queen Alexandra*. Vicky on princesses ('that dear Victoria . . .') *Empress to Sophie*. Maud ('as an all-round . . .') Anon, *The Private Life of the King*. Vicky on Maud, and Queen Victoria ('Alix, to whom . . .') Pope-Hennessy, *Queen Mary*. Charles ('lack of strings . . .') Michael, *Haakon, King of Norway*. Duchess of Teck on Charles, Pope-Hennessy, *Queen Mary*. Engagement ('the announcement . . .') Mallet, *Life with Queen Victoria*. Wedding ('never has a more charming . . .', 'the perfume' and 'Behind the door' London *Times*. Duchess of Teck on Maud, Pope-Hennessy, *Queen Mary*.

Chapter Eleven

Unless otherwise indicated, all quotations are from Victoria, *The Empress Frederick Writes to Sophie*. Wilhelm ('My mother and I . . .') Corti, *English Empress*. Von Bülow ('she believed . . .') *Memoirs*. Vicky on alliance ('such a thing . . .') Corti, *English Empress*. Sophie ('adorable . . .' and 'compare which . . .') Pope-Hennessy, *Queen Mary*. Alexandra on Greek royal family troubles, Pope-Hennessy, *Queen Mary*.

Chapter Twelve

Unless otherwise indicated, all quotations are from Victoria, *The Empress Frederick writes to Sophie*. Victoria on Queen Louise, Pope-Hennessy, *Queen Mary*. Food ('heavy . . .') F. Ponsonby, *Recollections of Three Reigns*. Stranger and three royalties, Christopher, *Memoirs*. Victoria and Danish family loyalty, Battiscombe, *Queen Alexandra*. Maud's home ('to reflect . . .') Anon, *Private Life*. Alexandra ('on no account forget . . .') Battiscombe, *Queen Alexandra*. Maud ('The Princess of Wales . . .) Mallet, *Life*. Observer ('it is indeed . . .') Tooley, *Life of Queen Alexandra*. Grand Duchess ('No! . . .') Pope-Hennessy, *Queen Mary*. Vicky on German anglophobia, Corti, *English Empress*. Victoria on Affie's death, Longford, *Victoria R.I.*

Chapter Thirteen

Edward's court, Marie of Romania, *Life*. Edward ('I don't know . . .') Magnus, *King Edward*. King's routine, Ponsonby, *Recollections*. King's career ('We shall not pretend . . .') London *Times*. Smoking, Ponsonby, *Recollections*. Nicolson ('Thank God . . .') Jullian, *Edward*. Female company ('What tiresome evenings . . .' and 'never happier . . .') Ponsonby, *Recollections*. King ('Stop calling me Sir . . .') Jullian, *Edward*. King and 'Underworld', Ponsonby, *Recollections*. Boer Anthem, Ponsonby, *Recollections*. Vicky ('There is not a kinder . . .') *Empress to Sophie*. Vicky's letters, Ponsonby, *Recollections*. Vicky's death ('who in dying . . .') Radziwill, *The Empress Frederick*. Vicky ('that understands . . .') *Letters*. Vicky's efforts ('to help others . . .') Gould-Lee in *Empress to Sophie*. Vicky ('Why we were . . .') *Letters*. Duke of York ('My room . . .') Pope-Hennessy, *Queen Mary*. Alexandra ('All my happiness . . .') Battiscombe, *Queen Alexandra*. King ('Marvellous . . .') Jullian, *Edward*. King ('their white arms . . .') Magnus, *King Edward*.

Chapter Fourteen

Unless otherwise indicated, all quotations are from Marie of Romania, *The Story of my Life*. Vicky on Marie's beauty, *Empress to Sophie*. Marie ('This one is divine . . .') and Sophie on Marie, Jullian, *Edward*. Garden party ('The Crown Princess . . .') Stancioff, *Recollections*. Vicky on Missy, *Empress to Sophie*. Bucharest ('an external veneer . . .') Hardinge, *Old Diplomacy*. Vicky on Nando, *Empress to Sophie*. King ('waiters at second rate . . .') Magnus, *King Edward*. Visit to Pope, Ponsonby, *Recollections*. King at theatre ('Mademoiselle . . .') Magnus, *King Edward*. Longchamps, Ponsonby, *Recollections*. Ambassador's comment, Magnus, *King Edward*. Entente and Cambon, Ponsonby, *Recollections*.

Chapter Fifteen

Alicky ('How I envy . . .' and 'The Empress Alexandra . . .') Buxhoeveden, *Life and Tragedy*. Holy Russia ('Church, dynasty . . .') Almedingen, *The Empress Alexandra*. Russian people ('deeply and truly . . .') Buxhoeveden, *Life and Tragedy*. Russian Empire ('in terms of . . .') Almedingen, *The Empress*. Cold rooms, Buxhoeveden, *Life and Tragedy*. Radziwill, *The Intimate Life of the Last Tsaritsa*. Love life, Mossolov, *At the Court of the last Tsar* and Eulalia, *Court Life from Within*. Ambassador ('I will say no more . . .') Hardinge, *Old Diplomacy*. Nicholas ('a great, never to be . . .') *Journal*. Observer ('I saw the Tsarevich . . .') Viroubova, *Memoirs*. Nicholas ('I don't think . . .') Mossolov, *At the Court*. Nicholas ('Lord how painful . . .') *Journal*. Alicky's letter to sister, Buxhoevenden, *Life and Tragedy*. Alicky on Duma, Almedingen, *The Empress*.

Chapter Sixteen

Maud's talk, Ponsonby, *Recollections*. Maud and family ('the habit . . .') Tooley, *Life*. Republicans ('like Garabaldi . . .') Michael, *Haakon*. Wilhelm ('Kings being dismissed . . .'), Edward ('am quite aware . . .') and Wedel's wire ('King Edward's furious . . .') Michael, *Haakon*. Edward on Maud and Charles ('have won golden . . .') Magnus, *King Edward*. Grand Duchess ('so Maud . . .') Pope-Hennessy, *Queen Mary*. Coronation journey, Michael, *Haakon*. Grand Duchess and Princess May, Pope-Hennessy, *Queen Mary*.

Chapter Seventeen

Vicky on Ena, *Empress to Sophie*. Beatrice ('I have heard . . .') Duff, *The Shy Princess*. Victoria on bull-fighting, Epton, *Victoria and her daughters*. Grand Duchess and Prince of Wales ('Beatrice is advised . . .') Pope-Hennessy, *Queen Mary*. Train de luxe and heat, Erbach-Schonberg, *Reminiscences*. Alfonso ('in five minutes . . .') Sencourt, *Spain's Uncertain Crown*. Ena ('I saw a man . . .') Erbach-Schonberg, *Reminiscences*. Prince of Wales ('I proposed . . .') Duff, *Shy Princess*. Duchess of Edinburgh, Erbach-Schonberg, *Reminiscences*.

Chapter Eighteen

For all information on the haemophilia of the Tsarevich Alexis, I am deeply indebted to *Nicholas and Alexandra* by Robert K. Massie. Victoria ('I do wish . . .') Pope-Hennessy, *Queen Mary*. Curse of Coburgs, Duff, *Hessian Tapestry*. Gilliard, *Thirteen Years at the Russian Court*. Nicholas ('We have got . . .') *Journal*. Dostoevsky, Massie, *Nicholas and Alexandra*.

Chapter Nineteen

Unless otherwise indicated, all quotations are from Ponsonby, *Recollections of Three Reigns*. Edward ('I have no wish . . .') and Nicolson ('the greatest diplomatic . . .') Magnus, *King Edward*. Corfu ('It is interesting . . .') and Sophie on the Kaiser, Hardinge, *Old Diplomacy*. Edward ('Alfonso has created . . .') Magnus, *King Edward*. Norwegians, Edward's policy and family ('there was no disguising . . .') Hardinge, *Old Diplomacy*. Edward and Nicolson, H. Nicolson, *Sir Arthur Nicolson*. Von Bülow, *Memoirs*. Edward ('The monarchy . . .') Jullian, *Edward*.

Chapter Twenty

Alexis ('Mama help me . . .') Buxhoeveden, *Life and Tragedy*. Alicky ('smiling and talking . . .' and 'distracted . . .') Gilliard, *Thirteen Years*. Rasputin's telegram, Viroubova, *Memoirs*. Alicky's letters, Massie, *Nicholas and Alexandra*.

Chapter Twenty-one

Mélas on Sophie, Mélas, *Ex-King Constantine and the War*. Sophie ('a great trial . . .') Dugdale, *Maurice de Bunsen*. Sophie ('extraordinarily distant . . .') Mélas, *Ex-King*. Roma Lister, *Reminiscences*. Valaority, Mélas, *Ex-King*. Sophie's orderliness and 'none of her children . . .' Mélas, *Ex-King*. Children ('Mama is just . . .') Nicholas of Greece, *My Fifty Years*. Sophie and Daisy of Pless, *Daisy, Princess of Pless*. Princess of Saxe-Weimar, Constantine I, *A King's Private Letters*. George ('I shall have reigned . . .') Christopher, *Memoirs*. Sophie and news of assassination, Gould-Lee, *Helen, Queen Mother of Rumania*. Marie on Alicky and proposed match, Marie of Romania, *Life*. Alicky ('You know how difficult . . .') Massie, *Nicholas and Alexandra*.

Chapter Twenty-two

Unless otherwise indicated, all quotations are from Marie of Romania, *The Story of my Life*. Constantine ('How was I supposed . . .') Mélas, *Ex-King*. Accusations ('using a veil' and 'We wanted to run . . .') Gould-Lee, *Helen*. Kitchener's visit and Sophie's pro-Germanism, Mélas, *Ex-King*. Sophie on England, Pless, *Daisy*. Christopher, *Memoirs*. King George V, Hourmouzius, *No Ordinary Crown*. Constantine ('How weary I am . . .') *Private Letters*. Sophie ('Can Belgium . . .') Gould-Lee, *Helen*. Marie ('I have health . . .') Daggett, *Marie of Roumania*. Englishman on Marie ('She was a flame . . .') Buchanan, *Queen Victoria's Relations*.

Chapter Twenty-three

Alexandra ('You have fought . . .') Alexandra, *Letters of the Tsaritsa to the Tsar*. Rasputin ('I need neither . . .') Paleologue, *An Ambassador's Memoirs*. Alexandra ('Be the master . . . etc') *Letters*. Marie ('Their hatred . . .') *Life*. Tsarevich in tears ('What is wrong . . .') Massie, *Nicholas and Alexandra*. Alicky's Englishness ('The Empress was very . . .') Buxhoeveden, *Life and Tragedy*. Marie ('very dangerous . . .') *Life*. Alexandra ('God have mercy . . .') *Letters*. Gilliard ('No one . . .') *Thirteen Years*. Alexandra ('You Russian ladies . . .') and news on abdication, Dehn, *The Real Tsaritsa*. George V ('Events of last week . . .') Nicolson, *King George*. Ambassador in Paris ('I do not think . . .') Massie, *Nicholas and Alexandra*. Alexandra ('I don't understand . . .') Kerensky, *Memoirs*. Soldier to Alexandra ('Did you know . . .') Buxhoevenden, *Life and Tragedy*. Nicholas to Kerensky ('I have no fear . . .') Bulygin, *The Murder of the Romanovs*. Marie of Romania, *Life*.

Chapter Twenty-four

Russian Minister ('The Greeks') and Constantine ('It is out of the question . . .') Gould-Lee, *Helen*. Christopher, *Memoirs*. Constantine's proclamation, Gould-Lee, *Helen*. Constantine's departure, Christopher, *Memoirs*. All quotations from Marie of Romania, *Life*.

Chapter Twenty-five

Sophie's telephone call, Christopher, *Memoirs*. Sophie on homecoming ('The level-headed . . .') Gould-Lee, *The Royal House of Greece*. Marie ('I have had many difficult . . .') *Life*. Marie to Ministers ('Gentlemen . . .') Daggett, *Marie*. Marie ('She is sweet . . .') Elsberry, *Marie of Romania*. Helen ('Had I listened . . .') Gould-Lee, *Helen*. Mrs Martineau ('Could this be . . .') *Roumania and her Rulers*. Constantine ('They have arranged it . . .') Gould-Lee, *Helen*.

Chapter Twenty-six

Unless otherwise indicated, all quotations are from Daggett, *Marie of Roumania*. Rosita Forbes ('Hollywoodesque') *These Men I Knew*. Marie's heir, Martineau, *Roumania*. Forbes ('The very spirit . . .') *These Men*. Mrs Martineau, *Roumania*. Visitor ('Why do you all . . .') Forbes, *These Men*. Count de St Aulaire, Martineau, *Roumania*. Marie's politics ('a positive genius . . .' etc) Martineau, *Roumania*. Marie's daughter, *I Live Again*. Marie on Mignon ('smiling, passive . . .') *Life*. Mignon's driving, Peter II, *A King's Heritage*.

Chapter Twenty-seven

Ena ('He tires . . .') Sencourt, *Uncertain Crown*. Grand Duchess Marie, *A Princess in Exile*. Duff-Gordon, *Discretions and Indiscretions*. Elinor Glyn on Ena and Alfonso, *Letters from Spain*. Eulalia on Ena and Marie, *Courts and Countries after the War*. Ena ('I long for the day . . .') E. Graham, *The Life Story of King Alfonso XIII*. Eulalia on Ena's Englishness, *Courts and Countries*. Alfonso ('Spain is great . . .') Sencourt, *Uncertain Crown*. Ibanez, *Alfonso XIII Unmasked*.

Chapter Twenty-eight

Unless otherwise indicated, all quotations are from Fjellman, *Louise Mountbatten, Queen of Sweden*. Prince Louis ('There is only one . . .') Kerr, *Prince Louis of Battenberg*. Swedish court ('uniform and bearskins . . .') Ponsonby, *Recollections*.

Chapter Twenty-nine

Marie ('George should never . . .' and 'my daughter and he . . .') Forbes, *These Men*. Communiqué, Gould-Lee, *Helen*. Marie in America, Packard, *Queen Marie's Visit*. Marie ('There are those . . .') Cornhill. Ileana on Ferdinand, *I Live Again*. Forbes, *These Men*. Michael ('How can Papa . . .') Bocca, *The Uneasy Heads*. Marie ('I have had such . . .') Forbes, *These Men*. Helen ('Suffering . . .') Gould-Lee, *Helen*. Eulalia on Sophie, *Courts and Countries*. Sophie and Ferdinand, Christopher, *Memoirs*. Alexandra, *Queen Alexandra, For a King's Love*. Sophie ('If we had to . . .') Gould-Lee, *Helen*. Funeral, Christopher, *Memoirs*.

Chapter Thirty

Ena ('And who . . .') Grand Duchess Marie, *Princess in Exile*. Alfonso, Thauraud, *Rendez-vous Espagnols*. Ena's last court, Pilar of Bavaria, *Don Alfonso XIII*. Ena ('I thought . . .') Sencourt, *Uncertain Crown*.

Chapter Thirty-one

Rebecca West, *Black Lamb, Grey Falcon*. Raditch ('What is more . . .') S. Graham, *Alexander of Jugoslavia*. Alexander ('The Queen . . .') S. Graham, *Alexander*. Mignon ('I really don't . . .' and 'I shall never be . . .') Forbes, *These Men*. Alexander ('You are happy . . .') S. Graham, *Alexander*. Alexander ('It's enough . . .') Peter II, *Heritage*. West, *Black Lamb*. Visits of Rosita Forbes. *These Men*. Mignon ('The monastery . . .') S. Graham, *Alexander*. Yugoslav Ambassador ('They have killed . . .') Peter and King's death, and Alexander ('What I require . . .') Peter II, *Heritage*.

Chapter Thirty-two

Unless otherwise indicated, all quotations are from Fjellman, *Louise Mountbatten, Queen of Sweden*. Eulalia, *Courts and Countries*. Wedding ('that indescribable . . .') Margaret Lane in the *Daily Mail*.

Chapter Thirty-three

Marie ('a hardhearted . . .' and 'If the instinct . . .') Elsberry, *Marie*. Marie ('I know nothing . . .') Nichols, *No Place like Home*. Marie and Beverley Nichols, *No Place*. Marie and fur cape, Marie's heart ('to bring their sorrows . . .' and 'Poor Doctor . . .' and 'There it stood . . .') Ileana, *I Live Again*. Marie's death ('a light . . .') Buchanan, *Relations*. Marie ('an outstanding figure . . .') Nichols, *No Place*. Grand Duke ('A star danced . . .') Buchanan, *Relations*. Receptionist ('Where was it . . .') Michael, *Haakon*. Maud ('I am so glad . . .' and 'far less pretentious . . .') Eulalia, *Courts and Countries*. Prime Minister ('warm and generous . . .') Michael, *Haakon*. Contemporary ('she indulged . . .') London *Times*. Mignon's conversation, Alexandra, *For a King's Love*. Peter ('What will happen . . .') Peter II, *Heritage*. Aspasia ('My dear Sandra . . .') Alexandra, *For a King's Love*. Peter on Marie, *Heritage*. Alexandra ('Accusations . . .') and Peter ('We're getting out . . .') and jewellery, Alexandra, *For a King's Love*. Mignon ('It has meant . . .') *Graphic*.

Chapter Thirty-four

Tourist ('I'm a storekeeper . . .') *Graphic*. Ingrid ('Good heavens . . .') Bocca, *Uneasy Heads*. Ingrid ('You just can't . . .' and 'Mother can charm . . .') Dwinger, *Portrait of the Queen of Denmark*. Frederick ('I have never . . .') Dwinger, *Portrait of the King of Denmark*. All quotations on Louise from Fjellman, *Louise Mountbatten*.

Epilogue

Eulalia, *Courts and Countries*. 'The crown has no meaning . . .', Cunliffe-Owen, *Elisabeth, Queen of the Belgians*.

Bibliography

Alexandra, Empress of Russia, *Letters of the Tsaritsa to the Tsar* 1914–1916. Duckworth, London, 1923.

Alexandra, Queen of Yugoslavia: *For a King's Love*. Odhams Press, London, 1956.

Alfonso XIII, King of Spain: *Diario Intimo. Recogido comantodo por J. L. Castillo-Puce*: Madrid, Biblioteca Nueva, 1961.

Alice, Grand Duchess of Hesse: *Letters to Her Majesty the Queen*. John Murray, London, 1885.

Alice, Princess: *For My Grandchildren*. Evans Bros. London, 1966.

Almedingen, E. M.: *The Empress Alexandra* 1872–1918. Hutchinson, London, 1961.

Anon: *All For Norway*. (Issued by the Royal Norwegian Government Information Office) J. M. Dent, London, 1942.

Anon: *Recollections of Three Kaisers*. Herbert Jenkins, London, 1929.

Anon: *The Empress Frederick: A Memoir*. James Nisbet, London, 1913.

Anon (One of His Majesty's Servants). *The Private Life of the King*: C. Arthur Pearson, London, 1901.

Anon: *The Royal Family of Greece*. Warwick Bros. & Rutter Ltd, Toronto 1914.

Arthur, Sir George: *Queen Alexandra*. Chapman & Hall, London, 1934.

Asquith, Margot: *Places and Persons*. Thornton Butterworth, London, 1925.

Balfour, Michael: *The Kaiser and His Times*. Cresset Press, London, 1964.

Barkeley, Richard: *The Empress Frederick*. Macmillan, London, 1956.

Battaglia, Otto Forst de: *Dictatorship on its Trial*. Harcourt Brace, New York, 1931.

Battiscombe, Georgina: *Queen Alexandra*. Constable, London, 1969.

Bennett, Daphne: *Vicky*. Harvill, London, 1971.

Benson, E. F.: *King Edward VII*. Longmans, London, 1933.

Benson, E. F.: *Queen Victoria*. Longmans, London, 1935.

Benson, E. F.: *The Kaiser and His English Relations*. Longmans, London, 1936.

Berggrav-Jensen, Elivind: *Mennesket Dronning Maud*. Glydendal Norsk Forlag, Oslo, 1956.

Bibesco, Princess: *Ferdinand de Roumania; une victime royale*. Les Amis d'Edouard, Paris, N.D.

Bismarck, Prince Otto von: *Reflections and Reminiscences* (2 Vols). Smith Elder, London, 1898.

Bismarck, Prince Otto von: *New Chapters of Bismarck's Autobiography*. Hodder and Stoughton, London, 1930.

Bocca, Geoffrey: *The Uneasy Heads*. Weidenfeld & Nicolson, London, 1959.

Bolitho, Hector: *The Reign of Queen Victoria*. Collins, London, 1949.

Buchanan, Sir George: *My Mission to Russia*. Cassell, London, 1923.

Buchanan, Meriel: *Recollections of Imperial Russia*. Hutchinson, London, 1923.

Buchanan, Meriel: *Diplomacy and Foreign Courts*. Hutchinson, London, 1928.

Buchanan, Meriel: *The Dissolution of an Empire*. John Murray, London, 1932.

Buchanan, Meriel: *Queen Victoria's Relations*. Cassell, London, 1954.

Bülow, Prince Bernhard von: *Memoirs* (4 Vols.). Putnam, London, 1931.

Bulygin, Paul: *The Murder of the Romanovs*. Hutchinson, London, 1935.

Burghclere, Lady (Ed.): *A Great Lady's Friendships*. Macmillan, London, 1933.

Busch, Dr Moritz: *Bismarck: Some Secret Pages of His History* (3 Vols). Macmillan, London, 1898.

Buxhoeveden, Baroness Sophie: *The Life and Tragedy of Alexandra Feodorovna*. Longmans, London, 1928.

Channon, Sir Henry: *Chips* (Ed. by Robert Rhodes James). Weidenfeld & Nicolson, London, 1967.

Christmas, Walter: *King George of Greece*, Eveleigh Nash, London, 1914.

Christopher, Prince of Greece: *Memoirs*, The Right Book Club, London, 1938.

Connell, Brian: *Manifest Destiny*. Cassell, London, 1953.

Constantine I, King of the Hellenes: *A King's Private Letters*. Eveleigh Nash & Grayson, London, 1925.

Corti, Egon, Count: *The English Empress*. Cassell, London, 1957.

Cowles, Virginia: *Edward VII and His Circle*. Hamish Hamilton, London, 1956.

Cunliffe-Owen, Sidney: *Elizabeth, Queen of the Belgians*. Jenkins, London, 1954.

Cust, Sir Lionel: *King Edward VII and his Court: Some Reminiscences*. John Murray, London, 1930.

Daggett, Mabel Potter: *Marie of Roumania*. Brentano's, London, 1926.
Dehn, Lili: *The Real Tsaritsa*. Butterworth, London, 1922.
Dubourg, Alain-Yves: *Royal Haemophilia*. (Abbottempo, Book 2). Abbott Universal Ltd, Amsterdam, 1967.
Duff, David: *The Shy Princess*. Evans Bros., London, 1958.
Duff, David: *Hessian Tapestry*. Frederick Muller, London, 1967.
Duff-Gordon, Lady Lucie: *Discretions and Indiscretions*. Jarrolds, London, 1932.
Dugdale, Edgar T. S.: *Maurice de Bunsen*. John Murray, London, 1934.
Dwinger, Jonna: *Portraits of the King and Queen of Denmark*. The Press Department of the Ministry of Foreign Affairs, Copenhagen, 1972.

Eckhardt, Tibor: *Regicide at Marseille*, American Hungarian Library and Historical Society, New York, 1964.
Elsberry, Terence: *Marie of Romania*. Cassell, London, 1973.
Epton, Nina: *Victoria and Her Daughters*. Weidenfeld & Nicolson, London 1971.
Erbach-Schonberg, Princess Marie zu: *Reminiscences*. Allen and Unwin, London, 1925.
Ernest II, Duke of Saxe-Coburg-Gotha. *Memoirs*. Remington, London, 1888.
Erskine, Mrs Steuart: *Twenty-nine Years: The Reign of King Alfonso XIII of Spain*. Hutchinson, London, 1931.
Esher, Reginald, Viscount: *Journals and Letters*. Ivor Nicholson and Watson, London, 1934.
Eulalia, Infanta of Spain: *Court Life from Within*. Cassell, London, 1915.
Eulalia, Infanta of Spain: *Courts and Countries After the War*. Hutchinson, London, 1925.
Eulalia, Infanta of Spain: *Memoirs* (Trans. by Phyllis Mégroz) Hutchinson, London, 1936.

Fabritius, Dr Albert: *Genealogy of the Danish Royal Family*. Ministry of Foreign Affairs, Copenhagen, N.D.
Fjellman, Margit: *Louise Mountbatten, Queen of Sweden*. George Allen & Unwin, London, 1968.
Forbes, Rosita: *These Men I Knew*. The Right Book Club, London, 1940.
Frederick III, German Emperor: *Diaries of the Emperor Frederick* (Trans. by Frances A. Welby) Chapman & Hall, London, 1902.
Fülöp-Miller, René: *Rasputin: The Holy Devil*. G. P. Putnam's Sons, New York, 1928.

Galiano, A. A.: *The Fall of a Throne*. Butterworth, London, 1933.
Gilliard, Pierre: *Thirteen Years at the Russian Court* (Trans. by F. Appleby Holt) Hutchinson, London, 1920.

Gladstone, Mary: *Diaries and Letters*. Methuen, London, 1930.

Glyn, Elinor: *Letters from Spain*. Duckworth, London, 1924.

Gore, John: *King George V*. John Murray, London, 1941.

Gould Lee, Arthur S.: *The Royal House of Greece*. Ward Lock, London, 1948.

Gould Lee, Arthur S.: *Helen, Queen Mother of Rumania*. Faber & Faber, London, 1956.

Graham, Evelyn: *The Life Story of King Alfonso XIII*. Herbert Jenkins, London, 1930.

Graham, Evelyn: *The Queen of Spain*. Hutchinson, London, 1929.

Graham, Stephen: *Alexander of Jugoslavia*. Cassell, London, 1938.

Graham, William: *My Friendship, and my visit to Her Majesty, the Queen of Rumania*. Lowton Church Echo, Crewe, 1925.

Grant, N. F. (Ed.): *The Kaiser's Letters to the Tsar*. Hodder & Stoughton, London, 1920.

Griscom, Lloyd C.: *Diplomatically Speaking*. John Murray, London, 1941.

Hardinge, Sir Arthur: *A Diplomatist in Europe*. Jonathan Cape, London, 1927.

Hardinge, Lord: *Old Diplomacy*. John Murray, London, 1947.

Hibben, Paxton: *Constantine I and the Greek People*. The Century Company, New York, 1920.

Hohenlohe, Prince Chlodwig: *Memoirs*. (2 vols, trans. by George W. Chrystal), Heinemann, London, 1906.

Hourmouzius, Stelio: *No Ordinary Crown*. Weidenfeld & Nicolson, London, 1972.

Hyde, Montgomery: *Mexican Empire*. Macmillan, London, 1946.

Ibanez, Vincent Blasco: *Alfonso XIII Unmasked*. E. P. Dutton, New York, 1924.

Ileana, Princess: *I Live Again*. Gollancz, London, 1952.

Jullian, Philippe: *Edward and the Edwardians*. Sidgwick & Jackson, London, 1967.

Kelen, Betty: *The Mistresses*. W. H. Allen, London, 1966.

Kerensky, Alexander: *The Kerensky Memoirs*. Cassell, London, 1965.

Kerensky, Alexander: *Russia and the Story's Turning Point*. Duell, Sloan & Pearce, New York, 1966.

Kerr, Mark: *Prince Louis of Battenberg*. Longmans, London, 1934.

King, Stella: *Princess Marina*. Cassell, London, 1969.

Kurenberg, Joachim von: *The Kaiser*. (Trans. by H. Russell & H. Hogen), Cassell, London, 1954.

Kurtz, Harold: *The Empress Eugenie*. Hamish Hamilton, London, 1964.

Lee, Sir Sydney: *King Edward VII* (2 Vols) Macmillan, London, 1927.

Lister, Roma: *Reminiscences*. Hutchinson, London, N.D.

Longford, Elizabeth: *Victoria R.I.* Weidenfeld & Nicolson, London, 1964.

Ludwig, Emil: *Kaiser Wilhelm II* (Trans. by E. C. Mayne) Putnam, London, 1926.

Ludwig, Emil: *Bismarck* (trans. by E. and C. Paul) Allen and Unwin, London, 1926.

Mackenzie, Sir Morell: *The Fatal Illness of Frederick the Noble*. Sampson, Low & Marston, London, 1888.

Madariaga, Salvador de: *Spain*. Jonathan Cape, London, 1942.

Madol, Hans Roger: *Christian IX*. Collins, London, 1939.

Magnus, Sir Philip: *King Edward the Seventh*. John Murray, London, 1964.

Mallet, Marie: *Life with Queen Victoria*. John Murray, London, 1968.

Mann, Golo: *The History of Germany since 1789* (Trans. by M. Jackson) Chatto & Windus, London, 1968.

Marie, Queen of Roumania, *The Country That I Love*. Duckworth, London, 1926.

Marie, Queen of Roumania: *The Story of My Life* (3 Vols.) Cassell, London, 1934.

Marie, Grand Duchess of Russia: *Things I Remember*. Cassell, London, 1930.

Marie, Grand Duchess of Russia: *A Princess in Exile*. Cassell, London, 1932.

Marie Louise, Princess: *My Memories of Six Reigns*: Evans Bros., London, 1956.

Martin, Sir Theodore: *Life of His Royal Highness the Prince Consort*. (5 Vols) Smith, Elder, London, 1877–1880.

Martin, Sir Theodore: *Queen Victoria As I Knew Her*. Blackwood, London, 1908.

Martineau, Mrs Philip: *Roumania and Her Rulers*. Stanley Paul, London, 1927.

Massie, Robert: *Nicholas and Alexandra*. Gollancz, London, 1968.

Maurois, André: *King Edward and His Times*. Cassell, London, 1933.

Melas, George M.: *Ex-King Constantine and the War*. Hutchinson, London, 1920.

Michael, Maurice: *Haakon, King of Norway*. George Allen and Unwin, London, 1958.

Milicevic, V.: *A King Dies in Marseilles*. Hohwacht, Bad Godesberg, 1959.

Mussolov, A. A.: *At the Court of the Last Tsar*. Methuen, London, 1935.

Nicholas II, Tsar of Russia: *Journal Intime de Nicolas II* (Ed. by A. Pierre) Payot, Paris, 1925.

Nicholas II, Tsar of Russia: *The Letters of the Tsar to the Tsaritsa 1914–1917*. Bodley Head, London, 1929.

Nicholas, Prince of Greece: *My Fifty Years*. Hutchinson, London, 1926.

Nichols, Beverley, *No Place Like Home*. Jonathan Cape, London, 1936.

Nicolson, Harold: *Sir Arthur Nicolson Bart*. Constable, London, 1930.

Nicolson, Harold: *King George the Fifth*. Constable, London, 1952.

Packard, Edward: *Queen Marie's Visit*. New England Essays, Cambridge Mass., 1927.

Paget, Walburga: *Embassies of Other Days* (2 Vols) Hutchinson, London, 1923.

Paleologue, Maurice: *An Ambassador's Memoirs*. (3 Vols) Hutchinson, London, 1923.

Palsbo, Susanne and Mentze, Ernst: *The Daily Life of the King of Denmark*, Danish Ministry of Foreign Affairs, Copenhagen, 1972.

Pares, Sir Bernard: *The Fall of the Russian Monarchy* .Vintage Books, New York, 1928.

Peter II, King of Yugoslavia: *A King's Heritage*. Cassell, London, 1955.

Petrie, Sir Charles: *King Alfonso XIII and His Age*. Chapman & Hall, London, 1963.

Pilar of Bavaria, H.R.H. and Chapman-Houston, Major D.: *Don Alfonso XIII*. John Murray, London, 1931.

Pless, Princess Daisy, *Daisy, Princess of Pless*. John Murray, London, 1928.

Pless, Princess Daisy: *What I Left Unsaid*. Cassell, London, 1936.

Pless, Princess Daisy: *From My Private Diary*. John Murray, London, 1931.

Ponsonby, Arthur: *Henry Ponsonby*. Macmillan, London, 1943.

Ponsonby, Sir Frederick: *Recollections of Three Reigns*. Eyre & Spottiswoode, London, 1951.

Ponsonby, Sir Frederick: *Sidelights on Queen Victoria*. Macmillan, London, 1930.

Ponsonby, Mary: *A Memoir, Some Letters and a Journal*. John Murray, London, 1927.

Pope-Hennessy, James: *Queen Mary 1867–1953*. George Allen & Unwin, London, 1959.

Poschinger, Margaretta von: *Life of the Emperor Frederick*. Harper and Brothers, London, 1901.

Radziwill, Princess Catherine: *My Recollections*. Isbister, London, 1904.

Radziwill, Princess Catherine: (pseud. Count Paul Vassili) *Behind The Veil at the Russian Court*. Cassell, London, 1913.

Radziwill, Princess Catherine: *The Empress Frederick*. Cassell, London, 1917.

Radziwill, Princess Catherine: *The Intimate Life of the Last Tsarina*. Cassell, London, 1929.

Rodd, Sir James Rennell: *Frederick Crown Prince and Emperor.* David Scott, London, 1888.

Rodd, Sir James Rennell: *Social and Diplomatic Memories* (3 Vols) Edward Arnold, London, 1922–25.

Rodzianko, M. V.: *The Reign of Rasputin.* A. M. Philpot, London, 1927,

Sanderson, Edgar and Melville, Lewis: *King Edward VII* (5 Vols) Gresham. London, 1910.

Sencourt, Robert: *King Alfonso.* Faber and Faber, London, 1942.

Sencourt, Robert: *Spain's Uncertain Crown.* Ernest Benn, London, 1932.

Stancioff, Anna: *Recollections of a Bulgarian Diplomatist's Wife.* Hutchinson, London, N.D.

Stephanie, H.R.H. Princess: *I was to be Empress.* Ivor Nicholson, London, 1937.

Stevenson, R. Scott: *Famous Illnesses in History.* Eyre & Spottiswoode, London, 1962.

Taylor, Lucy: *'Fritz' of Prussia.* Nelson, London, 1891.

Tharaud, Jerome and Jean: *Rendez-vous Espagnols.* Librairie Plon, Paris, 1925.

Tooley, Sarah A.: *The Life of Queen Alexandra.* Hodder & Stoughton, London, 1902.

Valti, Luc: *Mon Ami le Roi.* Les Editions de France, Paris, 1938.

Victoria, German Empress: *Letters of the Empress Frederick* (Ed. by Sir Frederick Ponsonby) Macmillan, London, 1955.

Victoria, German Empress: *The Empress Frederick Writes to Sophie* (Ed. by A. Gould-Lee) Faber and Faber, London, 1955.

Victoria, Princess of Prussia: *My Memoirs.* Eveleigh Nash & Grayson, London, 1929.

Victoria, Princess of Prussia: *Queen Victoria at Windsor and Balmoral.* (Ed. by James Pope-Hennessy) George Allen and Unwin, London, 1959.

Victoria, Queen of Great Britain: *Letters of Queen Victoria* (9 Vols) John Murray, London, 1907–32.

Victoria, Queen of Great Britain: *Leaves From the Journal of Our Life in the Highlands.* Smith, Elder, London, 1869.

Victoria, Queen of Great Britain: *Dearest Child: Letters between Queen Victoria and the Princess Royal* (Ed. by Roger Fulford) Evans Bros., London, 1964.

Victoria, Queen of Great Britain: *Dearest Mamma: Letters between Queen Victoria and the Crown Princess of Prussia.* (Ed. by Roger Fulford) Evans Bros., London, 1968.

Victoria, Queen of Great Britain: *Your Dear Letter: Private Correspondence of Queen Victoria and the Crown Princess of Prussia.* (Ed. Roger Fulford) Evans Bros., London, 1971.

Viroubova, Anna: *Memoirs of the Russian Court*: Macmillan, London, 1923.

Waddington, Mary: *Letters of a Diplomat's Wife*. Smith, Elder, London, 1903.

Waldersee, Count von: *A Field Marshal's Memoirs*. Hutchinson, London, 1924.

Wentworth Day, J.: *H.R.H. Princess Marina, Duchess of Kent*. Robert Hale, London, 1962.

West, Rebecca: *Black Lamb, Grey Falcon*. Macmillan, London, 1955.

Wilhelm II, German Emperor: *My Memoirs 1878–1918*. Cassell, London, 1922.

Wilhelm II, German Emperor: *My Early Life*. Methuen, 1926.

Witte, Count Sergius: *Memoirs*. Heinemann, London, 1921.

Woodham-Smith, Cecil: *Queen Victoria: Her Life and Times*. Hamish Hamilton, London, 1972.

Zetland, Marquis of: *The Letters of Disraeli to Lady Bradford and Lady Chesterfield*. Ernest Benn, London, 1929.

Newspapers and Periodicals

The Times, Daily Mail, Daily Telegraph, Graphic, Illustrated London News, The Sphere, The Tatler, The Observer, The Cornhill, Annual Register, Dictionary of National Biography, Almanach de Gotha, Royalties of the World.

Index